BRITISH AND AMERICAN COMMERCIAL RELATIONS WITH SOVIET RUSSIA, 1918 - 1924

BRITISH AND AMERICAN

COMMERCIAL RELATIONS

WITH SOVIET RUSSIA,

1918-1924

CHRISTINE A. WHITE

CHAPEL HILL & LONDON

THE UNIVERSITY OF NORTH CAROLINA PRESS

Manufactured in the United States of America

The paper in this book meets the guidelines for permanence
and durability of the Committee on Production Guidelines for
Book Longevity of the Council on Library Resources.

96 95 94 93 92   5 4 3 2 1

Library of Congress Cataloging-in-Publication Data

White, Christine A.

British and American Commercial relations with Soviet
Russia, 1918–1924 / by Christine A. White.

    p. cm.

Includes bibliographical references and index.

ISBN 0-8078-2033-4 (cloth : alk. paper)

1. Soviet Union—Commerce—Great Britain—History.

2. Great Britain—Commerce—Soviet Union—History.

3. Soviet Union—Commerce—United States—History.

4. United States—Commerce—Soviet Union—History.

5. Soviet Union—History—Revolution, 1917–1921.   I. Title.

HF3628.G7W46   1993   92-301

382'.0941047—dc20   CIP

Publication of this book was aided by a subvention from
Pennsylvania State University.

for Stephen

CONTENTS

TABLES AND MAPS

Tables

Maps

PREFACE

In the preparation of this book, I have had the good fortune to be allowed to work in a number of public and private archives and libraries. Many thanks are due to the tireless archivists, librarians, and staff of the Public Record Office and the British Museum in London; the National Archives and the Library of Congress in Washington, D.C.; the Library of the School of Slavonic and East European Studies at the University of London; the Library of Political and Economic Science, London; Cambridge University Library; the Bodleian Library, Oxford; the Slavonic Library at Helsinki University; the Butler Memorial Library at Columbia University; and the New York Public Library. I owe a special debt to Mr. David Crippen of the Henry Ford Museum, Dearborn; Mr. Edward Green of Midland Bank; Mr. Daniel Hartgrove of the National Archives, Washington, D.C.; Mr. Michael Jacobson, Dr. Elena Danielson, and Dr. Carol Leadenham of the Hoover Institution Archives, Stanford, California; Mr. Leo Van Rossum of the Internationaal Instituut voor Sociale Geschiedenis, Amsterdam; and Mr. G. J. Bawcutt of Kodak, Ltd., all who patiently endured my endless questions and provided me with valuable help and insight. I am also grateful to Mr. H. E. Scrope of Vickers, Ltd., who very kindly gave me permission to consult the Vickers Company archives before they were turned over to the Cambridge University Library. A collective—but no less heartfelt—thanks is due to the many other archivists, curators, and librarians of collections to which I was given access. A complete listing and citation of all archives and collections can be found in the bibliography.

Unfortunately, during the time which I was conducting research for this book Soviet archives had not yet been made generally available to Western scholars. I have attempted to counter this shortcoming by making use of Russian and Soviet collections, both published and manuscript, that exist outside of the USSR.

Over the years I have had the pleasure of the support and encouragement of a number of people. My greatest debt is owed to my supervisor, teacher, and friend, Mr. R. C. Trebilcock, whose patience and faith gave me the courage to go on. Both he and his former student, Geoffrey Jones, unselfishly shared their ideas and criticisms and provided me with intellectual sustenance and moral support when I needed it most, and on numerous occasions suffered my rantings with the good humor I could have expected only from friends. Richard Davenport-Hines gave needed advice and criticism; Alfred Rieber, Olga Crisp, and Barry Supple read early drafts of this manuscript and their comments were invaluable. The preparation of this manuscript would have been considerably more difficult had it not been for the tireless efforts of Lewis Bateman, Ron Maner, and Brian MacDonald of the University of North Carolina Press. Finally, my deepest gratitude and affection to my husband, Stephen Mackwell, who patiently read and critiqued each chapter, and without whose computer wizardry I would still be scribbling on paper with pencil.

The U.S. Board of Geographic Names system for transliterating Russian Cyrillic was employed in this work.

Needless to say, I alone am responsible for the interpretations, conclusions, and errors contained herein.

BRITISH AND AMERICAN COMMERCIAL RELATIONS WITH SOVIET RUSSIA, 1 9 1 8 - 1 9 2 4

INTRODUCTION

This study deals with the development of Soviet economic and commercial relations with Britain and the United States from 1918 to 1924—the period prior to the rapid expansion of imports into the Soviet Union that immediately preceded the First Five Year Plan.[1] Although the economic activity during the period immediately after the Bolshevik revolution was not as remarkable as the progress made under the First Five Year Plan, it was, nonetheless, significant in its own right. In addition to the expenditure of considerable sums of money in connection with the Allied intervention in Russia and the support of the various counterrevolutionary groups, both Britain and the United States also evinced a substantial interest in reviving and capturing what was perceived as a lucrative postwar market. This perception of Russia—Bolshevik or otherwise—as an eldorado stubbornly persisted in governmental as well as private business circles well into the 1930s. The trade and economic relations during this very early period did much to promote that belief.

At first glance, resources for the study of Soviet Russia during this period seem sparse, and the accuracy of existing economic data is often questionable. The conditions of civil war, intervention, and blockade, along with a predisposition to find the Bolsheviks loathsome, could not but help to color foreign observations. The relative absence of official representation of the Allied governments in Soviet Russia during this period also tended to produce infrequent and erroneous intelligence reports. Even so, through an examination of the vast amount of available material, it is possible to reassess the volume and value of immediate postrevolutionary Russian trade with Great Britain and the United States.

Nonetheless, it is difficult to establish with any accuracy the volume and value of this trade. With an essentially nonidentifiable gross national product (GNP) between 1918 and 1924, the conventional method of linking GNP with national imports and exports is not a useful one in analyzing the Soviet economy under War Communism and the first years of the New Economic Policy. One is therefore faced with the task of defining an alternative measure for determining trade levels. A defensible standard against which early Bolshevik commercial activity might be measured is provided by a comparison of the prewar and postwar trade statistics. Thus, returns for 1913 can be used as a yardstick for the assessment of postrevolutionary trade. The use of these data for such comparative purposes is commonly accepted. Quite simply, 1913 provides the last full year of prewar commercial conditions (although it can be argued that it represented a prewar peak in tsarist trading activity), while at the same time providing a relatively comprehensive set of fairly reliable data. Further, by comparing the level of Russian-bound exports from the United States and Great Britain as a percentage of the total exports from each country for both periods, one may obtain a better idea of the overall importance of that trade for these major economies. A similar comparison of Russian exports to those countries would also be enlightening—especially in the case of Great Britain.

Perhaps more important, however, is an assessment of the sectoral significance of commercial relations. Although overall trade figures may have been comparatively small, the question of the value of Russian trade to certain sectors of the national economies of Great Britain and the United States, as well as to individual companies or industries, cannot be ignored. A breakdown of exports ultimately destined for Soviet Russia according to product classification (e.g., agricultural machinery, textiles) and a determination of the percentage of the corresponding sectoral exports to total exports destined for Russia for both periods illustrate the impact of the loss of Russian trade on specific British and American industries and point out shifts in Soviet purchasing that may indicate product preference or credit arrangements.

From 1921 to 1924 Soviet Russia's trade increased steadily, despite the American policy of nonrecognition and the rather rough course of Anglo-Soviet relations during those years. This early period was a trial for both the Soviet government and Western business interests, and served as a prelude to the dramatic jump in the volume and value of Soviet foreign trade during the late 1920s. An examination of the contracts, agreements, and, later, the credit arrangements that were concluded during these early years, as well as a consideration of the Soviet government's record of fulfilling its foreign financial obligations, points to some of the possible reasons behind the rush to enter the Soviet market in the late 1920s.

In addition to examining the formal economic relations that developed between the United States and Great Britain and the Soviet authorities, this study analyzes the commercial exchanges that took place with those areas *not* under Bolshevik control, as well as the *unofficial* intercourse that occurred between certain American and British traders and commercial agents and Soviet Russia. Thus, this study outlines the formation of the economic policy toward the Soviet state that evolved on an official level in the United States and Great Britain and traces the development of trade, direct and indirect, on the private or unofficial level. The economic relations of individual traders and private companies that were carried out regardless of the political disposition of their respective governments toward the Bolsheviks, and independent of the state of official economic relations, reveal the attitudes of the business communities and the interactions of economics and trade with governmental policy making.

Both governmental and private commercial relations were closely linked and occurred under political circumstances radically different from those of any other period in history. The Bolshevik government, with its unorthodox proclamations and its total disregard for all that the Western nations held as axiomatic for the continued existence of civilization, was generally perceived as a despicable and repugnant body with which contact should be kept to a minimum. Moreover, the confusion surrounding the Bolshevik withdrawal from the war and subsequent bid for peace with Germany likewise served to discourage the Allies from officially approaching the Soviet government on any score. But neither the United States nor Great Britain could disassociate itself totally from Russia because of its economic interests that predated the revolution. Although the Allies desired to sever immediately all contacts with the unscrupulous Bolsheviks, they recognized the need to protect their nationals' interests in Russia and, perceiving Russia as having phenomenal economic potential, did not wish to forfeit completely the chance for any future dealings with the Soviet regime.

1

Prewar Economic Ties

In considering Russia's prewar financial ties to the West, Lenin does not appear far off the mark with his assertion that the empire was a "semi-colonial appendage of Western finance capitalism." This assessment especially holds true for the years after 1890, when the participation and, indeed, predominance of foreign capital in certain key Russian industries resulted in a delicate relationship between foreign loans and diplomatic alignments. According to currently accepted estimations, approximately 50 percent of all fresh capital invested in those industrial concerns doing business in Russia between 1880 and 1913 was of foreign origin. Further, for the quarter century preceding the war, foreign capital accounted for no less than 20 percent of the total common stock capital of these businesses; and by 1914, the proportion had risen to over 40 percent. Despite the fact that the presence of this capital in such preponderance was the result of a long-standing official policy to attract foreign participation in Russian industry, the tsarist government was, by the turn of the century, justifiably suspicious of the increasingly important position occupied by foreign capital in the Russian economy.

The participation of Western capital and entrepreneurial talent in the development of prewar Russian industry has been well documented elsewhere.[1] While considerable attention has been devoted to this aspect of Russia's financial relations, surprisingly little work has been done on the trade and commercial ties of the empire during the decade or so that preceded the war. A glance at the prewar Russian trade statistics quickly reveals that the country's commercial and financial relations were largely independent of one another. At the very same time that the Entente was being cemented with new loans and ever-greater French and British capital investments, there was a noticeable shift in Russia's trade that resulted in both France and Britain losing a significant proportion of the growing Russian market to Germany. A brief examination of the character and trends of prewar Russian trade relations from 1890 to 1913, followed by a more detailed assessment of the trends in Anglo-Russian and U.S.-Russian trade for both the immediate prewar and wartime years serves to illustrate the influence that these early relations had on the West's perception of the Russian market as a potential eldorado.

The composition and character of Russian exports changed little over the course of the half century before the war. Agricultural produce accounted for the overwhelming proportion of Russian exports, with foodstuffs alone making up no less than 50 percent of the total value of Russian exports during this period. Of this classification, cereals, primarily wheat and barley, were the primary source of foreign revenue; certain other agricultural products, notably eggs and butter, were also of considerable export importance.

Raw materials and semimanufactured goods provided the next most significant class of exports, with timber and wood products accounting for the majority of the value of this group. The importance of timber in the export trade of Russia was second only to that of grain, and the development of the Russian timber industry was to a large degree dependent upon the expansion of its export market.[2] Between 1900 and 1913 the volume of timber and wood products exported from Russia nearly doubled, and on the eve of the war some 25 percent of the total production was being exported. Further, it is significant that the corresponding value of timber exports increased by two and a half times during the last decade before the war.[3] Flax, hemp, tow, and linseed products accounted for the next largest return among goods of this classification. Russian flax was particularly important to Western Europe, because its linen factories were supplied almost exclusively with fiber from the Russian Empire.[4] Minerals, ores, and metals followed, with petroleum occupying a predominant position among these exported commodities. Although Russia

Table 1.1 Composition of Russian Foreign Trade (Percentage Distribution to Total Exports or Imports)

	Foodstuffs		Raw Materials and Semimanufactured Goods		Animals		Manufactured Goods	
	Export	Import	Export	Import	Export	Import	Export	Import
1894	56.9	18.4	37.5	54.4	2.0	0.7	3.6	26.5
1898	52.5	16.6	40.3	48.3	2.4	0.6	4.8	34.5
1903	61.3	20.1	31.9	52.5	2.0	0.8	4.8	26.6
1908	54.4	23.2	37.8	47.6	2.5	0.8	5.3	28.4
1913	55.3	17.3	36.9	48.6	2.2	1.3	5.6	32.8

Source: Pasvolsky and Moulton, *Russian Debts and Russian Reconstruction*, p. 100.

was the second largest petroleum producer in the world, and despite the fact that Russian oil exports were of considerable importance in the world petroleum market, they accounted for only 4 percent of total Russian exports immediately before the war.[5] Besides petroleum, manganese and platinum were the only other products of this class that were of any export significance, with Russian production providing for 99 percent of the world's platinum requirements. Manufactured goods were the least important group of Russian exports, and accounted for only 3 to 6 percent of all shipments abroad. These exports were largely composed of matches to Europe and cotton textiles destined primarily for Asian markets. Whereas the Russian economy was largely dependent upon its agricultural and extractive industries for its export revenues, raw materials and semimanufactured goods represented the largest percentage by value of all imports into prewar Russia. Metals and metal manufactures and raw and partially manufactured materials for textiles (such as raw cotton and spun wool) not only accounted for the majority of imports in this class but also represented a significant proportion of all Russian imports. In several instances, these imports amounted to more than 25 percent of the total value of goods purchased abroad.[6] Coal and coke made up the second largest import by value in this category, with some 20 to 25 percent of Russian solid fuel requirements being satisfied from abroad.

The distribution of Russian trade according to class, illustrated as a percentage of total imports and exports in Table 1.1, reflects very little variation over the twenty-year period before the war.

A comparison of the total imports and exports given in Table 1.2 shows

Table 1.2   Russian Trade, 1896–1913 (in Thousands of Roubles)

	Exports from Russia	Imports into Russia	Balance of Trade
1870	419,531	402,455	+17,076
1880	418,718	583,934	−165,216
1890	753,849	453,095	+300,754
1900	716,418	626,375	+90,043
1905	1,077,325	635,087	+442,238
1906	1,094,886	800,690	+294,196
1907	1,053,010	874,365	+178,645
1908	998,250	912,651	+85,599
1909	1,427,675	906,339	+521,336
1910	1,449,085	1,084,446	+364,639
1911	1,591,411	1,161,682	+429,729
1912	1,581,798	1,171,772	+410,026
1913	1,420,855	1,220,474	+200,381

Source: Worked from returns recorded in *Obzor vneshnei torgovli rossii po evropeiskoy i aziatskoy granitsam*, 1916.

a deterioration in the balance of trade between 1906 and 1908, followed by a sharp upturn in 1909, and a renewed slide from 1911 to 1913. While the Russian balance of trade remained favorable throughout the years preceding the war, imports measured year on year from 1909 were generally increasing at a faster rate than exports and, further, the value of exports was actually declining from 1911. This decline had a serious impact on the Russian economy because the trade balance was a basic factor in the economic structure of the country.[7] In this context, it is worth noting that Russia's economic relations with Western Europe were predominantly financial, whereas its relations with Central Europe were primarily commercial. Between 40 and 50 percent of the returns of the empire's direct exports to Western Europe were utilized as payment on Russian debts and for services. Conversely, nearly all of the Russian exports to Central Europe were used in the purchase of imports.[8]

Certain classes of imported commodities demonstrated a higher rate of growth than others. In the case of Russian purchases of foodstuffs from abroad, a comparison of the average values for the five year period 1902–6 against those for 1907–11 shows an increase of 33 percent. Over the latter period, imports of raw materials and articles partly manufactured were likewise 38 percent greater in value. The years 1909–13 present the most striking increase of imports in this classification. This growth is amply illustrated by a staggering increase of 67 percent in the imports of manufactured goods in 1911 as compared with the corresponding value for that class in 1910.[9]

Another, more subtle change occurred in the foreign trade of Russia between 1870 and 1913. The geographical direction of this trade underwent a distinct shift away from Western Europe, with a significantly greater proportion going to Central European countries, primarily Germany. The reasons behind this shift and Britain's reactions to it will be discussed in greater detail later, but it is important to note that Germany was both Russia's primary Central European trading partner and the predominant individual buyer and seller on the Russian market from 1900 onward.[10]

Geographically proximate and easily accessible through the Baltic ports, Germany had always been a primary Russian trading partner. Purchasing directly as well as via Holland and Finland, Germany served as the single largest market for Russian foodstuffs and raw and semimanufactured goods. As regards exports to Russia, Germany was quick to seize upon the opportunity presented by the Anglo-Russian estrangement during the Crimean War, and subsequently gained an even greater advantage in respect to sales of goods to that country. Germany provided Russia with almost three-quarters of the metal ores and metal manufactures and somewhat more than half of all the textiles imported during the quarter century before the war. Chemicals, paints, and varnishes came almost exclusively from Germany, and an increasing percentage of all finished goods, electrical equipment, and machinery imported by Russia was of German origin.[11] The trade statistics presented in Table 1.3 show that a growing proportion of all Russian trade was being handled by Germany. At the turn of the century Germany took roughly 26 percent of all Russian exports and supplied Russia with approximately 35 percent of all imports. But by 1913, Germany's share had increased to nearly 32 percent of all Russian exports and over 52 percent of all its imports. Although this expanded predominance may partially be explained by Germany's growing role as a reexporter of goods both to and from Russia, it is nonetheless clear that German produce provided the overwhelming percentage of Russian imports during this period, especially in the case of manufactured goods.[12]

The importance of Germany as a supplier of finished goods grew significantly between the turn of the century and the outbreak of the war. During this period Germany had captured by far the largest share of

Table 1.3 Russian Prewar Trade with Germany and Great Britain
(in Thousands of Roubles)

| | Exports from Russia | | | | Imports into Russia | | | |
| | To Germany | | To Great Britain | | From Germany | | From Great Britain | |
	Roubles	% of Total	Roubles	% of Total	Roubles	% of Total	Roubles	% of Total
1870	88,665	21.1	198,217	47.2	159,020	39.5	124,569	31.0
1880	133,426	27.8	143,480	29.7	264,983	45.4	145,706	25.0
1890	198,777	26.4	221,789	29.4	124,838	27.5	101,647	22.4
1900	187,635	26.1	145,576	20.3	216,853	34.6	127,144	20.3
1905	255,312	23.7	249,206	23.1	240,411	37.8	97,410	15.3
1906	284,675	26.4	225,447	20.7	298,422	37.2	105,726	13.2
1907	291,041	27.7	228,504	21.8	337,367	39.9	114,935	13.5
1908	278,992	27.9	220,514	22.2	348,426	38.2	120,286	13.4
1909	387,119	27.3	288,855	20.1	363,263	40.2	127,946	14.3
1910	390,640	27.0	315,476	21.8	449,794	41.8	153,847	14.2
1911	490,525	30.8	337,032	21.2	487,780	42.0	155,081	13.5
1912	543,178	29.9	327,811	21.5	532,346	45.5	142,356	12.2
1913	542,637	31.8	266,864	18.8	642,756	52.6	170,352	13.9

Source: Worked from returns recorded in *Obzor vneshnei torgovli rossii po evropeiskoy i aziatskoy granitsam*, 1916.

Russia's purchases of machinery, fittings, electrical equipment, and manufactures of all sorts. The extent to which Russia was dependent on German machinery—with the exception of complex agricultural machinery—on the eve of the war can be seen from the breakdown of the total imports of machinery and metal manufactures into Russia for 1910 and 1911 as indicated in Table 1.4.

Whereas German exports to Russia increased at an accelerated pace after 1900, imports from Russia remained relatively static, reflecting a much slower and steadier growth; and though Russia's trade balance was nearly always favorable with the principal countries of Europe, its balance with Germany more often than not registered a deficit. The type of relationship that existed between these two countries becomes clear from a comparison of the respective balances given in Table 1.5, and the exceptionally large deficits of 1912 and 1913 emphasize the virtual strangle-

Table 1.4   Russian Imports of Machinery and Metal Manufactures
(Value in Roubles)

	From All Countries	From Germany	From Great Britain
1910	196,894,000	104,874,000	20,414,000
1911	214,152,000	119,960,000	27,727,000

Source: Kennard, *The Russian Year Book*, 1913, pp. 306–7.

hold that Germany had acquired on the import trade of Russia during the twenty years preceding the war.

As a consequence, in addition to becoming gradually dependent upon Germany for equipment and repair parts, Russia became more closely tied to Germany through the introduction of German experts and mechanics necessary to supervise the installation and operation of specialized German machines.[13] The vulnerability created by this reliance did not go unnoticed, and on the eve of the war the Russians were making a concerted effort to interest other countries in their business. The obvious targets were Great Britain and the United States.

Although displaced from its position as Russia's primary trading partner during the 1860s, Great Britain remained the second most important buyer and seller in the Russian market. At the turn of the century, the United Kingdom took 20 percent of all Russian exports, while supplying some 20 percent of all that country's imports. A major purveyor of foodstuffs and raw materials to Britain, Russia ranked behind only the United States, Germany, and France, and by 1911 had surpassed even France in the value and volume of its exports to the United Kingdom.[14] Britain accounted for a significant proportion of all the exports of Russian foodstuffs, and for certain commodities continued to represent the major foreign purchaser throughout the period prior to the war. In the case of Russian grain exports, Britain's place as the largest single consumer was not eclipsed by Germany until 1898. Even then, the United Kingdom remained the principal buyer of Russian wheat and oats, taking an average of 19.5 percent and 43 percent of these exports respectively between 1908 and 1912.[15] Britain also provided the primary market for Russian butter, absorbing over half of all these exports, which in turn satisfied some 13 percent of its total butter consumption. Eggs were another important export in this class, with roughly one-third of all Russian eggs shipped abroad destined for the United Kingdom, where they satisfied 50 percent of the total requirements.[16] Although livestock generally did not account for a very large proportion of Russian exports, it is interesting to

Table 1.5 Russian Trade Balances with Principal Trading Countries
(in Millions of Roubles)

	Germany	Great Britain	France	Belgium
1894	+5	+42	+28	+10
1897	−27	+36	+36	+9
1900	−29	+18	+26	+14
1903	−9	+104	+48	+34
1906	−14	+120	+48	+34
1909	+24	+161	+39	+57
1910	−59	+162	+33	+60
1911	+3	+182	+34	+48
1912	+11	+186	+42	+54
1913	−100	+97	+44	+56

Sources: *Obzor vneshnei torgovli rossii po evropeiskoy i aziatskoy granitsam*; and
Pasvolsky and Moulton, *Russian Debts and Russian Reconstruction*, pp. 80–81.

note that approximately 32 percent of the horses exported went to the
United Kingdom where they accounted for almost half of the total number imported.[17]

Great Britain also purchased a substantial proportion of certain important Russian raw materials and semimanufactured goods. The Russian
Empire was a key supplier of timber and wood products to the United
Kingdom; on average, approximately two-thirds of all Russian timber
goods exported between 1909 and 1913 were destined for the British
market, where they in turn met over half of Britain's total timber requirements for that period.[18] Russia was likewise a major source for the European requirements of flax and hemp, and here again, the United Kingdom
purchased approximately 30 percent of all those exports. With regard to
other raw materials, Britain purchased a considerable amount of Russian
ores, metals, and minerals; iron, manganese, and, in particular, petroleum were the most important among this group.

Despite the fact that Russian oil production had suffered a sharp set-
back during the first decade of the twentieth century, the tsarist empire
was nonetheless one of the largest producers in the world. As an alternative to the increasingly monopolistic suppliers of the United States, Russian sources became even more attractive to the British—a fact that is
reflected in the increased amount of British capital invested in Russian oil
production and transportation.[19] This interest is also evident in the in-

crease in British petroleum purchases between 1909 and 1913, during which time Britain accounted for no less than one-fifth of the exports of Russian oil products.[20] More particularly, whereas the sale of Russian lamp oils to the United Kingdom shows a decline over that period, there was a considerable increase in the imports of lubricating oils and petroleum spirits. Over this five-year period, British imports of Russian lubricating oils had increased by 75 percent in volume and by some 250 percent in value; likewise, imports of Russian petroleum spirits had increased fourteenfold in volume and had doubled in value.[21]

Russia was the major purveyor to Europe of many of these goods, and its importance to Britain is amply demonstrated by the considerable proportion of British purchases supplied from Russian sources. There was, to be sure, a certain quantity of goods intended for reexport among these purchases, but as the returns in the *Annual Statement of the Trade of the United Kingdom* bear out, well over 90 percent was retained for U.K. consumption. While the absolute totals of Anglo-Russian trade (imports and exports) increased steadily throughout the nineteenth and early twentieth centuries, Britain's proportion of this trade declined considerably. Although it represented 39 percent of the total Russian turnover in 1870, the British share of this trade had fallen to approximately one-sixth of the total by 1913—the majority of this trade having been lost to Germany.

The annual variation in the proportion of Russian exports destined for U.K. ports was less than 5 percent between 1900 and 1913. The British share of the total exports to Russia, on the other hand, underwent a considerable decline over the same period. Although imports into Russia from all countries increased by some 300 percent between 1870 and 1913, it was imports from Germany that accounted for the largest proportion of this increase. In 1900 Germany exported on average rather less than one and a half times as much in value to Russia as did the United Kingdom. By 1913, however, imports from Germany were over three and a half times greater than those from Britain. Further, although British exports accounted for 13 percent of the increase of over 300 million roubles in Russian imports between 1909 and 1913, Britain's proportion of this trade actually declined.

Despite this relative decline, it is important to realize that Britain supplied Russia with a significant amount of raw and semimanufactured materials as well as certain manufactured goods. For example, the United Kingdom was a major supplier of solid fuels to Russia. During the five years immediately prior to the war, total coal and coke imports into Russia averaged 474 million poods and 59 million poods respectively (1 pood equals 36.1 pounds avoirdupois), for a value of some 87.5 million roubles.[22] Approximately half the quantity of these imports came from the United Kingdom, and on the eve of the war, Britain's share of this trade increased to 65 percent of the coal and coke supplies imported by Russia.[23]

The United Kingdom also provided the Russian Empire with a significant proportion of its imports of raw and spun wool. About 50 percent of the raw combed and worsted wool imported into Russia in 1913 came from the United Kingdom, and in the latter case, 40 percent of the 5 million poods of woolen yarns imported that year came from that source.[24] After Germany, the United Kingdom was the second largest supplier of finished woolen fabrics, accounting for one-sixth to one-seventh of all those goods purchased abroad by Russia.[25] Similarly, whereas Germany provided the overwhelming proportion of cotton goods and manufactures, Britain supplied Russia with about 45 percent of all its imports of cotton yarns.

The United Kingdom continued to be primarily an exporter of raw and semimanufactured goods to Russia throughout the period up to the war. As well as constituting the greatest percentage of British exports to Russia, this class of goods also accounted for 48 percent of the increase in Britain's export trade to Russia between 1909 and 1913.[26] Further, Britain's share in the sale of these goods to Russia remained relatively stable throughout the prewar period. In comparison, while British exports of manufactured goods to Russia did rise in actual value, Britain's overall share in this trade actually declined.[27]

A better picture of Britain's relative position as a supplier of manufactured goods to Russia can be seen in the example of exports of machinery and metal manufactures given in Table 1.4. Despite its heavily industrialized economy, Britain provided less than 20 percent of the manufactures of machinery (excluding agricultural machinery) and about 10 percent of the metal goods and semimanufactured machinery imported into Russia immediately before the war. Although it dominated the market for complex threshing machines and steam plows—accounting for 586,000 roubles of the 1,077,000 roubles worth of those machines imported in 1913—Britain provided only 12 percent of all the agricultural machinery purchased abroad by Russia during the immediate prewar period.[28] Even so, it is worth noting that rather more than 10 percent of the U.K. exports of agricultural machines and steam engines were destined for Russia. In the case of one of Britain's foremost manufacturers of these products, Ransomes, the Russian market was considerably more important, absorbing about 30 percent of that company's exports at the turn of the century.[29] Such circumstances, whereby the Russian market accounted for a substantial proportion not only of a firm's exports but also of its total production, were undoubtedly repeated for other manufacturers, and indeed for whole industries.

British merchants were justifiably alarmed by the growing German domination of the Russian market. There was considerable concern over how the Germans had managed to capture Russian sales; putting the advantage of geographical proximity aside, it was generally agreed that the German merchants had done much to adapt themselves and their products to the Russian market. Having batteries of local trading establishments complete with squads of traveling salesmen, German businesses had conquered the problem of distance, which the British, with only their city-centered offices, found so perplexing. Likewise, whereas British merchants continued to communicate with the Russians largely in English—both in person and through their brochures—giving the costs, weights, and measures in English with no benefit of Russian equivalents, German salesmen by and large spoke Russian and had their sales materials translated into that language, giving all specifics in Russian measures. More importantly, the Germans had also undertaken extensive advertising campaigns. Price was another major concern in the Russian market; although British goods were often of better quality, their higher prices put them at a distinct disadvantage to the wide selection of considerably less expensive German goods. While British merchants tended to take little note of the needs and requirements of the Russian market, the Germans not only took into account specific Russian needs, adapting their products to suit when necessary, but also accommodated the Russian preference for buying on credit. Despite the fact that long-term credits were an absolute necessity of economic life in an agricultural country like Russia, such business remained alien to British merchants and bankers. Finally, it is worth noting that the American companies of Singer and International Harvester had followed practices similar to those of their German counterparts in Russia and had equally great successes, dominating the sewing machine and harvesting machinery markets in that country.[30]

Although British merchants were repeatedly advised by Russian government and Chamber of Commerce officials, as well as by their own government's consular representatives, that these shortcomings were preventing the expansion of British business in Russia, little was done to redress the situation. Even so, a considerable commotion had been stirred by the growing awareness of the potential value of Russian trade, if only it could be wrenched away from the Germans. It is the resultant British drive to capture a greater share of Russian purchases abroad that best illustrates the early development of the notion of Russia as an inexhaustible market.

Finally, as a result of the shift toward closer commercial ties between Russia and Germany during the last quarter century before the war, Britain suffered the loss of substantial revenues from a decline in its "invisible exports" to Russia. British tonnage had long held the lion's share of the seaborne trade to and from Russian Black Sea and Baltic ports, as well as that shipped via the White Sea and Arctic Sea routes. However, despite the fact that British vessels continued to provide the major proportion of all prewar shipping tonnage entering and clearing Russian ports, Britain's predominant position was slowly being eroded. Accounting for more than half of all the shipping entering Russian ports in 1888, the British share had declined to only 35 percent by 1913–14, while German tonnage had risen from 9.5 percent to 16 percent.[31] This decline is particularly striking in the case of the Baltic Sea and White Sea routes. British tonnage servicing the Baltic in 1898 was nearly twice as great as the German registered tonnage, and in the White Sea exceeded German tonnage by some four times. By 1908, the Germans had managed to overtake the British share of shipping for both these routes, and in the case of the Baltic, outstripped British tonnage by 17.5 percent.[32] Further, while British interest in the Asiatic Russian trade routes remained relatively unchanged, the number of German vessels plying that route grew, and in 1908 accounted for the majority of all tonnage entering Vladivostok.[33] It was only in the Black Sea—where German shipping had virtually no interest—that the British predominance remained unscathed, accounting for a full 52 percent of the tonnage serving those ports immediately prior to the war.

The decline in Britain's overall share of Russian shipping was largely due to a shift toward the more frequent use of overland trade routes rather than any concerted effort by the Germans to capture this market.[34] A natural extension of the growing German domination of prewar Russian trade, overland transport routes accounted for an increasing percentage of all Russian foreign trade (Table 1.6). Particularly striking is the increase in Russian imports entering via European frontiers, with over half of all imports into Russia between 1909 and 1913 being received overland, as compared with 43.5 percent for the period 1881–90.

With the outbreak of the war and the closing of the Austro-German frontier to Russian trade, British shipping concerns quickly seized upon

Table 1.6   Percentage of Total Russian Imports and Exports via Overland Routes

	Exports	Imports
1802–4	12.0	22.0
1841–50	18.5	25.5
1871–80	29.5	39.0
1881–90	27.5	43.5
1909–13	27.1	53.8

Source: Soboleff, "The Foreign Trade of Russia," p. 303.

the possibility of recapturing this business. Russian commercial potential was perceived as virtually boundless, and with the removal of Germany at the outbreak of the war, British opportunities in particular were believed to be limitless. The British enthusiasm for entering full force into the cornering of this market met with only one obstacle: the American drive to do exactly the same thing.

2

American Competition and Wartime Opportunities in Russia

The Development of Russian-American Trade

After 1918, the commercial vacuum produced in Russia by the cessation of German trade was perceived in both British and American business circles as a timely opportunity.[1] The way was now clear to take over this trade; moreover, there was an obvious increase in the Russian need for manufactured goods as a result of the war. Despite the U.S. government's ostensibly neutral position toward Russia, American businessmen were just as keen as their British counterparts to take advantage of the commercial opportunities that the war had laid open.

Yet it is widely believed that the United States was largely indifferent to developing its trade with Russia prior to the war. With the exception of the well-known cases of International Harvester and the Singer Sewing Machine Company,[2] few other

American manufacturers are portrayed as having been particularly interested in the Russian market. Although those two companies were certainly pioneers in the American commercial penetration of Russia, the belief that American merchants and manufacturers generally were ambivalent toward that market is an over simplification and largely incorrect. Many American companies had long-established commercial relations with Russia, and a substantial number of them had sufficient business there to cause them to consider setting up Russian branch operations.[3]

Throughout much of the nineteenth century, the United States—like Russia—was primarily a supplier of raw materials to the industrialized nations of Europe. By the end of the nineteenth century, however, the character of the American export trade had undergone a significant change: domestic manufactured goods constituted an increasing proportion of all U.S. exports. While the total value of American exports had increased fourfold between 1860 and 1900, that of domestic manufactures alone had increased tenfold, accounting for 31.4 percent of the total value of exports in 1900 as compared with only 12.8 percent in 1860. The expansion of this export sector is even more striking between 1890 and 1910, when the proportion of manufactures increased from 14.8 percent to 44.9 percent of total exports.[4] The manufactured goods exported from the United States consisted primarily of iron and steel goods, copper, agricultural machinery and implements, mineral oils, chemicals, and leather goods—in short, just those manufactures that were being purchased in increasing quantities by Russia.

Although the United States lagged behind the United Kingdom in the value of its total trade turnover with Russia, the significance of this trade should not be underrated. Despite the fact that the value of the goods sold to Russia by the United States considerably outweighed its imports from that country, Russia was nonetheless an important supplier of certain raw materials. As with the United Kingdom, Russian exports to the United States were composed almost exclusively of raw materials and semimanufactures. According to Russian statistics, the total value of goods exported to the United States amounted to $4.84 million in 1910, of which raw materials accounted for $4.69 million, or about 97 percent.[5] Hides and skins, bristles, manganese ore, wool, and licorice root made up the bulk of Russian exports to the United States, and in all of these goods, Russia was a predominant supplier to the American market.[6]

After France and Germany, Russia was the third largest foreign source of raw and combed wool to the United States. As Germany frequently reexported Russian wool to the United States (which would often appear in the American returns as an import from Germany), Russia undoubtedly accounted for significantly more of that wool than is reflected in the returns.[7] Russia was also a major source of scrap rubber, manganese ore, flax, hemp, hides, and skins. According to the U.S. Department of Commerce returns, American imports of these goods from Russia were indeed greater than the Russian statistics would suggest. During the period 1906–10, for example, Russian trade figures indicate an annual average of 4.83 million pounds by weight of rubber waste being exported to the United States, whereas according to American statistics an average of 6.53 million pounds of scrap rubber had been received from Russia.[8] Similar discrepancies are evident with regard to Russian exports of manganese to the United States. Whereas the Russian Ministry of Trade and Commerce reported 24.3 million pounds as having been shipped to the United States, American returns show the receipt of 30.4 million pounds of the Russian ore. In the case of flax and hemp exports, the discrepancy is even more striking: according to Russian statistics, the annual average of flax exports to the United States during the period 1906–10 was 481,000 pounds, whereas the American returns show an average of 6,786,000 pounds for the same period. The corresponding figures for hemp exports are 241,000 pounds as opposed to the 1,624,500 average derived from the U.S. returns for the five-year period.[9]

The comparison in Table 2.1 of the yearly averages of Russian-American trade according to Russian returns on the one hand and U.S. returns on the other illustrates that such differences were not unusual. According to American statistics, the quantity of goods imported from Russia was about three times greater than the value registered in the official Russian returns. One cause for such discrepancies may lie in that goods exported to the United States were frequently invoiced through the local American consulate and were therefore more likely to show up in the U.S. returns. Moreover, it was the general practice in Russia to designate as the country of origin that country where the goods were purchased and which appeared in the invoice or bill of lading. As a considerable amount of American goods were purchased by Russia through Western European middlemen, a large proportion of this trade was subsequently credited to other countries—primarily Germany and the United Kingdom.[10] In this way, a substantial amount of Russian trade with the United States was "lost" altogether to both countries' statistics.

There was also a heavy dependence on foreign shippers and brokers to handle a large proportion of Russian-American trade as a result of the relatively undeveloped state of direct trade connections between the two

Table 2.1   Russian Exports to the United States (Yearly Average in Millions of Dollars)

	According to U.S. Statistics	According to Russian Statistics
1878–90	2.6	0.4
1891–1900	4.7	1.3
1901–10	11.9	3.0
1911–13	21.1	7.4

Sources: Figures for the United States were derived from the Department of Commerce returns and are for fiscal years. Russian averages are from the Russian Ministry of Finance, "Report on Trade with the United States," as cited in Sack, *America's Possible Share in the Economic Future of Russia*, p. 17.

countries. Because the "greater part" of the American-bound exports were handled in this way, the Russian Ministry of Finance admitted that the United States was undoubtedly playing a more important role in Russian trade than the Russian returns alone would indicate.[11] The fact that the records of the American consulates in Russia register merchandise to the value of more than $31 million as declared for export to the United States in 1912, compared with $9 million and $28 million reported in the official Russian and American returns respectively, goes far to show that Russian exports to the United States were indeed greater than either set of official data reflects.

Finally, it is interesting to note that, while Russian exports show a steady growth throughout the years prior to the war, exports to the United States increased at a substantially faster rate than Russian exports in general (Table 2.2). Comparing the yearly average of $547.21 million of total Russian exports for the 1901–10 period against the $297.22 million for the years 1878–90, total Russian exports show an increase of 84 percent, while exports to the United States alone increased by about 650 percent, from $0.4 million to $3 million. During the last three years before the war, Russian exports show a further increase of 39 percent, while exports to the United States increased by some 113 percent as compared to the 1901–10 average. If these figures are anything to go by, Russia was becoming a more important source of raw and semimanufactured goods to the American market, and all signs point toward the likelihood of continued growth in Russian sales to the United States had the war not disrupted this trade.

As a supplier to the Russian market, official returns put the United States as the third largest source of all goods imported. Though manufac-

Table 2.2   Russian Trade with the United States (Yearly Average in Millions of Dollars; from Russian Returns)

	Russian Imports		Russian Exports	
	Total	From the United States	Total	To the United States
1878–90	243.39	15.5	297.22	0.4
1891–1900	273.77	22.0	336.95	1.3
1901–10	393.27	28.3	547.21	3.0
1911–13	616.83	42.3	761.51	7.4

Source: Russian Ministry of Finance, "Report on Trade with the United States," as cited in Sack, *America's Possible Share in the Economic Future of Russia*, p. 14.

tured goods were being purchased in increasing quantities from the United States, raw and semimanufactured goods continued to account for the overwhelming majority of all American exports to Russia. Raw cotton alone made up the bulk of the value of these exports, accounting for over 37 percent of the average value of all U.S. exports to European Russia between 1896 and 1910. According to U.S. returns, Russia was the fifth largest foreign consumer of American cotton. Here again, however, it must be remembered that a considerable quantity of this export was purchased and shipped through European brokers—notably via Germany and the United Kingdom. In addition to the lack of direct trade connections, the role of the European middleman in American-Russian trade was made all the more important by the Russian need to purchase on long-term credit and to conduct the trade in commodities rather than in cash.[12] This procedure was especially true in the case of cotton, vast quantities of which passed through Germany en route to Russia.[13] A comparison of the 38.89 million pounds by weight of cotton that was reported in U.S. statistics as having been exported to Russia in 1910 with the Russian returns that record receipts from the United States of 164.95 million pounds demonstrates the striking discrepancies that occurred as a result. The United States undoubtedly accounted for far more of the cotton imported by Russia than is reflected in either the Russian or American statistics. It was, in fact, "conservatively estimated" in 1913 that the United States sold to Russia not less than $50 million a year in raw cotton, that is, nearly *ten times* the amount given in the official U.S. returns.[14]

Iron and steel manufactures and machines of all sorts held second place in U.S. exports to Russia, the total value of which was largely accounted

Table 2.3   American Exports to Russia (Yearly Average in Millions of Dollars)

	According to U.S. Statistics	According to Russian Statistics
1878–90	11.9	15.5
1891–1900	7.5	22.0
1901–10	16.7	28.3
1911–13	25.4	42.3

Sources: U.S. Department of Commerce, *Foreign Commerce and Navigation of the United States*; and Russian Ministry of Finance, "Report on Trade with the United States," as cited in Sack, *America's Possible Share in the Economic Future of Russia*, p. 16.

for by purchases of American agricultural machinery and implements. According to Russian statistics, these goods accounted for $2.73 million of the $3.23 total average annual value of American machinery imported between 1901 and 1905. Between 1906 and 1910, agricultural machinery made up an even greater proportion of all machinery imported from the United States by Russia, accounting for $4.43 million of the $4.94 million total. Here again, the American returns are somewhat greater than the Russian, recording an average annual value of agricultural machinery exported to Russia over the two five-year periods as $3 million and $5.17 million respectively.[15] Further, it appears that even the U.S. returns provide an inadequate reflection of the true value of these exports, as the American consul in Moscow estimated that this trade was actually worth perhaps $15 million per year to American agricultural machinery makers.[16]

A significant proportion of the third largest Russian-bound export from the United States—copper—likewise came to Russia through German and British agents. The amount of copper recorded in American statistics as being shipped directly to Russia was over twice that reported by the Russians as having been received from the United States.[17] The comparison of the Russian and American returns in Table 2.3 again indicates that a substantial portion of the total value of U.S. exports to Russia was "lost" to Russian returns through the use of European middlemen, and also gives rise to the suspicion that a certain amount failed to make it to either set of returns, having been accredited on both sides as an export to or import from a third country.

It is quite likely that Russian-American trade was substantially greater than either set of data alone would give reason to believe. In fact, the American consul general in Moscow declared in 1912 that the United

States sold "directly and indirectly" at least $80 million worth of goods to Russia annually during the years immediately before the war, and that it was likely that this trade "will come nearer approximating $90,000,000 a year." He went on to point out that such a reevaluation would place the United States second in the ranking of exporters to Russia, exceeding Great Britain in the value of its exports to that country.[18]

Other important American prewar exports to Russia included metal-working machinery and machine tools, zinc, oil products, and finished leather goods such as industrial belting and footwear. As mentioned earlier, these articles accounted for an increasing proportion of all U.S. exports, illustrating a trend toward increased exports of manufactured goods by the United States. Indeed, American manufacturers of such new and innovative products as the automobile, phonograph, photographic and cine materials, and telephonic and radio equipment had found ready sales in Russia, and the potential of the Russian market was not lost on these industrialists.

The commercial significance attached to Russia by American manufacturers became unmistakable between 1911 and January 1913—that is, between the time the U.S. government made the decision to terminate unilaterally the 1832 Russian-American trade agreement and the date at which that decision became effective.[19] Letters testifying to the importance of the Russian market were received by both the State Department and the Department of Commerce from a variety of U.S. manufacturers.[20] It is clear from these communications that a number of American manufacturers expected a bright future in the Russian trade; pharmaceutical and chemical goods producers, machine tool companies, and automobile manufacturers were among the many that lodged strong protests over the termination of the treaty. One of the more vocal lobbies was formed by the agricultural machinery and implement manufacturers who, to a certain extent, had become dependent on Russian custom. One-third of all U.S. exports to Russia—officially worth nearly $8 million a year—consisted of agricultural machinery and implements. This trade represented 32 percent of all exports from this sector between 1911 and 1913, so it is not surprising that this lobby protested against any action that threatened its access to the Russian market.[21]

Despite repeated attempts, all efforts to renegotiate a satisfactory treaty failed, and after 1 January 1913 Russian-American trade was conducted without the benefit of an agreement. American exports to Russia for the fiscal year 1912–13 not surprisingly declined somewhat, reflecting the uneasiness that was felt in American business circles over the conduct of commerce without an agreement. The Russians were likewise none too pleased with the American decision, finding it "incomprehensible that the United States should deliberately consider the sacrifice of a present and prospective market [worth] hundreds of thousands of dollars."[22] The termination of the agreement also came at a time when the Russians were exhibiting a keen interest in promoting more direct trade relations with the United States. Organizations such as the Russian-American Chamber of Commerce were chartered by the Russian government to foster better, more direct commercial relations between the two countries. A new commercial attaché was also sent to the embassy in Washington in 1913 with explicit instructions to assist American businessmen with any information they should require about trade opportunities in Russia; other officials dispatched to the United States frankly stated that it was their aim to encourage direct American contact as an effort to free Russia from German domination.[23]

While the Russians openly resented Germany's commercial predominance, the efforts to eliminate the European middleman from Russian-American trade were directed toward Britain as well. The outbreak of the war brought a sharpened fear that they would be exchanging German for British domination—a suspicion borne out by British moves to channel all Allied war purchases through London. With the soaring volume of Russian orders placed abroad, it was natural that the United States would likewise be wary of any attempts to limit the potential of American trade with that country.

The Effect of the War on Russian Trade

Never before had Russia experienced such a major upheaval in its foreign trade as that which resulted from the outbreak of World War I. Every aspect of Russian foreign commerce suffered some impact from the war. Most significantly, it effectively removed Russia's major trading partner, eliminating the source of roughly half of all its imports. It also closed those channels through which Russia shipped and received a large proportion of its trade. The effect of the blockade was immediate: a significant decline in the total Russian trade turnover is evident already in 1914, and by 1915 it had plunged to 53 percent of its prewar value. While the turnover did again reach prewar levels by 1916, the majority was now accounted for by imports at prices that were nearly double the 1913 value. The deficit that grew to phenomenal proportions between 1913 and 1917 illustrates the devastating effect of the war on Russian trade (Table 2.4).

Table 2.4   Russian Trade Balance, 1913–1917 (in Millions of Roubles)

	Exports	Imports	Turnover	Balance
1913	1,520.2	1,374.0	2,894.2	146.2
1914	956.1	1,098.0	2,054.1	−141.9
1915	401.8	1,138.6	1,540.4	−736.8
1916	502.0	2,488.4	2,990.4	−1,986.4
1917	488.3	2,498.8	2,987.1	−2,010.5

Source: Narkomfin, Institute ekonomicheskikh isledovaniy, *Narodnokhozyaystvo v 1916g.*, Vypusk VII, pp. 202–45.

The composition and character of this trade was also necessarily changed by the war. Raw and semimanufactured goods and articles that were wholly manufactured continued to make up the bulk of Russian imports and, despite a decline in 1914–15, had increased to account for 93.7 percent of all imports in 1916. Not surprisingly, manufactured goods alone made up 56.6 percent of the total value of Russian imports, with iron and steel manufactures taking first place.[24] With the exception of copper, finished leather products, and iron and steel manufactures, the types of goods that were being imported in increasing quantities from Britain and the United States during the war were not necessarily commodities that were purchased at all from these countries prior to 1914. The wartime trade was also artificially inflated with huge Russian purchases of munitions, as is evidence by the staggering growth in the import of explosives from the United States. Another change, apparent in Table 2.5, is the increased importance of the Asiatic ports of Vladivostok and Nicholaevsk in American trade with Russia. The rapidly expanding volume of imports handled through these ports not only reflects the necessity of establishing alternative routes to compensate for the restricted and severely congested state of trade via European frontiers, but also illustrates the growing importance of the United States as a source of supplies to Russia.

Russian export trade was likewise severely effected by the war. Foodstuffs, which had accounted for over half of all Russian exports in 1913, declined dramatically after the outbreak of the war. Here again, the removal of Germany, which had absorbed approximately one-third of all Russian exports, no doubt helped to effect this change. Equally important, however, was the closure of the Dardanelles, which prevented the exportation of grain and other foodstuffs that were normally shipped

Table 2.5   Trade of the United States with Russia in Europe and Asia (in Dollars)

	Russia in Europe		Russia in Asia	
	Imports	Exports	Imports	Exports
1910	12,687,797	18,463,598	1,140,468	1,070,163
1911	14,726,509	24,151,483	1,172,749	1,306,550
1912	26,279,295	26,098,377	2,067,575	1,216,760
1913	22,322,957	25,065,351	2,054,113	944,356
1914	12,306,334	22,260,062	2,263,063	5,696,275
1915	2,433,222	125,794,954	653,373	44,198,950
1916	4,478,990	309,806,581	4,139,705	160,701,673
1917	12,350,179	315,250,020	2,164,252	109,260,439
1918	6,784,603	8,902,449	3,975,404	8,433,069

Source: Data from U.S. Department of Commerce, *Statistical Abstracts of the United States*, 1921.

from Russian Black Sea ports. As the bulk of Russian corn was dispatched via this route, the war had effectively crippled the Russian export trade in grain. Although exports of raw and semimanufactured materials declined relatively little compared with those of foodstuffs, it must be noted that a number of Russian industries, notably the extractive industries, suffered severe setbacks as a result of the war. The inability to export because of a shortage of shipping tonnage and the closure of the straits, compounded by storage problems and labor difficulties, served to disrupt seriously a number of these industries and caused considerable long-term damage.

While the removal of Germany may have caused severe upheaval in the Russian economy, neither the preoccupation with the war in Britain nor that with neutrality in the United States prevented the anticipation of the seemingly boundless economic opportunities that presented themselves to the Allies in Russia. The wartime demand for finished goods in Russia promised a secure foothold in that market that would facilitate further commercial expansion after the war.

Despite, or perhaps because of, the necessity of more intimate Anglo-Russian relations brought about by the war, Russia was still anxious to develop better commercial relations with the United States. The Russian government wasted no time in pressing the United States to take advantage of the opportunity presented by the elimination of the German inter-

mediary in Russian-American trade.[25] Hopes for the speedy establishment of more direct trade relations were quickly dashed, however, when
negotiations for a new trade agreement failed to materialize.[26] The lack
of official commitment on the part of the Americans, combined with the
urgency of obtaining desperately needed supplies and war matériel, dictated the necessity of closer commercial and financial ties with Britain.

During the early months of the war, Britain was the major source of all
Allied war supplies. The demands placed upon British industry quickly
outstripped its capacity, however, and a growing number of Allied orders
were then placed in the United States—though the financing of these
purchases was still largely carried out in Britain. At a conference of Allied
ministers in February 1915, arrangements were discussed with regard to
the centralization and coordination in London of all Allied war orders
and their financing. Forced to acquiesce because of their dependence on
British credit, the Russians resented what they perceived as British attempts to control their war trade. Moves to circumvent this interference
and establish their own contacts led to the dispatch of an artillery commission to the United States in the spring of 1915, whereupon it made its
own purchases directly without the benefit of approval from London.[27]

Such independence on the part of their Russian ally was not appreciated in Britain, and in September 1915 the matter of procedure in placing
orders was again addressed. One of Britain's chief wishes, declared Chan-
cellor of the Exchequer MacKenna, was to establish a definite procedure
for placing orders with the United States. Britain and Russia, he asserted,
were competing against each other in the American market as well as for
the necessary funding in London. A virtual ultimatum was issued: as a
sine qua non for the receipt of further British credit, Russia was to concentrate future orders through Britain as well as keep the British government informed of the amount of payments, their destination, and the
dates the payments were due.[28] Russia was in no financial position to
refuse these conditions, and the agreement signed on 30 September 1915
provided the tsarist government with the desperately needed credit of £25
million per month. In return it was to surrender to Britain—on paper at
least—control over virtually every aspect of supplying its war effort.

Such conditions could only have made the Russians suspicious of
Britain.[29] They were afraid that the British would exploit Russian economic weakness and assume the position of dominance formerly enjoyed
by Germany. In the autumn of 1915, the Russians again struck out against
this control and established their own Procurement Commission. Created
to pursue independent lines of contact for the purchase of supplies, the
commission concluded contracts directly with American manufacturers

for such things as metals, chemicals, drugs and medical supplies, rubber, and machinery of all sorts. Even the financing was handled independently through an arrangement with Olaf Aschberg, the director of the Swedish-Russian-Asiatic Company.[30] Despite this attempt to exercise independence, the vitally important purchases of military supplies continued to be handled through the British who, not surprisingly, displayed a good deal of antipathy toward the Russian commission.[31]

Russian efforts to encourage direct relations with the United States were quite successful. Trade returns for the war period show that, although Britain had provided the majority of all Russian imports by value during the first full year of the war, the bulk of this trade had been lost to the United States by 1916. Russian-American commercial and financial relations had become more intimate by the end of 1915. As a result of the war, the United States had ceased to be a debtor nation, and instead was faced with a surplus of ready capital with which to pursue economic and commercial expansion abroad. The vacuum in Russian trade caused by the removal of Germany in combination with the huge profits to be made from the wartime trade naturally pointed to opportunities ripe for exploitation through the development of better Russian-American commercial relations.[32] Encouraged by the Russian government, American businessmen and financiers were also enticed by the promise of vast postwar prospects as well.[33] The Russian government, through the Russian-American Chamber of Commerce, did much to promote American interests along these lines and repeatedly used such organizations to invite American business to take a larger share of the Russian market.[34]

By 1916, the United States had succeeded in capturing the larger proportion of Russian purchases abroad. It had taken a more active role in directly supplying the Russian war effort and, indeed, in financing it as well. American capital was particularly coveted by the Russians as it was believed that, unlike British capital, it had no political strings attached. Russia had even managed to secure several small loans from the United States before that country entered the war. In October 1914, a credit of $90 million was made available to Russia by National City Bank of New York. Despite America's proclaimed neutrality and Wilson's refusal to grant government credit to any of the belligerents, National City Bank was informed that the methods used by private merchants in financing their trade was not the concern of the U.S. government. National City immediately extended an additional $5 million credit, though this time accepting Russian short-term treasury notes as collateral.[35]

The increase in the value of American exports to Russia even before the United States entered the war is staggering. Compared to the $31.3 million worth of American goods sold to Russia in 1914, U.S. exports had increased nearly tenfold by 1916, amounting to over $309.8 million. The future value of such trade was not lost on American businessmen or, indeed, on the U.S. government.[36] Dispatching yet another new ambassador to Petrograd in the person of David Francis, the United States made a fresh effort to conclude a trade agreement with the Russian government.

The Scramble for Advantage

The outbreak of hostilities in Europe prompted the growth of organizations and publications that were devoted solely to the task of enlightening the American public—particularly the industrialist and investor—about all aspects of Russia.[37] They generally bolstered the view that the war would not have any great or long-lasting effect on the empire; it was believed that Russia's vast natural wealth would cushion it against the hardships that the other belligerents would undoubtedly face after the war. To blossom, however, Russia needed only to combine its riches with American entrepreneurship and talent.[38] In its first issue, dated May 1916, the periodical *Russia* informed its readership that the tsar's domains offered a market that was potentially the size of Britain, France, Germany, and Austria-Hungary combined. With room for even further expansion, this market would provide American manufacturers with a vast outlet for their goods and products for years to come.[39]

Optimism and encouragement likewise emanated from governmental quarters. At an international trade conference in New York at the end of 1915, a Commerce Department representative declared that an urgent task stood before American capital. He pointed out the necessity of preparing the ground now for the acquisition of markets after the war, and went on to characterize Russia as a market that was "particularly deserving of serious attention on the part of every industrialist and exporter."[40] Private industry, however, needed no prompting. Representatives from a variety of firms were already traveling to Russia to investigate potential present as well as postwar business opportunities. Even such sober industrialists as Henry Ford had ideas for Russia. The report received from the corporate agent dispatched to assess the possibilities in that country was somewhat more than enthusiastic:

In Russia alone . . . once we get our factories started there, in automobiles alone we will do nearly as much as we are doing in America today.

You cannot realize the thing. It is so big it would stagger you. The country itself could stand half a dozen big assembly plants if the business is handled in the right way. . . . I would like to get into that country now and organize a Russian company while they are enthusiastic about American business men. . . . They want American manufacturers to come on the inside now and get busy. After the war will be too late, I think, to get the best kind of concessions to conduct our big business there.[41]

There were, however, some who were not content merely to speculate about such potential, and a number of ambitious American schemes to penetrate and capture the Russian market had been set afoot as early as 1915.[42]

Parallel to the awakening of a greater American interest in Russia was a flurry of activity in Britain that was likewise directed toward the firm establishment of British business interests on Russian soil. New commercial organizations such as the Russian Branch of the London Chamber of Commerce, the Anglo-Russian Trade Commission, and the Anglo-Russian Commercial Chamber in Petrograd were created to provide British manufacturers with "on the spot" reports of opportunities as they presented themselves in Russia, as well as advise on the best methods for securing the postwar trade.[43] These organizations assumed that there would be an unprecedented demand for imports in Russia after the war, and that its "natural resources and productive capacity" would pay for these imports in increased exports. The only question that remained was "who will get the benefit of it, and how, more particularly, can Great Britain get her share?"[44] Despite the fact that it was almost universally held that the future potential of Russian trade "could only be underestimated," and that "whatever might be imagined as Russia's requirements would fall short of her real needs,"[45] an acute jealousy nonetheless developed over this market.

With the outbreak of hostilities it was taken for granted in Britain that English manufacturers and traders would not only succeed in assuming the £60 million worth of Russian trade that was Germany's before the war, but that they could also "easily double" this figure once they put their mind to it. The vision of Russia as a passive market, waiting to be cultivated by British business, emerges in numerous tracts on the subject; the attitude was that it remained only for "British manufacturers to decide to occupy it."[46] But with American commercial interests becoming increasingly competitive in Russia, it was clear that Britain would have to fight for its share of that market.

Despite the common war effort created by America's entry into the conflict in April 1917, open competition and considerable suspicion continued to develop between the United States and Great Britain over the pursuit of what each believed to be its rightful share in the Russian market. Although U.S. government loans were made explicitly to finance the purchase of war matériel and related supplies,[47] there was a simultaneous burst of new activity directed toward enhancing postwar Russian-American economic and commercial relations. Chambers of commerce and other organizations stepped up their campaign to attract American business and capital,[48] and official economic missions—the Root Mission and the Special Russian Economic Mission, headed by the future Russian ambassador Boris Bakhmetev—were dispatched by the two governments to reinforce wartime relations and explore the possibilities of future American participation in Russian economic undertakings.[49]

The closer ties between Russia and the United States brought about by the war not surprisingly resulted in an increased American presence there. The burgeoning number of American businessmen, advisors, and philanthropists piqued the British, who were certain that this growing American presence was part of a larger plan devised to achieve a postwar monopoly in Russia.[50] Such fears were mirrored in the United States, where there was a general conviction that the British had grand designs to take Germany's place in Russian trade. It was, in fact, widely held that Britain was "trying to hog the commercial business of the world." The Americans, however, believed that they had the advantage as the Russians were "not asleep to the fact of what England is trying to do commercially."[51] The Russians, it was argued, would prefer to deal with the United States because it had no ulterior motives. Not content to trust the future of Russian-American trade to moral advantage alone, a number of highly placed U.S. representatives argued that definite action should be taken to safeguard America's position. The U.S. ambassador in Russia, David R. Francis, was in favor of encouraging American merchants and capitalists to get a "firm foothold" in Russia in order to offset what he saw as an Anglo-French conspiracy to capture the trade of Russia.[52]

The heightened competition that developed between the British and the Americans over their respective attempts to corner the postwar Russian market was based on wishful thinking. Preoccupation with windfall gains blinded both sides to the realities of the faltering Russian economy. The fact that Russia was exporting at maximum capacity before the war hardly weighed in their analysis of future demand.[53] Trade between 1914 and 1917 was necessarily inflated by exceptional import need and, further, did not consist of goods that would normally be imported in such quantities after the war. Nonetheless, the promise of gaining a substantial proportion of the trade that was conducted by Germany prior to 1914 whetted the appetites of the commercial and financial communities in both countries. In numerous cases, existing interests were significantly expanded during the war years; new branches and agencies sprang up in the larger Russian cities in anticipation of the huge postwar business to be done, and infusions of capital found a ready home in both new and existing locations within the mining, metallurgical, and manufacturing industries of Russia.

Prewar British and American trade with Russia was certainly not insubstantial, and the commercial opportunities presented there as a result of the war fired a great deal of enthusiasm and optimism in both countries over the prospects of the postwar potential of the Russian marketplace. However, it should have been fairly obvious from a variety of economic indicators that to pin such hopes on Russia was not merely overly optimistic but totally unrealistic. Nonetheless, the vision of an insatiable postwar market for manufactured goods promoted jealousy and suspicion between the two allies. Recriminations as to the motives and objectives of activities, whether governmental or commercial, were frequent.

The obsession with the commercial potential of Russia was augmented by the October Revolution. By the time the revolution erupted, both governments and capitalists alike possessed plans for developing their postwar interests in the country. The Bolsheviks were not initially perceived as an obstacle to these plans, and their successful bid for power did not immediately quell the excitement that had developed over Russia. Both official and business circles considered Bolshevism to be nothing more than a rather distasteful political aberration that would soon wane, leaving a more moderate government in its wake. Indeed, news of the Bolshevik coup was met with distinct casualness in the United States. So little was thought of the event that President Wilson chose to keep his appointment to play golf with his personal physician.[54] Convinced that the "next" Russian government would recognize and honor all previous debts, obligations, and contracts, there was a rush to "capture" whatever was possible while the power vacuum existed. A number of British firms, in anticipation of their future business there, had already appointed persons in Russia to act on their behalf—sometimes giving them agencies "for the whole of Russia."[55] There was also a brisk business in prewar Russian bonds and securities, with a number of investors hoping to profit from the sale of those bonds by less optimistic individuals. Stocks for at least eleven mines and nine combined Russian-English oil companies likewise continued to be quoted on the London exchange for some time after the revolution.[56] Not surprisingly, a clash of Allied interests occurred in Russia, as a result of which inter-Allied competition became even more intense, with ulterior motives and unfair advantage being suspected at every turn. Remarking on this state of affairs, the British Embassy in Washington pointed out that "the uncertainty and suspicion . . . among American businessmen as to our policy exists here in quarters where one would least expect to find it. Even the sober Gay [sic] spoke to me quite gravely about the bad feeling likely to be created here by our efforts towards trade development at this crisis of the war. The Department of Overseas Trade in particular is looked upon as something unsportsmanlike, devised to steal an advantage while the USA is busy winning the war to save democracy!"[57] While it was recognized that there was "bound to be mutual suspicion as to activities in the direction of trade expansion," the British government was equally quick to assume that "the Americans, of course, [were] out for as much as they can grab." It was felt that, in order to counter this, Britain should "continue working quietly and steadily for the extension of our export trade, by every possible means."[58]

The hostile ideological disposition of the new Bolshevik regime, combined with the more pressing concerns of the war and, in connection with this, the Bolsheviks' withdrawal from it, immediately jaundiced the relations between the Allied powers and the Soviet government. To be sure, unofficial contact with the Soviet regime was quickly established as the Allies attempted to secure the assurance of renewed Russian participation in a spring offensive.[59] It was only when these efforts failed to yield the desired unconditional guarantees of continued Russian participation in the war—ultimately manifested by the Soviet government's decision to opt for a unilateral peace with the Germans—that the Allied governments turned openly hostile. Instead of accepting withdrawal as a manifestation of the desperate need for peace in Russia, the Allies preferred to see the Bolshevik acquiescence to the harsh terms stipulated by Germany in the Treaty of Brest-Litovsk as an act of duplicity. Shortly afterward, the Bolsheviks initiated the policy now known as War Communism in Soviet-controlled Russia. The resulting nationalization and expropriation of private property and the repudiation of foreign debts were seen as unfriendly acts and subsequently put the Soviet government firmly beyond the pale in the eyes of the Allied nations. Diplomatic personnel in Russia were reduced to a bare minimum and shipments of war matériel and supplies were immediately halted.

As the events of 1918 unfurled, it became increasingly obvious to both the British and Americans that a cohesive approach was needed to deal with the so-called Russian question. As will be seen, the suspicion that each had for the other, the fear that one would "steal a march" and obtain an "unfair advantage" in a future—that is, non-Bolshevik—Russian market, and the lack of interdepartmental unity within each of the governments, combined to prevent the two Allies from ever attaining a united front on this issue.

3

The Allies,
the War, and
the Bolshevik
Revolution

Official British policy toward Soviet Russia underwent a radical change in the course of the three years following the October Revolution. From the actively hostile policy of the intervention and blockade in 1918–19, the British government made what appears to be a complete reversal by mid-1920. The unexpected announcement in January 1920 of the decision taken by the Supreme Allied Council to allow trade with the Russian cooperative societies was quickly followed by the extension of British diplomatic feelers on the possibility of opening negotiations with the Soviet government. By March 1921 British policy had shifted from its earlier stand of supporting the blockade and intervention against Bolshevik Russia to one that recognized the Soviet government as the de facto Russian authority, allowing for the conclusion of formalized agreements.

Unlike its British ally, the United States refused to reconsider its official position of nonrecognition until 1933. Even so, significant alterations in American policy occurred during the period 1918–21.

In the majority of instances, however, governmental decisions to relax or remove prohibitions on trade with the Bolsheviks were taken in direct response to, or in anticipation of, similar actions on the part of Great Britain. But in either case, governmental policy was not created in a vacuum, and the evolution of both governments' approach to the economic side of the Russian question was closely related to the major international political events of those years. Thus, the development of British and American economic policy in Russia between 1918 and 1921 can be examined in three stages: within the political parameters of the war; under conditions of the armistice and peace; and finally, under conditions of attempted accommodation with the Soviet government.

Until the conclusion of the Anglo-Soviet Trade Agreement in March 1921, neither government can be said to have any clear-cut or single official policy toward Russia. Even so, immediately after the revolution there was a virtually reflexive move to protect and promote their economic and commercial interests there on as wide a scale as possible. In this respect, both governments' overall economic objectives in Russia changed little throughout the period 1918–20. When these interests were threatened by Germany and, later, by the Bolsheviks, Britain undertook to convince the United States that the intervention and blockade were necessary protective measures. It was not by accident that British and American military and political involvements were greatest in those areas of Russia in which their economic interests were strongest. In the case of Britain, it is particularly apparent that the establishment of firm control over strategic raw materials was a primary motive behind the decision to intervene in Russia in 1918, and that this went on to form the basis for the economic policy that subsequently developed. Evidence points toward a preoccupation with the immediate need to keep Russian raw materials out of enemy hands—the reasoning employed to secure U.S. participation in the intervention—as well as with ensuring that an abundant supply would be available to Britain over the long run. It was officially maintained that the best way to keep Germany and, indeed, any other competitor from gaining an advantage in Russia was to promote British economic and commercial interests whenever and wherever possible. Consequently, many aspects of the policy expressed by the government at this time reflected the hope of strengthening considerably the British economic foothold there.

The formulation of any coherent Russian policy by either country was prevented by the existence of interdepartmental frictions and rivalries within the governments themselves. Further, the lack of communication even between bureaus within the same department frequently resulted in significant differences in the interpretation of policy. The Board of Trade, the Department of Overseas Trade, the War Trade Intelligence Department, and the Commercial Department of the Foreign Office were all in the habit of giving advice to traders. There was, however, "no effective connecting link between them and no organised consultation. The Ministry of Munitions were themselves carrying on very large trading transactions and giving advice. The War Office Contracts Department . . . was in the same position. The Ministry of Reconstruction had set up a large number of committees to examine important trade questions and were also giving advice to the trading community—frequently giving quite different advice to that given by other departments." Moreover, the Department of Overseas Trade—ostensibly responsible to both the Foreign Office and the Board of Trade—was reportedly able "to play one office off against the other and deal with practical matters unbeknown to either."[1]

Thus, it is necessary to undertake a reconsideration of the evolution of commercial policy on an official level and, further, the difference between the government's policy as it existed on paper and that which was actually effected must also be examined. It is also important to remember that virtually no one in either the British or American governments, including the diplomatic personnel in Russia, expected the Bolshevik regime to survive very long, and that this belief persisted in prominent, informed circles throughout the early 1920s. This conviction heavily influenced early governmental economic policy in Russia and thus also had a significant impact on the activities of private traders.

Commercial activities on the private level, as distinct from those of the government, will also be examined, as will be the activities and attitudes of private commercial concerns and business organizations that chose to trade with either Soviet or "White" Russia prior to 1921.[2] Although the antipathy of such groups as the Federation of British Industries and the New York Chamber of Commerce toward any commercial relations with the Bolsheviks is well known, these organizations did not represent business opinion across the board in either Great Britain or the United States. Because private trade interests not infrequently operated on lines quite independent from those laid down by the government, an examination of economic relations for the period 1918–20 must therefore be conducted on two planes: that of private commercial and trading interests, and that of the government.

Further, British and American attempts to capture the postrevolutionary Russian market have generally been described as singularly unsuccessful, and the existence of any significant level of trade with Russia as a whole during the three-year period 1918–20 has been dismissed out of hand. It is also usually argued that trade was hindered by a general disinclination on the part of traders to become economically involved in a country that was undergoing such volatile change. Although each government positively encouraged the commercial activities of its nationals in those areas of Russia that were free from Bolshevik domination, it is generally asserted that trade with these regions likewise never assumed any significant dimensions. This assumption requires qualification; it is interesting to note that the conventional judgments feature only exports to Russia, and, in particular, *direct* exports. The importance of Russian raw materials and foodstuffs to the United Kingdom and, indeed, to the economic well-being of Europe as a whole, is rarely mentioned except to describe the dearth of those goods available for export from Russia. On the contrary, the policy statements and memorandums issued by the Department of Overseas Trade and the Foreign Office show that British governmental interest was initially on Russia as a supplier. Despite Lloyd George's insistence that the way to tame the Bolsheviks was to ensure that Russia had an abundance of British-produced consumer goods, it must be noted that his primary aim in reestablishing this trade was to rehabilitate Russia as the European granary and major supplier of raw materials. The emphasis on the volume and value of exports to Russia in assessing the "significance" of Soviet trade for this period should therefore be reconsidered, and an evaluation of the importance of Russian exports to the United Kingdom in particular should be included.

Finally, the effects of the postwar economic slump played a vitally important role in pushing the governments closer toward an economic rapprochement with the Soviet Union. By the end of 1920, the recession had become a depression, with rampant inflation and unemployment in both Europe and the United States. Both governments were confronted with increasingly vocal industrial and commercial representations that pressured for the establishment of trading relations with the Soviet Union. Once again, Russia was cast in the role of the insatiable market, the panacea for both American and British economic ills. Pressure to conclude a trade agreement with the Soviets had pushed the British government full circle. The Americans, while continuing to mouth moral indignation, were fast on the British heels in their relaxation of the more obvious restrictions on trade with Russia.

1918: The Intervention

Whereas the Allies' political approach to the Bolsheviks was uncertain until well after the start of the intervention, there was no such confusion with regard to their economic policy in Russia.[3] The withdrawal of Russia from the war and the ensuing Soviet peace negotiations with Germany provided the driving force behind the Allied decision to defend their interests in Russia. There was a growing fear that the Germans would either capture militarily or acquire through the Brest-Litovsk Treaty supplies that would enable them to fuel indefinitely their war efforts on the western front. The goods and materials that had been shipped to Russia by the Allies throughout the war were an obvious and immediate concern. Hundreds of thousands of tons of such supplies had accumulated in the North Russian ports of Archangel and Murmansk and at the port of Vladivostok in the Russian Far East. By November 1917 goods and equipment amounting to 162,495 tons were laying at the quayside at Archangel alone; and in late March 1918, that is, after the ratification of the Brest-Litovsk Treaty by the Soviet government, these goods were reported to be disappearing into the interior of Bolshevik-controlled Russia at a rate of about three thousand tons per week.[4] A more serious problem was posed by the possibility of Germany gaining control over those areas of Russia from which strategic raw materials could be secured. Resources such as timber and flax from the Russian North, as well as oil, minerals, and grain from the Caucasus and the Ukraine had to be prevented from reaching the enemy. With the inability of the Bolsheviks to halt the German advance in the winter and early spring of 1918, and the conclusion of the Brest-Litovsk Treaty in March, it appeared that the Allies' fear of the German domination of Russia was being realized. The cession by the Soviet government of vast areas of the former Russian Empire to Germany and the conclusion of a trade agreement concurrent with the peace treaty served to give the Kaiserreich a position of undeniable advantage in Russia. Under the terms of the treaties, Germany could further curtail the already restricted volume of essential Russian raw materials that were still being exported to the European Allies and, ultimately, exclude Allied interests from Russia altogether. It is against such developments that the British and American governments' economic policy in Russia first took shape.

In neither the United States nor Great Britain was the Bolshevik revolution greeted with an immediate manifestation of ideological hostility. Little was known about the movement and certainly not enough to cause such sentiment. Rather, the deterioration of the Russian front since March and the course of the war generally had dictated that, in light of the further upheavals in Russia, all shipments of war matériel to that destination should cease. Purely a precautionary action, this move was taken to prevent matériel falling into enemy—then clearly German—hands. In addition, unofficial contacts with the Bolsheviks were immediately established by both Britain and the United States. Although unofficial representatives were dispatched initially to negotiate for the continued Russian participation in the war, this channel of communication was to remain open for almost a year after the Bolshevik revolution—that is, well after the manifestation of open hostilities.[5]

Many British and American officials, as well as numerous merchants, traders, and manufacturers with interests in Russia, continued to conduct their day-to-day business with the local Soviet authorities in much the same way as they did with the previous Russian government. Further, that Allied representatives remained at their posts and, for the most part, continued to function in their normal capacities during the first few months after the Bolshevik revolution served to calm any serious worries that the trader or businessman might have had toward continuing his commercial activities in Russia. There was, in short, an initial sense of assured continuity in Russia, an attitude that is evident in the general lack of reaction to the early Soviet announcements and decrees. Characteristic of this attitude is the Board of Trade's rather laconic observation regarding the Soviet denunciation in November of the Anglo-Russian Commercial Treaty of 1859: it was "assumed that the Treaty [would] terminate on the 24th October 1918, being twelve months from the date of the Russian note denouncing the Treaty."[6]

This attempt at "business as usual" pervaded the private sector as well during the early months after the revolution. Indeed, even the intervention did not deter the arrival in Russia of an informal British economic mission in June 1918. Although nominally headed by the comptroller general of the Department of Overseas Trade, the mission does not appear to have had its origins in the Foreign Office.[7] That it was viewed benevolently by the British government is obvious, however, from the Foreign Office's soothing response to the American ambassador's scathing criticism on the timing and desirability of the mission. Willing to take the responsibility for the dispatch of the commission, Balfour explained that it was only a small group of commercial experts who were "sent out with Lindley to Russia by H.M. Government to advise them as to the best means of restoring and developing British trade relations and interests in Russia and countering enemy schemes and commercial penetration."[8] Whatever oil was poured on the water to calm the Allied suspicions of the mission was immediately set alight when the group proceeded to Bolshevik-controlled Moscow in late July. The fact that it made the rounds of the various Soviet offices, discussing the possibility of trade and commerce with representatives of a regime against which hostile interventionist action had been taken by its own government, points to the remarkable state of the British commercial mind.

Nor did the extension of the blockade to include private trade to Russian ports do more than cause a minor inconvenience for a number of businessmen during those early months. It certainly did not prevent commerce with Russia, as trade through Finland was still quite unfettered.[9] The neutral countries of Northern Europe, not yet bound to honor the Allied blockade of Russia, also served as a major route through which both import and export trade passed. In the case of the United States, it is worth remembering that such transit routes handled a considerable proportion of prewar Russian-American trade and thus were quite familiar to its businessmen.[10] Indeed, as will be discussed later, transit trade was to play an essential role in the early development of the Soviet Union's commercial relations with the West.

A fair number of foreign-controlled businesses in Russia likewise suffered little disruption in their operations throughout this early period. Sales branches of the Kodak Company, Vauxhall Motor Company, and Ransomes, Sims and Jefferies all continued to do business for some time after the revolution. Indeed, Kodak continued to do a decent trade in its primary trading houses in Russia at least until the middle of 1918; its Odessa branch alone did an average of 1,200 roubles a week in business. Moreover, that company's branches in Soviet Russia were reportedly "all intact" as late as February 1920. Branch managers in Petrograd, Moscow, and Odessa quite simply "gave the Soviet Commissars a contribution to their funds and were allowed to continue their business without molestation."[11]

Certain British and American manufacturing firms with plants in Russia likewise continued their operations unscathed. In addition to the well-known American cases of International Harvester and Singer, the British-controlled Anglo-Russian Cotton Factories had also managed to escape expropriation by the Soviet government—at least temporarily. Although Raymond Robins has been credited with negotiating the fate of the two American firms in Russia, International Harvester and the Anglo-Russian Cotton Factories claimed that tactful management and the maintenance of good relations between their employees and management were the major reasons behind their successful evasion of nationalization.[12] Further, a number of companies were so confident that the Bolshevik regime would either collapse completely or soon evolve into a more moderate form of government that they continued with their plans to establish new branches even inside areas that were unquestionably under Soviet control. As late as 19 December 1917 the *Russkie Vedomosti* reported the opening of a branch of the New York City Bank in Moscow, which subsequently guaranteed to its depositors "the payment of their deposits even if they should be confiscated by the Bolshevik authorities, in which case they will be paid in Russian Currency by the Bank in New York. In the space of a month and a half the Petrograd Branch . . . received deposits of one hundred and fifty million roubles and in Moscow the deposits already amount to three hundred million roubles. One of the objectives of the Bank [was] to buy up as many undertakings as possible, especially metallurgical works."[13] In making note of this move, the Foreign Office remarked that the move was "a very smart stroke," and that "this [was] undoubtedly the way to do business." No doubt, the British government fully appreciated the bank's example of keen American acumen, for it appeared that the bank had exploited the instability of the Russian market to establish a firm advantage in the financial sector, allowing it to spread its economic influence through the acquisition of a substantial control over other areas of the Russian economy.[14]

Neither individual firms nor the British government proved averse to negotiating with the Soviets during the first few months after the revolution. One case that is significant for a number of reasons involves Vickers and its negotiations for the sale of the Tsaritsyn Ordnance Works to the Soviet government. The business transacted by this organization with the Bolshevik authorities throughout the first half of 1918 is so remarkable that the company memorandum on the subject deserves to be quoted at length.

> From the Great War onwards the necessity of making the Tzaritzin Ordnance Works a direct state concern became one of the chief features in the plans for the defence of the Country. . . . This idea was handed down from the Imperial Government to the temporary one and later was passed on to the Soviet Government without becoming any less momentous.
>
> One of the first questions of defence raised after the formation of the Soviet Government was the question of acquiring the Tzaritzin Works immediately after the 27th October 1917. The Commission [to negotiate the purchase of the Works] resumed its sitting under the Presidency of the Commissary for Naval Affairs and the representatives of the High Commission for Economic Affairs, and on 22nd

March 1918, the change of regime notwithstanding, it was decided to purchase the Tzaritzin Ordnance Works, and in April of that year, the transactions were duly concluded.

Simultaneously [with the sale agreement], Vickers Ltd. of London, through the Tzaritzin Ordnance Works Company, entered into an agreement with the Soviet Government similar to the special one it entered into . . . with the Tzaritzin Ordnance Works.

By this agreement, which was to act for 15 years, Vickers Ltd. agreed to carry out the supreme technical control over the manufacturing of heavy ordnance (16 guns) and of armour-piercing shells, and to apply their methods of moulding, forging, tempering, mechanical finishing and of testing and correcting gun shells.

In return for their works and the sole use of their methods and secrets of production, Vickers Ltd. were to receive a fixed commission, and in case of it being impossible for some order to be executed at the Tzaritzin Works because of their temporary lack of equipment, the order was to be executed at the English works of Vickers Ltd.

Vickers Ltd. were to participate to an exceptional extent in the setting up of the ordnance works at Tzaritzin; Vickers supplied the greater part of the equipment . . . paid out sums of money on [their] behalf . . . and even supplied guns to the Gunnery Department through the medium of the Tzaritzin works.

The agreement provided that Vickers Ltd. were to continue to supervise the technical side of the manufacture of heavy artillery and shells—as they had agreed to do with the Tzaritzin Company . . . orders for factory equipment and heavy guns, the latter through the Tzaritzin Works, fulfilled by Vickers, have not yet been paid. . . . That transactions are being made by the Soviet Government with the firm of Vickers Ltd., such as commercial orders for various machines etc, and since it is necessary to carry on regular relations with that firm the Soviet Government must pay the rightful claims of Vickers Ltd., especially since the representatives of that Government have previously recognised these claims by paying for the factory itself.[15]

The significance of the memorandum is threefold. First, it exemplifies the element of continuity in economic relations and that, "change in regime notwithstanding," business must go on. The company not only went through with the sale of the Ordnance Works, but also entered into a technical-aid contract in which it agreed to provide assistance in the various stages of armament production carried out at Tsaritsyn. Second, it must be noted that Vickers had concluded this contract in April 1918, that is, after the conclusion of the Soviet-German peace treaty, and was thus conducting armament trade with what was now considered to be, for all intents and purposes, a hostile government. This fact also goes to illustrate the growing divergence between the British government's economic policy in Russia and the interests of private business. Despite the adoption of an increasingly anti-Bolshevik government policy both on the political as well as the economic level, a number of British businesses continued to pursue their own interests in Russia irrespective of the government's policy. Finally, if the concluding statement of the memorandum is taken at face value, a precedent was set for the Soviet recognition of its own contractual debts when it paid for the Tsaritsyn Works. Although it appears from the records that Vickers was never paid for these services—if indeed, they were ever rendered—the company nonetheless continued to do business with the Soviet government. To be sure, the firm's assets in Russia were undoubtedly valuable enough to justify maintaining its commercial relations with the Bolshevik regime—if only as an attempt "to get back some of its own." Even so, the company's persistent interest in Soviet contracts throughout the 1920s suggests that Vickers continued to perceive the Russian market as a promising one.

While some prominent foreign firms like International Harvester and the Anglo-Russian Cotton Factories did manage to survive intact for a considerable period under the Bolshevik government, and others like Vickers continued to transact business with the regime during these early months, the majority of private business concerns both foreign and domestic suffered expropriation by the Soviet government or "spontaneous nationalization" by their employees. An interesting example of such confiscation can be found in the case of the Kyshtim Mines. One of the many mining interests of Leslie Urquhart's Russo-Asiatic Consolidated, the Kyshtim mines were confiscated by the Bolsheviks on 15 January 1918. Urquhart's correspondent at the mines informed the London office of the event in a rather enlightening telegram. Stating that the breakdown in transport had resulted in "total disorganisation" and that it was a "practical impossibility" to obtain fuel, food, materials, and wages, he went on to point out that the "stoppage of operations was inevitable and financing through coming months [would be] most difficult. Today's confiscation may make matters easier when order is restored."[16] Ambassador Lindley, who forwarded the telegram to the Russo-Asiatic Consolidated offices in London, informed the Foreign Office that he had "discussed the question of defending British interests" both with the French and Belgian ministers and had come to the conclusion that "as regards confiscation of Kyshtim Mines . . . and similar enterprises it must be remembered that it is better for owners to have their property confiscated with the chance of securing future damages than to be definitely ruined by a few more months working. This is the view of the local management."[17] Like Singer and a number of other firms operating in Russia during the war, the Kyshtim mines had been operating unprofitably for some time, and the expropriation was seen as a way of preventing future losses as well as providing a possible means of recouping some of the losses suffered over the course of the previous year or so. Further, the absence of strong representations by either the Foreign Office or the State Department protesting such confiscation of property tends to bear out that the governments largely concurred with the attitude of the owners on this issue.

Although such a stand could be taken to denote the governmental endorsement of a benign policy of cut-and-run, this is far from the case. On the contrary, the policy of commercial penetration in Russia was strongly advanced wherever possible. The Board of Trade energetically took up the question of Russia and, together with the Foreign Office, dispatched circulars to the consulates throughout that country sharply reminding them of their duty to keep their government informed on all manner of commercial and economic matters.[18] There was also considerable concern over the availability of a cadre of persons who were familiar with Russia. The Foreign Office worried over the "waste of good material" that resulted from the conscription of persons who "knew Russia, the Russian language and commercial conditions in Russia . . . when they might at any time be urgently required to forward our commercial interests in Russia." While it was recognized that the conditions that compelled British businessmen to leave Russia might also prevent them from returning, the Foreign Office went on to note that the government nonetheless wanted "to keep up British interests and influence in Russia, and get as many British subjects there as possible who are familiar with the language and conditions. The question is commercial rather than political." It was suggested that the Foreign Office should at least keep track of these men so that the government could "lay hands on them when the moment seems propitious for reconstruction and furthering our economic interests in Russia."[19]

By the spring of 1918 the British government's policy began to take on a distinctly anti-Bolshevik nature. A number of developments in both the Russian North and the Transcaucasian region had prompted the government to take decisive action to protect its substantial and long-standing interests there. The resulting policy of intervention was initiated in an

effort to protect, maintain, and extend if possible British economic interests in the area. However, attempts to realize this aim were carried out in
completely different ways in the two regions and, in the case of Siberia,
were met with considerable opposition by the Americans.

As early as December 1917 the British had approached the United
States with regard to Allied intervention in Russian affairs.[20] Wilson,
however, refused to consider such a move unless the United States was
specifically invited to do so by the Russian government. But by maintaining that there was "no Russian government to deal with" after the Bolshevik revolution, the administration effectively ensured that the United
States would "do nothing" with regard to Russia.[21] In order to provoke
an official reaction from the United States on the Russian question, the
Allies, particularly Britain, pushed and cajoled the Wilson administration. It was in this way that the president was finally made to agree to
intervention. Wilson, along with his secretary of war and chief of staff,
apparently remained unconvinced of the efficacy of the intervention and
agreed to the plans only in order to keep the peace with his Allies: "From
a military standpoint you [Secretary of War Baker] and General March
are clearly right but my trouble is that we are fighting a war with allies."
When pressure from that quarter intensified throughout the early months
of 1918, Wilson eventually succumbed and agreed to participate in the
action "upon which they have so much set their hearts."[22] However,
despite his continued hope "to limit the American contribution as far as
possible but still play the game," Wilson refused to give his blanket approval for operations in all the areas in which the British were proposing
intervention. In particular, the president remained firm in his stand that
the proposed joint American-Japanese action in Siberia would serve no
realistic purpose. It was only in July, when it became evident that Japan
was likely to act unilaterally, that the president took the decision to send
American troops to Siberia.

Just as Siberia was considered by the United States to be an area of
predominantly American interest, the British regarded the Murmansk
region as their preserve.[23] British naval presence in North Russia had
been a thorn in Russia's side since 1916, when that area—along with the
Black Sea—was put under the control of the Admiralty. With the Bolsheviks having secured a majority in the Archangel Soviet in February, the
already-uneasy relations between the British naval authorities in the region and the local government had become distinctly uncomfortable. The
conspicuous escalation of German naval activity in the White and Barents
seas and the reported appearance of German troops in Finland that spring
completely failed to assuage the growing truculence of the Archangel

Soviet toward the now-unwelcome British presence. The grim military situation and the potential advantage that control over the region would give Germany, combined with the increasing likelihood of an open breach developing between the local government and the naval authorities, were key considerations in the decision to land British troops in the Russian North that April. The one element that linked these factors together and provided the British government with the justification for the resulting intervention was the threat posed to the strategic raw materials produced in that region.

From the beginning, British economic policy in the North assumed an almost colonial nature. The charge that the British occupation of northern Russia was imperialistic came not only from the Bolsheviks but also from such unexpected sources as the American chargé d'affaires in Archangel who reported that there existed a general feeling among the American and French troops stationed there that the continued Allied presence in North Russia would "serve only British interests," which they suspected of being "imperialistic."[24] While the motivations behind each government's decision to intervene in Russia were certainly not entirely altruistic, American suspicions of British ulterior motives were confirmed by the events of the subsequent months.

For the duration of the occupation of the North, that is, from April 1918 to the withdrawal during the summer of 1920, British official policy in the region was directed toward complete economic domination. It was believed that "successful intervention" would be "more than paid for by economic concessions."[25] For the moment, however, His Majesty's Government had to be content with securing the readily exportable commodities of the Russian North. Indeed, during the 1918 navigation season thirty-seven steamships departed Archangel carrying some 63,475 tons of North Russian cargo on behalf of the British government, of which 59,180 tons consisted of flax and timber. In comparison, only 1,465 tons was loaded for private persons, and none of this cargo contained either flax or timber. In contrast, only 12,043 tons was loaded on behalf of the French government during the same period, while little over 5,000 tons of goods was exported to the United States from Archangel—all of which was loaded for private persons.[26]

These Russian commodities were considered to be increasingly necessary to Britain. In response to an inquiry from the Board of Customs and Excise concerning restrictions on imports from areas of Russia that were designated as being under "hostile occupation," the comment was made that "anything that comes from Russia now will be something that we want badly, such as flax, hemp, platinum and timber and we had better keep it wherever it comes from."[27] Some 50,000 poods (819 tons) of flax, for example, was contracted for by the War Office in 1918. No doubt some of the impetus for such contracts lay in the fear of losing control over supplies of materials that were necessary to the war effort. But as early as June there emerged a growing concern over future supplies from the North. Because of the domestic political upheavals in Russia and the disruptive effects of the war on Russian industries, the future supply of Russian exports to Europe was seen as uncertain at best. The scramble to purchase flax, for instance, was certainly prompted by the local consulate's warning that "in view of 40 per cent shortages of quantity sown you must act decisively if you wish to secure your future flax supply."[28] It is interesting to note, however, that the competition encountered from Allied quarters in securing these supplies was, more often than not, greater than that met from the enemy.

Along with flax, timber was another resource that Britain sought to control. Over half of Britain's prewar timber requirements were met by exports from North Russia. With the increased demand for this commodity caused by the war, the government moved quickly to secure that industry as well as the readily available supplies lying at the White Sea ports. In January 1918 the Foreign Office received a letter from a major British timber contractor who had extensive financial interests in the timber trade of Archangel. Given the uncertainty of the region's future, E. Schluter and Company desired to know if the government considered whether "further engagements would be warranted for the continuance of business." The minutes on Schluter's query are enlightening: it was pointed out that, although the government was "very anxious to maintain our present predominant position in the Murman Coast and at Archangel, we can hardly advise them to go on; at the same time it is advisable from our point of view that they should not stop. ? say that while Mr. Balfour cannot undertake the responsibility of advising them in the matter, he hopes that British predominance in the timber trade in North Russia will not be allowed to pass into other hands." Arthur Steel-Maitland of the Board of Trade likewise expressed a similar concern: "The white pine from Archangel is the best from anywhere. In the prospective scarcity of timber Russia is likely to be quite the greatest supplier and very important. Other nations are on the watch for the timber concessions there and I am told—though this is not yet confirmed—that Norwegians wish to get into it in competition with British enterprise."[29]

Both of these minutes are remarkable for what they fail to mention as well as what they state. In neither case, nor indeed in any of the minutes that accompanied the initial inquiry from E. Schluter and Company was the German threat to the area mentioned. There appears to be an overriding interest in cornering the industry rather than preventing it from falling into enemy hands. Despite the inadvisability of Schluter entering into any further business transactions with North Russian timber concerns, the government's response to the company clearly indicated that while it could not instruct on the matter it would not like to see the British position there weakened. The communication had its desired effect; E. Schluter and Company agreed to "hang on" as long as possible.

The government's overwhelming concern with exporting as much from North Russia as could be managed and with extending British control to as many of the key industries as possible did not proceed without impediment. The first and most obvious response was the reaction that this policy drew from the Soviet government. On 26 June 1918 Lenin stated that "if the English continue their robber policy we will fight them."[30] Strong words from the leader of a government that a mere four months before was compelled to conclude a harsh peace and an unfavorable trade agreement because of its inability to oppose any further German advance. But fight them Lenin did; the North was the area where the British interventionist forces suffered the worst casualties.

On another level, the British government's overzealous attempts to secure supplies of flax, timber, and hemp from the northern regions caused a multitude of problems for the very same private traders that they were proposing to encourage. One company ran into considerable problems exporting plywood from Archangel—including a consignment that the Timber Supply Department had a contract for—because it had been requisitioned by the British military authorities. As an essential component in the construction of aircraft, the plywood should have been ranked as a priority export—especially as it was under government contract! But the company was informed that though the military needed only "a small quantity," they desired "to hold back the entire lot," preventing the company's agents from shipping any of it out.[31] A number of other similar cases exist where private traders who did venture into the North Russian market found their efforts frustrated by the very government that declared its intent to foster such trade.

In the competition that developed between the government and private sector, that over tonnage was probably the most devastating to private commercial interests. While the availability of shipping facilities for goods to be imported into North Russia was limited, cargo space aboard ships sailing out of the White Sea ports was almost impossible to secure. The ships that arrived at Archangel generally departed carrying a cargo of timber or flax on behalf of the British government.[32] At a meeting held at the Ministry of Shipping in July 1919, it was even contemplated that the ships carrying private cargoes to the White Sea ports should be allowed to proceed only on the condition "that the shippers agree to bring home Government timber at specified rates to be laid down by the timber controller." It was hoped that this policy could be extended to cover neutral shipping to those ports as well.[33]

The one element that sets the British intervention and occupation of the Russian North apart from any of the other regions in which it became involved is the almost complete control exercised by the British authorities over the area. Tacitly recognizing British interests in the region, the United States did not contest its ally when it pressed for the overall military command in the Murmansk province. Along with this, however, the British also took over the administration and organization of nearly all aspects of the economic and even political life of the Murmansk province. The North Russian Provisional Government itself was created and set up by the British, and it was repeatedly forced to defer to the Allied command in the region. Further, the British authority's unilateral use of joint Allied relief funds for the region was a source of considerable friction between the United States and Britain. The British were accused of being "high-handed" with these Allied monies. In addition to employing the funds without consulting their Allies, the British provoked American irritation by attempting to claim credit for supplying relief to the region.

By the autumn of 1918, the British government felt it necessary to take charge of the economy of the North. The establishment of a stable currency was considered to be particularly urgent considering the vast expenditures on local labor and materials by the British command.[34] The initial attempt to bolster the currency took the form of an indirect loan to the North Russian Provisional Government. However, it was eventually decided to replace the rapidly depreciating rouble with a new British issued "rouble," backed by the Bank of England. In addition to arousing resentment among the local authorities, such control over the North Russian economy provoked considerable Allied suspicion as well. Though no protest was ever made over its adoption, the British-sponsored currency was widely considered to be no more than a means to enable the British to establish a financial protectorate and facilitate the commercial exploitation of that region. Reporting on the British currency plan for North Russia, Ambassador Francis stated that it would only "inure [itself] to the benefit of British commerce."[35] This fear was largely substantiated by the extent to which Britain controlled the commerce of the Murmansk province. Despite legitimate American and French interest in raw materials from this region, Britain had in practice preempted the lion's share of all materials available for export from Archangel.[36]

From the start, the British occupation of the Russian North undoubtedly had more of an imperialistic color to it than any of the other areas of Russia in which the Allied interventionist forces operated. Although it was asserted that the intervention was initially undertaken as a defensive measure, designed to prevent Germany from gaining control of essential war supplies, Britain continued to extend and consolidate its position in the North, exercising virtually complete economic and political control long after the armistice.

Major Allied interventionist activity took place in two other regions besides the North: the area between the Black and Caspian seas in South Russia, and Siberia. Although the occupation was initiated under the rubric of a joint Allied military operation, it was clear that in the case of these two areas the prevailing interests of Great Britain in Transcaucasia and the United States, in conjunction (or competition) with the Japanese, in Siberia would determine the nature of the intervention. However, even such a frank admission of the existence of spheres of influence did not preclude the development of governmental or private commercial competition and suspicion in either of these regions.

Prior to the revolution, British interests in Siberia were limited and, for the most part, tended to be concentrated in a number of mining concerns in western Siberia. Even so, the postwar potential of Siberia attracted considerable attention in both governmental and private commercial circles, and the opportunities presented by the prevailing chaos in Russia appeared ripe for exploitation. It was with genuine concern that the scarcity of British representation east of the Ural Mountains was realized by the government in the spring of 1918; "One wonders," mused Lord Cecil, "why Siberia has always been neglected by us in the past."[37] An examination of the possible benefits of an Allied occupation of Siberia was undertaken, the results of which hypothesized that such an occupation would result in the creation of an autonomous state not bound to German peace terms and destructive trade treaties. It was believed that this occupation would in turn promote a firm basis for the establishment of British trade in Siberia and, further, would allow for the "obtaining of concrete securities in concessions (railway, mineral, timber, etc.) against Russia's vast liabilities to the Allies." The possibility of dividing Siberia into spheres of influence was also discussed, "assuming British spheres of influence have been maintained at Murmansk and Archangel."[38]

The popular view of Siberia as a land of inexhaustible natural wealth with a vast potential as a market for a multitude of consumer goods held great temptation. While it was recognized that the organization and fostering of this trade would initially require infusions of capital—admittedly a "delicate point"—it was firmly believed that any risk would be more than offset by the returns and profits to be reaped. Typical of the vision is a comment made by a British consular officer, who remarked that "so much [?natural] wealth abounds everywhere that it is difficult to suggest anything on hard and fast lines—the thing is to be able to exploit and take advantage."[39] Indeed, finding a way to do this seemed to preoccupy the British, who were anxious that the Americans and Japanese should not usurp the market. In April, for example, it was suggested that the commercial penetration of Siberia was worth considering either as an alternative to or concomitant with the proposed intervention. In June it was likewise proposed that, in the event of Allied intervention taking place in Siberia, a British advantage could be established through a commercial arrangement with the Siberian Soviets to provide for the exchange of surplus stocks in Siberia and Russian Central Asia for goods that were urgently needed in the area.[40]

While the Allies were deadlocked over the issue of military intervention in Siberia, the British government had decided that "if we could not intervene with armies, we could at least promote a scheme (for political purposes), to which no one could object, for despatching supplies for the relief of the Siberian population." Although it was initially proposed that the program be undertaken on an inter-Allied basis, the Americans were clearly suspicious of being involved in a scheme in which they were admittedly to carry the majority of the financial burden.[41] Without waiting for a commitment from its Allies, the British government went ahead with its plans to set up a commercial organization in Siberia. It was decided that the commercial aspects of the intervention would be kept distinctly separate from the military side, and the Board of Trade was named as the department ultimately responsible for any arrangements under the program. In preparation for the trade that was to follow, the government also appointed additional consuls in various Siberian commercial centers during the summer of 1918.[42]

By September 1918 official commercial plans had been realized through the creation of the Siberian Supply Company. Leslie Urquhart, whose extensive business experience in Siberia had made him somewhat of an authority on the region, was chosen to set up and direct the company. Conceived of as a sort of clearinghouse for British trade in Siberia, the company's functions were to procure orders for goods from Britain and the empire, and to obtain and export Siberian goods in exchange for those imported.[43] As early as December, however, the Siberian Supply

Company was chalked up as at least a partial failure. British firms already operating in Siberia were less than pleased with the establishment of an official trade agency, which they tended to regard as government-sponsored competition. By the same token, firms in Britain were reticent to consign their trade to an agency that required that "any conditions as to selling price, etc. imposed by the British Commercial Commissioner at Vladivostok must be observed." It was decided that while the company should not be scrapped altogether—at least not yet—it was nonetheless necessary to make every attempt "to facilitate private trade," and to encourage manufacturers to use their own agents or correspondents wherever possible. In the general interests of British trade it was considered desirable that "British trade in both Eastern and Western Siberia should be developed to its fullest extent, through as many and as wide channels as possible." As one such channel, it was hoped that the Siberian Supply Company would still provide a means of introducing new British trade and manufacturers to the region, and help to cultivate goodwill for British goods.[44]

By the end of July 1919, the agency was reported to be "unable to transact business . . . due to difficulties in transport and exchange."[45] Effectively strangled by the conditions and restrictions imposed by the government that created it, the Siberian Supply Company managed to arrange for the delivery of less than £300,000 worth of goods to Siberia during its year in existence. An undeniable failure, the company was dismantled at the end of the year, leaving only a handful of existing commercial concerns to compete with their American counterparts.

The British government was apparently loath to risk its entire commercial future in Siberia on such a philanthropic enterprise as the Siberian Supply Company. Shortly after the Bolshevik revolution the government sanctioned a scheme to purchase shares in a number of Russian banking concerns, and as a result had managed to acquire 45 percent of the stock of the Commercial Bank of Siberia.[46] Control over such an institution had several advantages: in addition to providing a source of financing for British trade in Siberia, it also meant that whatever mining or manufacturing concerns that were owned or controlled by the bank were now effectively in British hands.[47]

Despite their unwillingness to embark willy-nilly on a policy of intervention, the Americans were certainly not ones to stand idle while the British captured the market they considered to be their own. Indeed, American capital and business investments in Russia during the war had tended to concentrate in Siberia and, while the absolute volume and value of these investments were comparatively small, American trading interests in that region were considerable. These interests were apparently so well entrenched that the British government was convinced that, even in the event that the Bolsheviks did emerge victorious in the civil war, those concerns would not suffer—and could possibly even gain from—the passive American participation in the Allied intervention in Siberia.[48]

The strong American commercial presence in Siberia was accompanied by a governmental preoccupation with the region from the standpoint of the U.S. global policy. Along with China and Manchuria, the Russian Far East now figured largely in the U.S. "Open Door" policy, particularly with regard to its application against Japan. So long as the Japanese refused to consider military intervention without American participation, Wilson was content to adhere to his moralistic policy of allowing the Russians to work things out for themselves. But in early April, in response to a local incident in Vladivostok, the Japanese made a unilateral decision to land troops which they subsequently showed no signs of withdrawing. For Wilson to abandon so abruptly his previous stand on the question would have been an admission of the suspicions he harbored against an ally. It was therefore with considerable relief that Wilson was able to latch on to the "plight" of the Czechoslovaks who had been caught up in Siberia as a justification for the dispatch of American troops.[49] Thus able to maintain his moral position of noninterference in Russian affairs and demonstrate his support for the gallant Czechoslovak "friends," the president was at once reconciled to take action in Siberia. The real reason behind Wilson's decision was not hard to discern; John F. Stevens of the U.S. Advisory Committee of Railway Experts to Russia observed that, through intervention, Wilson intended "to keep the 'Open Door policy' against our little brown brother and prevent him from grabbing the railroads."[50]

Japanese expansion was not the only cause for American concern over Siberia. The obvious enthusiasm that Britain expressed over the potential of Siberian trade was perceived as yet another example of the British government's intentions to extend its economic control over Russia. Spurning what was seen as an attempt to involve the United States in another British-dominated regional "relief" scheme, the Wilson administration refused to have anything to do with the organization and operation of the Siberian Supply Company. The existence of such an agency worried the government, however, and it was not long before the United States took action along similar lines. In October 1918 the War Trade Board of the U.S. Russian Bureau was established for the purpose of stabilizing the economic situation in Russia and promoting trade between the two countries.[51] Like the Siberian Supply Company, the Russian Bureau was to act as an intermediary between individual traders and the Russian market, facilitating the exchange of goods on both sides. But whereas Urquhart's company was a private organization that acted at the behest of the British government, the Russian Bureau was set up as a public corporation with an authorized capital of $5 million, the whole of which was subscribed by the U.S. government.

The Allies were informed of the creation and aims of the new bureau in the moralistic jargon that has since come to typify the Wilson administration. Reminding the Allies that Russia, in its present condition, had to be protected from exploitative commercial practices, the U.S. government went on to state its desire "to take advantage of the earliest opportunities to relieve in some measure the immediate economic necessities of the people of Russia." Accordingly, the bureau was devised "to permit its merchants to trade with Russia only under such direction on its part as will ensure the Russian people absolute fair dealings and complete protection against exploitative profiteering."[52] It is interesting to note that, despite such idealistic platitudes, certain business interests exercised substantial influence in the bureau. International Harvester, for example, undoubtedly benefited from the appointment of August Heid as the Russian Bureau's field manager in Vladivostok. Formerly the managing director of Harvester's operations in Siberia, Heid was certain to be partial to furthering that company's business through the bureau whenever possible.

The Russian Bureau was considerably more successful than its British counterpart. Although it was originally contemplated that the bureau would buy and sell goods, it was subsequently decided that "the best results could be achieved through the free movement of trade leading to the exchange of commodities."[53] Unlike the Siberian Supply Company, which suffered under the government's allocation of tonnage, the Russian Bureau worked to obtain shipping and commodities for this trade. By December 1918, the Russian Bureau, in conjunction with the U.S. Shipping Board, had facilitated the dispatch from American ports of five ships carrying goods destined for Russia. It also addressed the problem of financing large-scale Russian purchases by encouraging the import of a certain amount of Russian goods, which would be used to build a credit in the United States against which American merchandise could be purchased. In at least one case, the Siberian Cooperative Societies received special permission to ship to the United States consignments of furs and other Russian products worth an estimated $1 million, the proceeds from the sale of which would be used to purchase goods in America.[54]

The American role as self-appointed moral overseer in Russia becomes somewhat tarnished, however, in light of the government's economic pursuits in Siberia. While the Wilson administration was decrying the aggressive commercial practices of the British in North Russia it was busy trying to emulate them in the Russian Far East. Shortly after the Russian Bureau was organized, the government had begun to sound out certain of the larger American banking houses as to the possibility of opening a branch in Vladivostok. In addition to being a means to facilitate further U.S. trade with the region, such a bank would also provide the necessary foundation for any future issue of new currency should this be deemed necessary to stabilize the economy.[55]

Like the British, the Americans were also keen to acquire certain strategic goods from Siberia. There were, for instance, several expeditions dispatched to the Russian interior in 1918 for the purpose of procuring platinum for the Ordnance and State departments. One such expedition was reported to involve some 5,000 ounces of pure platinum that was purchased for less than $110 an ounce.[56] While there is nothing immediately controversial about these ostensibly simple purchasing expeditions (save the lower-than-market price paid), the manner in which they were conducted arouses a good deal of suspicion. Shrouded in secrecy, these expeditions were anything but straightforward. One in particular was combined with the opening of a Red Cross Mission; despite the cover, the agent involved warned the State Department that the "trip will be useless if this business is not done quickly and secretly."[57] So much for the government's moral rectitude. Further, it is clear that the Ordnance and State departments did not coordinate their procurement activities with other branches of the government that were interested in this metal. In a telegram to the chief of the Military Intelligence Branch dated 27 August 1918, the War Department confirmed that it understood "that a special mission *is supposed to be appointed* by the Secretary of War to act as agents for the War Department in securing platinum which the Secretary of Commerce has been authorized to purchase in Russia." This communication was sent more than three weeks after the agent involved wired the State and Ordnance departments, informing them of the existing opportunity to purchase the metal.[58]

Similar departmental friction plagued the operations of the Russian Bureau and, indeed, effectively prevented the dissemination of essential information concerning Russia. In particular, frictions between the State and Commerce departments hindered the exchange of commercial and political intelligence on developments in Russia, the result being that the Commerce Department was unable to provide current useful information or to assist efficiently American businessmen who were interested in trade with that country. A dramatic illustration of this friction can be found in the State Department's delay in forwarding a copy of the Soviet national-ization decree. Received by the State Department on 30 April 1918, news of this development was not relayed to the Department of Commerce until mid-June, and then it was transmitted under the routine heading "as of possible interest."[59] This slight caused an understandable outrage in the Commerce Department, but little was done to rectify the ever-widening interdepartmental breach.

The lack of interdepartmental communication not surprisingly had a devastating effect on the quality and reliability of information that was made available to the business community. Inquiries concerning the pos-sibilities of trade in Russia and how to initiate business in that market often received vague and sometimes irresponsible replies, and the advice that was tendered frequently differed considerably between the two de-partments. Moreover, the Russian Bureau—primarily responsible for pro-moting trade with the region—was dependent upon the State and Com-merce departments for its commercial intelligence. In short, local conditions throughout Siberia remained largely unknown, and the private trader was left pretty much to his own judgment when considering whether to attempt a commercial venture in Russia. Even so, a number of firms still took up charters to conduct import and export business with Siberia. Many businessmen were convinced that the Siberian market would "open up soon," providing a huge and ready market for those companies and individuals who exercised foresight and were prepared to take a risk to exploit it.[60] That this business was considered to be worth the risk is clear from the fact that, political and economic uncertainty notwithstanding, shipments to the Russian Far East continued to be made on short-term credit throughout 1918 and 1919.[61]

From the outset, the intervention in South Russia was significantly different from that which took place in either the Russian North or Siberia. Whereas in the latter two instances it could be argued that the intervention was genuinely perceived as a necessary wartime expedient, British intervention in the South took place only *after* the armistice, with the first troops arriving in Baku on 17 November. In a memorandum dated 13 November 1918, the War Office pointed out "the great impor-tance of insisting from the outset on the recognition of the supremacy of British interests in any undertaking in the North or South Caucasus or Don Country."[62] It was argued that there was an "imperial imperative" for the British military intervention in the Russian South and Transcaucasia. The disruptive influence of the war had convinced certain members of His Majesty's Government that it was essential to maintain some degree of political control over the area, and that "any sort of anarchy, disorder or

Bolshevism" in Transcaucasia would definitely pose a threat to Britain's entire imperial position in the East.[63]

However, a more likely immediate factor in the decision to dispatch an interventionist army was the threat posed by the war and resulting anarchy to the British oil interests in the region. The security of the Russian oilfields as well as the increasingly important petroleum-producing areas of Persia were of primary concern for the British. The Turkish occupation of the South Caucasus during the war and the Bolshevik-inspired labor uprisings in the Russian oilfields during summer of 1918 were viewed with alarm in the United Kingdom. While the necessity of defending the empire against immediate threat was seized upon as a compelling argument in favor of the dispatch of troops to South Russia, it soon became clear that other, equally compelling reasons were behind the decision to intervene. Indeed, by the end of 1919 it was openly admitted that parts of the region should be held "because of the immense value of the oil deposits."[64]

British commercial interests were deeply involved in Transcaucasia. The Russian oil industry alone had accounted for one-third of all the British capital invested in prerevolutionary Russia, some £18.1 million by 1916. By 1914 companies that were wholly or partly British owned accounted for half of the production of the Grozny oilfields, three-quarters of the oil produced at Cheleken, nearly all of the Maikop production, and the total oil production of the Emba region.[65] Though British investment in the industry was not especially profitable, the British role in exploration and the development of new fields continued to be significant.

The importance of British control over these fields was illustrated dramatically with the increase in military consumption during the war. The realization that crucial supplies could be cut off by the United States —Britain's principal supplier—caused the British government to go in search of other sources and encourage further entrenchment in areas where British interests in the industry already existed. It is in light of the ever-present threat of an "oil famine" that the British government was keen to secure its hold in the oil-bearing regions of Russia.

The prospect of the absence of any clear-cut authority in Transcaucasia immediately after the war presented an opportune moment for the British to gain unqualified control over the petroleum wealth of the region. The British wasted no time on this score, and on the eve of the armistice, the War Office issued orders to the British Command, Mesopotamia, for the occupation of Baku and its surrounding oilfields. By mid-November 1919 the War Office had extended its liability to include the Baku-Batum railway. It is also obvious that the purpose of the occupation was clear in the official mind: in December 1918, when the commander of the British occupying forces at Baku suggested that Georgia be included among those areas under British control, the War Office was instructed to remind the commanding officers in Baku and Batum that their task was to protect the railway and the pipeline that ran between the Caspian and Black seas, that is, between the oilfields at Baku and the port at Batum.

The official attempts to ensure a continued British presence—if not dominance—in this industry are striking. In one case, the government went so far as to block the proposed sale of a British petroleum company's interest in the Maikop oilfields, despite the fact that the company had been operating unprofitably there for some time. Throughout the autumn of 1918 the Anglo-Maikop Corporation had been in correspondence with the Board of Trade concerning the transfer of their properties and interests in the Maikop oilfields to the Moscow Narodny Bank. The company informed the board that the negotiations for the sale of the properties and assets in Russia were to be based on the condition that the corporation retain one-half of the properties and that joint control and management of the business was to remain in effect for a seven-year period after the sale. It was also pointed out that practically the whole of the oil produced by the companies associated with the Anglo-Maikop Corporation had been consumed domestically, the principal purchaser being the Russian government.[66] The total value of the transaction was put at £3 million; and the shareholders were known to be favorably inclined toward the deal, seeing that no dividends had been paid them for some time. Even so, the company's managing director was informed that the Board of Trade would oppose the transaction on the grounds that "a transfer from British to alien hands of the extensive oil properties in question would be undesirable in the national interest."[67] On 10 December the Petroleum Executive concurred with the view expressed by the Board of Trade: in the national interest, the sale of the properties and assets of the eight oil companies controlled by Anglo-Maikop could not, in their opinion, be consented to. It was further pointed out that "whatever the value the properties may possess today, it must be greater when conditions in Russia improve, so that the refusal can scarcely impose serious hardship to the companies."[68]

However, the Foreign Office, like the Treasury, had begun to question the initial stand taken on the proposed transaction. In a letter to the Petroleum Executive, Balfour examined some of the reasons why the deal ought to be allowed to proceed:

From the point of view of the oil requirements of the British Empire the refusal of the Board of Trade to sanction this transfer is undoubtedly correct. It is important to retain as much oil-bearing land in British hands as possible in order to prevent it from falling into alien, and possibly hostile alien, possession. From the political point of view, it is likely that the result of such a transfer would be the loss of a considerable amount of useful influence in Russia.

On the other hand . . . the Corporation are prepared to retain a controlling interest in the oil-fields, so that they could not fall into alien possession; and no doubt from the financial point of view it would be useful to transfer to the shareholders in London the sum of three million pounds of Russian-owned money now lying idle in London.

The Moscow Narodny Bank is the bank of the Russian Co-operative Association. It was not interfered with by the Bolsheviks but there is no other ground for thinking that it is a Bolshevik institution, nor is there any reason to think there is German influence behind it. His Majesty's Government has had extensive dealings with the bank, and the War Office recently paid it one million, five hundred thousand pounds for flax purchased in Russia.[69]

Despite the strengths of Balfour's reasoning, the Treasury's open support in favor of the sale, and the grudging change of heart by the Petroleum Executive at the end of December 1918, permission to initiate the negotiations was withheld for so long that by the time it was finally granted in the spring of 1919, the political, military, and economic conditions in South Russia had all changed so drastically that the terms that were originally put forward by the Anglo-Maikop Corporation were no longer possible.

Although the government was loath to entertain proposals that would involve any diminished British control over such extensive and strategic interests as those held by the Anglo-Maikop Corporation, it was certainly quick to support the bulk of applications for the issue of new capital by British concerns—notably by oil companies—that had operations in South Russia. Here again, Foreign Office minutes concerning such applications consistently reflected the overwhelming sentiment in favor of keeping the oilfields in British hands, even though conditions in the region argued strongly against such action being in the better interests of the company. Perversely, it was in this way that the government itself ultimately caused the most damage to British businesses in South Russia, and particularly to those concerned with the Russian oil industry.

Although it was undoubtedly the case that the oilfields were an immediate primary concern of the British government, complete economic penetration of the area was a longer-range objective that was dependent upon the success of British commercial agents in capturing the commerce and trade of the region. British commercial activity in the Russian South was certainly far more aggressive than in either Siberia or North Russia, a fact that did not go unnoticed in the United States. Unlike the other two areas of intervention, however, the Black Sea and Transcaucasian regions were not included in any prior Allied understanding as being a particular British "sphere," despite the British government's own view of the importance of the area and the absence of any American troops among the interventionist forces there. Even so, the Russian South was too rich in natural resources and abounded with too many opportunities promising profitable trade for either Britain or the United States to abandon its dealings there. Indeed, a sharp commercial rivalry soon developed between the two powers.

Private British commercial interest in South Russia took off quickly, and by the summer of 1919 competition there had already become so intense that the Americans were lamenting the fact that "all of the passenger accommodation on steamers for Russia are booked for some months ahead and in addition to the steamers leaving from Great Britain, arrangements have been made for businessmen to proceed to Constantinople and South Russia via Marseilles and Malta."[70] Such enthusiasm had from the outset received considerable official support from the British government. By maintaining or increasing the official commercial representation in the region, the government laid the foundation for an extensive economic intelligence network that would enable it to supply British merchants with information necessary for the conduct of trade. Support of a more direct nature was also made available: merchants were freely offered the assistance of the British interventionist armies. With the area predominantly occupied by British troops, the government was able to call upon its military—familiar with local conditions and needs—to aid private British businessmen. In this respect, the cooperation between His Majesty's Government and its nationals who traded in the region ran so close as to make the interests of the two appear indistinguishable. In fact, the local British consul assured the government that the safety of consignments shipped through Black Sea ports could be guaranteed provided that the business was done in the name of the British government and the goods were transported inland via the railway under a small convoy of British marines.[71]

Such collusion between the government and businessmen in Britain did not escape notice in the United States. American intelligence reports dwelt on the matter, noting bitterly that British military "assistance" often stretched to the commandeering of rolling stock for commercial loads, and that British officers often used their influence to secure export permits from the local representatives of the government of Denikin's Volunteer Army. In addition to the detrimental effect that such British influence had on American trade efforts in South Russia, it was also being used to create "a false impression about American sympathy with the Bolsheviks."[72]

The British government extended further assistance to its traders there in other ways as well. Measures to foster commerce with non-Bolshevik Russia generally were undoubtedly angled toward capturing the trade of the Caucasus and Black Sea regions especially. British business received the active participation of the government through the Department of Overseas Trade and the Board of Trade War Risks Insurance Office. It was through this latter office that arrangements were made in June of 1919 to "furnish covering insurance for inland risks upon British goods imported into Russia and goods bought by British firms for export from Russia."[73] These policies covered goods against loss or damage from "war risks, riots, civil commotions and other risks usually included in an ordinary policy issued by Lloyds," during shipment to South Russia and the northern Caucasus. Further, in instances where marine insurance was not furnished through ordinary channels, it was provided by the War Risks Insurance Office. This action by the British government achieved its purpose of encouraging banks to grant advances to merchants on shipments made to Russia; soon after its announcement a number of leading institutions indicated their willingness "to consider applications for advances against goods sent to Russia and insured by the Government." Where such advances were not available, the Department of Overseas Trade was authorized to assist directly British trade with Russia by providing intermediary payment for shipments.[74] Finally, in addition to advising merchants as to travel conditions in South Russia, the Department of Overseas Trade also kept lists of the more prominent Russian businessmen who had immigrated to Britain after the revolution. In the hope of recruiting their knowledge and experience to the benefit of British commerce, the department volunteered to put any interested firm in touch with these expatriates.

In light of what appeared to the American businessman to be a British conspiracy to eliminate competition and monopolize the market in South Russia, it is no wonder that the relative inactivity of the U.S. government was met with cries of indignation from a group who believed that they were being cheated. Indeed, that American business was not getting its fair share of the Russian market was a complaint made by private traders and the Commerce Department as well. With the exception of the War Trade Board's Russian Bureau—which relied on the financing from and the initiative of the private sector—the Wilson administration did not pursue anything like a coherent program of promoting trade with Russia, Bolshevik or not. As mentioned earlier, the Department of Commerce performed poorly in providing businessmen with the necessary information regarding Russian business conditions. A simple list of ships that plied between the United States and the ports of the "former Russian Empire" was, for a long time, unavailable to American businessmen, as was any information on travel, transport, and general economic conditions. Even the politically orientated trade with the White Russian forces did not come close to having the organization and support private British commerce received in South Russia.[75]

Although the ensuing commercial activity in South Russia was by no means overwhelming, it was nonetheless brisk. The character of the trade conducted on private account was simple: most goods exported to Russia from either the United States or Great Britain were for immediate consumption. Provisions, agricultural implements, hardware, woolen and cotton goods, boots and shoes were items of primary import, and were generally shipped on speculation rather than to order. In most instances, commercial transactions with the region approached barter. As foreign exchange was largely unavailable, merchants were forced to accept the rapidly depreciating Russian currency for their goods and quickly reinvest it in local products which were then exported.[76] Despite such obstacles, British and American merchants continued to pursue trade in the region, some with surprising results. In both these countries the commercial potential of the region was clearly regarded as promising. In the case of Britain, military intervention in the South was seen as providing an excellent opportunity to replace the German predominance there; it was believed that "when normal conditions return to Russia it should be possible for British traders to obtain a far larger share of Russian trade than in pre-war days."[77] To this end, numerous British firms sent representatives to the Caucasus to keep abreast of the development of business opportunities and to "be ready to proceed without delay into any new district which may become available for trade." British shipping concerns likewise took advantage of the growing trade; by mid-1919 there were seven steamship companies operating regular, scheduled services between Great Britain and the Russian Black Sea ports.

In comparison, the American efforts in South Russia were paltry. The Russian Bureau alone was not enough to compete with the swell of British commercial involvement in the region. While the sheer volume of inquiries received at the State and Commerce departments concerning the prospects of trade with the region reflects the development of a substantial private interest in South Russia, there was no real official effort to match the British there. Siberia remained the U.S. government's main focus of attention through 1918. It was not until the following year, when it became evident that there was a large and profitable business to be had with the White armies, that commercial competition in South Russia took off. Largely underwritten by governmental loans and guarantees, this business provided millions of dollars worth of contracts for a variety of American manufacturers. The American commercial community, however, was not content to remain idle while the British stole a march on it in Russia itself, and the ineffectual policy of the Wilson administration was met with a growing roar of protest from this quarter.

So long as the war continued, the blockade and intervention against Bolshevik Russia could be justified as a necessary response to immediate circumstances. The United States, initially committed to a policy of "doing nothing," was dragged along in the vortex of Allied—primarily British —decision making on the rapid flow of events in Russia. It is clear that the protection of existing interests and the promotion of further economic penetration figured largely in the development of the British policy toward Russia. Consequently, the need to counter potentially unfriendly activities on this level was certainly one of the aims behind the decision to dispatch troops to both the Russian North and the Transcaucasian region. But the advantages that were laid open to Britain by the political instability and disintegration of any remaining local governing authorities in Russia gave the policy of economic penetration an added impetus. That the government assumed a more decisive role in exploiting the situation in the North is perhaps the result of the absence of direct British investment in local industry. Private British interests in the Murmansk province were primarily those of traders and merchants. Thus, there was no existing basis upon which a successful policy of economic penetration could be built. It was no doubt hoped that private British investment and the already established extensive network of British commercial interests in South Russia would provide a firmer *existing* foundation for penetration. Given this prior capability, only military protection and official encouragement were needed. What the British government had not counted on was the failure of the Bolshevik regime to collapse and the difficulties that British representatives increasingly encountered in their dealings with the profoundly corrupt government of Denikin's Volunteer Army.

1919:

The Armistice and After

Although economic interests in Russia played a particularly important role in determining Allied policy toward that country, the end of the war significantly altered Britain's approach to the so-called Russian question. Throughout the period between the Bolshevik revolution and the end of World War I, Germany was the hinge upon which Allied policy toward Russia turned. The intervention in and occupation and blockade of Soviet Russia were all initially undertaken as wartime measures ostensibly directed against the Germans. Under the conventions of international law, the legal basis for the presence of Allied troops in Russia ceased with the armistice. Even before the armistice, the acting commander of the Allied interventionist army in North Russia, Brigadier General Ironside, described the "curious position" that he and his troops would face at the end of the war. With the removal of the German threat to the region, the Allied forces in the Russian North would "find themselves opposed to the Bolsheviks only. . . . We are now backing a White Russian Counter-Revolution against the Bolsheviks, and are actually committed to staying here in Archangel."[1] The interventionist forces in Russia dug in, and while no declaration of war was made on either side, there were—as Lloyd George noted—some four or five British forces on Russian territory, which "not infrequently shot Bolsheviks."[2]

The blockade policy likewise became overtly anti-Bolshevik. Unwilling to commit themselves to a concerted military effort against the Soviets, Britain and the United States supported a "cordon sanitaire" to tighten the blockade. Unlike the Black Sea or the North Russian coast, the Baltic was blockaded *after* the armistice. Although it was clearly directed against the Bolsheviks, the extension of the blockade was justified under international law as a means to prevent Germany from receiving war matériel from Soviet Russia, and hence to keep the Germans suppliant at the negotiating table.

The conclusion of the peace treaty with Germany in June 1919 removed this last shred of legal justification. As early as 7 June the Blockade Commission of the Supreme Economic Council advised the Council of Four that, as no state of war existed with Russia, international law would prohibit the continued maintenance of the blockade. Any restrictions that the Allied powers imposed upon the commerce of the neutral states would lose their validity with the conclusion of the peace treaty. While the Allies were free to prohibit exports from their own territories or in ships under their own flags, other states could not be prevented from doing so. Furthermore, even in the case of their own nationals, pro forma legislation was technically required. The Allies were faced with a rather prickly dilemma; whereas forbidding their own nationals from trading with Soviet Russia would deprive the Bolsheviks of major necessities, it would give unparalleled opportunities to Germany and other neutral states whose governments had no intention of imposing restrictions.[3]

Finally, in order to aid the "honest" Russians in their attempt to free themselves from Bolshevik tyranny, the Allied governments began a campaign of moral and, more importantly, financial support of the counterrevolutionaries. The continued presence of British troops in Russia after the war was essential to this support: by withdrawing its troops the British government believed that it would not only suffer "a serious loss of prestige" but would also be "letting down [its] friends."[4] While it was seen as impossible to maintain British forces in Russia indefinitely, the War Office urged that Britain should do everything possible "to give our friends a fair start" before withdrawing.[5] "Recent events have created obligations which last beyond the occasions which gave them birth. . . . New anti-Bolshevik administrations have grown up under the shelter of Allied forces. We are responsible for their existence and we must endeavour to support them."[6] While not prepared to launch an anti-

Bolshevik crusade themselves, Whitehall policy makers were determined to help the Russians to "stand by themselves" and were prepared "to do everything possible to support and strengthen existing [anti-Bolshevik] organizations."[7]

From the outset of the intervention, the U.S. government was disinclined to take any action unequivocally directed against the Bolsheviks. The United States was never an active participant in the blockade, and Wilson flatly refused to become involved in any scheme to extend it beyond the war. While he was undoubtedly sympathetic to Allied aims, the president was nonetheless compelled to point out that the continuation of the blockade after June 1919 constituted an act of war, which the United States was unable to condone.[8] Even so, the government continued to deny American nationals export licenses or clearance papers for their cargoes or ships bound for Soviet ports.

As to U.S. military presence in Russia, Wilson had always insisted that American forces were engaged in defensive operations only. While the American interventionist armies in Russia were indeed less openly hostile to the Bolsheviks than their British counterparts, the United States was far from a passive observer in the ensuing civil war. Like the British, the U.S. government tended to regard the emerging counterrevolutionary forces as charges under its protection. The president's avowed commitment to a democratic Russia ensured that a number of these groups received more than just his moral support.

The continuation of the intervention and the blockade after the armistice and the incessant meddling in the Russian civil war quickly revealed these actions for what they were—overtly hostile acts directed against the Soviet regime. Even so, it must be stressed that there was an absence of any unified Allied policy toward Russia and, indeed, a total lack of anything resembling a coherent policy within either the U.S. or British governments. The friction, confusion, and suspicion that arose over the Russian question produced the ill-defined and uncoordinated policy described as "no war—no peace," a tangle of confused political objectives, none of which commanded the full commitment of either government.

In contrast, British and American *economic* policy in Russia had always been more clearly defined than the political, and with the end of the war, it became still more sharply focused. Realistically or not, it was feared that Germany would attempt to recapture its former commercial domination in Russia. Instead of uniting against a common potential economic threat, however, the two powers competed against each other for the market.

Blockade and Stalemate

The anti-Bolshevik nature of the Allied approach to the Russian question was to result in 1919 being the worst year of diplomatic and economic isolation for the Soviet government. Far from writing the country off economically during this period, however, the British and Americans competed keenly to capture the trade of those parts of Russia outside of Bolshevik control. Although the end of the year failed to see the Bolsheviks overthrown, the commerce that accompanied the support of the counterrevolutionaries proved considerable—especially for the United States, whose exports to Russia in 1919 far exceeded any prewar level.

Russia had historically figured as a major supplier of raw materials and foodstuffs to Europe; however, with the end of the war, the task of restoring the country to economic viability took on a new importance. After the war, Russia was hailed as being of "very great importance to [Britain], if not the greatest, as a source of raw materials"; and Russian raw materials in turn were considered to be "indispensable" in postwar reconstruction.[9] It was considered essential to the national interest to extend British control over the source of these materials wherever possible or, failing that, to stockpile reserves against the potential loss of future supplies. The inability of Russia to supply Britain with grain, timber, petroleum, and other raw materials throughout much of the war had forced Britain to obtain these commodities elsewhere, and the heavily inflated postwar prices of these goods, especially those from America, gave added impetus to this policy.

After the armistice, Lloyd George's references to Russia stressed that the postwar recovery of Europe (and Britain particularly) depended upon the revival of Russia—not only as a supplier but as a market as well. The volume of exports to Russia achieved during the war and the requirements for the postwar reconstruction of the country reinforced the idea of Russia as a boundless postwar market, especially in light of the contraction in the world market generally and the loss of much demand from the primary producing economies. Given the "enormous potentialities of the country," "exceptional" commercial interests were seen as being at stake in Russia.[10] Britain's need for the vast Russian market was further emphasized when it was discovered that the U.S. government had set aside $1 million for the purpose of assisting postwar American export trade. Seeing the American move as an indication that British exporters were likely to meet "very powerful competition in their efforts to regain and extend trade in the older markets," the Board of Trade argued that it was now especially desirable "to endeavour to lessen present abnormal difficulties in the way of the development of Russo-British trade."[11]

Despite the government's commitment to encouraging this trade, inter-departmental frictions prevented the formulation of any uniform economic policy toward Russia.[12] Combined with the difficulties that arose from military operations and bureaucratic complications in occupied Russia, confused policy created further impediments to British trade. At an interview at the Foreign Office, representatives of the All-Russian Central Union of Consumers Societies stressed the devastating effect of these complications on developing Russian-British trade: at the same time that the British government was refusing to permit exports to areas under the control of non-Bolshevik governments in Archangel, Omsk, and Ekaterinodar, the United States was encouraging trade with those districts. Further, the Russian cooperatives had been unable to obtain permission to export goods from Britain to either Vladivostok or the Black Sea ports, though Vladivostok was "flooded with American goods" and some thirty thousand pairs of boots and shoes had already been cleared for export from the United States to Odessa.[13]

The United States was as determined as Britain to gain an economic foothold in Russia. Never having been as dependent upon Russian exports as Great Britain, it is not surprising that the United States was considerably less concerned with securing control over Russian natural resources.[14] Even so, British moves toward that end were viewed with the disapproval of the U.S. government and, on the private level, often encountered stiff competition from American business circles. In keeping with its tradition of the "Open Door" approach to trade, the U.S. government resisted attempts to exclude Americans from the opportunities in Russia. Indeed, Russia as a market for American goods had taken on a new importance during the war: imports from the United States had increased by a factor of seventeen. The business to be had from postwar reconstruction in Russia appeared to be just as promising, and government and merchants alike strove to ensure that the United States would secure its share of that market in the face of growing British competition. In light of this, the British government was warned that "American bankers and manufacturers . . . [were] fully alive to the possibilities of Russia as an inexhaustible market for American manufactures and as a great field for capital. They realise that, in view of diminished purchasing capacity, the intensified production and tendency to minimise imports in Europe, stagnation in the American export trade is bound to come and they rightly hope to find equivalents in Russia."[15]

In the case of both the United States and Great Britain, however, it should be stressed that all initial economic contacts were restricted to those areas of Russia outside of Bolshevik control. With all signs pointing to the imminent overthrow of the Soviet government, such restrictions on trade were perceived as temporary measures, effective only until order had been restored. In the meantime, the Allied governments worked hard to ensure that outcome by prohibiting trade and discouraging any contact with Soviet Russia.

With the legality and efficacy of the blockade coming increasingly under fire by mid-1919, both the United States and Great Britain were able to claim with some justification that "no blockade has ever been declared, or is being exercised, against any part of Russia."[16] Even so, the British especially managed to effect a degree of control over trade through Bolshevik ports. Though the Supreme Economic Council had ruled that trade with Soviet Russia would have to be permitted, albeit at the merchant's own risk, the *Daily Herald* speculated that this fact was being kept as quiet as possible in the hope that "a kind of 'bluff' blockade might be maintained—that people might refrain from sending goods to [Soviet] Russia because they thought they couldn't!" A Foreign Office minute on the article confirmed that "the situation in fact is exactly as described . . . there never has been a blockade of Russia and we are not at war with the Soviet Government; but any application to trade would have been turned down on one score or another, on account of the physical difficulties of reaching Central Russia."[17] Despite the official denial of the blockade's existence, British warships remained conspicuous in the shipping lanes to North Russia and the Black Sea.

More effective than the blockade, however, were the trade restrictions, licensing requirements, and credit limitations that both governments imposed on trade with Soviet Russia. Further, the questionable status of the Soviet government conveniently created difficulties over the legal title to Bolshevik exports, including gold. While the legality of such trade discrimination was debated, Allied merchants were prevented from doing business directly with Soviet ports throughout 1919.

Seen as only a temporary inconvenience, restrictions on Russian trade did little to dampen the enthusiasm of many British and American firms over the postwar business to be had there. Numerous firms had already begun investigating the market's potential and were anxiously waiting to start business. Until such time, however, those parts of Russia occupied by the Allied interventionist forces and counterrevolutionary armies were seen as providing a secure area in which they could begin trading without threat of expropriation or nationalization. Companies that coveted a prime position in the future Russian market saw an advantage to starting business in non-Bolshevik Russia in anticipation of the overthrow of the Soviet government.

Typical of this sort of business was the March 1919 agreement between the Ford Motor Company and Ivan Stacheef and Company for the purchase of four hundred Ford touring automobiles and some $25,000 worth of spares and repair equipment within a two-year period. Given the unsettled conditions in Russia at the time, the terms of the contract were remarkably liberal, a fact that Edsel Ford used to stress his commitment to this market. Stating that the agreement was "quite different from the usual form of sales agreement," Ford explained that "the Russian situation is extremely difficult to deal with, and for that reason [we] have given . . . more latitude than we ordinarily would."[18] In addition to providing attractive financial terms, the contract stated that both parties would assume equal responsibility for loss due to confiscation or destruction "brought on through acts of revolution or other uprising . . . due to the unsettled condition of the government and the socialist tendencies of the Russian people." The Stacheef contract also provided for the expansion of Ford's future Russian business: it was stipulated that, upon the contract's expiration, the possibility of further agreement be examined with a mind to "enter into the manufacture and selling of automobiles, parts and accessories, tools and machinery in European Russia, Siberia, and Central Asia."[19] Indeed, it is clear that Ford was cultivating the ground for future sales of its tractors in Russia. The Ford-owned *Dearborn Independent* articulated the company's intentions in an article declaring that "what Russia really wants is small mobile tractors . . . together with new modern agricultural machinery and implements on a large scale, sent with the necessary number of instructors who could show [its farmers] . . . how to use and operate these agricultural tractors, machines and implements." The company which met this need "would immediately conquer the Russian market."[20] Without doubt, Ford wanted to be that company and was in fact ready to deal with either faction in Russia in order to ensure that business.[21]

The imagined value of the Russian market was so great that it moved the two allies to fierce competition and mutual distrust. Each suspected the other of having ulterior commercial motivations behind their policy toward Russia. From the outset, the Americans were suspicious of what Britain hoped to achieve by intervening. As the end of the war removed the justification for the presence of troops in Russia, Britain's insistence on maintaining and even increasing its military presence could only heighten American suspicions. A frequent critic of British military policy in Russia, Secretary of War Baker was moved to state openly his belief that Allied troops in Russia were being used by the British to secure concessions and commercial advantage.[22]

The British government likewise treated the United States with increasing suspicion. The rapid proliferation of supposedly philanthropic American organizations in Russia was seen as a manifestation of the U.S. government's commercial aspirations. Determined not to be duped by the high-sounding principles emanating from the White House, the British were convinced that the Americans were out for all they could grab in Russia.[23]

Competition on a private level was also very much in evidence. There was mutual fear that the merchants of both nationalities—acting either privately or with the aid of their government—would gain an advantage in Russia. Reports that the Americans were offering Russian buyers lower prices and, more importantly, better shipping facilities were received with increasing frequency in Whitehall in early 1919. According to a letter from the Russo-British Cooperative Information Bureau, the United States was posing a serious threat to the important British cotton goods market in Russia. American goods costing some 50 percent less than the British equivalents were threat enough; in addition the bureau warned that unless something was done about tonnage availability Britain would lose this trade completely to American merchants.[24] Further, news that prominent Russian businessmen were being "entertained extensively in Paris . . . by American commercial interests" stirred a minor panic in the London Chamber of Commerce. Complaining that the British commercial community "does not learn of the arrival of leading commercial men from Russia until too late," the chamber pressed the Foreign Office to relay such news to them as soon as possible. "The matter is considered to be of very great importance in view of the enormous possibilities of trade with Russia in the future, which trade, in the present circumstances, is likely to go to other countries."[25] It must be noted that the suspicions and accusations were often justified. As will be discussed in greater detail later, neither government nor its respective nationals were reluctant to exploit any opportunity for a more secure footing in this most promising of postwar markets.

Even so, the British determination to secure their economic position in Russia prompted the government to consider undertakings far more sinister than merely employing British interventionist troops to their own economic advantage. One scheme, which was apparently considered seriously by the Foreign Office, was designed to put all of Russia under British political and economic tutelage. Proposed by the Russian banker Karol J. Yaroshinsky, the scheme suggested "that Great Britain should secure control of the big banks in Russia, of the transport companies and of the insurance companies."[26]

The acquisition of control over the large Russian banks was the first and most important step under this scheme, as the major Russian banking houses controlled many industrial and commercial undertakings, as well as mining, timber, and other concessions. In addition, these banks often had large, if not controlling, interests in the major transport and insurance companies in Russia. Control of the banks "would in itself alone be extremely beneficial to British economic interests, for the financing of British imports would be facilitated, and it would be possible to obtain easily and directly, and consequently in every way most economically, Russian raw materials." Further, by appointing carefully selected British subjects to occupy positions in Russian banks, trading houses, industrial enterprises, transport companies, mining companies, and forwarding and custom house agencies, Britain would also benefit from a dependable source of political and economic intelligence throughout Russia. The ability to keep a close watch over "every move made by our competitors in the Russian market" would ensure that British goods received priority and, "if necessary, obstacles placed in the way of that of competing goods."[27]

That the government gave any credence to this scheme is remarkable, but it was, in fact, seriously considered. Steel-Maitland remarked that it was a "proposition of great importance" which was "not . . . impracticable."[28] Minutes attached to the memorandum indicate that others at the Foreign Office shared this view and, further, concurred that "we should give general approval to the scheme provided it is pronounced by competent financial authorities to be sound."[29] Other than that, only three cautions were raised in connection with the scheme: "1) that we should not be mixed up with a failure, 2) that we should not excite the animosity of any other power whose animosity matters, 3) that we should not suddenly find ourselves participating in a scheme which has an inconvenient political colour."[30] While reason argues that the second point alone should have caused the Foreign Office to drop the scheme immediately, the minutes indicate the view that "this question did not seem to arise!"[31] France, with its large financial interests in Russia, was seen as presenting the only problem; but "so long as the promoters have her in mind" it was not necessary to worry on this score.[32] In light of Wilson's Fourteen Points, it is remarkable that U.S. opposition to such a scheme was not even considered. Whether the Foreign Office thought that such opposition would not occur or believed that American animosity was irrelevant is unclear. That the scheme was directed against powers other than Germany is certain, and the United States was clearly included in this company. Intelligence reports illustrating the extent to which American interests had "already been aroused to the possibilities of the Russian market" were presented as a "further argument in favour of the carrying through of [this] constructive scheme."[33]

The Americans were an increasingly important economic force in Russia, despite their lack of organized governmental support. The special relationship that developed between the United States and the Russian Provisional Government's ambassador, Boris Bakhmetev, combined with the concern over maintaining an American economic presence in Russia, should have ensured that the U.S. government took a more active role in supporting its nationals' business dealings in non-Bolshevik Russia. With the possible exception of the Russian Bureau, however, government involvement remained minimal. Members of Britain's business community, conversely, enjoyed their government's avowed support and aid. Indeed, government promotion of trade in certain parts of Russia did much to open up opportunities to British merchants who otherwise would have encountered the same difficulties as their American counterparts. Curiously, such support was not provided in an area of Russia where British control was the strongest—the Russian North.

The North

British governmental policy toward North Russia remained fairly consistent throughout 1918–19. Up to the withdrawal of the interventionist forces in September 1919, the government was primarily concerned with acquiring raw materials from the region. Britain's shortages of timber and flax prompted the government to protect its position in North Russia. Attempts to minimize American influence there reinforced America's impression that British policy was "imperialistic." The British government's preoccupation with securing its position in Russia vis-à-vis the United States as well as with obtaining the necessary quantities of raw materials essentially prevented the development of private trade in the White Sea district.

While the "bluff blockade" continued against Soviet ports in northern Russia, Britain was still faced with the problem of controlling the shipping to and from Archangel and Murmansk. With the opening of the 1919 navigation year in the North, the Foreign Office notified the Inter-Allied Trade Commission that "no vessel would be allowed to proceed to Northern Russia without having previously obtained a 'White Sea Permit.'" Permits were obtained from British legations or consuls, who "should

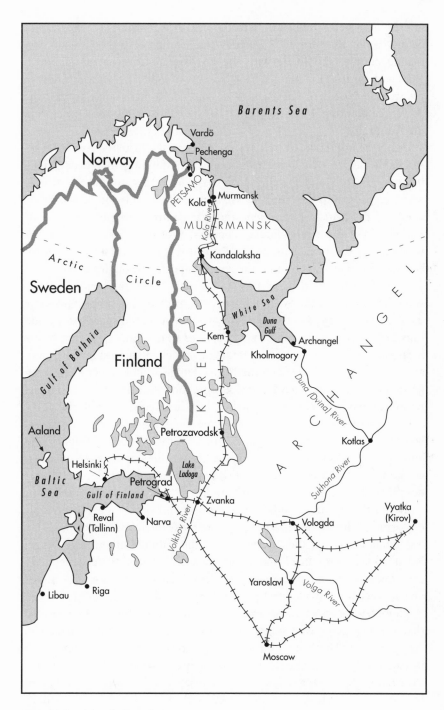

Map 4.1 North Russia

in every case refer applications to the British Admiralty and War Office before issuing the permit."[34] Despite American protests that control over issuing permits should lie with the Provisional Government of North Russia, the British maintained that "in view of military operations now in progress in Northern Russia, it was considered inadvisable to vest the powers of granting White Sea Permits in the hands of any body other than the Admiralty."[35]

Using the argument of military expediency, the British exercised a remarkable degree of control over trade and shipping to North Russia throughout 1918 and the spring of 1919. According to one Soviet estimate, 90 percent of the North Russian trade during this period was in the hands of the British government and was controlled at its discretion.[36] Exports from the region largely comprised local raw materials, which were purchased or requisitioned by the British authorities for government account. Likewise, the bulk of the goods imported through the ports was consigned to the British military authorities. While military and naval stores accounted for the overwhelming proportion of these imports—some 94,400 tons in 1918—the British government also dispatched 15,000 tons of "general cargo" and 67,750 tons of coal, which were sold to the local population.[37] Despite the growing commercial interest in the region, and regardless of advice from the British High Commissioner in Archangel that private trade should be encouraged for political as well as financial reasons, the government continued to deny free access through the port.

It was not until January 1919, some eight months after the initial landing of troops in the Russian North, that the War Trade Department announced its decision to allow export licenses for shipments of commercial goods to Archangel.[38] Although it was officially declared to be "highly desirable in the interests of British trade . . . [that] commercial relations with North Russia should be maintained and that . . . every possible opportunity should be seized to promote those interests," it was nonetheless made clear that the "exigencies of the military situation in North Russia" made it doubtful that shipping, wharfage, and warehouse facilities could be extended to private traders.[39] Such restrictions precluded any appreciable expansion of private commercial activities in the region.

Those few merchants who attempted commercial shipments discovered that their cargoes were subject to frustrating controls upon arrival in North Russia. The British military authorities in Archangel were under instruction to forward all freight received through that port directly to the British Supply Mission, regardless of the destination stated on the bill of lading. Such interference was not restricted to commercial cargoes only, as Inter-Allied relief shipments to Murmansk were likewise forwarded to a British agency. An imposition that particularly irritated the United States, this move was seen as an attempt by the British to manipulate supplies in order to "take all the credit" for the combined Allied relief and military supplies shipped to the North.[40]

British businessmen, however, were hamstrung by the limited shipping tonnage available to them and by the prohibitive requirements associated with securing an export license for northern Russia. Although the British government had apparently been successful in establishing a monopoly of control in the North, British merchants were nonetheless unable to compete with their American counterparts; of the 80,000 tons of combined commercial stores received at Archangel in 1918, 36,200 tons—approximately 45 percent—was exported from the United States.[41] This trend remained unchanged in 1919.

By January 1919, the increased American commercial presence in North Russia had given the British cause for concern. According to one source, there were nine American consuls in Archangel alone, all of whom were busy "sending out circulars and price lists and [were] doing an enormous barter trade." In comparison, there was only one British consul in Archangel, and he was "standing still, one reason being that no initiative is permitted him."[42] There were also fears that American businessmen were trying to capture the Scandinavian market—a move thought to be partly due to the advantageous position it would give the United States in its trade with North Russia. Both the British consul and chargé d'affaires in Helsingfors reported the arrival of vast quantities of American goods, which were being stockpiled in Finnish warehouses "for eventual reexport to Russia."[43]

It had become obvious by the spring that North Russian businessmen, cooperative societies, and the local government Supply Corporation were also increasingly "inclined to transact all their business with the United States directly, or indirectly." The British commercial attaché in Archangel warned his government that, until the same shipping facilities enjoyed by other countries were made available to British merchants, British trade with North Russia would continue to be at a disadvantage.[44]

Although this preference for dealing with American merchants piqued the British government, it took no action toward alleviating the problems of tonnage and credit. Instead, it held that it would be "to our advantage to keep *out* the Americans," enabling the British government to dispose of surplus supplies at a profit, which would, in turn, provide badly needed roubles to help finance its operations in the North.[45] Crude attempts were made by the British government to discourage American trade. In May 1919, for example, U.S. vessels carrying American goods and equipment purchased by the Archangel Cooperative Union were halted in the White Sea by British warships. Prevented from proceeding to Archangel, the merchantmen were forced to off-load their cargo on to British ships and the consignment's arrival in Archangel was delayed by four months.[46]

Despite such difficulties, businessmen in North Russia persisted in placing orders in the United States and Scandinavia, "avoiding the U.K. as much as possible." In the face of growing anti-British sentiment in North Russia, it was suggested by the commercial attaché in Archangel that "it might be well to see whether it would not be feasible to establish a commission, preferably in London, which would undertake the control of supplies for North Russia."[47]

With the removal in late February of the condition that British sellers be paid in sterling, British commercial interest in the area revived.[48] The shortage of tonnage available to private merchants still posed a stumbling block to this trade, however, even when North Russian orders would have meant considerable business for British firms. One factor behind the North Russian government's decision to avoid placing orders in Britain was the inability of the British to guarantee that goods ordered could be shipped and delivered. Even when Metropolitan Vickers was asked by the Archangel municipality to tender a bid for two turbines and two boilers for its electric station—an order which would have been worth 2.5 million roubles (over £500,000)—the government demurred. In reply to Lindley's request that he be allowed to inform the municipality that it need not anticipate tonnage difficulties, the Ministry of Shipping insisted that it would be "impossible to supply British requisitioned tonnage for other than military shipments."[49] In March, Lindley again forwarded a list of electrical machinery that was needed by the municipality, stating that it was "desirable to place this order in the United Kingdom for [the] sake of future orders which are likely to be extensive." The Russians, however, required an assurance of delivery, stipulating that the first shipment be dispatched in May. Unable to satisfy this demand, the British lost the business to the Americans, who had guaranteed delivery six months from date of order.[50]

The British government's reluctance to relinquish its hold over requisitioned tonnage may have been due to reasons other than pure logistics. The new rouble, issued by the British, was accused of making import so profitable as to be a "source of embarrassment" to the government. "One English trawler has disposed of a cargo for two million new roubles which means a loss of 1,300,000 old roubles to revenue of [the Russian] government." In addition, the diminishing stocks of raw materials readily available for export made it more likely that such losses would be incurred, as merchants were increasingly unable to reinvest their proceeds in goods for shipment to Britain. For these reasons, Acting Commercial Attaché Hoare recommended against any further promotion of this trade through the extension of the War Risks Insurance scheme—which already covered British trade to other parts of Russia not under Bolshevik control—to include the northern region.[51]

It was not until mid-July that the government allowed a few "free vessels" to engage in North Russian commerce. Even then, however, it was stated that "any trading which did take place would be subject to any restrictions which the Naval and Military Authorities might consider necessary at the time."[52] The liberal application of this condition provoked Lindley, who had learned "by chance" that permits allowing ships to proceed to the White Sea in order to export timber had been refused on the grounds that "no labour is available to load ships without interfering with naval and military requirements." Protesting that the decision was taken without consulting him, he demanded to know the justification for such a measure, which "cuts the ground from under our whole financial policy and stultifies all we have done to push the export trade."[53] The jealousy with which each government department guarded its own interests thus resulted in counterproductive policies that stifled any hopes of expanding this trade; the feeble efforts by British officials to assist private commerce in the area were far too few and much too late to redress the situation.

By the summer of 1919 Britain's position in the North was precarious; the antipathy toward the British and the growing sympathy for the Soviets among the local population ensured that Allied—that is, British—military operations in the region would receive little future support. Red Army victories and the growing wave of domestic disenchantment with the intervention prompted the British government to evacuate its troops from North Russia in the autumn of 1919. British control over Baltic and White Sea shipping was also terminated; the withdrawal of the Baltic fleet was made on the understanding that, barring any radical turn of events, a strong British naval presence would not be reinstated in the Baltic the following spring. The withdrawal of interventionist forces from North Russia reflected the Allied reassessment of the military and political situation. The collapse of Yudenich's North Western Army—the only viable counterrevolutionary force in North Russia—also compelled the British government to reevaluate its commitment to the region. The government expressed its views clearly on any future operations in the area when it informed the newly independent Baltic states that it could take no responsibility for protecting them against the Bolsheviks. Though abandoning the North as a field of operations, neither Britain nor the United States saw this action as abandoning Russia; rather, they realized the necessity of directing their support to the stronger, ultimately more successful counterrevolutionary armies in Siberia and South Russia.

Siberia

Unlike operations in the North, Allied military involvement in Siberia had always been passive and, after the armistice, was essentially limited to the supply and training of the local White Russian forces. In the case of the United States, however, this was a secondary consideration compared with their larger task of preventing Japanese expansion in eastern Siberia. The development of commercial relations with the various cooperative societies throughout Siberia was one means by which the United States hoped to counter the heavy Japanese military presence. Through the autumn of 1918 the U.S. government continued to increase the tonnage allotted for shipments to Vladivostok—from 10,000 tons in October to some 20,000 to 25,000 tons by December 1918. The enthusiasm for Siberian trade that predicated this expansion of shipping is reflected in the deluge of enquiries received by the State and Commerce Departments requesting information about commercial conditions, export licenses, and shipping facilities for this route. Concerned over the mounting number of speculative shipments arriving at Vladivostok, the American consul tried to temper this optimism. Warning that "most Americans have the wrong impressions," the consul informed the State Department that far less of the country was open to trade than was thought to be the case, and that the rail lines and warehouses were "hopelessly congested." Citing the lack of stable currency and exchange difficulties, he advised that only firms willing to confine themselves to moderate business opportunities in eastern Siberia, or those "able and willing to invest large sums in laying foundations for future business should be encouraged to engage in trade in Siberia at present."[54] Despite such warnings, little effort was made to inform merchants of the difficulties in this trade, and private commerce continued to be encouraged to provision and supply the region.

Undoubtedly cognizant of the immediate obstacles to trade in Siberia, several firms with long-standing experience in that region continued to do business there, and their reputedly profitable transactions excited further enthusiasm over the potential of the market. The representative of one import-export house, which had "a chain of stores throughout Siberia," declared that business was certainly possible in the Russian Far East.

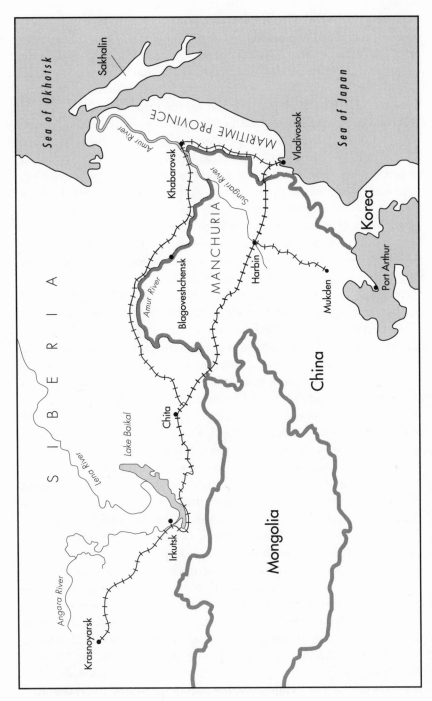

Map 4.2 Siberia and the Russian Far East

Reporting that it had already taken safe delivery in New York of $25,000 worth of furs it had purchased in Vladivostok, he stated that the firm had purchased an additional $250,000 worth of furs, hides, and horsehair for export to the United States.[55] International Harvester likewise continued to trade locally, and in one case was believed to have "sold for gold" some $600,000 worth of spare parts for agricultural machinery.[56]

Private American commercial interest was not limited to companies that had done business prior to the war; a number of firms had been incorporated specifically to conduct trade with postwar Russia. Two such companies, the American-Siberian Export and Import Company and Lied, were incorporated as early as 1918 in anticipation of the growth of the Siberian market in particular.[57] Though distrusted by the State Department, Jonas Lied's organization was well prepared for this business. A Scandinavian businessman with commercial experience in Siberia, Lied was not blind to the difficulties that limited this trade. Accordingly, his corporation was set up to operate on a barter basis—exporting American-made goods to Siberia, where they would then be sold in exchange for Russian and Siberian produce. Such barter trade was the preferred means of conducting business with the region, as goods were "much less uncertain than Russian roubles, and in fact, the market is so strong here for the raw materials that Russia can supply that firms entering into this arrangement are running not more than ordinary risks." The objectives of both the government and the private trader meshed perfectly: "The government's interest, of course, is in getting needed supplies into Russia; the interest of the firms sending the goods is in getting into the game early and earning good will, as much as immediate profit."[58]

That Siberia was considered by American merchants to be the more important area of non-Bolshevik Russia open to commerce is clear from the fact that the overwhelming proportion of U.S. vessels cleared for Russian ports were bound for Vladivostok: of the twelve ships that cleared the port of New York for Russia between 31 March and 12 July 1919, six were destined for the Russian Far East. Perhaps more illuminating, however, is the fact that those six ships accounted for 20,840 of the total 32,198 tons cleared—or nearly two-thirds of the net tonnage bound for Russian ports during that period.[59] Moreover, that Siberia was viewed as an exceptionally valuable future market for American manufactured goods is evident from the growing interest that banks and private financiers began to show. With an established branch in Vladivostok, the National City Bank faced competition from British and Japanese banks that opened branches not only in Vladivostok, but also in the nearby Chinese border city of Harbin. News that the British and Japanese governments were planning to establish a credit of £1 million each in these banks specifically for the purpose of facilitating Siberian trade prompted the suggestion that the U.S. government ought to consider setting up similar credit in the Vladivostok branch of the National City Bank—as its branch at Harbin had not yet opened.[60]

Under the auspices of the War Trade Board's Russian Bureau, the U.S. government not only continued to encourage American merchants to explore the business opportunities in Russia, but also concluded several deals with the larger of the Russian cooperative societies by the middle of 1919. According to the *Russian Outlook* of 19 July 1919, the U.S. government, through the War Department, supplied $15 million worth of surplus clothing and textiles directly to five Russian cooperative organizations, the payment for which was to "be made in the future" on a barter basis. Secretary of War Baker told representatives of the organizations that, by this action, the United States "hoped to create a widespread feeling among the Russian people that during the critical years it was found possible for the U.S. to regard the human problem above all others and to be of some assistance to the Russian people." A further credit of $5 million each was extended by the U.S. government to the Union of Siberian Cooperatives, Centrosoyus, and the Siberian Creameries Association to finance the purchase of goods to that value in America.[61] Unlike the previous arrangement, which provided for the repayment in local produce in the unspecified future, the terms for this credit were quite specific, requiring 10 percent of the purchase price to be paid upon shipment of the goods and the remaining 90 percent payable in installments within eighteen months.[62] In order to leave no doubt as to the question of the origin of these goods—as well as to ensure against possible profiteering—a further condition required that the merchandise be distributed to the civilian population under the supervision of agents of the U.S. War Department.[63] Although relatively little of this credit appears to have been taken up by any of the cooperatives in question, a further $5 million was extended to Centrosoyus, bringing the amount of government credit available to that cooperative for use in the United States to $10 million by the end of 1919.[64] The psychological effect that these extraordinary facilities were designed to have on the Siberian population should not be underestimated. By strengthening its position with the cooperative societies, the United States ensured its continued access to the Siberian market through the region's largest purchasing and marketing organization.[65]

Even though it had pushed for intervention in Siberia, Britain limited its military commitment in the region to equipping and training local Russian forces. After the armistice, the commitment was seen as a necessary responsibility to be kept up in the effort to combat Bolshevism. However, the desire to secure an economic foothold in Siberia was held to be so important that this goal was sometimes pursued to the detriment of larger political objectives in Russia. Even before the end of the war, the British commercial commissioner at Vladivostok reported numerous "far reaching schemes for economic and industrial development in Siberia" for which British government support was solicited. While recognizing that the persons involved were "presumably not entirely disinterested" and that any hint of encouragement from the government would "antagonise the more socialistic element in Siberia," which would suspect the British of exploitation, he was compelled to recommend that some sort of action be taken. The Japanese were "using every effort to secure valuable rights and concessions of all kinds and . . . American organisations are not beyond suspicion of a similar design. In these circumstances to decline to consider any such schemes will only result in their being presented to our allies who may thus secure a paramount position in [the] economic and commercial development of Siberia which may involve serious loss to British trade interests in [the] future."[66]

Similar concern over Siberian resources was expressed by the War Office. Within days of the armistice, the General Staff informed the Foreign Office that "whatever may be the ultimate decision of the Allies in regard to the general question of intervention in European Russia, no effort should be spared to prevent Siberia from relapsing into the hands of the Bolsheviks." Aside from the moral question of withdrawing support from those who have been encouraged to expect assistance, Britain would "be in danger of losing for an unknown period the resources of Siberia, which are indispensable for reconstruction after the war."[67] It is not surprising, therefore, that the government professed support for private firms that sought to preserve their interests in the region. It was desired that British companies provide supplies necessary to keep Siberian mines open, "otherwise the Japanese and Americans will certainly do so and will very likely obtain some form of control over the mining industry of the Urals."[68] To this end, the government favored applications from British owned Siberian mining corporations requesting permission to issue fresh capital.[69] Despite the government's commitment to these industries, by the spring of 1919 restrictions on the export of British capital to Siberia had caused considerable hardship. British mining interests in eastern Siberia especially were reported to be suffering from the inability of their London offices to remit capital to cover expenses. As American and Japanese capital was said to be widely available, the absence of British capital was "unfortunate."[70]

By January 1919 the British government had decided that "no useful purpose is served by continuing to treat trade with Siberia on the same footing as trade with European Russia since geographical and transport considerations make the danger of supplies sent to Siberia reaching undesirable destinations practically negligible." Exporters of goods to Siberia were allowed the same freedom as exporters to neutral countries outside the blockade area—subject only to the condition that any traders who were reportedly charging excessive prices to the Siberian consumers would have their licenses revoked.[71] Even so, it was recognized that Britain was, from the start, at a disadvantage to the United States in the region. In addition to having some 600,000 tons of their shipping on the Pacific coast, the Americans also had "infinitely larger stocks of materials then we can hope to provide." It was feared that the limited tonnage available to British merchants and the "very small amount, relatively, of goods that we can provide" would be "entirely swamped by American and Japanese competition."[72] Despite such realizations, however, nothing was done to address the larger problems that plagued British commerce with Siberia.

The concern over the strengthening American position, and the early failure of the Siberian Supply Company notwithstanding, the government remained adamant that the needs of the Siberian population should be "as far as possible provided by private enterprise."[73] To be sure, Siberia's potential trade prompted sufficient interest among private traders to lead to the formation of firms like Sibunion and Becos Traders, which were incorporated for the purpose of pursuing business in the region. There was also a renewed interest in the commercial activities of the Siberian cooperative associations, some of which had offices in London. Acting on behalf of the London agencies of the Siberian cooperatives Centrosoyus and Zakupsbyt, the Merchant Trading Company arranged the so-called Kara Sea expedition, which successfully delivered about 7,000 tons of goods for both organizations.[74] In light of the difficulties the Siberian cooperatives had met in their business dealings with the British as compared with the Americans, it is ironic to note that the Foreign Office instructed the British High Commissioner at Vladivostok to "impress upon the Siberian government that every facility should be accorded to this expedition in view not only of the military, political and commercial advantages but also of possible future developments of trading between Siberia and this country."[75]

Despite such rhetoric, Britain's total trade turnover with the Russian cooperatives in Siberia remained comparatively small. In light of the huge credits from the United States, it was argued that if British economic relief was to make any impression, Britain should do "as the Americans have done"—that is, to provide the cooperative societies with "large credits to be expended in England, taking their raw materials as security for repayment."[76] Despite the logic behind this argument, it appears that no action was ever taken along these lines.

Moreover, the increasingly aggressive American moves to capture the market, combined with the inability of British commerce—either private or government-assisted—to stem the American predominance in the region, caused the British to become highly suspicious of their ally. In particular, Britain made no secret of its mistrust of the ostensibly altruistic motives of the United States in Russia. While it was admitted that the government, through the Board of Trade, has "always had in view—and in a sense quite rightly—the policy of keeping British trade interests in Siberia well to the front," the duplicity of American activities there had nonetheless given them "every reason to have the deepest suspicions of the American YMCA and such like philanthropic institutions."[77] Reportedly under instruction "to send economic reports to their Consuls," the YMCA was especially suspected of engaging in "economic investigation" in Siberia.[78]

While it is clear that the British were unwilling to forfeit their share of the potential postwar Siberian market, the government was more than prepared to relinquish the military and financial burdens imposed by intervention in the region. As early as August 1919, the British commander in Omsk argued that, as the United States and Japan had economic interests in Siberia, those powers should assume responsibility for any further Allied commitments in the region. Echoing these sentiments, the War Office made clear its priorities by pointing out that Britain could "only make an adequate effort in one theatre. . . . The choice is between Siberia and South Russia and there can be no question on which it falls."[79]

The South

The British government's decision to dispatch an interventionist army to the South—its largest military involvement in Russia—was taken as an almost reflex action after the war. This decision involved none of the debate that had surrounded the action in other theaters[80] as the area was of primary strategic interest to the British. While the security of the empire has frequently been paraded as the driving justification behind the orders to secure the Transcaucasian and Transcaspian areas, it is interesting to note that British troops tended to be concentrated in those regions where British economic interests were the greatest. In the case of Baku, where the British had a considerable interest in the local petroleum industry, the British military authorities quickly assumed control of virtually the entire economic apparatus of the city. Mixed commissions were created and supervised by the British for the reorganization, repair, and operation of the ports and shipping, the railways, and local industries —especially oil. The determination with which they tackled the job is illustrated by the fact that, despite the extent of the damage done to the oilfields during the war and subsequent local uprisings, it took the British only one month to effect the repairs necessary to renew the export of oil from the Caucasus.[81]

British plans for the economic penetration of the South were quite different from their designs upon the North. There was a disinclination to become too involved in the commercial affairs of British merchants in the Caucasus and Black Sea areas. Further, intervention in the South took place only *after* the armistice, a condition that made the imposition of such control harder to justify. The relative importance of each region in terms of British direct investment is worth noting; while the Russian North lacked any strong British interest, South Russia had long attracted considerable British investment. The overwhelming proportion of direct British capital investment in prewar Russia was concentrated in the extractive industries of South Russia, and in the oil industry in particular. These interests, along with the existing commercial network in South Russia, were seen as providing the foundation for further British economic penetration of the region. The economic presence was already established, and only military protection and official encouragement were necessary to ensure its expansion.

The relative strength of the indigenous counterrevolutionary forces also figured in this difference of policy. The early defeat of the North Western Army and the growing Bolshevist tendencies of the North Russian Provisional Government posed an increasing threat to the British position. The realization that the British foothold in the North was, at best, tenuous not surprisingly led to the systematic plundering of the region and the removal of essential raw materials before the Whites suffered total defeat. In South Russia, on the other hand, the armies of Denikin and Wrangel were seen as a bulwark against Bolshevism, forces that would ensure the safety of British economic interests in the region.

Characteristic of the government's hesitation at involvement in southern trade was Balfour's response to the suggestion that an economic mission be dispatched to coordinate the provisioning of South Russia. He

Map 4.3   European and South Russia

declared that he had a "horror of missions," especially if they were sent for the purpose of "doing something."

> My own feeling is strongly against any avoidable extension to South Russia of Government control or trading operations. . . . I would far sooner see the suppliers on this side and the consumers on that side thrown into direct relations, if this can be done with a degree of safety. We know that, the moment the Blockade objection is removed, there are people who are only too keen to begin the resumption of such relations. . . . The Hudson Bay Company would be prepared, as soon as they were allowed to do so, to load a ship or ships and send them out forthwith, without waiting to ascertain what they could get in exchange for the goods on the other side. . . . As soon as the Blockade restrictions are removed, there ought to be no difficulty in getting direct enterprise under way.
>
> I hope very much that it will not come to a mission, if only for the reason that any mission to Russia, if it is to do anything at all, involves inter-Allied action, and that action will almost inevitably lead to the state of affairs which we now see in Siberia. I feel very strongly that the best course, if it can possibly be adopted, is to remove restrictions and encourage private enterprise by every means that we can.[82]

The government officially encouraged this trade and facilitated it wherever possible. Indeed, judicious governmental intervention did promote private commerce. The government instructed the British military authorities in the region to render whatever aid they could to British traders. As a result, British nationals faced fewer difficulties in transporting their goods and acquiring the relevant permits.[83]

While the government discouraged businessmen from traveling in other areas of Russia, South Russia was the subject of numerous reports and memoranda advising that merchants would benefit from visiting those areas under British or non-Bolshevik control. As early as 23 December 1918, the Interdepartmental Conference on Russian Affairs expressed its unanimous opinion that "it was most desirable that reputable British subjects willing to return to South Russia entirely at their own risk should be allowed to do so, as it was considered that the benefits associated with their return from the point of view of propaganda and the furtherance of British trade interests, were likely to outweigh any possible disadvantages."[84]

Despite the government's expressed desire to establish commercial relations with South Russia and the mounting pressure from private quarters to do so, the lack of interdepartmental cooperation and communication again frustrated attempts to reopen this trade. The Board of Trade particularly hounded the Foreign Office throughout January 1919 to persuade the Allied Blockade Committee to allow British commercial relations with the Black Sea ports of Novorossisk, Poti, and Batum.[85] The Foreign Office's refusal to press the issue with the committee in Paris was seen by the Department of Overseas Trade as the cause of the delay in resuming this trade, the effects of which were lamented by Steel-Maitland as being "great and harmful."[86] Pointing out that the present position had become critical with regard to relations with the area of Russia under Denikin's control, Steel-Maitland declared that it was

> unfortunate that divergent views between different Government Departments are causing indecision as regards the Government policy as a whole. . . . From a commercial point of view we are losing great opportunities, not only for the present, but for the future, through not being able to supply the population in General Denikin's area with the manifold articles that they need. From the political point of view, however, this failure is probably even more important. Bolshevism is largely caused by the want of necessaries of life. The supply therefore of these necessaries in full quantities to this particular area would be both the best safeguard against the spread of Bolshevism there and also avoid a contrast in the eyes of the Russia people with other parts of Russia. . . . Although the Dardanelles are supposed to be blockaded . . . I am assured that French and Italian vessels have passed through for the purpose of private trade.[87]

Trade was lost to Britain as a result of this continued prohibition, a point underscored by the news that the Georgian Economic Commission was in Stockholm negotiating the exchange of Russian raw materials for manufactured goods and other necessities. Since little could be done to prevent the neutrals from trading with the region, it was decided to invite the commission to Britain to discuss the resumption of trade, as it was "preferable to encourage the Georgians to trade with the United Kingdom rather than with Sweden."[88] In view of this admission, it is curious to note that appeals from British officials in South Russia for permission to allow local Russian businessmen "of good standing" to go to Britain for legitimate trade purposes had been ignored. As late as March the British consul in Odessa complained that, though many requests had been submitted to the Foreign Office, he had received no reply. This inaction caused "great dissatisfaction" in Russian business circles, where it was increasingly considered to be "impossible to try to develop business with England and that their trade relations with Germany must be resumed."[89]

By mid-1919 it had become apparent to many that the British position in the South was suffering as a result of the absence of any defined policy. Pointing out that the economic needs of the Caucasus were great, the representative of the Anglo-Persian Oil Company advised the Petroleum Executive that "if through British intervention some relief could be given it would certainly help to stop the tide of ill feeling which appears to be rising against us owing to our undefined policy towards Russia."[90]

Though the Foreign Office recognized that there was "a strong desire in this country for the resumption of trade with Odessa and other Black Sea ports" and admitted that conditions were such "that a resumption of trade within limits may now be possible," it was not until mid-February that the Department of Overseas Trade was able to announce that it was now permitted to accept applications for passage to South Russian ports.[91] From that point, however, "special endeavours" were made to promote trade with South Russia, the result being that during the two months between the department's announcement and 31 March, licenses had been issued for the export of £1.4 million worth of goods for Black Sea ports. Further, by early April, increasing numbers of businessmen were being sent to represent firms in the region. Private transport facilities were deluged with persons wanting passage to South Russia, and the main shipping lines reported that the Marseilles and Malta route was booked up to the end of that month.[92] It is significant that the tonnage shortage that plagued the development of private commerce of the North and Siberia was scarcely evident in the trade of the Black Sea region. In fact, the Ministry of Shipping had even arranged accommodation for some forty businessmen on the troop transport vessel HMS *Nile*.[93]

The British government clearly anticipated the development of considerable trade with South Russia. Once "normal conditions" returned to Russia it was hoped that British traders would "obtain a far larger share of Russian trade than in pre-war days." This situation would, in turn, "encourage firms who had not previously dealt with Russia to investigate the great potentialities of this market."[94] The volume of British commerce with South Russia was expected to be so large that direct shipment was to be advised wherever possible so as to avoid congestion.[95] That considerable importance was attached to this trade is evident from the fact that, in June, the Board of Trade extended its War Risks Insurance Scheme to cover inland risks upon both British goods imported into South Russia and goods bought by British firms for export from Russia. In certain cases the government also provided marine insurance where it would be otherwise unavailable. This positive government intervention encouraged banks to grant advances on shipments made to Russia. The British Trade Corporation, Lloyds Bank, the London County and Westminster and Parrs Bank, and the National Provincial and Union Bank of England all intimated that they were prepared to consider applications for advances on goods sent to Russia and insured under this measure. By mid-August these banks had formed the South Russian Banking Agency with a view to doing business in the area covered by the Insurance Scheme.[96] In addition, it was reported that certain British banks were considering establishing branches in South Russia, a move that would do much to facilitate the trade of the region. The scheme also encouraged a number of shipping companies, including Cunard, the Ellerman Wilson Line, Westcott & Laurence, and James Moss and Company, to provide tonnage for outbound as well as inbound cargo and to establish a scheduled service to the Black Sea ports. By the end of June there were seven regular services operating this route, with least five steamers a week departing Britain for Black Sea ports.[97]

As a result of the extension of the insurance scheme to cover trade with South Russia, the returns of exports to that area showed a marked increase during July and August, as did the volume of applications for assistance received by the Department of Overseas Trade from firms who sought to send representatives out to that region. Interestingly enough, the results that were produced by the War Risk Insurance Scheme had been obtained in a "rather negative way." Lloyds, upon discovering that the War Risks Insurance Office was prepared to accept insurance, began to offer policies at a rate that was one-half percent cheaper than the government's rates. It was supposed that the Lloyds underwriters had "acted on the principle that what was good enough for His Majesty's Government was good enough for them."[98]

There was no question that "quite a volume of business" was being done by the British in South Russia, and that this trade was highly profitable for some merchants.[99] The quest for huge profits in South Russia left an equal number of merchants disappointed, however. Largely unable to obtain payment in foreign currency, merchants were frequently forced to accept roubles in exchange for their goods and reinvest them in Russian produce, which was then exported. Such difficulties did not discourage those traders who accepted the Department of Overseas Trade's assessment that South Russia was one of the few areas where British business could expect the "greatest development in the future," with "the extension of business . . . likely to be quickest." Indeed, returns for the eight-month period from April to November 1919 were promising, with British exports to South Russia totally over £8.2 million. The problem, however, was that only £500,000 worth of goods was imported from the region during the same period. It became increasingly difficult for British merchants not only to obtain local goods, but to procure from the local government the licenses necessary for the export of goods already in their possession.[100]

Complications along these lines were encountered as early as March 1919, when the vice-consul of Novorossisk reported that some five hundred tons of Russian tobacco purchased by a British subject could not be loaded for export "because the Government of the Volunteer Army has put a prohibitive tax on tobacco." He went on to point out that considerable amounts of other goods that belonged to that government were "allowed to be shipped without [any] hindrance whatever, because by shipping those goods the Volunteer Army are opening a credit for themselves in England." British-owned goods were not shipped as "they would not be of any benefit at all to the Volunteer Army."[101] By August the Military Mission in South Russia felt compelled to warn the British government that nothing could be done "due to the corrupt nature of the [Volunteer Army Trade and Industry] Department and the obstruction in exporting goods from South Russia."[102] Conditions were such that British traders should be warned "not to send goods out to Russia except against prepayment or goods placed at their disposal actually on territory outside Russia."[103] The increasing frequency with which the Volunteer Army requisitioned local commodities earmarked for export, the inability to obtain export facilities and permits, the breakdown of inland transportation, rampant speculation, and an imprecise knowledge of quantities and even the whereabouts of commodities all combined to prevent a growing number of British merchants from receiving their return cargoes of goods, which they had been offered in barter.[104] By December, the British Mission in South Russia recommended that traders should "proceed with the utmost caution," warning that it was "extremely unwise to bring in unordered goods and sell them in the country before stipulating definitely for payment on return cargo. Once barterers get into the clutches of official Russia, they will be blackmailed *ad infinitum*."[105]

Whether commercial circles were convinced that the market would ultimately justify the risks encountered or whether they were simply not kept informed as to the difficulties inherent in southern commerce is unclear, but it is certain that British business continued to pursue this trade. Concurrent with warning against further commercial involvement in the area, the British consul in Rostov reported that "considerable shipments are on the way out, and several representatives of well known British firms, who are now here, have made large contracts, running into millions of pounds sterling, with the various Government Departments, railway and Co-operative Societies."[106] Regardless of the warnings and the lack of exportable commodities, however, British exports to South Russia over the last quarter of 1919 increased from £302,000 to more than £850,000; and by January 1920 the total value of goods for private trade at the port of Novorossisk alone was estimated at £3.5 million.[107]

Although no American troops were dispatched to South Russia, the United States was substantially interested in the region.[108] Like Britain, the U.S. government committed itself to support the anti-Bolsheviks in the South. By the winter, however, Denikin's defeats had cooled British enthusiasm for his cause; there was a real threat that further British aid would be cut off unless the fortunes of the Volunteer Army revived. Reluctant to extend further credit to Russia, the British government decided that supplies would subsequently be released only upon cash payment or in exchange for Russian goods to an equivalent value.[109] The American government had fewer reservations; during the autumn of 1919 the Russian Provisional Government's ambassador in Washington, Boris Bakhmetev, succeeded in arranging a $7 million credit for purchases in the United States. Further, throughout 1919, special "financial agents" attached to the Russian Embassy, S. A. Ughet and P. A. Morozov, had entered into numerous contracts with private firms as well as U.S. governmental agencies for supplies to the counterrevolutionary armies.[110] Between May and December 1919 over $19 million worth of goods and supplies was shipped to Denikin in South Russia, over half of which was dispatched in October and November.[111]

Despite this political commitment to the region, U.S. governmental interference in the development of private American trade with South Russia was minimal. The War Trade Board decided that commerce with the South would not be subjected to the same controls as those imposed on trade with Siberia, nor would it be required to use the intermediary agency of the Russian Bureau. Instead, South Russia was, from the start, open to general commerce.[112]

Although official interference in this trade was kept to a minimum, the U.S. government nonetheless took positive steps to support it. Consular representation in those areas of South Russia outside of Bolshevik control was substantially augmented. Britain, it was argued, had an immediate economic advantage because of its military occupation of that part of the country. The interventionist armies were accompanied by government officials "who kept the British businessmen advised as to commercial opportunities." If American business was to win any part of this trade, U.S. government representatives were required in the large trading centers of the region.[113] In addition, it was common for a newly appointed consul to be accompanied by vice-consuls, who were to be "distributed as opportunity arises in other districts."[114] Not surprisingly, the British watched this arrival of official American commercial representatives with trepidation.

Indeed, with news of the impending removal of the blockade of the Russian Black Sea ports, American merchants lost little time renewing commercial contacts. As early as March, the chargé d'affaires at the Russian Embassy in New York protested the delay in reestablishing steamship communication with the Russian ports on the Black Sea, pointing out that, in addition to the governmental supplies, there was a "great quantity of private goods" ready to be shipped to South Russia.[115] Exceptional measures were taken by firms to ensure that they would be able to compete in the region. Ford for one was reported to have concluded a deal with the Near East Development Corporation in April for the sale of four hundred tractors by contract. Noteworthy in terms of the sheer size of the order alone, the deal is more remarkable because Ford—who adamantly opposed giving even his own dealers credit—agreed to arrange the sale on a combined credit and barter basis.[116]

American businesses also began offering long-term credits and were "adapting themselves to the Russian character, customs and conditions." This penetration was done "very quietly with the aid of a very small but well organised group of agents, which make use of the Red Cross organisations and similar missions to spread their commercial propaganda." The British were convinced that virtually every large undertaking in the country was being scrutinized by the Americans, who were "not out for temporary business or bothering about small barter cargoes and quick turnover business after the manner of the greater number of British firms now active out here." Instead, the Americans had chosen to take advantage of the moment "to concentrate their efforts on permanent large investments without unduly worrying about the present status of the rouble or the other risks apprehended by the British firms."[117]

Accordingly, many Russian enterprises were believed already to be under American control. In particular, the Russian firm of Stakheieff and Company, which owned about seventy-five different concerns, was thought to be "financed entirely" by an American group that represented the huge Rockefeller and Armour interests. Surprisingly like the Yaroshinsky affair, the Americans apparently used this group to buy up primary interests in important Russian industries. British intelligence sources in Russia indicated that, over the course of one month, the Stakheieff group had bought up at least ten concerns in various parts of Russia and had acquired a large share in top-flight financial institutions such as the Volga-Kama Bank, the Russo-Asiatic Bank, and the Don-Kuban Bank. Unlike the British scheme, however, little or no cash was believed to have changed hands; rather, these transactions were primarily on the basis of shares in the new companies, with the American purchasers binding themselves to supply the requisite machinery and plant.[118]

Other far-reaching offers that were extended by this group included one that involved the supply of unlimited quantities of medical stores against raw materials, with the condition that they be sold at a 10 percent profit, which would be used to establish hospitals and medical research institutions. The offer also involved the opening of apothecary shops throughout Russia. Though initially demanding a 7 percent profit on the capital invested in these shops, the Americans eventually agreed "to do it all for nothing in the hope that the hold they secure on that trade will afford them the unrivaled and unassailable position for the disposal of their drugs and chemical preparations in the future." The same scheme also proposed that the group undertake sanitation works throughout Russia, with the Americans furnishing requisite materials and experts. While the Russian authorities expressed delight with the proposal, the British were not deceived by the philanthropic appearance of these offers: "As in the case of the majority of their Red Cross enterprises, the main concern of the Americans in this *soi-disant* charitable enterprise is the furtherance of commercial and financial interests."[119]

American interest also took less humanitarian forms. Negotiations were started for the construction of the Volga-Don canal and a pipeline from Grozny to the Black Sea, as well as the electrification of Dnieper Falls and the possibility of the exclusive right to construct future railway lines in the Don region on a profit-sharing basis. In "accordance with time honoured American methods," these schemes were all devised "to cover thorough commercial and industrial penetration." It was clear that the United States fully intended "to acquire a firm foothold in South Russia and cut out all competition."[120]

Nor were American merchants blind to trading opportunities in Russia. The local papers in Novorossisk announced that the United States was prepared to deliver "any quantity of goods" in return for tobacco and raw materials, and that an exhibition of American merchandise was planned to ensure that commercial relations between the two countries began auspiciously. American business found the Russian cooperative societies to be eager trading partners. The All-Russian Central Union of Consumers Societies had, as early as February, purchased 30,000 pairs of boots and shoes for export to South Russia.[121] The New York office of the Union of Russian Cooperative Societies had purchased some 620,000 poods—or nearly 9,000 metric tons—of goods in the United States for shipment to South Russia. Along with a large quantity of boots and sole leather, the Cooperative Society also purchased a variety of manufactured goods, including American agricultural implements "of the latest type." As in the case of British trade with the region, the majority of these transactions were conducted by barter, with the goods shipped when a corresponding value of raw materials had been received in the United States.[122]

The aggressive nature of American commercial activity in what was arguably a British sphere provoked hostility in London. As indicated already, the British suspected that the Americans either refused to distinguish between charitable and commercial enterprise or, at best, that American charity was "tempered with considerable commercial acumen." These suspicions were not without foundation. It was noticed, for example, that the Americans who had arrived in Batum to distribute foodstuffs to civilians were simultaneously actively securing orders from local dealers for "goods of every description."[123] Moreover, certain American relief organizations were unquestionably involved in trading activities. The Near East Relief Organization was known to have received a cargo of "trade goods" in South Russia. Although these goods were largely exchanged for foodstuffs from the region north of the Black Sea, it is nonetheless interesting to note that according to Hoover's own account, there were "some trade goods left over that Colonel Haskell used profitably."[124]

While the development of commercial relations in South Russia was undoubtedly regarded by both countries as highly desirable, neither government was willing to commit itself to protecting their nationals' commercial interests in the region.[125] The withdrawal of British troops during the autumn of 1919 and the encroachment of disruptive elements increased both governments' caution. However, in light of the growing American competition, two areas of British economic involvement were considered important enough to warrant governmental support long after the decision had been made to evacuate the interventionist troops from the area: the Chiatouri manganese concession and the Russian oil industry. The competition that developed over these South Russian resources caused the most friction in Anglo-American relations.

Both Britain and the United States were concerned over future supplies of Russian manganese. South Russia was a major source of the highest grade manganese ore, ferromanganese, which is essential in the production of steel and other tempered metals.[126] Though the industrialized nations of the West managed with poorer-quality ore from Brazil, Cuba, and India during the war, these ores were not an entirely satisfactory substitute for the Russian product.[127]

The British government's tacit support for the autonomous Georgian government was undoubtedly influenced by the need to ensure future supplies of this ore. Despite this sympathy, British manganese producers and exporters were forced to suffer exorbitant taxes and prohibitive export restrictions imposed by the Georgian government.[128] This industry presents a unique case, however, insofar as rivalry between British firms did more damage to British interests than any conflict with the local government. In September 1919 the Georgian authorities announced that they intended to place the export of manganese ore under government monopoly, whereby one firm or individual would be given the exclusive right to export.[129] Not surprisingly, this decision provoked protest from the British government as well as companies interested in the mines. However, when the government discovered that the British Trade Corporation was the firm chosen to receive the monopoly rights, official protests quickly ceased.[130] The Foreign Office wired in late November that they had "consulted with the Board of Trade and consider in the circumstances that every effort should be made to secure [the] monopoly for that body." Ironically, included in this communication were instructions "to do everything possible" to protect the interests of other private British manganese producers whose rights of export the British Trade Corporation had just usurped.[131]

Nor did this decision go unchallenged by the United States. The United States Steel Corporation and the Iron and Ore Corporation of America in particular expressed interest in the Caucasian manganese mining industry. News that the British Trade Corporation had been granted complete control over the export of that ore provoked consternation among steel producers in the United States. The overthrow of the Georgian government by the Bolsheviks in the spring of 1920 was viewed with satisfaction by some American firms, which lost no time in looking for a similar arrangement with the Bolsheviks.[132]

The competition that developed over Russian petroleum caused more serious friction between the two allies. The increasingly widespread use and application of the internal combustion engine had created an almost insatiable demand for oil, and growing military and naval requirements made this resource a strategic necessity. Given this growing demand, both

Britain and the United States were concerned not only with ensuring that adequate supplies would continue to be available to them, but also with securing a substantial—if not controlling—interest in petroleum-bearing lands wherever possible. Revolution and civil war notwithstanding, the oilfields of South Russia were the object of keen competition.

For the most part, British petroleum companies operating in South Russia shared with businessmen and government officials the illusion that the Bolsheviks were a passing phenomenon. Convinced that conditions in Russia would revert to normal, Royal Dutch Shell considered the possibility of undertaking drilling improvements in Baku as early as February 1919. Nor did this conviction waver, despite the government's decision in June to withdraw British troops and naval presence from the region by December. As late as October, Shell—with the support of the British military authorities in the Caucasus—had laid plans for reviving oil exports from Baku.[133]

Governmental policy did much to encourage this view among the British oil companies already operating in the Caucasus. Requests for permission to issue considerable amounts of new capital were looked upon favorably by the British government. The European Oilfields Corporation, the Ural Caspian Oil Corporation, Spies Petroleum Company, and North Caucasian Oilfields all sought and received permission to issue new capital shares that would enable them to continue operations in Russia.[134]

The extension of British control over oil-bearing properties in Russia was a principal aim of the government's policy of economic penetration in South Russia. To this end the government supported schemes designed to acquire control over these reserves wherever possible. As early as January 1919 the Anglo-Persian Oil Company reported that they had the opportunity to take over a "share in one or more Russian oil companies." The British company was not, however, "anxious to entertain the proposal unless its acceptance would definitely serve British national interests and was subject to the condition that British control was secured." Forwarding this communication to the Foreign Office for their opinion, the Petroleum Executive emphasized "the importance of extending British control over oil bearing areas."[135]

Although the oil companies and government agreed that a cooperative effort in the region was necessary to prevent Standard Oil from gaining a foothold, the Foreign Office nonetheless declared itself unable "to take the responsibility of advising British firms to establish themselves there." Pressure from the Petroleum Executive and the three major British oil companies—Anglo-Persian, Pearsons, and Shell—finally compelled the

Foreign Office to conclude that there could be "no harm in saying that H.M. Government will, in future, as in the past, give every assistance in their powers towards the protection and maintenance of the legitimate right of British enterprises established and working in foreign countries." Even the intractable Curzon, who was loath to commit the Foreign Office to any assurances whatsoever, noted that it was "most desirable that we should keep a footing in the Baku mines." Accordingly, he had "no objection to giving assurances in the terms indicated."[136]

Although Anglo-Persian was reluctant to commit itself in a country where "all was apparently chaos and confusion," the company nonetheless declared that it would be willing "to follow any policy in regard to the Russian oilfields which H.M. Government might eventually decide upon."[137] Despite the growing uncertainty over the future of the area and the difficulties that the Russian oil industry as a whole was experiencing throughout the spring, the government left no doubt as to its support for the British acquisition of Russian properties. Accordingly, the Petroleum Executive informed Anglo-Persian that while it recognized the commercial risks involved, the government would "view with approval" the company's continued attempts to purchase an interest in the Nobel properties.[138] Even the Foreign Office gave its grudging assent; by stating that it had no objection to Anglo-Persian entering into preliminary negotiations with the Russian firm, the Foreign Office noted that it had "already taken a first step in favouring efforts for securing British participation in the Baku area."[139]

There were two prongs of reasoning behind the government's drive to control these fields. The first and most obvious was to provide for Britain's increasing need for fuel oil. Producing only 2 percent of the total world supply of petroleum, the British Empire depended upon foreign production for its requirements. From the supply point of view, therefore, even the Foreign Office was convinced that it was "most desirable that we should secure, in some form, all possible control over oil bearing areas in foreign countries."[140] The intervention was seen by many as providing a "unique opportunity of getting most of the Baku oil fields under British control."[141] By so doing, the British would not only ensure the empire's supplies of petroleum, but would also free themselves from their dependence on the increasingly uncertain supplies of the expensive American product. The area had taken on new importance in view of the American producers' prediction that the output of petroleum in the United States would soon be exhausted, "leaving little if any margin for export." Further, it was considered "essential that a fresh supply should be opened up in view of the recent prices in America and the adverse course of the exchanges."[142]

The other, less obvious British motivation was to keep the American petroleum companies—especially Standard Oil—out. The Baku producers found themselves in an "extremely critical" financial situation after the war. The question was whether the assistance they received was to be British or American: "The principal producers . . . need financial support and they will get it either from us or from sources whose interests do not march with ours."[143] Standard Oil was clearly that other interest, and there was no doubt that it would present unparalleled competition in its attempts to secure a foothold in Baku. The government was warned that, should Standard succeed in its efforts, it would become, "in a very short time, a formidable competitor with us in our Eastern markets."[144] It was, therefore, "most necessary that the absolute control be in British hands. If we do not profit by the occasion offered it is the intention of these firms to get the money they require from American sources."[145]

Despite the fact that a number of government departments had evidenced a keen interest in the Russian oilfields, the industry was in danger of collapse throughout most of 1919 due to the inability of producers to export either crude petroleum or its products. Denikin's government was partially to blame for this crisis, having levied huge export taxes on the three major British concerns in Grozny. Rates had been increased by a factor of 200, and the conditions presented to the companies were either to agree to the new terms or, in effect, have their holdings confiscated. In addition, the companies were prevented from dispatching goods for export or sale in the Black Sea area until they had the equivalent value of goods imported for exchange; the situation was aggravated by the failure of the Denikin government to provide the companies with a list of the goods that were required. The Anglo-Maikop Oil Corporation complained to the Foreign Office about this predicament; they were operating at a loss and would continue to do so until they were able to export and sell their oil.[146]

Finally, the limited transport and pipeline facilities as well as the lack of tanker capacity combined to make the oil companies' situation critical. In July Anglo-Persian's representative in Russia grimly noted that, unless something was done to address the storage problem, the industry would be forced to shut down at the end of the year. "All export to the Volga, the natural outlet for 80% of the Baku production, is prevented by Naval Forces until the Bolshevik troops are driven away from that district. The only other outlet, by pipeline and rail to Batoum, is also under British control." Further, while offers to purchase large quantities of kerosene had been made by representatives of Italian and American petroleum companies, no corresponding offer had been made by the British who controlled the lines of transport. As a result, the British were increasingly blamed by Russian oil producers as being the cause of obstruction.[147]

Despite such accusations, it seems that nothing was done to alleviate this problem. It must be noted, however, that the War Office attached considerable value to the acquisition of these stocks. During the autumn, Shell succeeded in enlisting War Office support in its bid to organize the export of the entire quantity of petroleum available at Batum and Novorossisk, as well as to arrange for the purchase of petroleum from the recently formed Soviet at Baku. War Office participation was to be limited to the dispatch of a military mission to accompany the Shell representatives, though it was agreed that "no expenses [would] be charged to the Government in connection with the Mission."[148]

The scheme initially failed to elicit the support of the Foreign Office on several scores. The Foreign Office was curious as to why a military mission "should be sent back into this area which the War Office have just insisted upon evacuating" for no other discernible purpose than to push the interests of Shell and the territorial claims of Denikin. Further, it was noted that such collusion between the War Office and Shell in Mesopotamia had "already brought us into conflict with the Americans and the Standard Oil Company, and has taught us the danger of these military ventures in 'big business.'" Part of the proposal, which stipulated that an export tax be levied on the oil and the sum thus realized be paid over to the credit of Denikin's account in London, was declared to be "absolutely dishonest." "Baku . . . belongs to the Azerbaijan Republic, and Denikin has absolutely nothing to do with it."[149] By December, however, persistent goading by the War Office combined with moderate changes to the original proposal forced the Foreign Office into conceding that it had "no objection to the scheme in its modified form, provided it is conducted on a purely commercial basis and through the usual official channels." There remained, however, a strong hint of official collusion with Shell.[150]

From the start, the cooperation between the government and British oil interests in Russia had provided considerable cause for concern in the United States. Although only one American firm—the Standard Oil subsidiary Vacuum Oil of New York—had operated oil properties in Russia prior to the revolution, the South Russian oilfields had attracted substantial U.S. attention by 1919. The increase in the consumption of petroleum products during the war years had provoked a growing concern over future world supplies of this resource. As a major oil exporter, the United States was especially struck with the fear that domestic oil reserves were being exhausted, and a number of American petroleum producers and exporters likewise joined the scramble to gain access to foreign sources.

It was realized that the military occupation of South Russia had given Britain an undeniable advantage in the region, which effectively enabled it to assert control over the transport, storage, and disposition of the petroleum produced there. In light of their recently awakened interest, the United States had become extremely wary of any attempt by the British to secure a monopoly control over Transcaucasian oil. While this concern was undoubtedly one of the primary reasons behind the American refusal to recognize any new, autonomous government in Russia,[151] it did not prevent Standard Oil from entering into agreements with the government of Azerbaijan.

As early as January 1919 Standard Oil had taken steps to secure a share in the Russian oilfields by concluding a contract with the Azerbaijan government for the purchase of eleven plots of undeveloped land at Baku.[152] A more far-reaching attempt to gain substantial control over Russian oil-bearing land was launched by Standard Oil in November, when it initiated negotiations for the purchase of half of the Nobel Brothers' holdings at Baku. Despite the unsettled condition in the region Standard was "prepared to conclude agreements with the Russian firms now, and to await future developments."[153] The agreement with Nobel was concluded in July 1920, despite the fact that the Soviets had previously nationalized the oil industry and had occupied Baku four months earlier.

Standard Oil was also interested in purchasing quantities of Russian oil and kerosene with which to supply its Asian markets. Despite the critical need to relieve the overburdened storage of both Baku and Batum, Standard's attempts to purchase Russian kerosene were opposed by the War Office. In early April Standard Oil had inquired whether its representative could expect assistance from the British authorities in Batum. Relaying this request to the Foreign Office, the Petroleum Executive pointed out that, in view of the military occupation of the region, it was undesirable to refuse reasonable facilities in the way of safe conduct and the like. In addition to the need to redress the choked storage capacity, the Petroleum Executive noted that there were "certain negotiations in hand in connection with which it will be well to satisfy the Standard that we are not endeavouring to exclude them from legitimate spheres of activity."[154] Though the War Office replied that it was, in principle, prepared to grant facilities to Standard Oil, it was unable to condone the sale because of the problems associated with transport, and the need to meet "local requirements" and other "large demands" for kerosene.[155]

Standard Oil remained undeterred, however. Arriving in Baku in June with the U.S. Naval Mission, the company's representative immediately announced that Standard Oil "would buy at once large quantities of kerosene," and proceeded to make the offer through the Azerbaijan government. The agreement for the sale of 100,000 tons of this oil was effected in July, despite the attempts by the War Office to prevent it.[156]

The withdrawal of the British interventionist forces from Baku in the winter of 1919–20 did not lessen the determination of the various oil concerns to secure their position in the region. Despite the occupation of Baku by the Bolsheviks and the subsequent nationalization of the oil industry in April 1920, British and American oil interests continued to compete with each other for the wealth of the Russian oilfields. Bitter rivalries developed between the two oil giants—Shell and Standard Oil—over the control and disposition of this oil, as well as over essentially defunct ownership and leaseholds on oil-bearing property in Russia. Russian oil, and the trouble it caused, was to surface again at the future international economic conferences at Genoa and The Hague.

Both the United States and Britain had interests in postwar Russia beyond supporting the counterrevolutionary groups. The extent to which these countries were committed to pursuing their economic interests in Russia is apparent from the fact that the difficulties that developed between these allies over their Russian policies were, more often than not, the result of conflicting commercial interests rather than any political disagreement. Ulterior motives were often found beneath apparently politically motivated decisions. A striking example of this suspicion can be found in the remarks made by the U.S. commercial attaché in London, when he warned his government that "Great Britain, with her interests in Southern Russia through Denikin and her interests in Siberia through the financing of Kolchak, her control of the North West Government of Russia through her direct co-operation through Murmansk and Archangel, and her fostering of the new Western Russian Republics on the Baltic, show how serious Great Britain's intentions are regarding the trade of Russia."[157] It is significant to note that the possibility of this involvement being an expression of Britain's commitment to fight Bolshevism was not mentioned.

The focus of British interest shifted significantly during 1919—from that of Russia as a supplier, to the development of that country into a vast postwar market for British goods. Intervention was initially undertaken to prevent Russian resources and war matériel from falling into German hands, and after the armistice many argued that access to those resources was essential to rehabilitating Britain's postwar economy.

Britain's preoccupation with this concern was most evident in the Russian North, where the intervention resulted in strong governmental control over the local economy. The statistics on shipping that plied between Britain and the North Russian ports illustrate the highly exploitative nature of Britain's occupation of this region. Figures compiled from British shipping statistics show that of the 985 vessels—representing over 1 million tons of shipping—that arrived in Britain from North Russia in 1919, only 114, or 165,104 tons, were in ballast. Accounting for over £11.5 million of the nearly £16.4 million worth of Russian imports, North Russian timber and wood products undoubtedly claimed an overwhelming proportion of this tonnage. That the development of commercial trade with the region was a secondary concern is likewise evident from the fact that less than half of the tonnage departing British ports for Russia was registered as carrying a cargo for the North; and even then, the bulk of these vessels had been given over to the transport of supplies for the military authorities in Murmansk and Archangel.[158]

By the middle of the year, however, the potential Russian market had taken on new importance. The deteriorating postwar economies of Europe, Britain, and indeed, the United States had changed expectations of the Russian market. The increasing importance with which Britain viewed this market is clear from the recommendation that "the great potential value of the Russian market should be made widely known, and emphasis should be laid on its special importance to industrial Britain firstly, because it is a market which is practically certain for a great number of years to continue to expand, and secondly, because Russia is not likely, within any time which can be foreseen, to become a competitor in other markets for the sale of manufactured goods, or even to become industrially self-supporting."[159] With the onset of the postwar depression in 1920, the Russian market was undoubtedly regarded by many as being a panacea for Europe's economic ills.

The United States also regarded Russia as an increasingly important market for American manufactures. The need to open up "fresh outlets to replace other foreign markets for the moment lost to them" argued convincingly in favor of realizing the "boundless latent wealth of this country" by taking advantage of the "vast possibilities of trade with Russia."[160] The substantial volume of trade with Russia during the war demonstrated that the country could be an important market for American goods. American exports to non-Bolshevik regions alone had officially totaled nearly $82.5 million in 1919—a sum that far exceeded any prewar value and heightened American expectations of the so-called limitless Russian market.[161] The developing postwar economic slump and the subsequent evaporation of European markets could only sharpen the American competition.

While the absence of a strong existing British business community in the North necessitated continued military domination of the trade and economy of the region, the government's policy in South Russia and, to a lesser degree, Siberia tended to reinforce existing British interests in extractive industries. In the South especially, the government was concerned less with how British interests survived than with ensuring that the British presence survived at all. The government's encouragement of established British interests to maintain or even extend their business, regardless of whether this was an economically rational decision, shows the importance attached to South Russia by British officialdom.

The decision in June 1919 to withdraw British forces by the end of the year did not indicate diminished interest. Britain's vast imperial commitments after the war, and the disturbances in Ireland and India in particular, had required a growing number of troops to maintain the security of the empire. These demands, combined with the growing domestic unrest over delayed demobilization, forced Britain to reconsider the wisdom of maintaining troops in Russia. As early as 16 April 1919, Lloyd George had summed up the situation when he declared to the House of Commons that the military intervention in Russia was "the greatest act of stupidity that any government could possibly commit."

By the end of 1919, both Britain and the United States had come openly to question the wisdom of continuing to finance and supply the counterrevolutionaries in Russia. In terms of cost alone, this aid had strained the British Treasury. Total aid to all parties in Russia in 1919 had amounted to nearly £47 million—a sum that did *not* include the cost of British military operations.[162] Further, political sympathies among the population were frequently not of the variety anticipated by either the allies or the White armies, and the growing wave of Red Army victories had led the allies to doubt the efficacy of their support for these groups.[163]

More than anything else, however, it was the bankruptcy and corruption of the counterrevolutionaries that caused both Britain and the United States to cease economic dealings with them and consider alternative means of exploiting the vast Russian market. The shady dealings of the counterrevolutionary authorities, along with the countless consequent complaints from merchants, alienated official opinion in both the United States and Britain. Even the steadfastly anti-Bolshevik Foreign Office came to question the prudence of dealing with such organizations, noting in early 1920 that "fresh evidence to help us understand why the Whites have collapsed reaches us every day."[164] In the United States, supplies intended for the Volunteer Army were frequently scrapped by the Russians, and the Volunteer Army government's operations became so questionable that the War Department obstructed further aid shipments to South Russia. As early as November 1919, contrary to the wishes of Secretary of State Lansing, the War Department blocked such a shipment, declaring that "insecure credits, uncontrolled profits, distribution, etc." made its dispatch inadvisable.[165]

It had also become clear to both countries that their nationals were vulnerable to expropriation even in those areas of Russia that were ostensibly "safe" under non-Bolshevik control. At a meeting of the Allied consular corps in Vladivostok, the American consul stated that merchandise belonging to American citizens valued at "several hundred thousand dollars" had been requisitioned in 1918 and never paid for. In 1919, requisitions of American property had been "very much larger" and included a parcel of fine woolen goods valued at $330,000 alone. The British likewise complained of similar incidents: for the months of October and November, some £53,500 worth of British property at Vladivostok had been requisitioned.[166]

By the end of the year it was apparent that the Bolsheviks were a force to be considered. With the tide of the civil war having turned against the Whites during the winter of 1919, those British and American companies with holdings in Russia were compelled to deal with the Soviet government in order to safeguard their interests not only against the possibility of nationalization but against the encroachment of other foreign firms as well. This fear of being usurped is particularly illustrated by the friction that developed between the two major British and American petroleum companies that were interested in the Russian oil industry.

Finally, news that neutral countries—including Germany—had been conducting profitable trade with Bolshevik Russia prompted both the United States and Britain to reconsider their policy of refusing to allow their nationals to trade with those areas of Russia outside of White control. Concern was expressed over possible exclusion from this market, and renewed fears arose over what was perceived as a move by Germany to recapture its prewar position in Russia. Further, reports that the Bolsheviks were able to pay for their purchases in foreign currency or gold stirred excitement in commercial and government circles. Given the difficulties suffered in trading with the Whites, the lure of a cash sale, which apparently carried no more risk, enticed British and American merchants into surreptitious business with Soviet Russia.[167]

By the close of 1919 there was a stalemate between the Allied and the Soviet governments. The Allied failure to crush Bolshevism by either military intervention or economic isolation and the Bolsheviks' failure to spark a wider revolution had forced these enemies to come to terms with one another. The realization that each country had something that the other needed argued for a policy of coexistence, and the worsening post-war dislocation in Britain especially made the idea of trading with the Soviets more than palatable for many. It was with the aim of "opening" Russia that Britain embarked on the path that resulted in de facto recognition of the Soviet government and the conclusion of the trade agreement in March 1921.

5

Coexistence, Rapprochement, and the Anglo-Soviet Trade Agreement

By the end of 1919 the British government had come to the conclusion that however distasteful it may have found the Bolsheviks, a rapprochement with Soviet Russia was necessary. As mentioned previously, there was considerable pressure from both governmental and private circles for the modification of Britain's position on Russia. The vast postwar imperial commitments and their strain on the already overburdened public purse, the growing unrest over the slow postwar demobilization, and mounting popular sentiment advocating a "hands off Russia" policy had all taken a toll on the government. Britain had also expended the most in terms of both troops and money in its attempts to overthrow the Bolsheviks. That the counterrevolutionaries were further from victory now than in 1918 did much to convince the government that continued aid to these groups would be futile. However, it was the worsening economic situation in Britain and indeed Europe that provided the greatest pressure on the government to reconsider its policy toward the Bolsheviks.

One of the most eager proponents for this change was the prime minister himself. Lloyd George had never been convinced of the value of the intervention in Russia and had repeatedly expressed his doubts over the efficacy of continuing aid to the failing counterrevolutionary armies. By the autumn of 1919 Lloyd George had gained a strong ally in the Treasury, whose financial straits argued convincingly in favor of limiting further unsecured shipments of matériel to the Whites. The prime minister's annual speech at the Guildhall left no doubt as to his sentiments: Britain had, as far as possible, helped the Russians in their attempts to free themselves: "We cannot, of course, afford to continue so costly an intervention in an interminable civil war."[1] Responding to the subsequent charge that he proposed to abandon Russia in order to make peace with the Bolsheviks, Lloyd George undertook to clarify his position in the Commons. Insisting that he had no intention of entering into any negotiations with the Soviets, he went on to stress that it was of the greatest importance that peace should be brought to Russia. The settlement of the Russian problem was "essential to the reconstruction of the world. Russia is one of the greatest resources for the supply of food and raw material. The present condition of Russia is one of the contributing causes to the prevailing high prices, and high prices are undoubtedly in all lands the most dangerous form of Bolshevik propaganda."[2]

By 1920 the economic necessity of renewing trade relations with Russia had become both the cause and the justification that ultimately pressured the government to place its relations with the Soviet regime on a new footing. A representative on the Supreme Economic Council, E. F. Wise of the Ministry of Food, had greatly influenced Lloyd George with his argument that it was essential to European economic well-being to restore Russia to its former place as the granary of Europe. Moreover, the British economy was beginning to feel the effects of the postwar recession, and Russia—both as a producer and a consumer—was increasingly looked to as a means of alleviating the economic dislocation. By the beginning of 1920, a surprising number of British merchants and manufacturers were already calling for a normalization in trade relations with Russia. The fortunes of the civil war, however, had left Britain little choice other than to come to terms with the Soviet authorities if it hoped to gain access to Russian grain and resources as well as to open the vast Russian market to British manufactures.

Even so, while Britain was clearly anxious to trade with Russia, it was not yet willing to deal with the Soviet government. It was argued that, by trading with Russia only through the cooperative societies, Britain would not only avoid the question of recognition but would also facilitate the exchange of goods by dealing directly with what was, before the war, the largest network of marketing organizations in Russia. The failure of this policy to result in much trade led the government to reconsider yet again its restrictions on trade with the Bolsheviks. News that substantial Soviet orders were being placed in Scandinavia and Germany provided the final push that convinced the government of the necessity of inviting a Bolshevik trade delegation to Britain.

This movement toward a normalization of relations with the Bolsheviks by no means enjoyed universal support within either the government or Britain's commercial and financial community. The impact of those elements that were strongly opposed to any sort of rapprochement with the Bolsheviks must certainly be taken into account when considering the development of Anglo-Soviet relations during 1920. Further, the interdepartmental frictions that had plagued British policy making on Russia persisted in muddying the waters throughout this period. The friction between the prime minister and the Foreign Office was particularly harmful. Although this problem largely resulted from the personal animosity between Lloyd George and his secretary of state for foreign affairs, Lord Curzon, the Foreign Office was nonetheless excluded from the mainstream of governmental policy making.

Throughout the period January 1920 to the conclusion of the Anglo-Soviet Trade Agreement in March 1921, the British government moved slowly but steadily toward the recognition of the Bolshevik authorities as the de facto government of Russia. The economic necessity of coming to terms with Soviet Russia was the primary motivating factor behind the British government's gradual shift toward a rapprochement with the Bolsheviks. It is significant to note that the normalization of trade and commercial relations preceded—and indeed, preempted—any moves toward a political rapprochement, and that de facto recognition through the trade agreement was extended purely as a means of facilitating trade.

The evolution of the policy from a stalemate with the Bolsheviks to the de facto recognition of the Soviet government went through three distinct stages. Encompassing the period from January to about March 1920, the first period was heralded by the Supreme Council's decision to allow trade with the Russian cooperative societies and was characterized by Britain's eagerness to trade with Russia while at the same time maintaining its distance from the Bolsheviks. The second period, roughly from April to October, was characterized by the government's capitulation to various parties who pushed for the initiation of negotiations with the

Soviet trade delegation. The government, however, still by and large used these negotiations as a political weapon, and the conclusion of a trade agreement was by no means taken for granted. There was a gradual shift in the objectives of this policy over the course of 1920 as well. Initially concerned with regaining British access to Russian resources, the government was soon compelled by domestic economic conditions to consider placing its trade relations with Russia on a more conventional footing and, consequently, it undertook to negotiate directly with Soviet representatives. By the end of the year, the number of unemployed in Britain had reached unprecedented levels. Trade with Soviet Russia was seen as a palliative to the depression, and the conclusion of a trade agreement was increasingly viewed as not only essential but inevitable as well.

Although it officially refused to consider any modification of its official position toward the Soviet government, the United States closely followed British developments. Maintaining its self-righteous political position by refusing to deal with the Bolsheviks, the United States government nonetheless made moves to relax its restrictions on Russian trade. Official American decisions to liberalize trade with Russia were largely responses to British policy shifts in this direction and were essentially aimed at preventing British merchants from "stealing a march" on American merchants. Ensuring that American goods had an equal chance in the Russian sian market became an increasingly important consideration as the depression deepened toward the end of 1920. While there was an undoubtedly strong and vocal group that lobbied for better Soviet-American relations, U.S. policy toward Russia in this period was primarily a response to British policy.

"No War–No Peace"

In its communiqué released to the press on 17 January 1920, the Supreme Council announced that it had decided "to give facilities to the Russian Co-operative organisations which are in direct touch with the peasantry throughout Russia, so that they may arrange for the import into Russia of clothing, medicines, agricultural machinery and other necessities of which the Russian people are in sore need, in exchange for grain, flax, etc., of which Russia has surplus supplies."[3]

Trade with the Russian people through the medium of the cooperative societies provided a means through which the Allies could open the much needed market of Russia while avoiding any of the moral and diplomatic complications of dealing with the Bolshevik authorities.[4] Despite the

wave of Bolshevik nationalizations, the two largest cooperative bodies
—the Centrosoyus and Selskosoyus—as well as the cooperative bank,
the Moscow Narodny, appeared to have maintained their independence
for some time after the revolution. Originally not included in the Bolshevik decree of 20 December 1917 that nationalized Russian banks, the
Moscow Narodny—as well as other specialized banking and credit institutions that served particular branches of production or industry—was
allowed to continue its operations relatively unscathed. Even after their
nationalization in December 1918, the cooperatives and their financial
organs were left to operate much as they had before.[5] Further, the network of Russian cooperatives was quite extensive and served as the main
commercial agent through which the Russian peasant and city dweller
alike received their goods.[6] More importantly, however, the cooperatives
were the primary vehicle through which the Russian peasantry marketed
its produce, organizing the collection, transportation, sale, and even export of local goods. A large existing network that enjoyed the trust of the
peasantry, the cooperatives were undoubtedly seen as providing the most
expedient means through which the Allies could acquire much needed
produce from Russia.

British firms also possessed considerable experience in trading with the
Russian cooperative societies. As well as handling a substantial prewar
trade, these organizations also conducted a fair amount of business after
the revolution. In 1919, for example—that is, during the period of the
blockade—the London office of Centrosoyus alone exported goods to
the value of £700,000; and the total exports of all foreign branches
reached a value of £1,220,000. Other cooperatives likewise developed a
"considerable turnover" with Britain during the postwar period: the
Zakupsbyt (the Union of Siberian Cooperative Associations), which had
established its London agency only in 1918, had succeeded in effecting
the purchase of over £350,000 in 1919.[7] As early as July 1919, an
agreement described as "the first of its kind" was concluded between the
Cooperative Wholesale Society and "a large group of Cooperative Societies" in South Russia for the "direct interchange of goods." It is also
interesting to note that, despite the substantial size of the initial transaction
—some £300,000 worth of goods—the British Cooperative Society felt
it safe enough to dispatch these goods without any cash payment from the
Russian organizations.[8]

Finally, the cooperatives were also financially solvent outside of Russia,
thus eliminating the absolute necessity of barter trade and alleviating
problems in connection with credit and deposits against orders. The
Central Union of Consumers' Cooperatives, "Centrosoyus," was the or-

ganization with which the bulk of British trade was planned. In addition to its primary status as the largest and most extensive of the Russian cooperative societies, Centrosoyus had access to a considerable amount of capital deposited outside of Russia. Cut off from the main office in Moscow by the blockade, the representatives of Centrosoyus abroad had used their capital to build up independent organizations and establish head offices in London and branches in several other major foreign cities. By 1919 Centrosoyus reportedly had between 20 and 25 million kroner on deposit in banks outside of Russia.[9] The organization's close ties with the Moscow Narodny Bank, which also maintained a major branch in London, made this cooperative a natural partner in British trade.

Like the cooperative societies, the Moscow Narodny Bank had suffered little interference from the Bolsheviks. The activity of the bank immediately after the revolution reflected "no change in tempo." In fact, London banks quite happily continued their dealings with the Moscow Narodny throughout the period of the intervention. Although British banks were prevented by "present government restrictions" from making loans against roubles, the London City and Midland Bank was able to confirm in mid-1918 that the terms governing the Moscow Narodny's account with them were the same as those quoted to the bank when it applied for its account in September 1915.[10]

Even so, the intervention and the civil war had caused considerable difficulties for the bank. Consequently, in 1919 its London office was converted into a limited company with an authorized capital of £250,000. Established with a view to facilitating the export and import operations of the central cooperative organizations of Russia that traded on the foreign markets, the Moscow Narodny Bank was able to obtain advances for collecting raw materials and help attract foreign capital by giving guarantees or by accepting bills of exchange of the cooperative organizations against proper securities.[11] Indeed, the new limited bank appeared to have little trouble in obtaining sizable overdraft and credit facilities to finance its commercial operations.[12] That it was effective in facilitating this trade is clear: while the total turnover of the Moscow Narodny had represented some £4 million in 1919, this figure had increased to over £19 million in 1920.[13]

Despite the fact that the council clearly stated that its decision implied "no change in the policy of the Allied governments towards the Soviet government," many in Britain nonetheless saw it as the first step toward peace with the Bolsheviks. No matter how the decision was put, the government could not "at the same time open up trade relations with Russia and go on hitting her."[14] Even the Foreign Office, which agreed with the assessment that the Soviets had "some time ago abandoned their repeated attempts to absorb the cooperatives," nonetheless recognized that trade with Russia could not be accomplished without the approval of the government in Moscow.[15] The Soviet authorities were, in fact, looking increasingly toward the cooperatives "to assist them in the distribution of commodities especially in recently conquered Siberia and South Russia." Therefore, the "situation created by this announcement . . . must either lead to something approaching formal relations with the Soviet government or to an attempt to use the cooperatives as a substitute for Kolchak and Denikin in the struggle with the Soviet government."[16]

The British government's Russian policy had clearly evolved from one that was concerned primarily with overthrowing the Bolsheviks to one that was aimed at gaining access to Russian resources, especially foodstuffs. The worsening economic conditions in Central Europe and the effect that the absence of one of the world's major suppliers of corn and raw materials was having on the economy of Europe generally provided Lloyd George with the evidence he needed to convince the Supreme Inter-Allied Council of the necessity of reopening Russia to trade regardless of that country's politics.

Lloyd George had been influenced greatly by the arguments of E. F. Wise, whose memorandum of 6 January presented a grim analysis of the future of Europe—and Britain in particular—if the trade was not renewed. Declaring that the vast resources of the Russian Empire "were a factor of enormous importance in the economic stability and organisation of the world," Wise left no doubt as to what would happen if they were not again made available. The civil war and the blockade had "cut off these vast supplies from the rest of the world and are one of the main causes of high world prices. Europe has been forced to get her breadstuffs and her fats from America at American prices or to starve." American grain prices, he pointed out, were higher than they had ever been; news of substantial exports from Russia would not only bring prices down but also have the possible effect of making the American government more agreeable to supply Europe on credit.[17]

Further, Wise saw the health of the British economy itself as being at stake: Britain had been a primary consumer of Russian wheat and flax prior to the war. Russia had also supplied no less than one-third of all the butter imported into the United Kingdom prior to the war, and there was "no hope of supplying an adequate ration until these sources are again open to us." In addition, Russia was seen as an increasingly important purchaser of U.K. goods: "The demand of the Russian market for goods as soon as trade is possible will undoubtedly be on a colossal scale, and will be limited by the power of Russia to organise exports for payment." It was, however, essential that this trade be opened to Britain as soon as possible, as there could be "no doubt that the longer reopening of trade with Russia is delayed, the more formidable will be German and American competition. . . . Our relative advantage in both respects tends to grow less each month."[18] A panacea for European and British economic ills, the opening of trade with Russia would "go further than any other factor to reduce the cost of living, to put right the American exchange, to reduce freight rates, and to ease the general shipping situation."[19] In such a light, trade certainly was, as Lloyd George argued, "the best way . . . to ruin Bolshevism."[20]

The Supreme Council's announcement should have left little room for confusion in the development of the resulting British policy. Strictly speaking, the decision to allow trade officially removed the existing blockade of Soviet Russia—a measure that had been imposed in 1918 and, despite its dubious legality, never lifted. Although the Allies had published their decision in the press, the British government apparently made no subsequent effort to clarify this point to either the neutral governments of Northern Europe or the Admiralty forces enforcing the blockade in the Baltic.[21] Combined with the absence of any statement concerning a cessation of hostilities between Britain and Soviet Russia, the government's failure to inform those interested parties had resulted in it being able to maintain effectively the appearance of a blockade throughout the spring of 1920.[22]

British business circles were also left in considerable confusion as to what exactly their government's policy was toward trade with Russia. Although the Interdepartmental Russia Committee stated that "the re-opening of trade on the lines proposed must inevitably involve at an early date the re-opening of ordinary commercial intercourse," it was nonetheless agreed that it was "not at present possible to inform private traders that they are free to trade wherever they like and with whomsoever they like in Russia."[23] Further, while the government's stated policy was to encourage British trade with the Russian cooperative societies, there remained a number of officially induced obstacles that effectively hindered the development of these officially sanctioned commercial relations. The shortage of tonnage available to ship commercial goods to Russia continued to hinder those who were willing and ready to trade. The Shipping Board jealously guarded the disposition of vessels under its control and frequently used the excuse that unswept mines in the Baltic made the danger too great to risk available tonnage on such ventures. Licensing requirements for exports to Russia remained ill-defined and were often arbitrarily applied. Cloth, for example, had been a major export to Russia throughout 1919 and 1920, and licenses for its export were generally granted with no difficulty. On several occasions, however, companies with large consignments of woolen material for Russia were refused export permits or officially discouraged from shipping them on the grounds that the goods were considered to be "more important to those Eastern Armies than arms or ammunition," and whose export was thus considered to be "contrary to the interests of His Majesty's Government."[24] Customs officials were also instructed to refuse clearance papers to any vessel that declared a Soviet port to be its final destination, despite the fact that British citizens were free to trade at their own risk with Russia, and though the goods that were being shipped to the Baltic States for the cooperative societies were known to be ultimately bound for Soviet Russia. Finally, while the Department of Overseas Trade was entrusted with the task of informing British commercial interests that trade was now permitted with Soviet Russia, no such official public declaration can be found in either the *Board of Trade Journal* or in the British press. The resulting policy of "no blockade—no trade" was largely brought about by the attitude of the Foreign Office, which maintained that no actual machinery for handling the trade had ever been set up by the government, and that any impending negotiations with Soviet Russia would have to be confined to determining the extent and possibility of trade.[25]

Such contradictions characterized much of British policy toward Russia throughout the spring of 1920. In considering the development of British policy since May 1919, even the Foreign Office was compelled to note the confusion:

The events of the year . . . have not demonstrated which of the two policies [peace or war] was the more right or the more expedient. Perhaps they would have done so if it had been practicable for either course to have been more definitely adopted or more resolutely applied. The somewhat sluggish current of opinion has, however, been flowing in the direction of peace rather than war, and policy has flowed with it.

The complex nature of the present situation is illustrated by the following facts: The United Kingdom is not at war with Soviet Russia, but the fleet in the Black Sea has orders to take offensive action against the Bolshevik forces. The United Kingdom is not at peace with Russia, but it is her declared policy actively to promote commerce between the two countries. Although it is her declared policy to promote commerce, British subjects are not allowed to go to

Russia, nor are Russians admitted to the United Kingdom nor are any goods allowed to be exported to Russia from this country. . . . His Majesty's Government have publicly declared the blockade of Russia to be at an end and the navy have been instructed to allow ships to proceed to Bolshevik ports. His Majesty's customs officers are, however, instructed to refuse clearance to vessels proposing to sail to Russia, although such refusal would be illegal and would expose them to damages. His Majesty's Government do not recognise in any way the Soviet Government as a government, but they correspond directly on a variety of political and commercial subjects with the persons in Moscow alleging themselves to be members of that Government.[26]

No doubt many of the contradictory aspects of British policy during the beginning of 1920 were due to the fact that certain government departments were not informed of crucial changes in ministerial thinking. The prime minister's blatant refusal to involve the Foreign Office in any decision making on Russia provides a particularly striking example of the damaging effects that this exclusion had on Britain's Russian policy. Relegated to the sidelines at the Paris Peace Conference, the Foreign Office continued to be left largely out of the picture in Lloyd George's postwar government. In fact, the Foreign Office had been kept in complete ignorance of the discussions in Paris that led to the Supreme Council's decision to allow trade with the Russian cooperatives. Further, as late as two days after the decision had been made public, the Foreign Office itself had still "received no official notification of any kind either as to the extent of the decision or the motives which prompted it."[27] On 20 January, Hardinge wired Curzon in Paris requesting such guidance, pointing out that it was "desirable" that the decision be officially "confirmed and amplified as soon as possible."[28] Curzon, however, was just as surprised by the decision as the Foreign Office in London. Embittered by Lloyd George's calculated efforts to keep him out of such affairs, Curzon informed the Foreign Office that the "decision of the Prime Ministers in Paris with regard to trade with Soviet Russia was taken by them in the absence of any Foreign Office representative." Further, Curzon also complained that, although an account of the proceedings that led to the decision was available through Hankey's minutes of the meetings, these were withheld from him: "[The] Prime Minister took the line in private conversation that this was not the affair of the Foreign Office, but of [the] Food Ministry, who should control procedure." Curzon advised the Foreign Office that it should, therefore, seek its answers from Hankey and Wise.[29]

Nor was the Foreign Office the only government department to experience such isolation. The Department of Overseas Trade, which should have been primarily concerned with this decision, had likewise received "no information until late on the previous evening [prior to the announcement] that the question of the resumption of trading relations with Bolshevik Russia was under consideration in any form."[30]

The immediate difficulties arising out of Lloyd George's secretiveness were obvious: the Foreign Office was "assailed with requests for fuller information" about the scope of the decision, but was "unable to say anything."[31] It is also significant that British diplomatic and consular officials abroad learned about the decision through its announcement in the press. The lack of guidance from Paris and the inability of the Foreign Office to advise its diplomatic representatives abroad did much to damage that department's credibility. The British Embassy in Washington wired London that the "State Department feels rather hurt that [the] decision should have been reached and announced without consulting America."[32] General Keyes, the British military representative attached to Denikin's forces in South Russia, had likewise learned of the Allies' decision only through the press. The effect of his being "kept in the dark" inevitably soured relations. "Anti-British feelings are sure to develop among the White forces now," he complained, and requested that, in the future, he "be informed of such major decisions beforehand so as to avoid such embarrassment." The Foreign Office minute appended to Keyes's telegram is enlightening and displays the diplomat's irritation with the government's secretiveness: "General Keyes can hardly expect to learn important decisions otherwise than through the Press when this Department obtains the same information through the same channels."[33] Such a blow to the pride and dignity of the Foreign Office could only heighten the tension between its officials and the negotiators in Paris. Nor did it make the diplomats any better disposed toward the Ministry of Food. Finally, the prime minister's blatant snub of the Foreign Office sharpened existing animosity between Lloyd George and Curzon. The effects of this friction were to become evident over the course of the ensuing months.

Despite the government's apparent attempts to persist in disassociating itself from any dealings with the Bolsheviks, an undeniable change was taking place in Britain's relations with the Soviet government even during the early part of 1920. Negotiations concerning the exchange of prisoners had been under way for some time between British and Soviet representatives, though it was not until 12 February that this potentially explosive issue was at last defused with the conclusion of an agreement.[34] There was also a distinct disinclination on the part of the British government to become embroiled in any future conflict between Soviet Russia and those independent states that bordered on Russia. On 24 February, at the prompting of the British prime minister, the Allies resolved that they could not accept the responsibility of advising those states "to continue a war which may be injurious to their own interests. Still less would they advise them to adopt a policy of aggression towards Russia."[35]

Further, the government's claim that it was dealing only with representatives of the Russian cooperatives was also beginning to wear thin. In February, a number of cooperative officials had been "recalled" to Moscow and were quickly replaced by trusted communists.[36] Headed by such loyal comrades as Krasin, Litvinov, and Nogin, the composition of the new delegation appointed to take over negotiations with the West left no doubt as to the nature of the Russian trade delegation. Even so, the British government continued its charade of pretending to have nothing to do with the Soviets.[37]

Road to Rapprochement

In April, however, British policy toward commercial relations with Russia underwent a distinct change.[38] The Conference of the Supreme Allied Council at San Remo had decided to permit direct trade negotiations with the Bolshevik representatives.[39] Accordingly, the British government had begun to consider issues of a more general nature in connection with the opening of trade with Soviet Russia. While it was generally accepted that it was desirable to enter into direct negotiations with the Bolsheviks for the purpose of normalizing official relations, it was realized that such negotiations would necessarily mean the de facto recognition of the Soviet government. It was this latter situation that the British government sorely wanted to prevent, but could not easily find a way to avoid.

> The resumption of commerce between England and Russia would in the course of a short time involve virtual *de facto* recognition of the Soviet Government, and perhaps some kind of "peace negotiations." We are anxious that trade should be resumed without recognition, or at least that the resumption of trade should precede a general settlement with the Bolsheviks. In order to decide upon a policy it is necessary to reach conclusions upon the following questions:
>
> Do the Bolsheviks want locomotives so badly that they will agree to a resumption of trade with us without a general settlement or in other words can we get Russian grain without giving recognition?

Can we afford to do without Russian grain or must we have it even at the cost of recognition?

. . . In my judgment the answer to the first question is that they would withhold their grain and do without our locomotives for the present. . . . [As to the second question] we must decide which of the factors is most dangerous to the existing order of society in Europe and to the security of the United Kingdom, namely virtual recognition of the Soviet government or starvation and disease in Europe on an unprecedented scale.[40]

For many, the lesser of the two evils was not at all clear during the spring of 1920, and to a number of men in prominent positions in Britain, the latter situation was preferable to the recognition of the Soviet government. Nonetheless, the logic of the projected sequence of events following the initiation of trade relations seemed irresistible, and trade with Russia seemed "almost inevitably the first step on the road to the recognition of the Soviet Government." Since trade with Russia—as opposed to official commercial relations with Soviet Russia—was viewed as essential, it was generally thought to be only a matter of time before direct relations with the Soviet government would come about. Until that time, however, Britain would "be able to trade with Russia indirectly, and . . . shall accordingly have a certain breathing space in which to see the effect [of trade] on Bolshevik Russia as distinguished from the Soviet Government."[41]

By the spring of 1920 the British government was firmly committed to opening negotiations for commercial relations with Soviet Russia. The prime minister reaffirmed his government's decision "to open up trade relations with Russia and to give every facility for the purpose with a view to sending in peaceable material to Russia and obtaining the surplus of Russia's food supplies and raw material for the rest of the world."[42] It is also interesting to note that, as reflected in Lloyd George's statement, the goal of opening the Russian market to British manufactures was increasingly cited as the government's first priority. Although British moves to reopen trade with Russia had initially been undertaken with the aim of regaining access to Russian foodstuffs, the government's objectives in this trade had shifted considerably by the middle of 1920.[43] Further, this shift is also apparent in the government's attempts to justify its commitment to the establishment of trade relations with Soviet Russia. Always viewed as a vast potential market for British manufactures, Russia had attracted special interest from British suppliers as domestic economic conditions in Britain worsened. By the middle of 1920 British industry was already showing the strains of the postwar slump, which was ultimately to result in massive unemployment and severe economic dislocation at the end of the year. At the same time, the loss of major trading partners in Europe made the prospects of trade with Russia all the more appealing. Finally, the prime minister's argument that the Bolsheviks could be "tamed" by means of exposing Russia to the civilizing influences of foreign trade had gained considerable support during this period.

Throughout the summer of 1920, other, more subtle changes were taking place in the government's approach to the Russian question. There was a fair amount of concern that goods exported from Russia to England as payment for Soviet purchases could be attached or would be liable to other similar legal difficulties with regard to ownership and title. In response to Lloyd George's query about the possibility of a British citizen successfully litigating for possession of Soviet gold, raw materials, or securities in Britain, the Law Officers tendered advice that is rather remarkable—especially given the strong lobby groups that were opposing the opening of trade with the Bolsheviks on just those legal grounds:

Assuming that the Soviet Government is to be considered as the *de facto* Government of Russia, and that the gold or goods in question have been nationalised, requisitioned or confiscated by or under [the] authority of that government, we are of opinion that a British subject could not successfully initiate litigation to obtain possession of gold or goods sent to this country. . . . The validity or propriety of the nationalisation, requisitioning or confiscation of the gold or goods, being the executive act of a *de facto* foreign government, is not a matter into which the Courts of this country would, in our opinion, have jurisdiction to inquire. The remedy, if any, of persons aggrieved is, we think, exclusively diplomatic and not legal.[44]

Such an assumption that the Soviets were the de facto government of Russia is itself novel among any of the branches of the British government at that time; further, the contention that solutions to the individual claims against the Soviet government should be sought in the realm of diplomacy instead of in the courts presented an effective means of removing the question of the title to Soviet gold and goods, and thus would solve the problems that had heretofore been used as a major argument against the reestablishment of trade relations.

But the persistent interdepartmental differences and the prevailing lack of a cohesive policy among the governmental offices remained a principal stumbling block with respect to the acceptance of Soviet goods—especially gold—as a means of payment. The Treasury, wanting to keep clear of any subsequent court battles that might have developed over title, notified the Foreign Office that "on financial grounds, Their Lordships consider it essential that exports to Russia should not be paid for in gold so long as there is any possibility that creditors of Russia in this country could successfully initiate proceedings to obtain possession of or an injunction against the disposal of such gold and they would be glad if the particular attention of the Law Officers could be directed to this point."[45] While it was admitted that the "whole subject may have to be reconsidered in the event of an agreement being arrived at for the resumption of trade with Russia," the government's policy on the acceptance of Soviet gold was to remain unchanged throughout 1920.[46] Though the importation of gold to the United Kingdom was not in itself prohibited, no licenses were granted for the melting down of such gold, or for its reexport. Nor was the Bank of England willing to accept Russian gold in the absence of a guarantee of title by the government—a guarantee that His Majesty's Government was not prepared to give. Further, the Bank of England was prepared to pay only the mint price for any gold it purchased, that is, 77s/9d per ounce, as compared to the world market price for gold, which stood at approximately 116s/1d per ounce in mid-1920.[47] This policy effectively prevented any significant quantity of Russian gold from being legally imported and realized in the United Kingdom, and subsequently did much to hinder the development of direct official trade with Soviet Russia. As will be discussed later, however, the amount of gold exported from Russia during that year points to the existence of a substantial amount of indirect trade with that country.

The Foreign Office likewise still tended to discourage trade with Russia. In response to inquiries concerning the resumption of trade, the Foreign Office repeatedly advised against entering into any commercial arrangements with Soviet representatives. In some early cases, the Foreign Office even stated that British citizens were "not permitted to do any business until the British government's policy in regard to Russia had been formulated," despite the fact that there was "no longer any embargo on trading with Russia except as regards arms and ammunition."[48] A number of firms had lost substantial contracts to other countries as a result of such instructions received from the Foreign Office; and though they protested against the government's prohibitive policy, the damage had already been done.

Similarly, the Board of Trade was prevented by the Foreign Office from effectively promoting this trade. In late May, on the initiative of Curzon, the Cabinet agreed to "defer the publication of the proposed press notice as to the resumption of trade with Russia until [Curzon] held certain conversations with Russian delegates now here or coming to this country." Robert Horne pointed out, however, that the Board of Trade had on occasion received

> applications for licenses to export goods to Russia which we can see no valid ground for refusing. . . . I do not know whether your [Curzon's] objection to publishing the proposed notice extends to the grant of such licenses. . . . I should also mention that the customs have hitherto refused clearance to any shipping to a [Soviet] Russian port. I believe in this they have acted at the request of the Foreign Office, but they are fully aware that their action has no legal warrant and may be successfully challenged at any time. I should therefore, be glad to know if you see any objection to the Customs granting clearance to ships carrying cargoes for Russia which the Board of Trade has granted licenses. It seems evident to me that the present position has become untenable. . . . The matter is urgent from a practical administrative point of view.[49]

The Foreign Office, however, remained firmly opposed to allowing trade. The Board of Trade was seen as "splitting hairs"; it was clear to the Foreign Office that the Cabinet's decision that "no notice permitting trade should be published" meant that trade was not to be permitted. Horne was accused of "begging the question" by stating that he saw "no valid reason for refusing licenses."[50]

Trade through neutral countries was also discouraged by the Foreign Office. It was common knowledge that a proportion of the goods exported to Northern Europe and the Baltic was ultimately bound for Soviet Russia. Although the Foreign Office had no legal means of preventing this tertiary trade, it did attempt to block it whenever possible. Receiving notice that the firm of Graham Brothers of Stockholm was interested in subcontracting to British manufacturers for various parts needed in their contract with the Nydquist and Holme Company, which had agreed to supply the Soviet government with one thousand locomotives, the Foreign Office declared that it could not "authorise any export to Russia, therefore we can not agree to Messrs Graham placing their particular contract in England." Curiously, the Foreign Office did suggest that if Nydquist and Holme desired to place orders in Great Britain, they would not discourage companies from accepting such offers! Even Sir Eyre Crowe was puzzled as to the "real sense of this cryptic proposal. On the surface it reads as if we are quite ready to supply Bolshevik agents in Sweden direct whatever they order, but we will not allow the order to go through the (apparently) British firm of Graham at Stockholm."[51]

It was not until the end of the year that the larger political questions associated with Anglo-Soviet commercial relations were worked out. The defeat of the remnants of the counterrevolutionary armies left the Bolshevik government as the only remaining viable authority in Russia, forcing Britain to face the necessity of officially recognizing—at least as de facto —the Soviet government as the representative government of Russia. The resolution of other significant points of friction took place as well; a settlement of the Soviet-Polish hostilities had been achieved, and the exchange of prisoners between Soviet Russia and Britain had considerably eased the tension between the two governments. To be sure, friction did still exist, notably over the issues of propaganda, compensation for confiscated British property, and the recognition of the debts of previous Russian governments. But by the end of the year, even these sticking points in the negotiations did not seem insurmountable. Along with the gradual resolution of some of the troublesome issues that had previously hindered Anglo-Soviet trade discussions there was a shift in the government's overall approach to the negotiations.[52] Despite the stalemate over Soviet propaganda activities and the problems connected with financial restitution, the government had shown itself increasingly disinclined to break off negotiations.[53]

While public support for the resumption of trade with Russia had long been in evidence, by the end of the year popular opinion was overwhelmingly in favor of the conclusion of a trade agreement. Undoubtedly the result of the worsening economic conditions in Britain, the widespread belief that trade with Russia was necessary in order to put British industry back on its feet was no longer seen as merely a manifestation of the liberal press or, worse, the product of Soviet propaganda. In fact, by December, even the *Times* had published a series of articles expressing the need for a speedy conclusion of a trade agreement and decrying its delay. It is interesting to note that the Foreign Office was widely seen as the origin of the delay—an accusation not without some basis.[54]

The records indicate that the Foreign Office was indeed responsible for many of the hitches in the resumption of trade during the last months of the year. The conflict between Lloyd George and his secretary of state for foreign affairs had become so heated during the last weeks of November and early December that the prime minister decided to entrust the British side of the negotiations entirely to Sir Robert Horne of the Board of Trade. The Foreign Office also remained in a position to discourage British traders from dealing with Soviet Russia, advising those companies that made inquiries that, although there were no longer any restrictions on imports from Russia, exports to that country were still subject to prohibitions.

However, even the Foreign Office began to view Britain's trade with the Soviets in a more favorable light by the end of the year. There was a general acceptance of the prime minister's argument that it was possible to moderate the extremism of the Bolshevik government through trade. The growing unrest—domestically as well as in those states bordering on India—likewise helped to convince a number of these officials that an agreement of some kind was desirable. It was believed that an agreement would provide a political lever, which could be used to prevent the Bolsheviks from exploiting disturbances in or around the empire; and the volume of Russian orders that would be placed in Britain subsequent to an agreement would help abate the pressures on the home front by alleviating somewhat the problem of unemployment. Finally, the specter of commercial competition was beginning to become more than just a threat to British plans for the economic penetration of Russia. Having never been informed of either the Supreme Allied Council's decision in January or of the government's arrangements to open trade negotiations with the Bolsheviks, the neutral governments announced during the spring that they no longer felt bound by their earlier commitment to respect the blockade of Russia. Even before the neutrals made this decision, however, unofficial trade was being conducted on a significant scale between their citizens and Soviet Russia. The legitimization of this competition and all that went with it only promised an increase in that trade.[55] The growing fear that American and German competition would displace Britain from any future share of the Russian trade also figured largely in this shift. More than anything, however, it was the worsening state of the British economy and the swelling ranks of the unemployed that pushed the government to reestablish normal commercial relations with Russia as quickly as possible.

Unemployment, Foreign Trade, and the Russian Siren

By the end of 1920 both Great Britain and the United States had begun to suffer seriously from the recession. In the United States the slump was registered most clearly by the drop in production for both manufacturing industries and agriculture. But in Britain, the collapse of the postwar boom had wider repercussions. Inflation was rampant, with commodity prices in a few instances peaking well over three times their prewar values.

The percentage of unemployed swelled to alarming proportions in a matter of months, and with an increasing number of plants and factories cutting back or even suspending their operations altogether, the situation showed little hope for immediate improvement. The continent was in economic ruins, and the prospects of restoring anything like normal trade relations with Europe—let alone with a shattered Germany—seemed to be a thing of the distant future.

The Russian market took on a new importance in both Britain and the United States during this period. Ever since the outbreak of the war the British government and merchants alike had their eye on capturing the bulk of Germany's trade with Russia. The Bolshevik revolution and subsequent civil war and intervention served to retard British commercial penetration in Russia. But with the lifting of the blockade of Russian ports in January 1920, the British once again, albeit very cautiously, began to pursue the chimeral market. Through the use of neutral third-party agents and by shipping their goods via intermediary countries that catered to this transit trade, merchants were able to sound the commercial potential of Soviet Russia.

By March 1920 confidence was such that the use of agents in neutral countries was no longer the sole means of gaining access to the Russian market, though, to be sure, a significant number of merchants apparently still preferred to deal through agents in the Baltic states and Scandinavia. British commercial representatives were by this time operating in London on behalf of the Russian cooperative societies as well as for the newly established Russian trade delegation. It was increasingly common for a British agent to enter into negotiations and arrange contracts with the Soviet purchasing organs on behalf of clients.[56]

The significance of this early trade has been considerably underestimated in terms of its perceived importance as well as in the absolute value of the business conducted. While it certainly came to nowhere near the prewar levels, the indirect trade between Soviet Russia and Great Britain was recognized by even the British government as being "considerable."[57] Aside from the aspect of sheer volume and value is the effect that this trade—or lack thereof—had on a number of industries. Particularly striking examples can be found in the textile industry of northern England and the tea brokerage business in London. In the latter instance, the Board of Trade was notified of an abnormal accumulation of stocks; by October 1920 the India Tea Association had in its bonded warehouses in London some 224 million pounds avoirdupois of tea as compared with approximately 113 million pounds in 1914. This surplus was attributed to "the elimination of Russia as a buyer."[58]

A similar dependence upon Russian demand is evident in the case of the Yorkshire woolen industry, although in this case orders from Russia continued. The textile industry was one of the hardest hit by the depression, and the situation at the close of 1920 did little to hearten the government. According to the *Special Weekly Report on Unemployment*, the position appeared to be "growing worse in both the cotton and woollen textile industries. Practically all woollen and worsted firms are now on short time."[59] In fact, the only mills that were working full time in Yorkshire in December were three concerns that were engaged in work on a contract for two million yards of woolen cloth for Russia.[60] The importance of these contracts was pointed out to the Foreign Office by the Board of Trade in order to stress the necessity of concluding a trade agreement with the Soviet government: "As to what Yorkshire would lose if Russian orders were stopped, we can assume that practically the only limit on Russian demand for cloth in the present circumstances would be their capacity to pay. One of our experts here estimates that an order for two million yards at, say 8/- per yard, or £800,000 in all, to be manufactured from raw wool up to cloth would take, say four months on full time and employ approximately 4,000 hands." At a time when unemployment already stood at almost 700,000, there was "no doubt about the attitude which mill hands in Yorkshire would undertake towards a rupture of Russian trade negotiations."[61]

The absence of imports of Russian raw materials was likewise seen as being a major factor inhibiting the recovery of certain industries and causing short-time working and redundancies.[62] In the case of flax, this relationship was obvious. Britain had suffered a shortage of flax since Russian supplies had been cut off during the war. As discussed earlier, this commodity constituted a major export from the Russian North throughout the period of the intervention—largely to the account of the British government.[63] Receiving the overwhelming proportion of its flax requirements from Russia, Britain's linen and thread industry was particularly hard hit by the postwar shortage of Russian flax, and in 1920 the majority of those plants in Belfast and Dundee were at best half employed.[64]

It was the promise of a lucrative market that did the most to argue successfully for the conclusion of the Trade Agreement in March 1921. Reports were received in the spring of 1920 concerning several large orders for manufactured goods that were placed in Scandinavia by the Soviet trade envoy, Leonid Krasin, as he waited there for permission from the Foreign Office allowing him to proceed to Britain. The fear of losing out on a promising market—and one that demanded most eagerly the products of the industries hardest hit by the depression—caused a considerable number of Midlands and northeast industrialists to come down firmly in favor of negotiating with the Soviets.[65] Combined with the news of these orders, Krasin's arrival in England in May and his immediate efforts to get in touch with manufacturers raised the hopes of British industrialists far beyond reasonable levels. Even so, while the attention of the government was focused on the developments of the Polish crisis throughout the late summer and autumn of 1920, Krasin was busy cultivating business. The results of his activities can be seen in a number of orders that he managed to place for textiles, boots and shoes, and assorted machinery, the value of which was estimated by the Board of Trade to be worth £1,788,500 by September 1920.[66]

While the repugnant nature of the Soviet regime was never questioned, business opinion was certainly split over the desirability of trading with that government. With the notable exception of the British Federation of Industries and some of those businessmen who had suffered large losses at the hands of the Bolsheviks, the attitude of the British commercial community ran from ambivalence to wholehearted support for the resumption of trade relations. Indeed, by the autumn of 1920, the Russian trade delegation "had a fairly powerful group in the City behind it." A number of firms, including the Slough Trading Company, Marconi, and Armstrong-Whitworth Company, had started negotiations for substantial business with Soviet Russia. In the case of Armstrong-Whitworth, the preliminary agreement for the repair of some three hundred Soviet locomotives over a five-year period was conditional upon the conclusion of a general trade agreement with the British government. The fact that the contract would provide work for an estimated three thousand unemployed on Tyneside provided the firm with motivation enough to support the conclusion of the agreement.[67]

The electrifying effect that these orders had on the outlook of the beleaguered industries far outweighed the value of the actual sales involved. It was widely believed that, once opened to trade, Soviet Russia would prove an antidote to the economic ills of Britain.[68] The liberal press, closely associated with the industrial Midlands, mounted a renewed campaign against any possibility of a disruption in the negotiations due to a break over the Polish crisis. Editorials in the *Manchester Guardian* and the *Daily News* had from an early date criticized the government for failing to come to terms with the Bolsheviks and were now urging the rapid conclusion of the trade agreement. Even the usually circumspect *Times* offered its support in a number of editorials undoubtedly sanctioned by Lord Northcliffe, a close personal friend of Lloyd George.[69] The government, however, was not as convinced as to the wisdom of such a move as the prime minister would have liked. In an attempt to sell the advantages of the agreement, particularly to the London financial circles and to the Conservatives within his government, Lloyd George expounded on the long-term potential of the Soviet market. Wise enough to realize that this potential trade alone would not be enough to counter the hostility harbored by the Conservative members of the House, a number of whom had themselves suffered some sort of financial loss in Russia, he also dwelt on the "civilizing" effect that opening that country to trade would have on the revolutionary regime.

On the first score, that of the potential of the market, the Board of Trade remained skeptical. In an attempt to pour cold water on overexcited expectations for this trade and its impact on the British economy, Sir Robert Horne, president of the Board of Trade, pointed out that such hopes were clearly false, as Soviet Russia had nothing with which to trade, and that it would be "years and years" before one could expect the exchange to approach anything like the prewar levels. Even so, Horne came out in favor of the trade agreement, assuring the Conservatives that the government was not ignoring the question of Russia debts and obligations, but rather was providing for its settlement as part of a future peace treaty. In the meantime, however, trade should be encouraged, as it was the sole means of restoring the Russian economy; and without such recovery, creditors had very little hope of ever recovering their claims from Russia.[70]

The Foreign Office, however, was more hesitant about any policy that even hinted at a rapprochement with the Soviets. It was widely held in the Northern Department that the conclusion of an agreement with the Bolsheviks would eliminate one of the bargaining chips with which the Foreign Office sought to control Soviet excesses. It was believed that once these "chips" were spent, the task of successfully negotiating the points of friction between the two countries would be much more difficult.[71] But by the end of 1920 the advocates of rapprochement among those members of the public who knew anything about the Anglo-Soviet negotiations, as well as among members of the government, significantly outnumbered the detractors.[72] Even the Foreign Office had by this time revised its stand somewhat, though not because of any change of heart concerning either the nature of the Bolshevik regime or the efficacy of the trade agreement. Rather, as H. F. B. Maxse of the Foreign Office argued, the British government could reap political advantages from the conclusion of the agreement whether or not it produced the economic results that its supporters so hoped for. If it was successful and a significant amount of trade did follow the signing of the agreement, the obvious benefits would be in the form of reduced unemployment and a healthier economy. Any improvements would also have the less obvious benefit of denying the Soviets the fertile ground that social and economic unrest would provide for their revolutionary propaganda. He further maintained that any increased contact with the outside world, such as through improved trade relations, would serve as a moderating influence on the Soviets. On the other hand, Maxse suspected that "the trading agreement by itself would be quite insufficient to promote trade." Russia lacked the necessary quantities of exportable commodities; trade, therefore, would be dependent on credit. Since the agreement made no provision for credit facilities, and since it was improbable that credits would be forthcoming from private British quarters, it was unlikely that an appreciable amount of trade would result. In either event, Maxse pointed out that it would

> be no longer possible for the Soviet Government to excuse its own failures at home on the ground of capitalist blockade, or to claim sympathy from abroad. Once the Soviet Government is robbed of its martyr's halo it will have to stand or fall on its own merits. If then, no trade results, we shall have weakened the Soviet position in Russia, and we shall have drawn the teeth of the most dangerous opponents of our institutions at home. One point however must be emphasised, it is only by absolutely open and honest dealing on our part that this result can be achieved; any restrictive measures on trade, any action which could be construed as a "capitalist boycott" would only strengthen the Soviet hands at home and add fuel to our internal troubles here.[73]

Nor was the Foreign Office alone in its thoughts along these lines. At a Cabinet meeting in November, Bonar Law went on record as saying: "We are in for bad unemployment. There is some business to be got in this way. If we make no agreement the effect on the public mind of the imaginary volume of trade which would never take place, but which they think would take place if there were an agreement, would be very bad."[74]

Finally, it appeared that the Soviet government was to prove Lloyd George correct in his assertion that the Bolshevik regime could be tamed through its exposure to the West. According to reports received concerning the debates that were raging in Moscow throughout the early spring of 1921, it appeared that the Soviet government was on the brink of abandoning communism in favor of something the Bolsheviks called "State Capitalism." On the day after the trade agreement was signed, the Soviet government officially announced the adoption of the so-called New Economic Policy (NEP). The prime minister was sanguine. There was, he declared, a "great change in Russia itself . . . from the wild extravagant communism of . . . even a few months ago . . . a complete change in the attitude of the Bolshevik Government to what is called capitalism, towards private enterprise . . . towards nationalisation."[75] As events would prove, Lloyd George was somewhat less than correct in his prediction of the abandonment of communist principles by the Soviet government.

The Anglo-Soviet Trade Agreement was concluded in London on 16 March 1921.[76] The agreement left many issues unresolved, relegating even the volatile subject of Russian debts to the future negotiations for a "formal general peace treaty."[77] Negotiated and signed on behalf of His Majesty's Government by Sir Robert Horne (of the Board of Trade), and by Leonid Krasin on behalf of the government of the Russian Socialist Federated Soviet Republic, the agreement is perhaps more important for its de facto recognition of the Soviet government than for its attempts to resolve any major outstanding differences. The extent to which the success of these negotiations can be attributed to the fact that they were conducted without Foreign Office representation is a matter for speculation. Despite its being headed by the Bolshevik-baiting Curzon, the Foreign Office by and large shared Lloyd George's assessment of a moderating Soviet government.[78]

On the Soviet side, the decision to come to some sort of agreement with the British was by no means taken with the unanimous support and approval of the Politburo.[79] The Bolshevik leadership generally regarded foreign trade as an instrument of Soviet foreign policy to be used to achieve both diplomatic and economic objectives. The necessity of balancing diplomatic against economic goals was illustrated in the development of Soviet policy toward the United Kingdom during the summer of 1920, with the issue of encouraging foreign investment in Soviet Russia provoking one of the hottest debates among the members of the Soviet Central Committee.[80] Although the desirability of soliciting foreign capital had been discussed in governmental circles as early as 1918, it became a fixed policy only during the winter of 1920–21. Even then, the opposition to the trade agreement and commercial relations with Great Britain was strong among the Social-Revolutionaries and the extreme left of the party. Radek and Bukharin were both vociferous opponents of any retreat from communist principles. Arguing that Lenin was proposing to allow Russia to be exploited by the Western capitalists, Radek asserted that "no honorable communist will agree to the conditions demanded by Lloyd George. . . . We know perfectly well what England means by her commercial negotiations with Soviet Russia. . . . The English only want to force themselves into Russia in order to overthrow the Soviet system."[81] Lenin, however, with the support of key figures like Trotsky, Litvinov, and Chicherin, managed to convince at least some of the dissenting members of the necessity of establishing regular trade with England. "Our purpose at present is to arrange a trade agreement with England and to start regular trade, so as to be able to purchase as soon as possible the machinery required . . . to re-establish our national economy. . . . We do not for a moment believe in lasting trade relations with the imperialist powers; what we shall obtain will be simply a breathing space."[82] With both governments ultimately convinced of the necessity of such an accord, the Anglo-Soviet Trade Agreement was signed, marking the end of the open hostility that had existed between the two countries for over three years.

Though it was argued within the Soviet government that a trade agreement with Britain "was of the highest value" and would open the door to markets in other countries, an agreement with the United States was seen as being eminently preferable. Trotsky, though he ultimately argued in favor of the trade treaty, nevertheless believed that the United States would emerge as the new center of world economic activity—a factor that he saw as detracting from the political value of an Anglo-Soviet agreement.[83] Lenin expressed a similar view by declaring that the Soviet Union desired to conclude economic agreements with all countries—"but especially with America." "We shall need American industrial goods —locomotives, automobiles, etc., more than any other kinds of goods from other countries."[84] This preference was not lost on the British: "The position of the Soviet government with regard to the United States is to be noted. Just in the same measure as they are hostile towards the British and French, they are friendly disposed towards the Americans."[85] The United States government, however, remained unmoved.

United States policy toward Soviet Russia took shape during the months immediately after the Bolshevik revolution. Politically, this policy was based on the tenet of nonrecognition, a stand that no U.S. administration of either political party was willing to change until 1933. American economic policy, however, underwent minor but significant modifications during the course of 1920, shifting from a policy of blockade and "cordon sanitaire" to one that allowed merchants to trade at their own risk. Initially undertaken as a response to Allied—particularly British—moves to liberalize trade with Russia, the Wilson administration found itself under increasing pressure to relax American commercial relations with Soviet Russia. The impact of the postwar depression on U.S. industry during the winter of 1920 provided the final push the government needed to remove the remaining barriers to the development of unrestricted and direct U.S.-Soviet trade.

The Supreme Allied Council's decision to allow trade with the Russian cooperative societies was viewed very unfavorably in the United States. It was argued that commerce could not fail to lead to political relations and, thus, that the move to permit trade with the Soviet-controlled cooperatives was "preparatory to dealing with [the] Soviet Government." The British ambassador in Washington noted that the United States clearly regarded Britain as the driving force behind the decision and that "adverse comment is likely to become increasingly anti-British in tone. Action will be represented as being mainly an effort to secure Russian trade in spite of attendant political risks."[86]

While the government saw the Allies decision as a breach of the concerted policy of a cordon sanitaire, American business circles tended to regard it as a calculated effort on the part of the British to "bring back trade" to their country. The commercial community shared the suspicion that the move amounted to opening up direct relations with the Soviets: "We have no confidence in the mere statement that this trading is to be done only with Russian Co-operative Association." As these organizations were known to be firmly under the control of the Bolsheviks, the announcement was a "subterfuge," made with "the distinct idea of gaining an advantage. Trade is [Britain's] life blood and she is not going to stop at anything to get it back."[87] While American businesses continued to declare their loathing of "Bolshevik principles," they were nevertheless quite opposed to being excluded from the market on mere moral grounds.

As British talks with the Soviet representatives progressed during the early spring, pressure from business circles as well as within the government itself had resulted in the Senate's resolution that the United States should seek to establish "more friendly relations" with Russia. While the United States continued to disapprove of any hint of recognition of the Soviet government, and preferred to ascribe the recent decision taken by the Supreme Council at San Remo to the influence of the Labour party and a "wish to secure trade advantages," there was nonetheless a distinct revision of the "uncompromising hostility towards Soviet Russia."[88] Undoubtedly hoping to moderate Britain's pursuit of Russian trade, the U.S. government subsequently proposed that the Allies once again consider formulating a common policy toward the Soviets.[89] Believing that Britain and the United States were "on the eve of a commercial war of the severest sort," Wilson expressed his fear that Britain would prove "capable of as great commercial savagery as Germany." There was little doubt that the vast markets of Russia would be the object of particularly severe competition.[90] None of the Allies showed any interest in the American proposal, however, and the United States was compelled to consider an independent policy. While the government was still loath to have any dealings with the Soviets, it was recognized that this approach was now probably the only way that America could compete with "the monopolistic arrangements of the British."[91] Indeed, the United States wasted no time in deciding its own path. Concluding that it was now necessary to remove the embargo on private trade with Soviet Russia, the government informed the British that they proposed to do so on 10 April, that is, three days later. Not surprisingly, this quick reversal was the source of concern and irritation in the British government. Having somewhat disingenuously promised to keep the United States government informed on the progress of their negotiations with Krasin, the British clearly did not appreciate American efforts to anticipate their decision "and allow American traders to get a start on our own."[92]

Although it had informed the British of its decision to remove its embargo on trade with Soviet Russia, the U.S. government made no attempt to enlighten either the business community or the majority of its representatives of this fact. Indeed, government policy remained just as obscure as it had during the previous year, when the State Department declared that no blockade of Russia existed.[93] There continued to be little cooperation between the State and Commerce departments, despite William Redfield's resignation as secretary of commerce and the appointment as his replacement, of J. W. Alexander.[94] The jealousies and competition that characterized so much of the government's early dealings with Soviet Russia continued to disrupt the formulation of American "policy." Particularly illustrative of the antipathy between these two departments is a sharply worded Commerce Department memorandum concerning the release of information to the press.

> Insofar as the State Department pre-empts all official utterances on the political situation in Russia, fair enough. It would appear at the same time within the province of this Bureau to indicate to the press unofficially any non-political matter which is in harmony with the American diplomatic attitude and commercial policy toward Russia and which the specialists in the Bureau consider reliable and devoid of propaganda. If, on the other hand, the State Department prefers a policy of censorious obscurantism toward the whole Russian situation in both its economic and its political phases, this Bureau might as well surrender for good its heretofore undisputed function of supplying American business men with data on Russian conditions,

because in a country where trade and industry are nationalized it is hard to see how any reference can be made to commercial matters without grazing the political situation governing them.[95]

Not surprisingly, this situation led to considerable confusion among even the government's own representatives. In March, the acting U.S. commercial attaché in Paris asked the Commerce Department whether trade between the United States and Russia was permitted: "From the contradictory reports which we have received we assume that official sanction has not yet been given by our government with regard to trade with Russia. . . . We desired only to receive a little light on what now seems to be a most confused situation." The commercial attaché hastened to remind the department that since the "first comers in Russia will undoubtedly receive the cream of the business there," it was "very much to the interests of our business people to take the earliest possible advantage of the resumption of trade" with Russia.[96]

A significant number of American businessmen shared this view.[97] As early as January 1920, the American Commercial Association to Promote Trade with Russia was formed. Asserting that it was "ridiculous that American businessmen are forced to stand aside impotently while their European rivals skim the cream off this tremendous market," the association went on to argue that American businessmen who wished to trade with Russia should be granted every opportunity and facility to do so.[98] While they were quick to protest against any apparent restriction on this trade, American businessmen—like their British counterparts—found it difficult to ascertain exactly what their government's policy was. The secretary of the Association to Promote Trade with Russia complained that his organization had tried to secure a concrete statement of Russian policy from the administration for four months and that they were "still totally ignorant."[99]

On 7 July 1920 the U.S. government took its first step toward the normalization of trade relations with Russia. Forestalling the British, who were still negotiating terms with Krasin, the State Department announced that the "restrictions which have heretofore stood in the way of trade and communication with Soviet Russia were today removed by action of the Department of State." It was stressed, however, that this action "neither granted nor implied" political recognition of the Bolshevik government, and that the "individuals or corporations availing themselves of the present opportunity to trade with Russia will do so on their own responsibility and at their own risk."[100] While the government did nothing to dispel the impression that it had removed all obstacles in the way of trade, the development of normal trade relations was inhibited by a number of restrictions that were clearly set out in the release: no passports were to be issued for travel between the United States and Soviet Russia, nor any change made in visa regulations; no postal communications were to be established; and the existing prohibition on the importation of Russian bullion was to remain in force.[101]

Any illusion of a thaw in U.S.-Soviet relations that had been created by the State Department's action in July was quickly shattered by the so-called Colby Note in August. The Secretary of State hoped to remove any doubts concerning the U.S. government's continued commitment to its policy of nonrecognition. Declaring that since the existing regime in Russia was "based upon the negation of every principle of honor and good faith and every usage and convention underlying the whole structure of international law," the government had found "no common ground" upon which it could stand with a power whose conception of international relations were so alien—indeed, "utterly repugnant," to its own.[102]

Such a political stand did not prevent the United States from stealing a march on Britain commercially, however. In December 1920, under growing pressure to reopen commerce with Russia, the U.S. government lifted the prohibition on the acceptance of Russian bullion, coin, and currency, ostensibly removing the last remaining obstacle to trade with Soviet Russia. Even so, the use of "Bolshevik gold" as a commercial instrument remained impossible due to the refusal of the Treasury Department and Assay Office to accept it. In each case, a certificate was required from the seller declaring clear title to the gold.[103] While the question of title continued to prevent both the Treasury Department and the Assay Office from accepting any gold that was clearly of Russian origin, this problem was easily circumvented by the restriking of the gold by neutral countries —a process that had been used by the Soviets for some time. Further, it is clear that the State Department, the Treasury, and the Assay Office were well aware of this action; and that the State Department had advised the Treasury that the Assay Office might accept gold of Soviet origin "if it possessed the coinage or mint mark of a friendly nation."[104]

Although Soviet attempts to approach the new Harding administration were rebuffed, the government was nevertheless compelled to reconsider its policy of refusing to recognize "any proper basis for considering trade relations" while at the same time desiring to get its fair share of the market.[105] Harding's new secretary of commerce, Herbert Hoover, was more concerned with promoting U.S. trade than attempting to influence the Soviet government by withholding it. He believed that American merchants were losing out to foreign competition and unless there was an effort to facilitate this trade, the Russian market would certainly be lost to the United States.[106]

The government's policy of nonrecognition had done little to discourage the growing number of businessmen who favored trade with Soviet Russia. There had been a substantial interest in the potential of Soviet trade as early as 1919.[107] Despite the government's open hostility toward the Bolshevik regime, the activities of Ludwig C. A. K. Martens, head of the "Soviet Bureau" in New York, had attracted the attention of a number of American firms. In March 1919, Martens wrote to the State Department, communicating his government's desire to establish friendly relations between the two countries. Expressing his government's wish to initiate American-Soviet trade, Martens listed the commodities that Russia was prepared to buy and sell, indicating that $200 million in gold would be deposited at European and American banks to cover initial credits. He further proposed that negotiations be undertaken to "insure a basis of credits for additional Russian purchases" in the United States.[108]

In spite of the general distaste for the Bolsheviks, there appeared to be no shortage of American firms willing to enter into cash contracts with the representatives of the Soviet Bureau. When the bureau's offices were raided and searched in May 1919, the intelligence personnel of the Army and Treasury Department found an eighteen page list of the 941 firms and companies that had indicated a desire to do business with Martens.[109] The list included the large meat-packing houses of Chicago, the Ford Motor Company, Packard Motor, General Ordnance Company, Bausche and Lomb Optical Company, and a number of American agricultural machinery producers. The values of a number of these Soviet contracts were substantial: Elia Barlow of New York had concluded a contract in July 1919 for $3 million worth of boots and shoes; Weinberg and Posser Engineering Company had taken orders for machinery and tools worth $3 million; there was a contract for $3 million worth of underwear from Fischman and Company; the National Storage Company had negotiated for the sale of $10 million of miscellaneous goods; and the Bobroff Foreign Trading and Engineering Company had concluded contracts worth a total of nearly $6 million for the Soviet Mission—of which $4.5 million was accounted for by the Lehigh Machine Company's contract to supply one thousand printing presses.[110] By mid-November 1919, Martens claimed to have negotiated contracts amounting to more than $20 million with American firms and business houses, "mostly with the largest business houses in the United States," and declared that he was getting "more and more support from business interests" that were dissatisfied with the present state of relations between the two countries.[111] Indeed, Martens could not have been far off the mark, as only six months later Soviet contracts negotiated with American businesses were estimated to be worth approximately $300 million.[112]

A number of other prominent New York businesses were reported to have extensive dealings with Martens and the Soviet Bureau. The import-export firm of Gaston, Williams and Wigmore, "who did a large business with Russia during the war," were known to be acting as "fiscal agents" for Martens in 1919. Likewise, the Guaranty Trust Company acted as a "depository for persons financing Martens," and Henry Sabin, president of the bank, was believed to be "personally interested in Martens and his work."[113] There were quite a few prominent American businessmen who expressed more than a casual interest in the development of trade with Soviet Russia. In addition, the growing number of newly incorporated companies in New York that all dealt specifically with that business indicated that such interest would not pass quickly.

In a number of cases, these early dealings were the start of a long association with the Soviets. As early as April 1919, the Soviet Bureau had requested a meeting with Henry Ford. The bureau's representatives believed that they could make Ford understand that "Soviet Russia is inaugurating methods of industrial efficiency compatible with the interests of humanity."[114] The bid was apparently successful, as the secretary of the Soviet Mission received an appointment to see Ford's personal secretary, E. G. Liebold. Having only the previous month concluded the agreement with Ivan Stacheef and Company, Ford was clearly not content to let the fortunes of the company's Russian business ride indefinitely with a single agent.

Ford's initial foray into the Soviet market also coincided with the worsening depression in America.[115] By November 1920, Ford was already anticipating a substantial business with the Soviets, indicating the possibility of a "large order which may total 1,000 autos, trucks and chassis for shipment to Russia."[116] Like many other businessmen of the period, Ford saw the expansion of his foreign market as a means of compensating for weak periods in domestic sales. With Europe in equally desperate financial straits, Ford began to look to new, relatively undeveloped markets for his products.

Faced with deportation proceedings at the end of 1920, Martens was forced to leave the United States in early 1921. American business with Soviet Russia was in no way hindered by his absence, however. An extensive network for trade had been established: in addition to the Soviet Bureau, three purchasing organizations were now operating in the United States on behalf of the Soviet government. Centrosoyus America Incorporated, the Products Exchange Corporation, and the People's Industrial Trading Corporation were all American companies, incorporated under the laws of New York.[117] The Hammer family's Allied American Corporation was also linked to the Soviet Bureau as early as 1918, when Martens turned to Julius Hammer for "interim financing" for the bureau's operations in exchange for which the Allied American Corporation was given a license for U.S. trade with the Soviet Union.

Further, the transit trade network, which had been used extensively by American merchants and businessmen before the war, was once again in operation. Although not officially sanctioned, transit trade was openly pursued as a means of trading with Russia. To be sure, while shipments to Reval could be made "in accordance with the State Department's War Trade Board ruling of July 20, 1919," the State Department was quick to note that these rulings did not "contemplate that goods exported under them will be resold into Soviet Russia."[118] Such warnings had little effect, however, especially as the Commerce Department was at the same time openly suggesting that merchants interested in Russian trade use the Baltic states or other intermediary countries.[119] Nor were the opportunities presented by such trade lost on American businessmen; by the summer of 1920 a considerable volume of Soviet-bound American trade was already being conducted through intermediary states.

In the case of both Britain and the United States, it was economic—not political—necessity that drove them to closer relations with the Bolshevik regime. Whatever moral reservations the two governments had in allowing their merchants to trade with Soviet Russia were soon outweighed by economic conditions at the beginning of 1921. Further, the move toward relaxing these trading relations was hastened by the growing competition between the two countries for the limited markets of the world and the threat of losing whatever advantage they had in Russia should the other country agree to terms first.

Initially undertaken as a response to British moves to reopen normal trading relations with Russia, U.S. policy soon achieved its own momentum in the form of a growing lobby that not only pressured for the normalization of commercial relations with Soviet Russia but increasingly favored a political rapprochement as well. Although the U.S. government firmly adhered to the policy of nonrecognition until 1933, it was not so dogmatic where commerce and trade were involved. The economic policy of "trade at your own risk" underwent a subtle but significant change; by the end of the year, the government had clearly shifted its attention away from the risks, refocusing instead on the trade to be had in Russia.

The evolution of the British policy was marked by key events that defined the slow but firm progress toward agreeing to terms with Soviet Russia. However, the government's policy on the issue of trade with Russia was never clear-cut. Although this certainly retarded the conclusion of the trade agreement and, ultimately, the development of official trade relations, it nonetheless had the effect of promoting the establishment of a network for indirect trade between British merchants and Soviet Russia.

The successful conduct of this transit trade by merchants of both countries had a considerable impact on the development of future commercial relations with Soviet Russia. It was during this period that the Soviet government gained its reputation for shrewd negotiation and sound credit. Despite its importance, little is known about this early trade. Official returns are often cited as an indication of the economic isolation of the Bolshevik regime, yet there is evidence that the value of transit trade was almost as large as—if not larger than—the officially registered trade of either country with Soviet Russia. An examination of this trade will not only provide a more accurate assessment of the actual volume and value of this commerce, but will also measure its effect on Britain's economic relations with the Soviet Union. In this respect, a comparison of British and American trade returns for the years before and after the agreement must include a consideration of this transit trade as far as possible.

6

Trade at Your
Own Risk

The increased risks and marginal profits involved in trade with non-Bolshevik Russia soon discouraged British and American merchants from becoming too involved in commerce with the Whites. Attention shifted toward transit trade with Soviet Russia, which offered a more lucrative market that not only promised to pay in cash or gold but also held less risk for the merchant. There is substantial evidence that—government prohibitions notwithstanding—manufacturers, brokers, and trade agents found the potentially huge Soviet market too tempting to resist. Even companies that had suffered expropriation or nationalization by the Bolshevik authorities reopened business relations through agents in neutral countries and, in some cases, tendered bids for substantial Soviet orders, well before commercial relations with the Bolsheviks were put on a normal footing.

More than anything else it was the successful conduct of a considerable volume of indirect trade that prompted the West to accept Soviet Russia as a responsible trading partner, opening the way for the rapid expansion of Soviet purchasing abroad during the mid-1920s. Although the postwar depression had pressured growing numbers of British and American merchants into indirect transactions in 1920–21, it was the Soviet government's scrupulous observation of its commercial obligations and its efficient handling of business dealings that kept Western businessmen coming back for more.

Transit trade played an essential role in early Soviet commerce, accounting for a substantial volume of the goods that reached Soviet Russia during 1920 and 1921.[1] A consideration of goods in transit to Soviet Russia through Reval—the only Baltic port for which any records have been discovered—reveals the extent to which the British and American returns for the two-year period understate the total volume of trade. Though certainly not an attempt to provide comprehensive trade statistics, an estimation of this transit trade shows that British and American trade with Soviet Russia was substantially greater than is conventionally assumed.

The significance of this early trade to Western European industries hard hit by the postwar depression must also be taken into consideration. As discussed previously, certain industries had concluded large contracts with the Soviet government as early as 1920 and attached considerable importance to this trade. It is worthwhile, therefore, to assess where possible what share of total exports from these industries was purchased by Russia.

Finally, the fear of being displaced from the Soviet market by a resurgent Germany, combined with the continuing Anglo-American commercial rivalry in Russia, helped to wear down governmental resistance toward liberating this trade. In this connection, the Soviet government's political goal of establishing *direct* trade relations wherever possible was largely realized. Merchants and governments alike wished to recapture the profits lost to the European middlemen who conducted the transit trade.

Transit Trade: The "Gateway to Russia"

Transit trade through Scandinavia and Northern Europe in particular had traditionally played an important role in Russian foreign commerce. Prior to the war, both Britain and the United States made extensive use of this cheap and easy way of conveying goods to the Russian Empire.[2] With the revolution, Russia ceased to be a belligerent, and it was not long before Scandinavia was again seen as the best route through which merchants could transport goods to Russia. As early as July 1918 it was suggested that "goods might be shipped from the U.K. to Gothenburg, and thence forwarded in a neutral ship via the Baltic Sea." Not only was the Scandinavian route the shortest, it also offered the most economical disposition of tonnage and probably the safest means of transporting goods to Russia at that time.[3]

The neutral states had maintained friendly relations with the Soviet government up until 1919, when Allied pressure forced them to adhere to the blockade. Sweden in particular enjoyed a profitable commercial relationship with the Bolsheviks immediately after the revolution, having exchanged some 9.25 million kroner (over £509,000) worth of manufactured goods for Russian raw materials by mid-1918.[4] Denmark and Norway also renewed their economic relations with Soviet Russia soon after the Bolshevik revolution. Although the Soviet government was not officially recognized by Denmark, the Danish government continued to encourage this trade and even sanctioned the formation of a Danish-Russian Chamber of Commerce in Petrograd to promote trade with "all parts of Russia."[5]

Though disrupted by the blockade in early 1919, unofficial transit trade with Soviet Russia had begun to reappear by the middle of the year. With the ratification of the peace treaty, the neutral states—along with Germany and the newly independent Baltic republics—quickly reassumed their role as intermediaries in Russian trade. As Allied trade with these countries was subject to few restrictions, it was quickly realized by those who wished to trade with Soviet Russia that the transit routes were a convenient way to circumvent any official difficulties encountered in obtaining export licenses and customs clearances, while at the same time providing a secure base from which to conduct commerce without the fear of expropriation. Further, the use of neutral shipping also enabled merchants to sidestep the difficulties associated with the tonnage shortage in Britain.

Businessmen from many nationalities were swift to exploit this opportunity. German, British, and American merchants and commercial representatives had surfaced in Scandinavia, Northern Europe, and the Baltic states by mid-1919, many of whom were known to be in touch with the local Soviet trade representatives. As early as July, Danish merchants were again playing "a large part as agents for general trade between Russia and foreign countries," and were reportedly "engaged in negotiations with a view to acting as commercial intermediaries between Russia and America."[6] Copenhagen especially was extensively used by the United States in its preparations for the renewal of trade with Russia and the Baltic. Ford was one company that made considerable use of this Copenhagen corridor: Ford cars, trucks, and tractors were shipped in a dismantled form to Copenhagen, where they were assembled and forwarded into Norway, Sweden, Finland, the Baltic countries, and Germany. The importance of this transit route to Ford's foreign sales of tractors is apparent from the fact that while France and Sweden received 150 and 42 Fordson tractors respectively during the second quarter of 1919, Denmark received 305. That Ford was particularly interested in the Russian market is apparent from a report concerning the development of the company's foreign business in which Russia was described as an area whose territory was "not yet closed." An agent was subsequently instructed "to organize Germany, Poland and Baltic Russia, just as soon as political (and economic) conditions warrant."[7]

Ford was clearly not alone in his plans to utilize Copenhagen as a convenient transit point for Russian trade. As early as November 1918 the U.S. trade commissioner in Stockholm had proposed that an American-Baltic terminal company be established in Copenhagen with the aim of constructing centralized terminal buildings, warehouses, and assembly plants "to handle American goods only for transshipment to and from Denmark, Norway, Sweden, Finland, Russia and possibly Germany." It was suggested that "direct American connections should be built up through the terminal company by giving agencies in various Baltic ports for lines of American manufactures and producers centralized in the terminal." In this way, "American control of American commerce in the Baltic would be secured. . . . Such centralization would furnish American trade in the Baltic with strong means of combatting competition and would cut out foreign cartels and middlemen."[8] While this particular proposal never got off the ground, there were a number of companies eager to share in this growing trade.[9] Some Danish firms even acted as agents for the Soviet government; the International Clearing House of Copenhagen, for example, purchased a variety of goods in Great Britain for shipment into Soviet Russia.[10]

Sweden likewise had shown an interest in handling transit trade and had tried actively to recruit British and American financial backing. Although Britain had long neglected commercial relations with Sweden —probably due to the "presumed insignificance of its small population" —there were nonetheless "trading interests far beyond the borders of Sweden," which could best be developed by "utilising Swedish corporations." Sweden was "anxious to do business in Russia and the Baltic provinces," and if Britain chose not to participate with the necessary backing, Germany and America would "remain alone in the field."[11] Indeed, the Swedes were clearly unwilling to let the future of this business rest entirely with the British; it was declared that Sweden's "first and greatest task" was to become the "natural go-between [for] American industry and the new trading district" in the east. It was in Sweden's interest to promote this transit trade, as resulting profits would largely benefit Swedish merchants and shipping companies. American business, however, needed little prompting; from an early date they had sought to establish relations with Swedish firms "for ultimate trading in Russia."[12]

Though ostensibly at war with the Bolsheviks, Finland was also used as a transit point for goods destined for Soviet Russia.[13] The construction of an international free port at Abö was proposed in the summer of 1919 in the hope of diverting the Russian perishable goods traffic that passed through the lower Baltic ports and Copenhagen.[14] While plans for Abö never materialized, trade passing through Helsingfors was great enough to cause congestion there. By the early autumn of 1919 Finnish Customs was reported to be experiencing "great difficulties in regard to the quantities of goods—mostly American—that are arriving in Helsingfors for eventual re-export to Russia."[15]

The considerable interest exhibited in trading through the neutral states quickly led to the establishment of a network of commercial agents, brokers, banks, and insurance underwriters who were willing to assume the risks associated with trading with the Soviets.[16] As will be discussed, it was also through these countries that the Soviet government circumvented the obstacles in the way of the acceptance of its gold as payment abroad.

The Baltic became increasingly important for the transshipment of goods to Soviet Russia during the first half of 1920. Prior to the war, the Baltic ports of Riga, Reval, and Libau were used extensively for the transit of goods to and from Russia. Part of the former Russian Empire, this area provided Russia with the much needed "window on the west"; the harbor facilities of the Baltic provinces were excellent, and their proximity allowed the inexpensive movement of goods by rail between them and the cities of northern Russia.[17] Until German activities in the Baltic Sea halted shipments, the region served as an important transit area for Russian trade with the West. Although largely cut off during the war and blockade, it is important to remember that this transit trade had played a major role in the prewar economy of the Baltic cities and, indeed, had served as a primary channel through which Russia conducted its foreign dealings. However, under the conditions of the Brest-Litovsk Treaty, Soviet Russia was compelled to relinquish the Baltic provinces as well as other western portions of the former Russian Empire.

With the end of the war, the governments of the newly independent Baltic states were particularly concerned with the possibility of being engulfed by the Bolsheviks. Consequently, they supported General Yudenich's counterrevolutionary North Western Army. As the civil war progressed it became clear that neither Yudenich nor any of the other

White Russian leaders were prepared to recognize the independence of the Baltic states from Russia. The Soviet offer of Baltic autonomy —conditional upon the withdrawal of support for the North Western Army—came at a time when Bolshevik victories were mounting and the promise of Western aid appeared remote. Agreeing to this condition, the governments of Estonia, Latvia, and Lithuania indicated that preliminary discussions should begin no later than 25 October.[18] However, a last attempt by the North Western Army to capture Petrograd prevented these negotiations from taking place. Repulsed by the Red Army, Yudenich retreated into Estonia; with the remaining fragments of the force hit by typhus, the North Western Army was all but wiped out by the end of November 1919. Though Trotsky was anxious to pursue Yudenich across the Estonian frontier, both Lenin and Chicherin firmly opposed such a move, the latter pointing out that it would "only rouse the English Liberals and moderate Tories against us" and "save a tottering Churchill."[19] More to the point, it was realized that future trade through Estonia would be endangered by such provocation. That this trade corridor was the Bolshevik's primary concern becomes evident from the fact that a similar argument was not employed by the Soviet government to prevent the Red Army from invading Poland in 1920.[20] Estonia further cleared the way for peace with Soviet Russia by complying with the Bolsheviks' demand for the disarming of the defeated counterrevolutionary army. The armistice, signed on 31 December 1919, was followed by the conclusion of a formal treaty of peace between the governments of Estonia and the Russian Soviet Federated Socialist Republic (RSFSR) on 2 February 1920.

The Dorpat Peace Treaty laid the foundations for an early renewal of trade through Estonian ports. Under the terms of the treaty, Soviet Russia was given "free economic access to the sea" through Estonia, and it was stipulated that all goods in transit to Soviet Russia through Estonia were to be free from transit and import duties. The treaty also provided for the negotiation of a commercial agreement as soon as possible after the conclusion of the peace.[21] In exchange, the Soviet government agreed to pay Estonia 15 million gold roubles, which was to stand as security for Estonian and other foreign credit.[22]

It is clear that Estonia needed Russia as much as the latter needed the ports of the Baltic states. The events and series of compromises that led to the conclusion of the Treaty of Dorpat in February 1920 demonstrate that peace and the subsequent reestablishment of Estonian-Russian transit trade were high priorities for both governments. On the Estonian side, this accord required compromises on a number of issues, including the decision to negotiate a peace treaty independent of the other Baltic states, and an agreement to disarm the North Western Army after its retreat across the Estonian border. The Soviets, on their part, extended the recognition of Estonian independence; more significant, however, was Lenin's support of Chicherin in his refusal to let Trotsky upset the negotiations by pursuing Yudenich and his already decimated forces across the border.

Finally, it should be noted that as early as August 1919—a month after the Estonian government had initially agreed to open peace negotiations with the Soviets—commerce through Reval was already taking place. A London commercial journal noted that a "healthy stream of trade" had begun to flow through the port, and that the "vast gateway of Russia" was once again open for the transit of trade to Russia:

> The road to Petrograd, to Moscow, and every industrial centre of Russia, lies open to the trade of the world. Commodities sorely needed by the 170 million people inhabiting the Russias can pass freely at this moment through Esthonia's Capital, Reval, which is but eight hours distant from Petrograd. . . .
>
> Since the War Great Britain has been opening trade with Esthonia through the port of Reval and already has a fleet of some sixteen ships running there. . . .
>
> A steamship line direct from New York to Reval is already in organization. The first ship will shortly depart.[23]

Remarking that in making peace with the Baltic, the Bolsheviks had gained an intermediary through which they could carry on trade with the outside world, Lloyd George certainly anticipated the development of British transit trade by this route. Indeed, the way for it was left open, as the British government had imposed no restrictions on commerce with the Baltic.[24] Even so, trade with Soviet Russia through the Baltic was, for the most part, "in the hands of Swedish merchants who are backed by Americans. American goods are arriving in the Baltic Provinces and are also being delivered to Russian Bolshevists with the aid of German merchants in Letland. English goods are said not to be able to compete with American prices."[25] Further, the British noted an increased American presence in the region during the last months of 1919. In addition to a new commissioner and consul at Riga, an extensive Red Cross organization was being set up in the Baltic, members of which were reported to have joined for the opportunity of "finding trade openings." Clearly, the Americans had "their eyes open for possibilities of trade with Russia."[26]

By the end of 1919 a number of U.S. merchants had gone to considerable lengths to secure openings in the Baltic. The Lithuanian government was approached by the Manhattan Trading Company with a proposal for the organization of goods traffic between Germany and Russia through Lithuania. The draft agreement, drawn up by the company's general representative and the Bolshevik representative in Berlin, Victor Kopp, proposed to run two trains each way daily, with goods to the value of about 3 million marks per train. The American firm agreed to supply twenty locomotives, two hundred trucks, and all other necessary material, all of which was eventually to become Lithuanian property.[27]

The rapid restoration of the Baltic to its former position as a transit trade channel signified as much the West's eagerness to begin trading with Soviet Russia as the Estonian and Soviet governments' desire to promote it.[28] A symbiotic relationship developed between Soviet Russia and the Baltic states as a result of the mutual need for the renewal of this trade. In addition to welcoming the Soviet trade delegation—which had begun its operations in the Baltic in early 1920—the Baltic states accommodated numerous local companies, which were authorized to act as agents for the Soviet government. As will be discussed, extensive banking facilities had even been provided by the Baltic states to promote this business—services that were widely utilized by Western merchants in their Soviet trade operations.

Whereas the Baltic provinces had played an important part in prewar Russian commerce, they were crucial to the conduct of early Soviet foreign trade. In 1913 the five busiest Baltic ports (excluding Petrograd) had handled 13 percent of the Russian exports and 24 percent of the total imports into Russia across all frontiers.[29] In comparison, as much as 80 percent of the goods that entered Soviet Russia between 1920 and 1924 were believed to have passed through Baltic ports.[30] The first Baltic state to make peace with the Bolsheviks, Estonia acted as a major conduit through which the Soviets transacted much of their foreign trade in 1920. Estonia accounted for over 76 percent of the volume of all Soviet imports during the period from May to the end of December 1920, with imports via Narva totaling over 24,000 tons—or nearly 29 percent of the total tonnage imported into Soviet Russia during that year.[31]

While Estonia certainly handled an increased proportion of the transit trade tonnage, it did not account for a matching proportion of its value. Handling primarily finished and manufactured goods, Scandinavia—and Sweden in particular—continued to account for a large proportion of the value of Soviet Russia's foreign trade during the preagreement period. Over 28 percent of the total value of Soviet Russia's imports for 1920 were shipped from Sweden.[32] A large proportion of these "Swedish" imports were goods in transit from other countries, primarily the United States and Great Britain.[33] The American consul in Reval was fully aware of this situation, remarking that the countries of shipment were "not always the countries of origin, and this is particularly true of goods shipped from Sweden."[34] Further, a considerable amount of tertiary trade with Russia was conducted through Sweden, with British manufacturers and exporters doing business in the Baltic cities—principally Reval —through a number of financial and industrial concerns situated in Stockholm.[35]

That traders would use these transit routes was not only taken for granted by the British government but encouraged as well. As early as mid-1919 representatives of the Department of Overseas Trade were dispatched to the Baltic with the aim of promoting British trade with the region. Further, the government intimated that by developing commerce in the Baltic, British merchants would encourage the reopening of trade with greater Russia and, indeed, that the renewal of economic relations with Soviet Russia was dependent upon "such temporary arrangements as the political situation admits."[36] By the end of February 1920, when it had become apparent that the cooperative societies were under the complete control of the Bolsheviks, this "temporary measure" represented the only remaining way of trading with Soviet Russia while at the same time ignoring its government.[37] Accordingly, the British commissioner in Riga was officially notified of his government's intention to reopen trade with Russia "principally through the Baltic ports."[38]

Perhaps more significantly, however, it was recognized that once the Bolsheviks made peace with the Baltic states—a move the British government had advised at least Estonia to undertake—the blockade would be impossible to maintain.[39] Further, there was no doubt about Estonia's willingness to assist in removing the remaining restrictions on trade with Soviet Russia. On 21 January 1920, well before the ratification of the Soviet-Estonian peace treaty, the Estonian government announced that "in consequence of information from the Supreme Council to the effect that the Blockade of Russia has now been raised," it had decided that "goods in transit passing through Esthonian territory shall be free from customs and transit duty."[40]

Though the British government supported the Baltic states' claims to independence, it is clear that Britain's interest in the region was of a "strictly commercial" nature.[41] In themselves of little commercial importance to Britain, the Baltic states were nonetheless valued as a means of gaining an early entry into the Russian market.[42] That Western merchants would stand to benefit from the Soviet-Estonian peace was noted by Gukovsky, the Bolshevik representative in Estonia: the Entente, he declared, was "only making use of the peace between Esthonia and Russia to get a market for its wares."[43] Indeed, it was openly recognized by the British government that, because the embargo on direct trade with Russia remained officially in force until March 1921, British business with that country was "largely transacted through the intermediary of countries with which trade was possible—viz., the Baltic States and Sweden."[44] "It has, of course, always been and still is open to anyone to send medical stores or any other commodities from the U.K. to Moscow by simple means of consigning them to an agent in Reval, whence they would be forwarded by rail into Russia. Similarly there is no obstacle to anyone sending goods of practically every kind to Russia direct or over Reval from America or other countries in Europe."[45]

Government and business circles alike in Britain seemed convinced that the Baltic would be for some considerable time the primary conduit for Soviet foreign trade and that the country which captured the "distributing trade in the Baltic" would be in a "very advantageous position for trading with Russia." At the end of December the Foreign Office received a plan that was designed to "create a kind of monopoly for British traders as against foreign traders."[46] Presenting its "Baltic Development Scheme" to the government, the National Metal and Chemical Bank of London declared that it had—at considerable cost in immediate profits—"transacted business on such terms as more or less preclude competition in the immediate business offering in the Baltic and has striven to cement a bond between British interests and the Baltic States, in the conviction that a secure footing at the Northern gateway to Russia is a national advantage to this country which will amply repay British traders in the long run. In August last [1919] provisional arrangements were made with the new states whereby the handling of the main import and export trade of these countries was secured to this country."[47]

Noting that the scheme would provide British interests with a "powerful hold" on the major Baltic ports, the Foreign Office concurred that such control would undoubtedly have an "important effect on the development of British trade in the interior."[48] This control was apparently considered important enough for the Foreign Office and the Board of Trade to recommend that the government declare itself ready to use its influence to ensure that "arrangements made with their approval are recognised and carried out by the existing government ... or by *any government which may in the future absorb or replace the present governments of the Baltic Provinces.*"[49]

Despite the thaw in Anglo-Soviet relations and the initiation of negotiations for a trade agreement, British merchants preferred to conduct their trade with the Soviet government through the intermediary of neutral countries. As late as 25 November, protesting against a possible reduction in the status of British representation in the Baltic, the Board of Trade made clear that it believed the Baltic would continue to play an important role in British trade with Russia. Asserting that any trade with Russia would "necessarily be done for some time to come largely through Latvia and Esthonia," Sir Robert Horne pointed out that the commercial importance of those states would be greatly enhanced. The Russians were "establishing important missions at Riga and Reval, no doubt for commercial purposes," and it was considered essential that Britain should "do nothing at this moment which might impair our influence in those states."[50]

With access to the Russian market made relatively easy and comparatively risk-free via the intermediary countries, the volume and value of indirect trade with Soviet Russia increased sharply over the course of 1920.[51] As early as April, a "general resuscitation" of trade in the region had occurred, the full effects of which were expected to be felt once the ice cleared the Baltic ports completely. Concerned by the activity of American and European firms in the Baltic, the British government instructed the Admiralty to render "every assistance" to facilitate the operations of British businessmen in the region.[52] British efforts to secure a firm economic foothold there had a definite impact on the character of Baltic transit trade with Russia: British goods soon accounted for an average of 30 percent of the total volume of transit trade shipped through Reval to Soviet Russia. So successful were these early experiments that British trade brokerage houses and import-export firms were quick to offer their services as agents on behalf of traders of other countries, including the United States.[53] It must be remembered, however, that the country of manufacture was not always accurately represented in the returns, as the origin of the cargo was, as a matter of course, ascribed to the last port of shipment. Such inaccuracy was particularly true in the case of British goods, which were frequently shipped to the Baltic via Northern Europe or Scandinavia.

Even so, it is interesting to note that the percentage of transit trade through the Baltic that was recorded by the Soviets as having originated from Great Britain increased substantially during the last quarter of 1920. By the middle of the year, tension over Poland and Wrangel's successful offensive prompted the British government to discourage merchants from dispatching goods to the Baltic if they were obviously meant for ultimate Bolshevik consumption. Though it recognized that no license was required for the export of goods to the Baltic or any other non-Russian destination, the Foreign Office was nonetheless anxious to prevent certain

articles from reaching Soviet Russia via these channels. Cloth—khaki
and woolen fabric in particular—was seen as especially important to the
Red Army, and several substantial orders for these fabrics had been placed
with British firms by Soviet purchasing organizations in the Baltic.[54]
While neither the Board of Trade, Customs, nor the Foreign Office had
any legal power to prevent the export of these consignments, Curzon was
firmly of the belief that "no means should be spared" to prevent these
transactions from being consummated and urged the Board of Trade to
"put pressure upon the intending exporter in order to prevent the cloth
from being exported."[55] The Board of Trade concurred with such sentiment, declaring that it constantly tried to impress upon traders and
financial houses concerned in such operations that "in the present circumstances" such shipments were "contrary to the interests of His Majesty's Government." However, the board warned the Foreign Office that
"such representations may not be effective when the firms are willing to
disregard them."[56] Further, the government also informed its representative in Reval that, although no legal means existed for preventing the
export of goods consigned to Reval but known to be intended for ultimate delivery to Russia, it was nonetheless the policy of His Majesty's
Government "to prevent acquisition of such articles by Bolsheviks if they
can, and you should therefore discourage agents who have approached
you so far as you properly can."[57]

While such official representations undoubtedly stalled some of these
Soviet contracts, it is certainly the case that a number of British businessmen chose to continue to deal with the Bolsheviks through other, less
obvious routes, such as Sweden and Denmark. It is significant, however,
that with the final defeat of the counterrevolutionary forces and the turn
of events in the Soviet-Polish hostilities, governmental pressures to curb
the Baltic trade were relaxed. As Table 6.1 illustrates, Soviet-bound British exports through the Estonian port of Reval increased dramatically at
the end of the year, indicating Britain's strengthened position in the "peace-
ful penetration of Soviet Russia through Esthonia."[58] More generally, the
growing importance of Estonian ports to Soviet foreign trade is amply
illustrated by the fact that the total value of trade that passed through
Reval alone more than doubled during the last quarter of 1920.

On the surface, the United States appeared to have little part in this
growing trade with Bolshevik Russia. However, despite the State Department's attempts to discourage the export of goods that it suspected of
being ultimately destined for Bolshevik Russia, American commercial
interest in the Soviet market remained undaunted and Soviet-American

Table 6.1   Transit Trade with Soviet Russia via Reval*

1920	October	November	8–29 December
From England	$26,760	$247,257	$1,331,786
As % of total	1%	6%	27%
From Sweden	$1,168,131	$2,017,979	$1,564,214
As % of total	58%	47%	33%
From Denmark	$442,725	$235,714	—
As % of total	22%	5%	—
From Germany	$377,668	$1,203,900	$1,796,300
As % of total	19%	28%	38%
Other	—	$606,742	$99,429
As % of total	—	14%	2%
Total	$2,015,284	$4,311,593	$4,791,729

Source: Worked from returns given in reports filed by Charles Albrecht, American Consulate, Reval, no. 102, Enclosure, "Values of Transit Goods Passing through Reval Customs House, October 1920," 29 December 1920, NARG 59, 660i61/1; no. 111, "Transit Goods through Reval to Soviet Russia for the Month of November 1920," 14 January 1921, NARG 59, 660i.00251/9; and no. 125, "Transit Trade through Reval for Period 8–29 December 1920," 3 February 1921, NARG 59, 660i.00251/7.

*Values are converted from Estonian marks at the cited rate of 70 EM to $1.

trade remained brisk. That the Soviets hoped, "by indirect transactions, to make purchases" was certainly taken for granted in American business circles; what was surprising, however, was the scope of these transactions. As early as May the acting director of military intelligence remarked that "it would seem that [the Soviets] are making fair progress in such transactions with the United States, both with individuals and firms, and it is definitely known that the Soviet Bureau has made contracts for many millions of dollars worth of supplies and materials."[59]

More than the blockade, the U.S. government's restrictions on the trade of its citizens with Bolshevik Russia prevented any truly significant development of early direct economic relations between the two countries.[60] Even so, numerous American manufacturers were not prepared to lose a lucrative market simply because their government imposed restrictions on trade with Russia. International Harvester, for example, had seen its Russian sales increase dramatically, soaring from $1 million in 1916 to some $8 million in 1919.[61] Considering the company's predominant position prior to the war, and the fact that it continued to enjoy an understanding with the Bolshevik authorities that allowed it to operate unmolested in Soviet Russia, International Harvester was understandably unwilling to forgo a market in which the demand for agricultural machinery could only increase. Permitted to trade openly only with non-Bolshevik regions of Russia, businessmen interested in pursuing opportunities in Soviet Russia had to be content to deal through an agent in a neutral country.

Northern Europe and the Baltic continued to play an essential role in Soviet-American commerce even after the blockade had ostensibly been lifted. Although there were no restrictions on American trade with the newly independent Baltic states, the State Department had nonetheless made it clear that it did not contemplate that exports made under Special Export License RAC-77 would be reshipped into Soviet Russia. Even so, American merchants were routinely informed that they were able to divert cargoes that were consigned to order and manifested at Reval, provided that the goods were not landed.[62] While some American firms —like International Harvester—felt obligated to inform the State Department of their suspicions that certain of their shipments dispatched to Estonia had found their way "farther east," there is no indication that this possibility discouraged those companies from pursuing further such transactions.[63]

Such punctilious behavior was the exception rather than the rule, however, and American merchants and manufacturers were quick to seize upon the Baltic as an indirect means of doing business with Soviet Russia. As early as April 1920, U.S. businessmen were already returning from Reval where they had reportedly undertaken negotiations with the Soviet Mission for the sale of American goods.[64] Even the Ford Motor Company was not averse to using the Baltic as a means of furthering its interests "in the interior of Russia." Ford's agents in the region—the People's Industrial Trading Corporation—had declared themselves to be "working very hard to place some Fords in Russia." To that end, the corporation had three representatives engaged solely upon the task of "working their way into [Soviet] purchasing organizations in the Baltic." While the objective was to introduce Fords into Russia as soon as possible, it is interesting to note that both Ford and the People's Industrial Trading Corporation wanted to achieve that task in a manner that would "build up future business."[65]

In addition to those cargoes that were shipped from the United States directly to the Baltic ports at the initiative of American business, there were also numerous instances where goods were either purchased by a foreign agent in the United States or consigned to an agency or individual in yet a third country. Indeed, it was not unusual for American goods to pass through two ports before arriving in Soviet Russia; in this case, the invoices were frequently made out in the names of the immediate consignee and shipping agent, with the primary origin of the goods—on paper at least—being obscured. One example, reported by the American consul at Reval, involved a shipment of over $10,000 worth of morphine sulfate to Reval. The bill of lading was from Moller and Persson to Oscar Stude, Reval, to the order of the Allied Drug and Chemical Corporation. The morphine was of American origin, sold by the B. Brown Export Corporation (New York) to Brown and Krieger in care of the Allied Drug and Chemical Corporation, and was originally shipped to Stockholm whence it was dispatched to the "Centrosoyus, Russia," by the Allied Drug and Chemical Corporation through Oscar Stude, Reval.[66] Taking into consideration only the last port of shipment, the Estonian Customs House registered this consignment as "transit goods from Sweden" to Soviet Russia. This practice makes impossible any systematic breakdown of American export trade to Soviet Russia. Even so, U.S. State and Commerce Department records give a fairly good idea of the types of commodities sent forward by American firms. Inquiries, usually concerning restrictions, were almost always accompanied by a list of goods that were ordered or sold; raw cotton, cotton goods, shoes, clothing, soaps, chemicals and medical supplies, agricultural machinery, and manufactured goods made up a large percentage of the articles that were shipped from the United States to the Baltic and Scandinavian countries and ultimately forwarded to Soviet Russia.[67]

While little of this early trade was directly attributed to the United States, Soviet statistics credit that country with having provided 21 percent of the total value of goods imported between mid-April and mid-October 1920. The United States was, in fact, the third most important supplier of goods to Soviet Russia after Britain and Germany, which provided 29 percent and 25 percent respectively of all Russian imports during this period.[68] The majority of this trade was undoubtedly conducted indirectly. According to official U.S. returns, for example, American exports to Russia amounted to $28,728,000 in 1920; yet for the five months January to May 1920—that is, before that government removed its restrictions on trade with Soviet Russia—the U.S. consulate in Reval estimated that American goods to the value of $22.8 million had already been dispatched across Russian borders.[69] Indeed, certain government officials suspected that the total value of trade via these routes amounted to at least double that officially recorded.[70] Considering that a single shipment by the Allied Drug and Chemical Corporations was worth over $10,000, such an estimate is not as farfetched as it initially seems.

On 7 July 1920 the Department of State announced the removal of sanctions on trade and communication with Soviet Russia, thereby permitting the direct shipment of goods to Russian ports.[71] Despite the elimination of the more obvious restrictions on trade and economic relations with Soviet Russia, the majority of American as well as British goods bound for that country continued to pass through the medium of the Baltic ports and agent countries. While the continued use of intermediaries was at least partially due to the general distrust of the Bolshevik regime, there is nonetheless evidence of an increased willingness on the part of both British and American businessmen to deal directly with Soviet Russia in 1920.[72] Indeed, by the end of the summer of 1920, the Soviet trade delegation had already established direct contacts with British merchants and businessmen. Arcos, the first Soviet export-import organization, had begun its purchasing operations in Britain in October and by the end of the year had placed orders amounting to nearly £2 million.[73]

A far more important factor in determining the continued utilization of Baltic and Scandinavian middlemen was the difficulty that both British and American businessmen encountered in accepting Soviet gold as payment for their goods. Greater American leniency in regard to trade with the Soviets did not extend to permitting the importation of Russian gold and currency. Even when these restrictions were ostensibly removed in December 1920, the use of "Bolshevik gold" as a medium of exchange was impossible due to the refusal of the U.S. Treasury Department and Assay Office to accept it. British merchants likewise ran into difficulty in accepting Russian gold in payment. Although there were now no restrictions concerning the actual import of this metal, the uncertainty over the legal title to the gold made it difficult to dispose of in Britain. The Baltic and Scandinavian countries, in addition to the role they played as "agents" for transit trade, also performed the invaluable service of converting Soviet gold into an acceptable medium of exchange for the Western powers. That is, they provided not only a channel for trade but a sort of transformer for currency.

The Means to Trade

The role of gold in the development of Soviet trade relations was a critical one. The Bolsheviks relied on gold throughout the period prior to the conclusion of the Anglo-Soviet agreement as the only means with which to conduct trade with the West. Easily transported and converted, gold was also the one commodity over which the Bolsheviks had control of a large and accessible supply.

The unsettled conditions immediately after the revolution necessitated that trade with Russia be carried out primarily on a barter basis. There was a disinclination to extend credit for trade with even those areas of Russia that were occupied by the Allies or counterrevolutionary armies. Rampant inflation also discouraged Western merchants from dealing in the local currency; it was not uncommon for a merchant to have his profits—and perhaps a good part of his initial capital—wiped out before he could reinvest the roubles earned in a previous transaction. In addition, graft and corruption among the local counterrevolutionary governments had become so widespread by 1920 that Western businessmen were refusing to deal with them. Yet there was an acute awareness of the existence of a potentially vast market in Russia, one that was also known to be paying in convertible currencies or gold in its transactions with German, Scandinavian, and other Northern European businessmen.

The circumvention of the legal restrictions imposed by the governments of the United States and Great Britain on the acceptance of Russian gold provides an insight into the determination with which the traders competed for a share of the Soviet market. It also reveals that the two governments largely turned a blind eye to this activity. It was widely known and accepted that a number of neutral governments, the Swedish in particular, assayed and reminted a staggering amount of Russian gold in 1920 and 1921, and that the Baltic states acted overtly as intermediaries in numerous transactions that involved Soviet gold. Indeed, as one of the largest producers of platinum and gold, Soviet Russia's problems in financing trade went only as far as the difficulty that it had in realizing these metals on the world market, and the individual merchant's predisposition toward accepting them on deposit or in payment for their goods.

The fear of an impending shortage of both gold and platinum in 1918 prompted the British and American governments to purchase and export as much as they could from Russia, even to the point of competing with each other. During the spring of 1918 the belief that a platinum "famine" was imminent and that current supplies would last only until June 1919 if the British government did not "act now to try to gain a reserve of that available from Russia" prompted the Restriction of Enemy Supplies Department (RESD) to advocate that "all possible amounts should be purchased."[74] Platinum was essential in the manufacture of military and related supplies such as sulfuric and nitric acids, fuses, and firing charges for large caliber guns; it was also a necessary component in the manufacture of magnetos and other electrical components, and was used extensively for telephone, telegraph, and wireless installations.[75] In addition to meeting the military requirements for this metal, the purchase of Russian platinum was perceived as necessary in the effort to deny the stocks to Germany. The Admiralty pointed out that "notwithstanding the heavy cost of the material, there would appear to be little reason to apprehend that purchase would involve any loss to the Treasury, while on the other hand it would serve not only to safeguard to a large extent the supplies which this country will require in the future, but also to prevent the enemy from obtaining supplies of which they are in great need." Everything pointed to the "desirability of purchasing platinum whenever and wherever possible."[76] And purchase they did: from renegades like Gregory Semenov, who no doubt stole it; from Kolchak and Denikin; and even from the Bolsheviks.

By mid-1918 it was reported that all large stocks of platinum were under the control of the "Russian Government." Related correspondence indicates that the government referred to was indeed that of the Bolshevik authorities.[77] Thus, it is significant that subsequent arrangements made by the British and Americans to purchase platinum from this government required that payment for this metal be made in sterling in London.

Moreover, as early as 1918 the Bolshevik authorities were already disposing of this metal through neutral countries. The Soviet agent in Stockholm reportedly had twenty poods (722 pounds) of platinum available for sale shortly after he arrived there in September 1918. In addition to this amount, Swedish intermediaries informed the British Consulate in Stockholm that they were able to arrange shipments of additional platinum, of which there was some two hundred poods reportedly available. It is interesting to note that the British representative forwarding this information advised that unless his government "urgently desire to obtain more platinum in this way it is not in our own interests to encourage these exports by Bolsheviks which will procure for them large credits outside Russia."[78] This heavy purchasing of platinum irrespective of its source continued throughout 1918 and 1919 and could not have failed to place a considerable sum of foreign currency at the disposal of the Bolshevik government.

In addition to the sale of platinum, the Bolsheviks had other means of acquiring foreign currency. The sale of diamonds and other valuables gave the Bolsheviks needed funds abroad.[79] Kamenev ingenuously admitted that the Bolsheviks had for some time been selling diamonds and jewels when they were in need of "assets in foreign countries."[80] The large diamond producing and marketing firm of DeBeers was known to have a strong interest in these sales. During the course of 1920 the market prices of both DeBeers shares and the diamonds themselves had fallen nearly 50 percent. In order to restore their value, DeBeers was reportedly "buying up as far as possible" all the diamonds the Russians had for sale.[81] If American intelligence is to be believed, over £2 million worth of diamonds had been smuggled into Britain by the Bolshevik trade delegation by November of 1920.[82]

The money spent by the British forces in Northern Europe and Russia also provided another possible source of sterling. It was reported that the British Fleet spent about £5,000 per week in Bjorkö. While it was not certain where this money went, military intelligence suggested that it was not at all unlikely that it was bought up by the Bolsheviks.[83]

The legitimate sale of bonds and securities on foreign markets also helped to raise currency. Some £14,000 was acquired by the Moscow Narodny Bank in 1920 through the sale of a number of Chinese 1913 series 5 percent Gold Bonds on the English stock market. Undertaken with the full knowledge of the British government, the sale of these bonds was permitted on the condition that the proceeds would be used by the Bolsheviks to purchase drugs and medical supplies in England.[84]

It was the realization of the Russian gold reserves, however, that largely enabled the Soviets to carry on trade during 1920 and 1921. An estimated $600 million remained in the Russian gold reserves after the revolution. By 1922 the Federal Reserve of the United States maintained that there was "no question that the major part of the Russian gold has found its way into the reserves of other countries and most of it ultimately into the Federal Reserves."[85] Nor was there any question that this gold was primarily used to "pay for indispensable imports."

Breaking the Gold Blockade

By late 1919, the neutral states had already undertaken to act as agents for the sale of Russian gold as well as to provide for its use in establishing credits for the conduct of Soviet trade. They provided the invaluable service of "washing" the gold by assaying, reminting, and ensuring its title. This process enabled the Soviet government to realize a considerable amount of gold that would have remained virtually useless for trade because of the British and American governments' reluctance to accept it and the restrictions imposed on its disposal once it had been imported. The ability to sell their gold for foreign currency enabled the Bolsheviks to pay cash for their purchases from firms and businessmen who, under other circumstances, would have shied away from trading with Soviet

Russia, and thus freed the Soviets from the necessity of trading exclusively through intermediaries in neutral countries.

The amount of gold that was involved in both direct realization and the establishment of credits in Northern Europe and the Baltic states was considerable. Numerous reports concerning the movement of vast sums of Russian gold bullion and coin were received by both the State Department and the Foreign Office. Indeed, the U.S. government was particularly interested in keeping track of Russian gold and requested that its representatives abroad relay any information they may discover on the subject.[86] Reports sent back to the State Department indicated that a considerable proportion of the gold imported from the neutral and Allied countries was suspected of being of Soviet origin. Gold received from the Netherlands, for example, was highly suspect. Although Dutch law forbade the export of gold "except by special permission," gold in transit was not effected, and over four million kilograms of this metal were assayed, restruck, and exported to the United States under this provision.[87]

The French were likewise suspected of having extensive dealings in Russian gold. Despite their protest that the dispersal of Russian gold would decrease their chances of recovering the debt owed to their bondholders, the French government nonetheless looked through its fingers at the smelting and reexport of the metal.[88] Indeed, the U.S. consul in Paris noted that between May 1921 and January 1922, over $57 million of Russian gold was invoiced through the Paris consulate for shipment to New York.[89]

But it was Sweden that served as the primary *point d'appui* for Russian gold. As early as January 1919 an American intelligence agent noted the arrival of "millions after millions" of gold roubles: "For many months past the Bolsheviks . . . have used Sweden as a base of translating their stolen money and property into the coin of other countries and in securing machinery and other articles."[90] By 1920 the Swedish press bristled with reports concerning the arrival of Russian gold in Stockholm. According to official Swedish customs statistics reproduced in Table 6.2, Russian gold bullion and coin accounted for 98 percent of the 278 million kroner worth of gold imported into Sweden during that year.[91] The director of the Royal Swedish Mint reported that a total of nineteen tons of Russian gold had been assayed, melted, and restruck with the Swedish seal in 1920. Moreover, Soviet efforts to dispose of this treated gold were highly successful: by the beginning of December, export licenses had been issued for nearly £10.5 million worth—or 90 percent—of the Russian gold imported up to that time.[92] Further, that this gold was accepted by a growing market is borne out by the dramatic increase in the amount

Table 6.2   Gold Movements in 1920–1922 (according to Customs Statistics of Sweden; in Kroner, Par Value = $0.268)

	Imports of Gold		Exports of Gold	
	Total	Of This, from Russia	Total	Of This, to the United States
1920	278,018,158	274,487,078	59,090,911	17,356,071
1921	683,980,619	670,028,251	934,396,353	327,546,154
1922	296,666,667	295,244,352	330,371,692	218,417,524
Total (3 years)	1,258,665,444	1,237,759,681	1,323,858,956	563,319,749

Source: Worked from data given in "Gold Movements in 1920–1922 according to Customs Statistics of Sweden, Switzerland, France and the United States," *Russian Gold*, Amtorg Information Department, 1928.

reprocessed by the Swedish Mint, from the nineteen tons in 1920 to seventy tons during the first quarter of 1921 alone.[93]

Another important development became evident by May of that year: the United States was becoming the primary recipient of this "treated" gold. That the British had reason to fear that the United States was ultimately receiving the "major part" of the Russian gold delivered to the Swedish Mint for "treatment" is borne out by the returns in Table 6.2.[94] The ability to import, assay, and sell gold bearing the mint mark of a neutral country allowed American banks and financial institutions to purchase a large proportion of the gold that had been "washed" of its Soviet origins in Sweden.[95] Indeed, the United States received a full 30 percent of the gold exported from Sweden in 1920. Although the official American share of this export was to increase by only 5 percent in 1921, the actual value of gold received increased five and a half times, from nearly $16 million to over $87.8 million.

The suspension of the restrictions placed on the importation of Russian gold to the United States in December 1920 was understood by a number of businessmen to mean that the Russian metal could now be used in commercial transactions with the Soviets, prompting an increase in the importation of Russian bullion and coin. The American business community soon learned, however, that the U.S. Treasury, Mint, and Federal Reserve Board continued to refuse to have anything to do with gold from Soviet Russia. Ostensibly, it was the Treasury's fears of becoming entangled in a dispute over the title to the gold that prompted this policy. Gold that was obviously of a Russian origin or that was suspected of having a "Soviet taint" was not accepted by the Assay Office, and without an official assay of its purity, the Treasury Department would not purchase it.[96] Since the U.S. Treasury was the only institution that would be interested in such large quantities of this metal, the businesses that did accept it as payment were essentially in possession of an inconvertible—and therefore useless—asset.

The easiest way around this problem was to remove any visible signs of its Russian origins, a service that was already being provided by the Swedish, Swiss, and Dutch mints, as well as private assay firms in France, Belgium, and Denmark.[97] Even so, the Assay Office was justifiably suspicious of the origin of the gold that arrived from the Allied and neutral states bearing no distinguishing stamp other than that of the private assaying firm that refined it. Gold of this sort was reported to be arriving in the United States from France and England at the rate of some $10 million per week. That this gold was probably of Russian origin is evident from the admission that, if an affidavit were required of the American consignees on these shipments, the banks would "likely refuse to accept it."[98]

The U.S. government turned a blind eye on the import of gold from Sweden, though it was aware of its origin. As the Swedish government refused to issue licenses for the export of gold of Swedish origin, and since Russian gold made up the overwhelming proportion of the gold imported into Sweden between 1920 and 1922, the American government must have been aware that the gold exported was predominantly of Russian origin.[99] Remarkably, it was even proposed officially that those gold roubles that had already found their way to the United States should be "returned to Sweden . . . to have them melted in the Swedish Government Mint, and stamped with the Government stamp. The U.S. government will accept gold so stamped without inquiring into its origin."[100]

One explanation for this practice may lie in the growing concern over the apparent depletion of U.S. gold reserves at this time.[101] A more likely possibility, however, was the belief that it would be "useless to try to prevent the export of Russian gold"; that it would "leak out" anyway, and eventually "get beyond control." According to this view, it was a wise move for the Allied nations to get control of this gold while they could.[102]

The prospects of purchasing "unlimited quantities" of the Russian gold at approximately 17 percent below New York prices quickly drew customers like the Guaranty Trust Company, First National City Bank, and the Equitable Trust Company, as well as numerous other smaller concerns.[103] Shipments of Russian gold were said to be going forth to the

United States "by nearly every sailing of the Swedish-American Line."[104] According to incomplete records, several of the major New York banking houses had purchased over $94 million of gold in the Stockholm and London markets during the first six months of 1921 alone.[105] The Equitable Trust Company appeared to be the single largest American buyer, with nearly three million kilograms of this gold reportedly invoiced for its account through Sweden and Switzerland by August 1921.[106] Since the American banks were usually willing to pay a better price for the gold, the Swedes naturally preferred to deal with them, and especially preferred them to the British, whose mint and bank were willing to offer only 77s/9d per ounce—some 30 shillings per ounce less than the market price.[107]

British policy toward the use of Russian gold for trade was self-defeating. The government was, on the one hand, clearly anxious to promote unofficial trade between Russia and Great Britain. British merchants were told that there were no restrictions on their importing Russian gold, and the Foreign Office hastened to assure the Moscow Narodny Bank in the spring of 1920 that any amount of Russian gold could be brought into Britain with no threat of claim by His Majesty's Government. Likewise, the government was clearly anxious that the gold be realized in or through Britain.[108] Despite a similar desire by the Bolsheviks to utilize the British gold market in order to establish credit, the Soviet government was effectively prevented from doing so on any large scale throughout 1920. Foreign Office assurances notwithstanding, the question of title to the gold remained a contentious issue among the various governmental offices. The Treasury for one still considered it essential that "exports to Russia should not be paid for in gold so long as there is any possibility that creditors of Russia in this country could successfully initiate proceedings to obtain possession of or an injunction against the disposal of such gold." Much to the chagrin of the Foreign Office, the Treasury had also taken it upon itself to prevent transactions in Russian gold whenever possible—despite the fact that their actions were in direct opposition to the government's instructions.[109] Moreover, the Bank of England would pay only mint price for gold of Russian origin; and further, once it had been imported into the United Kingdom, the reexport or melting down of the gold was prohibited.[110] The loss of about 27 percent on each transaction in gold in the United Kingdom was more than enough to discourage the Soviets from disposing of it in London.[111] The damaging effect of the government's stand on Russian gold did not go unnoticed; even the Foreign Office bitterly noted that "while we are quibbling over the legal title of the gold and hoping for a return of the halcyon days of the gold standard other countries are getting the trade."[112]

While Russian gold was subjected to certain restrictions that made its sale in Britain difficult, gold exported by the Estonian government itself was regularly bought by the British government. The logic in the government's action escaped even its servants, as the vast majority of Russian gold was known to be exported via Reval. It was also well known that the Estonian State Bank, as well as other private banks in Reval—such as Scheel's Bank—acted as the agent of the Soviet authorities, and it was therefore "logical to assume that the gold exported by that bank was Russian in origin."[113] Even on the eve of the signing of the trade agreement, the British government reported that, so far as their records go, there was "no trace of Russian gold coming to or being sent from this country." They did admit, however, to having received nearly £3 million of Estonian gold, but His Majesty's Government did not consider this to be of Russian origin.[114]

Nonetheless, a substantial volume of Russian gold in the form of unmarked bullion was known to have been shipped to Britain directly from Reval. Unidentifiable fine gold was worth 105s/8d per ounce to the trades, and with Russian gold averaging 900/1000 fine, this bullion produced a price of 95s/1d per ounce. Even after the usual commission for remelting and assaying, this price was far better than the mint rate of 76s/2d per ounce quoted by the Bank of England in March 1920. It was noted by the Moscow Narodny Bank that in order to sell fine gold in England it was not important how crudely the melting was carried out, provided that the gold was rendered unrecognizable as coin.[115] Between October 1920 and August 1921 the Bolshevik government sent to Arcos in London £6 million worth of gold. Prior to that "considerable" shipments of gold were made to Krasin and Klishko in London in small parcels. According to Scotland Yard, reminted bars of Russian gold were sent from Stockholm to New York, where a Soviet agent sold them and credited the proceeds to Klishko's account at the London branch of the Guaranty Trust Company. Some $25,000 was sent forward in this fashion *each week*. The total value of gold sent to Great Britain up to August was estimated between £8 to £10 million.[116]

By December the government's reasoning behind the restriction on Soviet gold was being brought into question. There no longer appeared to be any constructive purpose in the maintenance of the policy, and the official prejudice against Soviet gold was recognized as having a detrimental effect on Anglo-Russian trade. Hopes that the impending conclusion of a trade agreement would bring about more favorable terms were shared by both sides. Moreover, it was generally recognized that the "gold question was not only an economic one, it was also a political matter. It, in fact, involved the *de facto* recognition of the Soviet government."[117] With the signature of the trade agreement a certain measure of public recognition would have to be given to the Soviet government to ensure that the British courts would "recognise the nationalisation of private property and consequently the title of the bona fide purchaser of such nationalised goods in the United Kingdom."[118] This recognition would, of course, affect the disposition of Soviet gold in Britain by freeing it for reexport and allowing it to fetch full market value in Britain. The complication of the issue by the successful litigation for possession of imported Russian plywood in late 1920 served to retard the progress toward a resolution of the gold dilemma, and it was not until after the conclusion of the agreement that the British government accepted any responsibility for the gold.

By the end of the year it had become clear that the "dubious title" had become "less and less of an obstacle to trade."[119] Although the difficulties surrounding the acceptance of this gold had effectively hindered the development of direct trade with Russia, they certainly did not discourage the acceptance of Russian gold as collateral by British and American merchants. Businessmen were known to have concluded contracts whereby the Soviets had deposited as security a sum of gold in an agent bank in a neutral city such as Reval.[120] With their reserves of gold being rapidly depleted, the Soviet government endeavored to use the gold increasingly as security to obtain foreign credit. These credit arrangements often provided for payment in goods, or in currency raised through the sale of goods. Significantly, it was remarked that the Soviets "appeared in no doubt as to their ability to . . . export considerable quantities of grain and raw materials." The sale of these goods would allow a "revolving" credit system to be established, whereby goods could be ordered against the security of gold credited to the account of the manufacturer. Under this arrangement, should the Bolsheviks fail to meet their obligations within the specified time, title to the gold would revert to the creditor. Upon the successful completion of a contract, the gold would again be put forward as a tangible asset to be offered as security in another deal. In this way, the Soviets would be able to prevent the further depletion of their gold reserves while at the same time using it to effect trade.[121]

The Bolsheviks met with early success in establishing this "revolving credit." In May 1920 the Foreign Office received notice that an agreement had been entered into between Krasin (Centrosoyus) and the Russian Corporation, which provided for the deposit of £5 million in gold in Reval. Having consulted with the leading bankers in London, the Russian

Corporation stood advised that "British banking institutions would be prepared to give the necessary credits to enable trade to be resumed, secured on the gold, provided same was moved from Reval to a safe place for which purpose Copenhagen is approved. I would add that a large part of the credit granted would be utilised to cover purchases of British goods for export to Russia."[122] Such arrangements provided the Soviets with a line of credit in Britain through British banks, as opposed to relying on individual manufacturers accepting Russian gold on deposit. Similarly, British merchants were also known to ship Russian gold to the United States, where it was "used to create credits for the payment of goods exported to the U.K. [for ultimate delivery to Soviet Russia] — thus diminishing the loss on exchange."[123]

By the end of 1920 the Soviets had established a fund of about £50 million in gold to be used as security against which they hoped to place contracts up to £100 million.[124] Throughout the period prior to the agreement, British and American merchants and banks had made extensive use of the Soviet's system of revolving credit to the apparent satisfaction of both parties. Indeed, there is no record of any complaint or protest lodged with either the State Department or Foreign Office concerning any failure by the Soviets to meet the obligations incurred in this way.[125]

However, concern over the Bolsheviks' propaganda activities caused the British and American governments to regard this outpouring of gold from Russia with considerable trepidation. Fears that the funds would be used to foment unrest and spread revolutionary ideas prompted both governments to keep a close watch on the ultimate disposition of the metal. In response to its many requests for information on this subject, the Foreign Office received numerous reports that maintained that the gold coming out of Russia was being used almost exclusively to finance Soviet trade. Noting that the government was following the gold transactions as closely as it could, one Foreign Office official observed that there was no indication that this gold was being used for anything other than commercial transactions.[126] He went on to remark that "politically, the chief question is whether or not any of this gold is being used for the purposes of propaganda. . . . We continually receive reports showing that comparatively large contracts are in [the] process of negotiation by Soviet agents in various countries and we receive from the Baltic States statistics showing that a certain amount of goods are being supplied to Soviet Russia. It is, therefore, probable that the major portion of this gold is being used for legitimate trading purposes."[127]

The U.S. government also made efforts to keep track of the Russian gold. American authorities, however, were less concerned over the possibility of its use in seditious activities, primarily because "every effort is made to control the despatch and destination of the gold."[128] A number of prominent American businessmen likewise maintained that this threat was exaggerated: Roy W. Howard, president of Scripps-Howard Newspaper Service, informed Reeve Schley, the vice-president of Chase National Bank, that he personally thought "the menace of Bolshevism in the United States is about as great as the menace of sunstroke in Greenland or chilblains in the Sahara."[129] Even the former manager of the Russo-Asiatic Bank in Petrograd—potentially someone with a political ax to grind—supported the view that the proceeds of the gold sales would be used by the Bolsheviks "for the purpose of purchasing commodities in the various countries, and that the money will not be used for Bolshevik propaganda."[130]

With the assumption that the overwhelming majority of this gold was being realized in order to finance foreign trade—a belief that was expressed by both American and British representatives—these data on gold provide an insight into the amount of unofficial trade that was conducted with Soviet Russia. Although no direct correlation can be made between the shipments of gold and the total value of Soviet purchases made abroad, it is nonetheless clear from the volume of gold exported that the Soviet government had substantial means with which to conduct foreign trade. It stands to reason, therefore, that the successful realization of the Russian gold reserves indicates that a certain, not inconsiderable amount of trade *was* conducted. The nearly £68 million worth of Russian gold officially received at the Royal Swedish Mint during the three years 1920–22 serves as a "bottom line" estimate of the assets available to the Soviet government.[131] This figure is, without doubt, a cautious one, considering that substantial quantities of Russian gold were also known to have been shipped to Holland, Switzerland, Norway, Belgium, and even Japan.[132] Indeed, the total value of gold of Russian origin imported into the United States between 1920 and 1921 inclusive was "conservatively estimated" at approximately $350 million.[133]

With the extension of limited credit facilities in both Britain and Germany by mid-1921, this gold became especially important in Soviet trade with the United States, where credit remained largely unavailable until 1924. This importance is particularly evident from the fact that the United States became the primary recipient of gold "treated" in Sweden shortly after the conclusion of the Anglo-Soviet Trade Agreement. Here again, while official U.S. statistics record the receipt of only $85,000 worth of Russian gold in 1921, American intelligence records put the value of such gold at over $42.5 million—a sum dwarfed by the estimated five million kilograms that were believed to have been exported to the United States during that year.[134]

The Bolsheviks' success in selling this reminted gold illustrates two things: that the Soviets had a pressing need for foreign currency and that there was a market for this gold, even though it was known or at least suspected of being of Soviet origin. The inability to deal directly with Russian gold did not stop either American or British merchants from pursuing this trade, but rather, merely forced them to deal largely through intermediaries in the Baltic and Northern Europe "with consequent disadvantage to both parties."[135] Although merchants were initially "willing to dispose of their accumulated stocks on reasonably low terms," and "likewise willing to forego a fair proportion of their profit in order to turn Soviet gold into cash," they nonetheless came to resent the profits lost to Scandinavian and Baltic middlemen in the conduct of this trade.[136]

7

British and American Policy toward Russia, 1921–1924

For well over a year after the conclusion of the trade agreement, there were no incidents that seriously marred Anglo-Soviet relations. Even the instances of propaganda and subversion that did provoke the British government to formal protest did not develop into the full-blown crises that later dominated Anglo-Soviet relations. The question of the Soviet government's recognition of the debts and obligations of previous Russian governments—while recognized in principle and ostensibly shelved pending the negotiation of a general peace treaty—received a good deal of attention. But again, the issue failed to have any overall damaging effect on existing relations. Although neither of these contentious points served to disrupt the trade that had developed, the issue of debts was a sore point that effectively blocked the development of more extensive commercial relations. The linchpin in any attempt to expand the trade was credit, and the obstacle preventing the extension of credit to Russia was the unsettled question of debts owed by Russia to its former creditors, public and private, and the restitution or compensation due to foreign owners for the losses suffered from the nationalization or expropriation of their property by the Soviet government.

Despite these problems, Anglo-Soviet trade relations did improve following the conclusion of the agreement. Though certainly not attaining anticipated levels, there was nonetheless an increase in the overall volume and value of trade. These increases largely resulted from the outcome of two cases in the British courts concerning the legal title to goods and gold received in the United Kingdom from Soviet Russia. By recognizing the title of the Soviet government to these goods, the judgment handed down on these test cases had the effect of transforming the agreement from a primarily academic instrument into one that provided the Soviets with the ability to trade directly with Britain.

The United States again figured prominently during this period, though its official policy toward the Soviet government remained largely unchanged. After withdrawing its interventionist armies from the Russian North and Siberia, the government seems to have preferred to ignore Russia rather than deal with the Bolsheviks in any way. As a rather jaded article in the *Times* pointed out, "Relations with Russia are a part of the greater problem of foreign affairs, and in this neither the Senate nor the House is really interested."[1] The United States continued to maintain its official relations with the representatives of the Russian Provisional Government through the 1920s. With the exception of a few congressmen and senators who advocated coming to terms with the Soviets, the wisdom of these relations was left unchallenged.[2] While the United States had followed Britain in lifting the blockade in 1920 and had anticipated the conclusion of the Anglo-Soviet Trade Agreement by removing the more obvious restrictions on American trade with Russia, the U.S. government was certainly not disposed to accommodate the Soviets any further.

Despite the American government's coolness toward the Bolshevik regime, unofficial relations continued to improve during the period 1920–22. The renewed pursuit of the Russian market by American businessmen provided stiff competition for British traders. The trade agreement notwithstanding, the value of Soviet-American trade closely rivaled—and in some instances surpassed—the amount of trade done by Great Britain. Further, Soviet negotiations with Hoover's American Relief Administration and the subsequent dispatch of American aid to those areas of Russia worst hit by the famine brought unofficial U.S.-Soviet relations as close as they ever had been. The appearance of American relief officials in Russia combined with the receipt of vast amounts of provisions and the extension of $20 million in credit was a significant development in the course of Soviet-American relations. Finally, with regard to the increasingly predominant position occupied by the United States in Soviet Russia's foreign trade, a comparison of the British and American approach to famine relief operations does much to explain the shift in Soviet preference from British to American manufactured goods.

The international economic conferences at Genoa and The Hague during the spring and summer of 1922 marked the zenith of this period in Anglo-Soviet relations. The hopes that were placed in these conferences for the resolution of some of the larger economic issues and ills of Europe and Russia especially seem, in retrospect, to be more than slightly optimistic. Nevertheless, in the spring of 1922 these hopes were genuine enough. By the opening session of The Hague Conference in June, however, both Britain and Soviet Russia were skeptical of its chances of success; and by its conclusion in early July total disillusionment had occurred. Anglo-Soviet relations were to become increasingly strained through the autumn of 1922, and the threat of a rupture had, for the first time since the signing of the agreement, become a permanent element in their relations.

The conferences also marked the beginning of a significant shift in Soviet foreign policy; never again would Britain be afforded such an opportunity for the favorable settlement of the Russian debt question. With the improvement of the internal economic situation in the RSFSR by the end of 1922, the Soviet leadership was increasingly loath to compromise its principles in order to attract foreign capital. In this connection, Lenin's refusal to ratify the long-negotiated Urquhart concession goes far to illustrate the degree to which the Soviets were now willing and able to sacrifice the prospects of securing foreign capital in their pursuit of foreign policy goals.

The Trade Agreement and After

Although recognition was not specifically mentioned in the text, the Anglo-Soviet Trade Agreement effectively stood as de facto British recognition of the Soviet government. Any doubts were removed by the Law Officers of the Crown when, in response to a query from the Foreign Office, they stated, "It would be correct [to say] . . . that His Majesty's Government recognise the Soviet Government as the *de facto* Government of Russia."[3] This judgement served as the basis for two legal decisions that ranked as important test cases in the establishment of Soviet title to goods exported from Russia. The first case, that of *Luther v. Sagor*, involved the reversal of an earlier ruling on the title to a consignment of Soviet plywood. Originally decided in favor of the British claimant in December 1920, the judgment was overturned in May 1921, primarily on the evidence of the Law Officers' pronouncement. Lord Justice Bankes declared that, since the Soviet government was recognized by the British government as being the actual authority in Russia, the acts of that government must be given "all the respect due to the acts of a duly recognised foreign sovereign state." With the question of title firmly settled in favor of the Soviet government, Russian raw materials and other commodities could be freely exported to the United Kingdom and the British purchaser able to take possession of them without fear of the consignment being attached.[4]

The second test case concerned the title to Russian gold imported as payment for British goods. Arrangements had been made months in advance in preparation for the hearing of this case. Discussions between Horne and Krasin in early January resulted in the so-called Gold Letter, which was attached to—but not officially a part of—the trade agreement.[5] In the letter, Horne suggested that the Soviet government "bring a small parcel of gold to this country as a basis for a test action." Clearly anticipating no problem in establishing the Soviet title, Horne went on to outline the conditions for the subsequent import, sale, and reexport of the gold. Indeed, the outcome of the test case in July appears to have been assured from the beginning. The court's decision was based on the rather dubious application of a tsarist law that denied state bondholders any legal claim to the state gold reserves.[6] The extension of this law to cover the tsarist state gold reserves under the control of the Soviet government was questionable, to say the least, but it goes far to illustrate the importance that the British attached to this issue. It was taken as understood that the object of the arrangement was to "facilitate and extend trade between the United Kingdom and Russia in accordance with the Trade Agreement," and that "all gold imported under these arrangements [was] to be used to pay or to secure the payment for goods purchased in the United Kingdom and in particular for goods the product or manufacture of the British Empire."[7]

The decision in favor of the Soviet title and the relaxation of export licensing requirements for goods shipped directly to Russia (excepting shipments of war matériel) removed the last of the legal hindrances in the way of Anglo-Soviet trade. Further, the agreement also provided the Soviet government with the legal basis to claim the capital held by unfriendly Russian trading and financial institutions. Krasin advised the Union of Siberian Creameries that, because of the "reciprocal legal relations" between Britain and Soviet Russia, that organization would soon "be forced by the courts to deliver up the public co-operative capital" in their possession, and he then invited them to do so voluntarily.[8] More generally, Soviet optimism is reflected in a report filed by Krasin and published in the Soviet press: "The work of the Soviet Trade Delegation . . . has been carried on in quite favorable circumstances. . . . The moment the trade agreement was concluded the atmosphere in which our commercial work was carried began to improve. Until the signing of the agreement, many firms entered into no dealings with us. . . . Now . . . we have dealings only with first class firms, and our work has assumed a much healthier tone."[9]

The British were likewise hopeful; the New Economic Policy made a strong impression in Great Britain. Remarking on its effect, Krasin observed that the British saw it as a sign that the "Bolsheviks have at last come to their senses and that it is now possible to have dealings with them."[10] The government, however, was still generally more cautious in its hopes for the trade agreement than were British businessmen. Even Lloyd George had considerably tempered his earlier ebullient predictions by the autumn of 1921. In reply to a speech by a member of parliament who had recently returned from Russia, the prime minister contested the view that the Soviet need for manufactures was so great as "to provide employment for everyone" in Britain. Statements like that, Lloyd George said, were only misleading. Although he had used just such an argument only months before to support the agreement, the prime minister admitted that this tactic was merely designed to ensure its successful conclusion. He knew "perfectly well that unless there was a trading agreement and every facility was given for trade, it would always be said 'why do not you open Russia?' . . . We knew there was some trade but not trade to the extent of the anticipations of some."[11] Even so, the trade agreement was admitted to have had "substantial results," and the amount of trade done since its conclusion was stated to be of a "very considerable quantity."[12]

While Anglo-Soviet commerce subsequent to the trade agreement failed to achieve anything like the prewar levels—a fact that its detractors repeatedly pointed out—the influence of the agreement on the development of Anglo-Soviet relations cannot be overlooked. In addition to its effect on the volume and value of trade, the psychological impact of the normalization of relations should also be considered. The agreement represented a political triumph for the Soviets. Through the negotiation and the conclusion of the trade agreement, the Soviet government had finally achieved recognition by a major power. Further, the agreement was an important precedent that marked the beginning of a general movement toward rapprochement with the Soviet government; the conclusion of each new agreement served to reinforce its claim to treatment as an equal by the rest of the world.

On the British side, the agreement put the Soviets within the law—or so it seemed. Now that the Soviets were party to a legally binding agreement, it was believed that the issues that had previously disrupted relations would either be eliminated, as with hostile Bolshevik propaganda, or postponed, as with question of debts. Further, the agreement bestowed upon the Soviet government an official legitimacy without which a number of merchants would have continued to refuse to do business.[13] The results of the two legal test cases reinforced the notion of legitimacy and Anglo-Soviet trade was increasingly seen as enjoying the benefit of the full protection of the British government. British merchants became more confident in the use of the usual commercial apparatus; checks, bills of exchange, and other documents covering values in trade could once again be used in their dealings with Russia. Arcos, the Soviet trade organ in the United Kingdom, was also given an improved commercial position in the City and was able to command credit in the way of a business. London quickly became a center for Soviet financial operations, with a number of the state banking organs maintaining balances of "very considerable amounts" with the joint-stock banks there.[14]

In light of the overall expansion of Soviet purchases abroad, Anglo-Soviet trade would have shown some increase in 1921 regardless of the trade agreement. Even so, the question remains as to whether the Anglo-Soviet Trade Agreement made any positive quantitative difference in the amount of trade conducted between the two signatories. Unfortunately, official British returns do not readily provide an answer. The first and most obvious difficulty involves the variations encountered in the geographical definition of "Russia." The Board of Trade itself used no less than four different definitions to describe that country between 1919 and 1921.[15] It is quite vexing to discover further that the data from more than one—and sometimes as many as three—of these classifications were used in one table alone![16] It was not until 1921 that the practice of employing the prewar geographical classifications was scrapped and returns were recorded as trade with Russia "as now constituted." The difference that this redefinition made on the value of that trade is striking, as illustrated by the recorded annual returns listed in Table 7.1.

A more accurate picture of Anglo-Soviet commerce both before and after the conclusion of the trade agreement can be found in the month-by-month account of Arcos's purchases in Britain during 1921. These returns, reproduced in Table 7.2, show a significant increase in the value of

Table 7.1 Statistics of United Kingdom Trade with Russia

	Imports from Russia	Exports of U.K. Produce	Reexports to Russia	Total Exports	Turnover
1913	£40,270,539	£18,102,683	£9,591,270	£27,693,953	£67,694,492
1920	33,522,892	11,992,083	4,841,300	16,883,383	50,356,275
1921	2,694,674	2,181,007	1,210,283	3,391,290	6,085,964
1922	8,102,829	3,640,624	970,403	4,611,027	12,713,856
1923	9,266,100	2,491,650	1,989,476	4,481,126	13,747,226
1924	19,773,842	3,860,385	7,212,144	11,072,529	30,846,371

Source: Compiled from U.K. Parliamentary Papers, *Annual Statement of the Trade of the United Kingdom.*

direct Soviet purchases in the month following the agreement. These statistics reflect certain inevitable seasonal fluctuations: the increased export of grain in the autumn and the effect of the navigational season are among the most obvious causes of such fluctuations in Russian trade. The burst of purchasing in September is no doubt a reflection of the increased purchasing power of the peasant in the autumn. This period was traditionally the one during which major purchases of agricultural equipment were contemplated—a fact that did not go unnoticed by Ford.

The Soviet statistics in Table 7.3 likewise illustrate the dramatic growth in both the volume and value of direct Anglo-Soviet trade over the period 1920–22. Although this increase is undoubtedly a reflection of the overall expansion of Soviet trade that had begun in 1919, these statistics are nonetheless also indicative of the growing confidence that British traders had in their ability to deal directly with the Soviet representatives in Britain.

The significance of the increase becomes apparent, however, when British returns are taken in conjunction with the Soviet statistics in Table 7.4. A comparison of the proportion of Soviet imports from Great Britain as against those from the United States and Germany confirms that the British data reflect a real increase in the volume of Anglo-Soviet trade.

That the trade agreement served to increase the volume and value of the direct trade seems at least probable. However, the immediate development of this trade did not occur along the lines originally anticipated by either country. The returns in Table 7.1 show that the value of Soviet purchases in the United Kingdom remained relatively constant between 1921 and 1923, while the sale of Soviet goods in Britain accounted for a growing proportion of the total trade turnover. The hope that the normal-

Table 7.2   Arcos Purchases Made in the United Kingdom, 1921*

Month	Purchases
January	£56,844
February	212,271
March	126,995
April	627,885
May	354,361
June	844,522
July	440,997
August	303,404
September	1,096,928
October	282,498
November	227,489
December	203,724
Total	£4,777,918

Source: Klishko to Gregory, no. J.B./13923, 23 November 1922, Enclosure, annotated article, "Russia's Foreign Trade for 1921," in *Russian Information and Review*, FO 371/8176.

*Goods purchased by Arcos at the beginning and end of the year were not necessarily shipped during 1921.

ization of commercial relations would open up the Russian market and provide a measure of relief for unemployment and the growing unrest in Britain failed to materialize. This failure was due in no small part to the fact that credit was not forthcoming; and it was exactly on that score that the major objective of the Soviet government in signing the treaty had been frustrated. None of the £26 million in British government guaranteed export credits were made available to cover trade with Russia. Their depleted gold reserves and worsening internal economic situation made the Soviets unwilling to expend gold in financing increased imports from the United Kingdom.

The high cost of British goods—as against German and American —also served to discourage the Soviets from placing extensive orders with British firms. Krasin admitted openly that he had intentionally "set aside" an order for forty thousand tons of rails to be placed in Britain "so as to convince people in Great Britain that the agreement was having practical results." The cost of these rails was so high in Britain—some 36

Table 7.3 Anglo-Soviet Trade, 1919–1921/22 (Direct Trade Only)

	1919		1920		1921		1921/22*	
	1,000 Tons	1,000 Gold Roubles	1,000 Tons	1,000 Gold Roubles	1,000 Tons	1,000 Gold Roubles	1,000 Tons	1,000 Gold Roubles
Imports from Great Britain	14	27	1,152	6,018	317,390	61,752	596,185	53,111
Exports to Great Britain	—	—	—	—	104,051	9,344	282,154	17,988

Source: From returns given in Vneshtorg, *Vneshnaya Torgovlya*, 1918–40, pp. 449–70. The values in this table were recorded at current prices in prewar gold roubles where 9.46 roubles = £1.

*Soviet fiscal year.

percent higher than the German product—that Krasin was forced to abandon the idea.[17] Further, the absence of any credit had prompted the Soviets to decide against placing any long-term orders in Britain and to limit themselves to the purchase of manufactured goods.[18] Even so, the Soviets apparently thought it important to convince the British of the efficacy of the agreement. The Russian trade delegation in London published a number of accounts concerning the "preponderance" of British goods imported into Russia during the months immediately following the conclusion of the agreement. Indeed, according to one such report, British goods accounted for 45 percent of the total volume of Soviet imports in May and 39 percent in June.[19] The Soviets had undoubtedly channeled an increased proportion of their purchases to Britain for political reasons. But it is not until the autumn of 1921, when the famine in South Russia reached disastrous dimensions, that the degree to which politics entered into these calculations becomes obvious.

More than anything else, the famine put the Russians against the wall. The remaining gold reserves were needed to pay for imports of foodstuffs and relief supplies. British intransigence on the issue of extending the Export Credit Guarantee Scheme—let alone a governmental loan—did much to damage relations in the long term as well as to deflect Soviet purchases to other countries, primarily the United States.

Table 7.4   Soviet Imports for 1921 (First Nine Months)

	Germany		Great Britain		United States	
	Thousand Poods	% of Total Imports	Thousand Poods	% of Total Imports	Thousand Poods	% of Total Imports
January–March	416.6	14.1%	164.7	5.5%	1,514.0	52.1%
April–June	1,717.5	18.8%	3,309.6	30.6%	313.0	16.4%
July–August	6,082.5	23.0%	8,116.3	32.6%	5,067.4	19.5%

Source: *Ekonomicheskaya Zhizn'*, 6 November 1921.

Despite its official aloofness in its dealings with Soviet Russia, the United States government was one of the first to respond to Russian appeals for famine aid in July 1921. An agreement providing for the delivery and distribution of aid was concluded between the Soviet government and the American Relief Administration in August, and the first shipments of American foodstuffs to South Russia were reported to have been dispatched by the end of the month.[20] Though the ARA was ostensibly a nongovernmental organization, the U.S. government clearly assisted in facilitating American relief efforts. The administration itself was set up and managed by Secretary of Commerce Hoover. The government also volunteered to suspend the prohibitions on the acceptance of Russian gold, allowing the Soviets to deposit $12 million in the United States for the purchase of famine relief supplies.[21] The Congress also moved quickly to provide an initial $20 million in credit to finance further relief purchases in the United States. By February 1922, nearly $53 million had been made available to the ARA for the relief of the Russian famine.[22]

To be sure, the activities of the ARA were not entirely altruistic, and the U.S. government made little effort to hide its ulterior commercial purpose. As a private organization, the ARA was able to provide commercial intelligence "without the risk of implication through government action."[23] The Soviets likewise recognized that American offers of assistance "were not entirely inspired by philanthropic motives"; the idea of "getting a footing in the Russian market" undoubtedly provided a good deal of the motivation for providing aid.[24] Undeniably, however, U.S. efforts to assist to the famine stricken regions of Russia were to some extent genuine; and the relief provided by over $60 million worth of ARA subsidies was very real indeed.

In comparison, the initial reaction of the British government to the news of the famine was one of skepticism. Despite reports from the

British representative in Moscow confirming that the famine was "a real one" and that "relief should be given," British officialdom continued to harbor the suspicion that the crisis was being used "merely as a ploy by the Soviets to gain goods under bogus pretence."[25] Hodgson warned that, having recently entered into an "agreement with a view to commercial advantage," His Majesty's Government would be "placed in an invidious position by standing aloof," and further, that the "neutral attitude" of allowing private organizations to render assistance without government approval seemed "to have nothing in its favour."[26] Despite the potentially devastating propaganda value of such a policy,[27] the British government continued to await the results of a study by the Supreme Council, though that body had not yet even appointed a commission to study the question.[28] Relations were further soured by the British insistence that any extension of credit to the Soviet government, even for use in the purchase of famine relief supplies, should be dependent on Bolshevik recognition of Russian debts and liabilities. After his return from the Paris meeting of the Supreme Council, Lloyd George made a speech in Parliament which did much to arouse Soviet suspicion and resentment. Pointing out that famine relief would have to "come from outside," the prime minister declared that the Soviets would not be able to get these supplies unless they recognized all debts and obligations.

> I am not putting that because I want to take advantage of the famine, in order to get recognition for debts that have been incurred; merely to use the famine for that purpose would be diabolical. I put this because I know it is the shortest road to relief. . . . If the Soviet Government want to create confidence, if they want to get the trading community to come to assist them at this juncture, they must say they will recognise all these obligations. . . . I do not want to take advantage of this dire calamity for the purpose of obtaining acceptance of this principle, but I know this is the best way of dealing with the matter.[29]

The Foreign Office supported the prime minister's decision, though perhaps for slightly different reasons. The appeal by Dr. Nansen's Russian Relief Commission was similarly rebuffed. It was argued that the principle of "non-intervention in Russian affairs ought to be absolute" and credits would simply be intervention in another guise—this time propping up the Soviet government.[30] The "full recognition of debts" and the "provision of real tangible security" were set down as basic requirements for any extension of credit: "If once governments were prepared to ignore the elementary principles upon which credit is given all the world over, they would be striking at the very foundations of confidence between nations."[31] Nansen's attempt to "get around" the issue in order to secure credits for famine relief was seen by the Foreign Office as "simply encouraging the Soviet Government to refuse the only conditions on which Russia's economic recovery are possible."[32]

While at the same time refusing to extend credit for famine relief and donating a mere £194,431 in surplus government medical supplies, there was an increasing British indignation over the American "monopoly of all the relief work in Russia."[33] The United States was seen as elbowing out the British, overshadowing their relief efforts with "piles of dollars."[34] That the Americans were getting all the credit for the relief operations as well as reaping commercial benefits through their less-than-totally philanthropic agencies riled the British considerably.[35] As the returns listed in Table 7.5 show, British relief efforts compared poorly with the proportion of American and German exports that were registered as "non-commercial"—a fact that undoubtedly had much to do with the Soviet government's renewed efforts at improving their relations with the United States. Further, Soviet displeasure over the British policy is apparent in the decline in British exports to Soviet Russia during 1922. As can be seen in Table 7.5, the proportion of Soviet purchases placed in both Germany and the United States increased substantially in 1922, and in the case of Germany, exports of nonrelief goods increased by 59 percent. On the surface, however, diplomatic relations remained unaffected by these developments, and the year 1921 came to a close with the promise of the resolution of the remaining outstanding differences between the Soviet and British governments.

The Year of the Great International Conferences

The lack of any appreciable economic recovery in Europe and the concomitant increase in social unrest prompted the Supreme Council to meet in Cannes in January 1922 to consider the problem of economic reconstruction in Europe. Its resolution made very promising reading for the Soviets, who viewed with satisfaction their invitation to the pending conference. Heartened by the decision to provide for the discussion of credit for the Soviet Union, the Bolshevik authorities were also pleased by the council's admission that the success of the conference depended upon the recognition that "nations can claim no right to dictate to each other regarding the principles on which they are to regulate their system of

Table 7.5   Soviet Trade: Imports according to Origin (in Thousands of Gold Roubles at 1913 Prices)

Country of Origin	Total Imports		Commercial Imports		Noncommercial Imports	
	1921	1922	1921	1922	1921	1922
Great Britain	67,326	58,556	60,561	50,788	6,765	7,768
Germany	58,864	128,145	54,360	91,666	4,504	36,479
United States	49,002	151,279	39,794	38,937	9,208	112,342
Sweden	14,895	14,506	14,249	10,399	601	4,107
Latvia	2,518	23,767	2,022	14,223	496	9,544
Estonia	8,443	13,690	8,377	12,899	66	791
All countries	232,429	458,360	210,003	273,807	22,426	184,553

Source: Hodgson, Moscow, no. 221, Annual Report, "Economic Situation in Russia during 1922," 26 March 1923, FO 371/9364.

ownership, internal economy and government. It is for every nation to choose for itself the system which it prefers in this respect." It was in the closing comments of the resolution, however, that the Soviets found the greatest promise: "If, in order to secure the conditions necessary for the development of the trade in Russia, the Russian government demands official recognition, the Allied powers will be prepared to accord such recognition only if the Russian government accepts [certain] stipulations."[36] It is not surprising that these stipulations included the principle of Soviet recognition of Russian debts and liabilities to foreign creditors and investors. But this provided no problem for the Soviet government, which had in principle already recognized these debts under the terms of the trade agreement.[37] Despite these initial impressions, Lenin nonetheless felt compelled to warn the Allies that "all attempts to impose terms upon us as if we were vanquished are outright nonsense and not worth answering." Chicherin echoed these sentiments, declaring that "we must guard Russia's independence, permitting neither the violation of her sovereign rights nor interference in her domestic affairs."[38]

Though tempered with frequent self-admonitions against expecting too much from the Genoa Conference, Soviet optimism ran high. The hope of gaining credit and expanding trade was obviously a major objective. In his speech at the opening session of the Eleventh Congress of Soviets, Lenin left no doubt as to Soviet aims at Genoa: "We are going to

Genoa not as Communists, but as merchants. We have to trade and so have they. We wish to trade to our advantage and they to theirs. . . . We are going to Genoa with the practical objective of developing our trade and creating favorable conditions for it. . . . I must say that, at the most sober and cautious estimates of the prospectives of Genoa, one can judge without exaggeration that we shall attain this objective."[39]

Britain had also pinned its hopes on this conference. The restoration of normal international trade was imperative to the United Kingdom, whose economy was largely dependent on trade and the servicing of international commerce. A final settlement of the debt problem and the reopening of Russia's full economic potential was seen as a prerequisite for the overall scheme to promote European—and particularly British—recovery. The importance attached to the conference by Britain is reflected in the caliber of the members of the delegation; not content to trust the representation of His Majesty's Government to anyone else, especially the Foreign Office, Lloyd George attended the conference himself. The British delegation was also accompanied by representatives of such business interests as the Russo-Asiatic Consolidated (Leslie Urquhart) and the Becos Trading Company (A. G. Marshall). Indeed, these special advisors far outnumbered Foreign Office representation, which accounted for only three or four of the ninety-one members of the British delegation at Genoa.[40]

The atmosphere of confidence that characterized the beginning of the conference was quickly soured by the private discussions that took place between the Allies at the British villa. Existing Soviet suspicions of Anglo-French collusion and German fears of isolation and Soviet duplicity were intensified by these pourparlers at the Villa d'Albertis. In an attempt to ensure that the Russians would not likewise conspire with the Allies to press for reparations, the Germans reopened the Berlin Treaty negotiations with the Soviet delegation. The resulting conclusion of the Rapallo Treaty caused considerable discord among the conference participants and provided the Allies with fresh evidence of Soviet duplicity.[41]

But it was the question of the settlement of Russian debts and the granting of credit that quickly created the impasse at the Genoa Conference. The Soviet sine qua non for the recognition of any of the debts incurred by the previous Russian governments was the assurance of credit. The Soviets were frustrated, however, by the British insistence upon securing the recognition of debts before even discussing the possibility of credits.[42] Soviet counterclaims against the costs and damages suffered at the hands of the Allied intervention and involvement in the Russian civil war were also brought up by the Soviets. The reciprocal right to claim damages was included in the 1921 trade agreement, providing the Soviet government with a legitimate right to press its claims against Britain—a point that was apparently discounted by the British government. After a cursory discussion amongst the Allied experts (from which the Russian plenipotentiaries were barred), Sir Philip Lloyd-Greame informed the Soviets that the Allies "could accept no liability for the counter claims"; but taking into account the serious economic state of Russia, they were prepared to recommend that the Russian war debt owed by their government "should be reduced to a percentage to be agreed upon."[43] This compromise allowed the negotiations to progress somewhat. Though Chicherin maintained that the terms of the suggested moratorium be defined and the percentage of the debt to be written down should be clearly stated before his government could consider the proposals any further, he was apparently well enough satisfied with them to agree that the finer details be left for the "experts" to settle at a future date.[44]

The Bolsheviks also agreed to pay Russia's prewar foreign obligations, providing that these, too, were reduced considerably and that the Allies consented to grant credit. The argument that it would be useless for the Soviet government to accept the liabilities of such a debt when they were unable to make the payments failed to move the British, who remained firm in their insistence that the Soviets recognize all debts before the subject of credits was discussed.

Compensation and restitution were the issues that caused the conference's ultimate failure. Fundamental disagreements between the Allies precluded the possibility of a broader settlement of the Russian question. French and Belgian intransigence over the issue of full restitution drove a wedge between them and the British, who were willing to consider Soviet compensation along the lines of a concession. Hesitation over breaking an ostensibly united Allied front prevented the British from taking any independent action, causing them to miss an opportunity to settle with the Soviets—at least partially—some of the more contentious issues.

The British memorandum of 2 May put the Allies' differences in relief, with Belgium refusing to sign it and the French withholding their full approval. Declaring that no progress could be made until the Soviets recognized their liabilities, the memorandum outlined the British conditions for any further discussions. It is interesting to note that the terms of the memorandum were considered even by members of the Foreign Office to be unreasonable. Remarking that the memorandum demanded "everything—or practically everything—and offers practically nothing in return," O'Malley went on to point out that "the Russians could not possibly accept it." The only course left open to them would be "to

make it appear that they are not primarily responsible for the failure at Genoa."[45]

Not surprisingly, the Bolshevik response to the British memorandum was bitter. Pointing out that the Allies had consistently ignored their efforts to discuss the possibility of credits or a loan, the Soviets asserted that the conference had "started wrong by imposing the condition that Russia must accept the liability of government debts and individual claims before the examination of this question." It was clear from the number of foreign businessmen engaged in trade and negotiations with the Soviet Union that acceptance of this liability was not necessary for successful commerce. On the settlement of debts, Russia's "good faith" on the question was "shown by her desire not to assume engagements which she cannot carry out. More than one of [the] states at Genoa have repudiated debts [and] have confiscated property of foreigners or own nationals without [the] ostracism meted out to Russia." Citing a number of historical precedents, the Soviets concluded with the assertion that Russia could not be "compelled to assume that responsibility to foreign powers and nationals for annulment of public debts and nationalisation of private property. . . . Legally, Russia is not bound to pay past debts." In the spirit of conciliation, however, and in accordance with the condition of reciprocity as put forward in the third Cannes resolution, the Russian delegation was "prepared to accept [the] liability for public debts, with the exception of war debts."[46]

The Allied response to the Russian memorandum of 11 May was to propose another conference at The Hague in June for the purpose of dealing with "all outstanding questions relating to debts, private property and credits." This proposal was, in effect, an open admission of the failure at Genoa, as *all* questions remained outstanding.

Britain had gone to Genoa with the primary task of securing Soviet recognition of Russian debts and liabilities. It can be assumed from the manner in which this matter was approached that the British were fairly certain that, in light of the economic conditions in Russia, Chicherin would not be able to return to Moscow without some sort of arrangement for foreign assistance. The Rapallo Treaty removed any such pressure, if it ever existed, by bringing the Soviet Union and Germany closer together. Failure to adjust for this development further contributed to the inability to reach a settlement. Even so, it appears that with Chicherin's acceptance of the terms put forward by Lloyd-Greame on 21 April, most of the problems could have been resolved if only the Allies would have agreed to discuss credits. The British government's refusal to recognize the Soviet sine qua non served to back the Russians into a corner and leave

them no acceptable means of reaching a compromise. Finally, the British memorandum of 2 May and the subsequent Soviet reply illustrated the growing rigidity in the positions of both those governments, with the result that whatever progress had been made was quickly lost.

Genoa and the Politics of Oil

While the Genoa Conference did little to improve the state of affairs between Britain and Soviet Russia, it had put considerable strain on inter-Allied relations. Contention over the issue of Russian oil went far to disrupt what remained of the united front against the Bolsheviks. Although the United States refused to participate in the conference, American interests certainly did not go unrepresented. The question of Soviet compensation and restoration of properties was a major concern for the two oil-producing giants of the world—Shell and Standard Oil—and it was the competition between these two companies that provoked much of the irritation between the Allies at Genoa.

Undeterred by the withdrawal of British troops from the region at the end of 1920, both Shell and Standard Oil continued to vie for control of Russia's petroleum resources. Competition between British and American oilmen had become so fierce by the middle of 1920 that the Foreign Office remarked that "oil [was] thicker than blood."[47] By the autumn of 1921 representatives of Shell and the Soviet government had begun serious discussions concerning the possibility of the company operating vast tracts of oil-bearing lands under a new concession. Declaring itself to be anxious to help Shell "as much as possible" in its attempts to regain control of its Russian properties, the British government was nonetheless restricted by the fact that it could not intervene on behalf of a primarily Dutch-owned company. However, once the Russian companies in question were transferred to British control, the Petroleum Department was "prepared to take the necessary steps to afford [Shell] governmental assistance."[48]

By the same token, there was considerable British anxiety over the rumor that Standard Oil had entered into negotiations with the Soviets for a similar concession. The British government attached great importance to "getting this concession into the hands of people who are under [British] influence rather than that of the Standard Oil Company"; to that end, the government offered Shell its "full approval and support" in the company's negotiations for the three Russian oilfields of Emba, Grozny, and Baku.[49] While the government had made sure that Krasin was well

aware of its position, it nonetheless was concerned that "the negotiations between the Shell and the Russians should not become known."[50]

From the outset, the Genoa Conference "fairly oozed oil."[51] Both Shell and Standard dispatched officials to Genoa to ensure that their interests were properly represented at the conference. According to the press, Genoa was "full of carefully camouflaged representatives of one of the biggest interests in Russian . . . oil."[52] There was much jockeying for advantage among governments and oil companies alike at Genoa—each jealously guarding against any possible encroachment on their Russian petroleum interests. Rumors that a comprehensive agreement had been concluded between Shell and the Soviet government, combined with the British government's definition of a "previous owner," which, according to its memorandum of 2 May, conveniently precluded Standard from claiming the Nobel properties the company purchased in 1920, provoked Standard to make strong representations to the State Department.[53] Protesting against "any recognition of any nationalization of privately owned oil properties or any disposition of oil properties so nationalized," Standard Oil went on to request that the State Department intervene "for the protection of American interests in Russia."[54] Despite denials by both Shell and the Soviet government that any such deal had been struck, the State Department nonetheless issued a statement which declared that "the United States will never consent that any scheme whatsoever, national or international, shall be applied unless it takes account of the principle of the open door for all and recognizes equal rights for all."[55]

Officially, however, the British remained obtuse. Though assured by Shell that the "rumoured deal [was] entirely without foundation in fact," the government still refused "to be forced by the Standard into making any public statement about the alleged Shell concession."[56] Pointing out that there was "nothing to show that our attitude has altered" since the British government undertook to support Shell in its negotiations with the Soviet government, or that His Majesty's Government would "not welcome and support the kind of agreement which the press alleges actually to have been come to," the Foreign Office advised against issuing any denial that could be taken to mean official disapproval of such a concession in principle.[57] It was decided that it would be "undesirable to say anything which might hamper us in the future from supporting the Shell's application for an inclusive concession of this kind. I have no doubt the Standard would take a concession for the whole of the four Russian oilfields if they could get it. . . . It is entirely to our interest that the Shell rather than the Standard should be in this strong position."[58] Despite the initial stand taken against Standard, the absence of "a definite and consis-

tent oil policy" plagued the British government not only in its policy toward Standard Oil but in its relations with the United States as well. While it was considered to be particularly important "to disabuse foreign and especially American opinion of the idea that the government used the oil companies of London as pawns in a game of commercial imperialism," the essence of the struggle over Russian oil nonetheless boiled down to whether Britain could "afford to fight the Standard Oil Company or whether we must continue to submit to their blackmailing methods."[59]

It was, of course, natural that the governments of both Great Britain and the United States were concerned with promoting the interests of their nationals. In the case of Shell and Standard Oil, however, there is evidence that this concern was intimately connected with the governmental hopes of acquiring control of strategic oil reserves—to the exclusion of the other if possible. Petroleum interests were seen as playing a "very important part in the future settlement of the economic questions in Europe," and the "three main interests [were] American, British and Russian." Competing for this resource on the "same ground for the first time," these two companies—backed by their respective governments —came into open conflict at Genoa. While neither interest got what it wanted out of Genoa, the Soviets undoubtedly benefited from this contest over oil. The division and squabbling among the Allies and associated powers at Genoa served to emphasize the importance attached to this resource, ultimately strengthening the Soviets bargaining position and giving them the ability to play one concern against the other.

The Hague Conference

Unlike Genoa, there was a distinct lack of enthusiasm for The Hague Conference and more skepticism than optimism over what it might achieve. Positions on the basic issues had hardened on both sides, with neither showing any tendency toward compromise. Further, the failure to invite German participation, combined with the exclusion of any Soviet representation whatsoever from the preliminary meeting at The Hague on 15 June appeared to be a calculated effort to weaken the Russian position vis-à-vis the Allied powers.[60] Though warned by an old Genoa hand against preparing "a cut and dried plan" for presentation to the Soviet delegation, the British nonetheless undertook to settle all outstanding differences among the Allies before the conference was convened, enabling them to present the Soviets with a fait accompli.[61]

As the policy of the Allied governments remained largely unchanged, a

settlement at the Hague would have been possible only if the Soviets had radically modified their previous position. While it was hoped that the famine and the worsening internal economic situation would force the Bolsheviks into a more compromising position, it is apparent from the composition of and the considerably restricted powers accorded to the British delegation that His Majesty's Government entertained little serious hope on this score.[62] Unwilling to risk his reputation on yet another potentially disastrous international conference, Lloyd George stayed safely away from The Hague, sending instead representatives from the Board of Trade and the Foreign Office.

The atmosphere in Russia prior to this conference was described as one of nervousness and uncertainty.[63] With Lenin temporarily incapacitated by the first of the strokes he was to suffer, and with the economic situation in Russia showing little improvement by the summer of 1922, the Soviet government was preoccupied with other, more pressing problems. Although it was officially stated that the government expected little from The Hague Conference, there nonetheless remained the vague hope that an agreement with Western Europe could yet be reached.[64]

The Soviet government, however, firmly adhered to the conditions set forth in its memorandum of 11 May, declaring that "unless credits were discussed, any discussion of debts would be pointless."[65] But the first session, while underscoring the increasing truculence of the Allies, tended to show that the Soviets were somewhat less intractable than their official statements suggested. Communications received at the Foreign Office from British representatives at The Hague pointed out that in public the Soviets maintained the position that they could not admit any principle of restitution or compensation and refused to recognize debts except on the condition of obtaining credit.[66] Their speeches at the conference, however, were in "marked contrast to those which the Russians made at Genoa." Further, it seemed "fairly clear" from the private conversations between the British and Soviet representatives at The Hague that the Russians were "prepared in practice to go very far towards meeting [British] requirements, if they can be convinced that by so doing the credit resources of Western Europe will be made available to them."[67]

Despite Krasin's more amenable disposition, there remained the difficulty of the French and the Belgians, whose intransigence again proved a major stumbling block in the conference.[68] Any joint settlement with the Russians depended upon these two allies who would undoubtedly be very reluctant to come to any agreement which could in any way be held to imply recognition of the right to nationalise property.

If they continue to maintain this attitude the question will at once arise as to whether we are to continue the Conference without them. If we do, I have little doubt that we shall arrive at a satisfactory settlement. If we do not, every country will be automatically freed to make its own arrangements with the Russian. Again, I have little doubt that if this course is taken, we can make a very satisfactory arrangement with the Soviet Government.[69]

The question was whether Britain would be "prepared to make a deal with Russia if she offers terms which [the British] consider reasonable and which the French do not." With Anglo-French relations already dangerously strained over the Greco-Turkish war, it was decided that the risk of further alienating the French by making a separate deal with the Russians was not worth any of the potential benefits that such a settlement might yield.[70]

With this decision, the negotiations at The Hague were once again hopelessly deadlocked over the same issues that brought the Genoa Conference to an impasse. Stating that no further progress was possible, the Subcommission on Private Property declared an end to its sitting. By 14 June all three of the subcommissions had ceased their discussions, and The Hague Conference was likewise in jeopardy of ending in failure. It was at this point that Litvinov insisted on the convening of a plenary session in which he aired a fresh proposal: if the delegates were amenable, he would inquire of Moscow "whether the Russian government consents to recognize the obligations of the former Russian Governments to foreign citizens even if credits . . . would not be available at the present time."[71] A similar inquiry was made concerning compensation for nationalized property as well. Heralded as being of "extraordinary importance" and as representing "a new epoch in their negotiations," Litvinov's proposal to wire for fresh instructions along those lines appeared to have broken the deadlock.[72] Despite the interest expressed, the non-Russian delegations met and declared The Hague Conference closed only one day after Litvinov had agreed to wire his government—that is, without waiting to hear Moscow's answer. It was this decision that removed any hope of Britain reaching a satisfactory settlement on the questions of debts and compensation.

Anglo-Soviet Relations: An Uneasy Coexistence

The failure of The Hague Conference marked the beginning of a decline in Anglo-Soviet relations. Negotiating from a position of increasing strength by the end of 1922, the Soviet government was no longer forced to compromise its principles in order to survive. With the more immediate and pressing demands of the famine having been alleviated by a good harvest, the first signs of recovery in the Soviet economy had begun to make themselves felt.[73] It was now up to Moscow to decide "whether it was worthwhile to pay the price for foreign assistance."[74] That the Soviet government had begun to consider this price too high can be seen in Lenin's refusal to ratify the extensive concession agreement negotiated with Leslie Urquhart.

In September 1922, after over a year of discussions, a contract was drawn up by Urquhart and Krasin for the return of the Russo-Asiatic properties as a concession. Described as a breakthrough in Anglo-Soviet relations, the contract was seen as proof that politics could be put aside when "two practical men" talked business.[75] Political developments quickly overshadowed the future of the agreement, however, as the contract was presented to Moscow for ratification at the same time as the crisis over Turkey threatened to cause a breach in Anglo-Soviet relations.[76] On 9 October the Sovnarkom voted overwhelmingly against the ratification of the contract.[77] The "unsatisfactory nature of the political relations existing between Soviet Russia and Great Britain" was stated as being responsible for the rejection of the Urquhart agreement. This decision was clearly meant to be "regarded as punishment for British action in the Near Eastern Question."[78]

The more secure position of the Soviet government permitted it to be increasingly selective in its foreign purchasing as well as in the concessions it was ready to consider. Prepared to wait for credit, the Soviet government considerably decreased its cash purchases abroad in 1923.[79] Moreover, Soviet purchases generally were being channeled away from Britain in favor of the United States and Germany. During the last quarter of 1922, U.S. and German exports to Soviet Russia were respectively four and three times greater than those from the United Kingdom.[80]

The fall of Lloyd George's coalition government in October 1922 marked the beginning of the Conservative government's "frost-bitten diplomacy" with Moscow.[81] Power was restored to the Foreign Office, and Curzon —finally free of Lloyd George's short lead—was able to pursue what he saw as a more decisive policy with regard to the Soviets.

By January 1923, relations had already deteriorated to the point where

Krasin was compelled to inform his government that "practically we have no political relations at all with England at the moment, and as I expected, Bonar Law and his Cabinet colleagues display no wish to meet or negotiate with us."[82] Concerned over the increasingly strained state of Anglo-Soviet relations during the spring of 1923, Commander J. M. Kenworthy accused the government of going "out of its way to pin-prick and annoy the Russian government," and called for a debate in the Commons on "the present policy of this country with regard to Russia."[83]

Relations had reached a new low at the end of March, when news of the trial and forthcoming execution of ecclesiastics in Soviet Russia caused the British representative in Moscow to lodge an official protest. The reply to Hodgson's note was unreservedly hostile, accusing Britain of interfering in Russian affairs and declaring that His Majesty's Government was guilty of far worse sorts of political executions. Pronouncing the Soviet response unacceptable, Hodgson refused to receive it.[84] Having debated for some time the merits of breaking off relations with Moscow, the British government decided to consider this move. Not surprisingly, the Foreign Office supported such a route. On 5 April Gregory noted that "we appear to have reached a point where a definite rupture would have a very serious prospect of damaging the Soviet government and, if not immediately bringing it down, at least of creating a situation which may ultimately lead to its dissolution from within. . . . It is a chance which may not readily recur, and we ought not to let it slip."[85]

The situation came to a head on 8 May when the Soviet government was presented with the so-called Curzon Ultimatum. Charging the Soviets with violation of the trade agreement through their continued propaganda activities in Asia, the British government threatened Moscow with an immediate rupture in relations unless it undertook, within ten days, "to comply fully and unconditionally" with British terms.[86]

The fact that the British note was in the form of an ultimatum took the Soviets "completely by surprise." It was interpreted as "denoting a fixed intention to break with Russia whatever the reply might be."[87] Although it undoubtedly stirred considerable resentment and indignation in Soviet Russia, Moscow was not prepared to risk severed trade negotiations with Britain, and its reply was largely conciliatory.[88]

On 22 May, in the middle of the crisis, Bonar Law was succeeded by Stanley Baldwin. The change in leadership was seen as having a moderating influence on the anti-Bolshevik "diehards," like Curzon, who were pushing for a rupture.[89] Himself a businessman, Baldwin was credited with being "alive to the dangers involved for this country in the breaking-off of relations with Russia. His influence may, therefore, be counted upon to combat the possibly unintentional but undoubtedly provocative stiffness of our Foreign Office in its dealings with the Soviet Republics."[90]

On 23 May the British government was further placated by the receipt of another conciliatory note from Moscow. Agreeing to pay all claims of compensation raised in the Curzon note, and offering the "unqualified withdrawal" of the Narkomindel's communications with Hodgson, the Soviet government had settled on all issues except that of propaganda, which it suggested should be discussed separately. Having achieved what it perceived as a victory over the Bolsheviks, the British government declared itself satisfied on 20 June, and "normal" relations were resumed.[91]

There was, however, an increasingly vocal group that felt that Anglo-Soviet relations should be placed on a more satisfactory footing. A growing number of large, respected businesses and industrial concerns were coming out in favor of de jure recognition of the Soviet government, arguing that their expanding interests in Russia might be better served by closer diplomatic relations. To be sure, there remained a fair number of bondholders and conservative organizations that stood fast against such a move; signatories of the so-called Paris Resolution (which included such organizations as the Association of British Creditors, the London Chamber of Commerce, and the British-Russia Club) continued to demand that recognition of the Soviet government be postponed until guarantees of restitution and compensation were given. Even so, it became apparent early on that there would be a "stiff fight" between the bondholders and the industrialists over this issue.[92] By the end of the year, even a number of those organizations which had previously opposed recognition had changed tack, coming out in favor of the government "taking such steps as would enable trade between the two countries to be developed and extended as rapidly as possible."[93]

The official disposition to extend recognition to the Soviet government was substantially modified by the Labour party's victory in the general election of 1923.[94] On 1 February 1924, having faced considerably less opposition than one would have imagined, MacDonald's government extended de jure recognition to the government of the USSR.[95]

Curiously, recognition was to herald the beginning of another, more serious deterioration in Anglo-Soviet relations. The continued refusal to extend the Export Credits Scheme to cover trade with Russia—though there was nothing to prevent the British government from doing so—caused resentment in Moscow, and contributed to the feeling of uncertainty and growing isolation that developed during the period immediately after Lenin's death in January 1924.[96] Further, the failure of the British government to ratify the laboriously negotiated Anglo-Soviet Commercial Treaties in late November confirmed the belief that Soviet Russia must be "prepared to manage without the foreigner."[97] This atmosphere of uneasy coexistence rapidly deteriorated toward the end of 1924, erupting into open hostility over the "discovery" of the "Zinoviev Letter." Anglo-Soviet relations were plunged into a new era of suspicion, which was ultimately to result in the Arcos raid in 1926 and the severance of relations in 1927.

The American Answer to the Russian Question: A Policy of Inaction

Official U.S. policy remained virtually unchanged during this period. Nonrecognition and a laissez faire attitude, which permitted trade at the businessman's own risk, formed the basis of American policy toward the Soviet government until 1933. Although nonrecognition remained de rigueur, the emphasis of the policy shifted noticeably from "risk" to "trade," and by 1923–24, there was a marked increase in the number of governmental officials who favored some sort of trade agreement with the Soviet government while avoiding recognition.

The change in administration in 1921 had given rise to Soviet hopes of a thaw in U.S.-Soviet relations; however, Harding was quick to reaffirm the policy of his predecessor: "International good faith forbids any sort of sanction of the Bolshevist policy. The prosperity of American citizens in Russia, honestly acquired under the laws then existing, had been taken without the color of compensation, without process of law, by the mere emission of countless decrees. Such a policy challenges the very groundwork of righteous intercourse among peoples and rends the basis of good faith everywhere in the world."[98]

When Coolidge took office in 1923 the Soviets again approached the United States with the hope of negotiating a settlement. Any aspirations were quickly dashed, however, as that administration had much the same message as Harding. In response to Soviet feelers, Secretary of State Hughes asserted that if the Soviet government intended to comply with the American conditions, nothing prevented negotiations; in the meantime, however, no reason for negotiation existed.[99]

Although the U.S. government stood firmly against having any direct dealings with Soviet Russia, it nonetheless remained strongly committed to allowing every opportunity for its citizens to do business there. Secretary of Commerce Hoover effectively encouraged American firms to trade with Russia by informing them that they need not "anticipate interference on the part of this government."[100] Officially confirming this position in

December 1923, President Coolidge stated that the U.S. government offered "no objection to the carrying on of commerce by our citizens with
the people of Russia."[101] Moreover, as early as mid-1921, the Commerce
Department had begun to take positive steps to aid American concerns
interested in Russian trade. Apparently prompted by the fear that the
Anglo-Soviet Trade Agreement would give the British an edge in the
market, the department even undertook to remind commercial circles of
the possible business opportunities in Russia.[102]

American merchants interested in doing business with Soviet Russia
undoubtedly had a strong ally in Secretary of Commerce Hoover. Often
at odds with Secretary of State Hughes (who opposed any direct relations
with Soviet Russia whatsoever), Hoover pushed incessantly for greater
freedom in U.S.-Soviet commercial relations. He was convinced that direct U.S.-Soviet trade was a necessity if there was to be any hope at all of
preserving the "future Russian market for U.S. domination."[103] Hoover
disagreed especially with Hughes's position of allowing American business to continue to be conducted primarily through European middlemen; any permanent American foreign commerce, he argued, should not
be based upon the reshipment of American goods by other nationals.[104]

By the middle of 1921 the Soviets were anxious to reduce the importance of intermediaries in Russian foreign trade and had begun to divert
trade from Estonia and the other Baltic states to Britain and Germany
"where direct purchases can be made." The "Bolsheviks [were] tiring of
the practice of paying high commissions upon goods, particularly in
Esthonia."[105] The British and American merchants who had engaged in
such transit trade certainly shared these sentiments. While it was noted
that this indirect business had undoubtedly helped "to put the Baltic
States on their feet" it also had the effect of increasing the cost of the
goods sold, as well as resulting in a consequent loss of profits to the
merchant.[106]

The situation was considered by many to be unsatisfactory, and from
1921 onward, the once-small lobby that supported closer relations with
the Soviet government gained in numbers and strength. The Americans,
like the British, tended to ascribe considerable importance to the Russian
market as a means to boost employment in the United States. In addition
to those businessmen who saw themselves losing this trade to other countries or—at best—losing money through the use of European middlemen, an increasing number of government officials was also supporting
this move. There had long been a small group of senators and congressmen who openly advocated recognition. Senator Borah, one of the most
vocal of this group, repeatedly used trade conditions to convince his

audience of the necessity of "normalizing" these relations. American merchants he asserted, were suffering because of the government's policy. There were "fourteen nations that are doing business with Russia, have their diplomatic missions in Russia, are trading and carrying out business with Russia, and they are not losing any money." American merchants, however, were compelled to do their business with Russia "through another country"—primarily Britain—and were consequently losing money because they had to pay a commission.[107]

While the argument for recognition continued to fall on deaf ears, the logic behind allowing American merchants more direct contact with the Soviet purchasing organizations had apparently struck home. By 1923 there were five Soviet purchasing agencies operating in America with the blessings of the U.S. government: Arcos America, Centrosoyus America, Selskosoyus America, the Products Exchange Corporation, and the Import and Export Company of America.[108] There were also several American firms, like the Allied American Corporation, which had agreed to act as commercial agents for the Soviet government. Direct trade was further facilitated by an agreement between the State Bank of the RSFSR and the Guaranty Trust Company, whereby the latter had agreed to act on behalf of the State Bank in the United States. In addition to securing the services of the Guaranty Trust, a number of commercial banks in New York had also been named as correspondents.[109]

The absence of any formal agreement certainly did not hinder the development of American trade with Soviet Russia. Indeed, U.S. exports to Russia had nearly doubled between 1921 and 1922, increasing from $15.6 million to $29.9 million. It is also interesting to note that the value of U.S. exports for 1922 was some $3.8 million greater than that for 1913. Moreover, the value of American exports to Russia had overtaken that of both Britain and Germany during that year.[110] This gave ample ammunition to those who opposed recognition: it was argued—with considerable justification—that no significant difference in trade would be made by either a trade agreement or recognition.[111]

The Soviets were more than willing to do business with American merchants and industrialists despite the U.S. government's policy of nonrecognition and the general absence of credit. At least partially the result of the worsening relations with Britain, the growing number of orders placed in the United States also represented an attempt to cultivate closer Soviet-American relations. Trade was increasingly being used as a political lever: it was observed by the Foreign Office that "when important orders are under consideration, political interests may outweigh commercial considerations. Orders may be placed with countries where it is desired to secure support in view of pending political negotiations and ostentatiously canceled if political disputes arise."[112] Indeed, the absence of a U.S.-Soviet agreement was considered by some to be a distinct advantage; that American traders got "all the business because the U.S. government *has not* recognised Russia."[113]

More important, however, was the Soviet predilection for all things American. Hoover was not far off the mark when he observed that Americans were "infinitely more popular in Russia" than any other nationality.[114] This affinity was certainly reflected in the Soviet preference for American goods. Indeed, it was no secret that, while European offers were "acceptable," "American orders [were] preferred."[115] This preference was to a large extent due to the fact that the Soviets "identified" with the United States: "The basic elements of the Soviet economy—vast areas and populations and an increasing demand for goods—creates a situation which American experience is especially fitted to meet." To this end, the Soviets saw the United States as "a model of industrial technique" and endeavored to "develop its industries along American lines."[116] In particular, the Soviets were obsessed by Ford's assembly line method, and "Fordizatsia" quickly became synonymous with efficient and modern production techniques.[117]

Despite this preference, even the United States was not spared from feeling the effects of the Soviet government's growing confidence. In September 1922 the State Department made preliminary inquiries concerning the dispatch of a commission to Russia "to investigate the economic conditions of that country so as to be better prepared to aid potential investors and be armed with relevant information for trade." Having refused Soviet Russia the reciprocal right to send a commission, the State Department was informed that there were already enough American "advisors" and "commercial" people on Russian soil.[118] No longer in such dire need of the capital or credit of the Western countries, Soviet Russia was able to exercise a greater degree of autonomy in the pursuit of its foreign—and even its domestic—policy.[119]

By 1924, official nonrecognition notwithstanding, a "long list of American manufacturing concerns" were reportedly engaged in "supplying [Russia's] post-revolutionary needs on a credit basis with the backing of American banks." Moreover, Britain's recognition of the Soviet government had the effect of boosting American interest in the Russian market. The Allied American Corporation noted that, since British recognition, it was receiving "twice as many inquiries from American concerns desirous of marketing their products in Russia" as compared with before.[120]

Hoover, however, believed that the "really important problem confronting American businessmen with respect to Russia [was] not that of trade but of investment. Without a large investment of foreign capital as a means of restoring production, the prospects are that, at least for some years to come, there will be even less opportunity to sell goods to Russia than in 1921."[121] Accordingly, Hoover maintained that "the hope of our commerce lies in the establishment of American firms abroad, distributing American goods under American direction, in the building of direct American financing and, above all, in the installation of American technology in Russian industries." Moreover, he had no doubt that it would be Americans who would "undertake the leadership in the reconstruction of Russia when the proper moment arrives."[122]

But the majority of both American and British businessmen were unwilling to invest money into what was as yet an unknown market, preferring instead to limit themselves to the more immediate returns of commerce. Even so, the capacity of the market seemed endless, and the Soviet's prompt discharge of all obligations did much to erase the memory of confiscation and repudiation.

8

The Pursuit
of the New
Eldorado

Growing British confidence in the Soviet
market was somewhat soured, however,
by the rather rocky course of Anglo-Soviet
political relations throughout the early 1920s. Outrage over the Bolshevik treatment of Russian ecclesiastics and the seizure of British trawlers, combined with the increasing friction over the Soviet
violations of the conditions of the trade agreement,
brought the possibility of a rupture to a head in the
early spring of 1923. Despite such trouble on the
diplomatic front, Anglo-Soviet trade continued to
expand during this period, and merchants and industrialists who did do business with the Soviets
had few complaints. To be sure, Foreign Office records do contain a number of letters relating particularly disastrous encounters with the Russians;
it was, however, "the usual rule for British firms to
abstain from giving any information unless they
happened to find themselves in difficulties."[1] It is
evident from the wave of protest from commercial
and industrial circles over the possibility of a breach
in Anglo-Soviet relations that successful business
dealings far outweighed those that elicited complaint. Protests against such action were received

from numerous firms and organizations that had considerable interest in the maintenance of good relations.[2]

That commercial opinion mattered is evident from the Foreign Office's concern over the possible charges that could be leveled against the government if it broke off relations. Accordingly, Gregory pointed out that a rupture in relations was a weapon that could only be used once, and therefore should be used "for striking at the propitious moment to upset the Soviet Government." Until that time, however, he advised that any official protest "should take the form of withdrawing all of our people from Russia, but here only ejecting the actual officials of the Russian Trade Delegation . . . while leaving Arcos untouched. If we do this, we can meet the criticism that we are totally destroying all trade with Russia and we can say that we have no objection to trade being carried out at the risk of the trader—as in fact is the case now as far as Americans and French."[3] Although obviously concerned with appearances, the Foreign Office nonetheless justified its stand by asserting that Britain had not benefited from the trade agreement. Indeed, it was maintained that "British business interest in Russia is at present so small that it need not be taken into account in considering the political case for or against a rupture."[4]

The Foreign Office was quickly disabused of this opinion. The Board of Trade, for one, remained unconvinced of the desirability of such a move. Arguing that the negation of the trade agreement would have detrimental effects on direct trade relations, the board went on to name a number of specific contracts and deals that would undoubtedly suffer. The Foreign Office was also reminded that a rupture would jeopardize London's growing role as the financial center for Russian foreign banking business and, further, discourage those "older firms" who were only just beginning to interest themselves in Russia again.[5]

Considerable opposition to the policy of a breach manifested itself early on in Parliament as well. Ramsay MacDonald believed that for Britain to negate the trade agreement would be "foolish in the extreme." Citing some £12 million per annum in trade, MacDonald declared that Anglo-Soviet trade was "not exactly a trade to be thrown away in a reckless way as if you could afford to do without it. . . . [The trade agreement] keeps the doors open." Having mentioned a letter from Ruston and Hornby in which that firm protested any rupture in relations, MacDonald was challenged by Undersecretary of State McNeill, who declared that his inquiries had found that the "great preponderating mass of instructed, expert business opinion" maintained that, if the agreement were to be terminated, "it would not have any harmful effects upon our trade and employment." This view elicited considerable parliamentary scorn and disbelief, with shouts from the benches demanding "Who are they?" and comments such as "They are not the cloth people nor machine people either."[6]

The position of British industrialists and traders on the issue of normalized relations with Russia was increasingly "diametrically at variance with the British politicians."[7] Those firms and industries that stood to lose from any disruption in Russian trade were quick to express their concern and opposition to the government's move to sever relations. While it was admitted that, as late as 9 May, "no letters have so far been received from important commercial bodies in support of the Russian policy of H.M. Government other than the letter from the Association of British Creditors," the number of protests against the policy swelled as the crisis over the Curzon Ultimatum developed.[8] Indeed, by 28 May, the Foreign office had received over two hundred resolutions and some fifty private communications *opposing* the proposal to cancel the trade agreement with Russia.[9] A large number of contracts with a variety of manufacturers and commercial concerns were declared to be at stake, the loss of which would cause "definite and grave injury" to the businesses concerned.[10] Appalled by the government's proposal to cancel the trade agreement with Russia, Sir Allen Smith of the Engineering Employers' Federation pointed out that such an action would separate the British trader from "what might be our very best and most profitable market." These concerns were particularly valid for the interests Sir Allen represented: "In view of the work being done for Russia here and the orders we have recently received for manufactures, I hope that we shall not lose the only sheet anchor we have."[11]

Russian business was clearly still seen by many as a palliative to Britain's economic ills. It was believed that the improved economic conditions in Russia would permit the development of that market, the expansion of which was seen as essential in relieving unemployment in Britain. Further, it was increasingly argued that the absence of normal diplomatic relations with the Soviet government stood as a "serious impediment to the development of commercial relations," which "consequently contributed to the aggravated volume of unemployment" in Britain. Indeed, it was maintained that the unsatisfactory state of Anglo-Soviet relations had "greatly interfered with the machine tool industry and with other sections of the engineering industry."[12] While the British government was refusing to negotiate with the Soviets for a reasonable settlement of past differences, there were "two million unemployed and partly-employed workers in this country, and there are millions of Russians desirous of purchasing products, the manufacture of which in this country would lessen the number of those unemployed and relieve the dead weight of unproductive expenditure upon the State."[13] It was "only for want of credit" that Soviet orders to the value of many millions of pounds were not being placed in Britain.[14]

Despite the official position, London financial circles had evidenced a distinct change in attitude by the autumn. Although the City was "still sore" about the repudiation of debts, banks had begun to offer credit on ordinary commercial lines to firms trading with Russia.[15] Birch Crisp of the British Bank for Foreign Trade had even described Russia as "one of the bright spots on the commercial horizon." Noting this softening, the *Financial News* remarked that while the circumstances may not have changed politically, they certainly had changed commercially.[16] Nor was the City's change of heart lost on the Soviets, who were quick to point out that while the British politicians continued to maintain the position that the Soviet Union did not "deserve confidence or credit," the banks thought otherwise. "Negotiations with the chief London banks and branches of American banks for credits amounting to tens of millions of roubles are in a satisfactory state; when it is not a matter of politics but of a good rate of interest bankers are not against granting loans."[17] In short, British financial circles had begun to see the "enormous" possibilities of the Russian market, and it was "certainly not in the national interests—financial, commercial or economic—that we should see it fall into other hands."[18]

Similar sentiments were expressed by the engineering industry, a sector particularly hard hit by the postwar economic slump.[19] Ruston and Hornby, for example, was forced to lay off nearly two-thirds of its work force and sell its machinery below cost in order "to keep in business at all."[20] Formerly "much interested" in trade with the Ukraine, the company was "very anxious to secure a fresh foothold" in what was described as a "most promising agricultural area," which was expected to "absorb a heavy proportion of the better class of agricultural machinery" imported by Soviet Russia.[21] But it was the huge task of rebuilding Soviet industry that was seen as presenting the greatest opportunities for British business. The Russian petroleum industry was of particular British commercial interest: the Russian oilfields needed large quantities of tin plates, wire rope and piping, machinery, boilers, and other plant. It was anticipated that, "as the Russians are anxious to work the field fully there should be good openings." Engineering firms like Vickers, Babcock and Wilcox, Ruston and Hornby, and the Leeds Forge Company—as well as a number of manufacturers of steel wire rope and piping—were all quick to take advantage of this need.[22]

Becos Traders, an association representing some eighty "important engineering works," was especially interested in developing the Russian market. In August, the organization decided to dispatch a delegation to Russia in order to examine the possibilities for business there.[23] News that filtered back from the Becos delegation visiting Russia that summer fired considerable interest among British manufacturers. Themselves no lightweight industrialists, it is unlikely that the members of the mission would have been susceptible to any propaganda the Soviets may have attempted. Even so, the delegation declared itself "unanimously optimistic as to the future": Russia, it concluded, would provide an "enormous market . . . for British goods of all classes."[24]

By the autumn of 1923 it was noted that contracts were being entered into in such numbers that it would have been "incredible without the fullest confidence of each of the contracting parties in each other."[25] Even the Foreign Office was forced to admit that British trade with Soviet Russia "may be said to be satisfactory." The Soviets had "invariably promptly carried out their engagements. A number of firms who have had considerable experience have not hesitated to grant trade credit for as long as a period of 6 months against bills endorsed by Arcos, or alternatively, by the Russian State Bank. No case of protest on maturity has been recorded. . . . Trade terms and methods have not been called into question."[26] Indeed, Arcos had "established a reputation for fair trade and fulfillment of obligations which has justified British firms in granting credit facilities."[27]

Even certain of those firms which had suffered expropriation or nationalization at the hands of the Soviets now saw fit to extend credit. As early as September, Vickers had concluded a contract with the Soviet government for the construction and equipping of power stations in Russia, the terms of which allowed credit up to seven years.[28] Although Vickers was admittedly "one of the most enterprising firms in capturing Russian business," this measure caused considerable surprise. Even the Foreign Office, which had been told "some time ago that this was on the tapis," knew nothing of the seven-year credit.[29] The company's early decision to extend long-term credit was undoubtedly a determining factor in their successful bid for this contract. That both parties found their business relations to be satisfactory is evident from the fact that equipment and plant for eleven of the seventeen power plant projects undertaken by the Soviet government between 1920 and 1930 were supplied by Metro-Vickers.[30]

Like many other engineering firms, Vickers had suffered a sharp fall in profits in 1922, a condition largely due to the decline in British foreign trade generally. All of Vickers's departments had watched orders as well as profits drop off during that year, and conditions at the company's shipyards at Barrow were reportedly the worst in the firm's history.[31] The possibility of large Soviet orders was certainly not unwelcome; while at the same time offering Vickers a chance to recoup some of its earlier losses in Russia, this business was also seen as a means of redressing its more immediate economic difficulties.

In addition to promoting its other Soviet business interests, Vickers had put considerable pressure on the government to allow the realization of a number of Soviet contracts for war materials.[32] Applying for permission to export five hundred submarine mines to Soviet Russia in the spring of 1923, Vickers pointed out the serious shortage of work at their naval construction works at Barrow, declaring that the condition would be "considerably relieved" if they were permitted to carry out the order. Moreover, Vickers assured the Admiralty that, if the contract was not placed in Britain, there was "every probability that it [would] be placed on the continent."[33] While this position was noted as being the "usual Vickers argument," the firm was undoubtedly concerned over the loss of this business to "less scrupulous" nations.[34] Although the Soviets were "trying their best to place orders in England," the policy of His Majesty's Government had "helped a good many large orders to go away to works in other countries." Because of the "obstacles placed by [British] authorities," Vickers was losing "frequent and large orders for Russia, which could have alone solved the unemployment problem in England."[35] Britain was, the company complained, "very much behind others with regards to obtaining Russian orders." There was apparently considerable truth in this: during a three-week period, the Soviet government had placed orders in France for the delivery of armaments and war matériel to the value of seven million gold roubles.[36]

Despite the official position on the export of armaments to Soviet Russia, Vickers continued to negotiate openly with the Soviets for the sale of armament matériel.[37] Moreover, on at least two occasions during the spring of 1923, that company had successfully pressed for the issue of export licenses for goods that clearly fell under government prohibitions. In both cases, Vickers informed the government that negotiations had reached the stage where the assurance of an export license being granted was required. The company emphasized the "great importance of such licenses being granted"; pointing out its continued problem of unemployment, Vickers stressed that if the licenses were to be refused, it would be "obliged to discharge men owing to the impossibility of keeping our factories at work."[38] Broad hints were also made that governmental interests would be affected should this business be lost. The successful culmination of negotiations for the delivery of six hundred Vickers machine guns to the Soviet government would not only "create very considerable employment" in Britain, it would also ensure the continued operation of those works:

> This material is not manufactured in this country by others than ourselves, and such contracts enable us to keep in constant employment those technical experts and skilled mechanicians requisite to the manufacture of this material for H.M. Government.
>
> This contract would provide employment for approximately one thousand men over four months, to be followed by an order giving employment to 1400 men over ten months.
>
> We venture to conclude, from a consideration of the above points, that you will aid us in every way to obtain the export licenses within the period stipulated, failing which the contract would be lost to a foreign armament firm.[39]

This approach apparently worked — at least with the MacDonald government — as in both instances Vickers received the licenses required to export the matériel to Soviet Russia.

However, the change of government in the autumn of 1924 made it more difficult for such contracts to be carried out. Although it was viewed favorably by the outgoing MacDonald government, Vickers lost a "firm offer" for the supply of arms and ammunition to the value of £7.5 million because it "would be inconsistent with the attitude towards Russia taken up by members of the present government during the recent general election to sanction the equipment of Soviet Russia with arms and ammunition of British manufacture."[40] Even the new conservative government was not prepared to lose the armament business completely, however. Having inquired whether the government's position would prevent it from "executing any orders whatever in the way of armaments for Russia," Vickers was informed that individual cases would be considered on their own merits. The government was forced to admit that "what the Soviet government cannot order in this country, they will order abroad — and with the present severe unemployment in heavy industry we ought to assist where we can do so without sacrificing the principle that Soviet Russia must not equip herself with [British] arms and ammunition." Vickers lost no time in requesting permission to export ten "Virginia" airplanes which could "not be described as civil machines," and informed the government that there was also a number of other "various small orders" in view.[41]

Vickers's continued efforts to negotiate the sale of arms to the Soviet government—the export of which was ostensibly prohibited—goes far to illustrate the determination of those stricken firms to capture this business. However, the full potential of the Soviet market was put well out of reach of the majority of British manufacturers by the competition met from American business.[42]

Despite the Anglo-Soviet Trade Agreement and the subsequent extension of British de jure recognition, Britain failed to secure a commercial advantage in Soviet Russia. Instead, the balance of Russian trade remained overwhelmingly in favor of the United States. American trade with Soviet Russia more than doubled its prewar value during the course of a decade. By the end of the 1923–24 Soviet fiscal year, American exports to Soviet Russia had surpassed those of Britain and Germany combined. Although it accounted for only a little more than 11 percent of the total Soviet trade turnover between 1921 and 1924–25, the United States provided nearly one-fifth of all Russian imports during that period. By the 1924–25 fiscal year, the American share of this business had increased to nearly 28 percent.[43] Indeed, while the total U.S.-Russian trade turnover in 1924 was 10 percent less than it had been in 1913, the value of American exports to Soviet Russia had risen to over $42 million as compared with $26.5 million in 1913.[44]

As early as 1919, American commercial interest in Russia had been so great that the Bureau of Foreign and Domestic Commerce saw the need to establish a separate office devoted entirely to that country. By the end of 1921 the bureau was providing confidential information to those businessmen who inquired about Russia, and many bureau division chiefs were openly advocating this business. Particularly excited by the prospect of Soviet orders for American automotive manufacturers, Gordon Lee of the Automotive Division of the Commerce Department requested that a circular be issued, declaring that "if there is any business to be gotten for American motor truck manufacturers, we want to help them [even] if they are to be sold to the polar bears."[45] Soviet-American trade statistics had begun to appear regularly in commerce reports and trade supplements, and by 1923 demands for information had become so frequent that a confidential circular concerning trade with Soviet Russia was prepared by the bureau.

While the U.S. government remained officially aloof, it was nevertheless "very much interested in any trade relations with Russia." Indeed, the Director of the Bureau of Foreign and Domestic Commerce, Julius Klein, had been instructed to inform American manufacturers that the Commerce Department had "not the slightest objection" to American goods being shipped to Russia. It was, in fact, "only too glad" to see American manufacturers get the business.[46]

American business did not seem to be particularly disturbed by its government's refusal to recognize the Soviet government. That is not to say that those firms interested in this business were indifferent to the state of official relations between the United States and Soviet Russia. On the contrary, American manufacturers of heavy industrial and other engineering goods were vitally concerned that commercial relations be as favorable as possible. As was the case in Britain, this sector was particularly hard hit by the postwar depression, and Russia was seen by many in both governmental and private business circles as a convenient spillover market for American products.[47] Manufacturers of highly specialized equipment and machinery for which there was a demand in Soviet Russia—such as machine tools, agricultural machinery, oil-drilling equipment, and printing presses—had for some time lobbied for better commercial relations with Russia. Organizations like the Committee on Russian Trade and the American Commercial Association to Promote Trade with Russia were formed, the membership of which included "a number of representatives of large American business and banking interests." Avowedly "impartial regarding all political conditions in Russia," these organizations were formed solely for the purpose of mobilizing American trade with Russia.[48]

Although considerable enthusiasm over this trade was expressed even among such corporate giants as the Radio Corporation of America, General Electric, Dupont, Allied American, International Harvester, and Ford, American manufacturers on the whole remained surprisingly apolitical in their pursuit of Soviet business.[49] Few American firms openly lobbied for recognition of the Soviet government in the 1920s. Indeed, the larger U.S. firms could afford to deal with Soviet Russia regardless of their government's position and so tended to regard recognition as unnecessary—or even undesirable, as it would permit greater competition in the Russian market.[50] Apparently satisfied that the government supported their efforts to capture a share of that market, U.S. manufacturers were, at least for the moment, content to conduct business without the benefit of official rapprochement.

Most U.S. firms, however, continued to prefer to deal with the Soviets indirectly, usually through an agent with offices in London or the Baltic. The Dollar Trading and Finance Corporation was one such agency that represented the interests of a number of American manufacturers.[51] As early as May 1922, the Dollar Trading Corporation informed the U.S. commercial attaché in London that the firm was "willing to do business with the Soviet government on a credit basis." The company offered to take the goods of bona fide American manufacturing firms at cost and sell them to the Soviets at an 80 percent profit which was to be divided equally between the firm selling the product and the Dollar Trading Corporation. In exchange, the company would secure orders, the terms of which would be 25 to 40 percent cash, with the remainder given in credit or taken in produce. These arrangements were apparently acceptable to a number of American firms, as the company acted as an agent in Russia for the Sullivan Machinery Company, International Harvester, and "about 20 other concerns in the U.S. selling agricultural machinery."[52]

Armand Hammer's Allied American Corporation was another agency to which a number of prominent U.S. manufacturers entrusted their business in Soviet Russia. Hammer had established a close working relationship with the Soviet government in 1921, when he went to Russia to assist in famine relief efforts. His success in securing much-needed medical and food supplies for the Soviets had put him in an undeniably advantageous position with regard to further business undertakings with that government. Indeed, Hammer's unique position was recognized by the U.S. government as early as 1922, when the Department of Commerce began recommending the services of the Allied American Corporation to businessmen interested in Russian trade. By the end of 1923, Hammer's favor among top Soviet officials had borne fruit in the form of a variety of concessions, the most profitable of which was that for a trading concession.[53] Under the terms of the agreement signed in July 1923, the Allied American Corporation was given the right to handle one year's trade between the United States and the Soviet Union, independent of the jurisdiction of the Commissariat for Foreign Trade, in return for which the firm agreed to pay the government 50 percent of its profits.

By 1924 Allied American represented at least thirty-eight major American firms in Russia, including Ford, U.S. Rubber, Union Twist Drill, Advance Rimely Thresher Company, the American Tool Works, and Westinghouse Electric. The "big increase" in Russian-American trade that was anticipated after the conclusion of the concession agreement had materialized "beyond expectations." The stipulated annual minimum turnover of $2.4 million had in fact been exceeded after only six months, and it was fully expected that the amount of business handled by Allied American during the first year of the concession would exceed $10 million.[54] Moreover, a fair proportion of even this early business had been conducted on credits of six months to two years or on a basis of cash and credit and, as Hammer stressed, "the contracts entered into thus far have been without loss and there has been no defaulting."

Already handling a considerable volume of trade by January 1924, Allied American was to benefit further from the British decision to extend de jure recognition to the Soviet government. The British move had sparked fresh concern among American manufacturers: officials of the corporation noted that, since recognition, Allied American was receiving twice as many inquiries from American concerns interested in selling their goods to Russia as before. However, because of the more liberal attitude taken by British banks toward extending credit to the Soviets, a considerable amount of the business handled by the corporation continued to originate in the British market. Some $1 million worth of American cotton, for example, had been bought by the corporation in Britain and shipped to Soviet Russia.[55]

In early 1922 the Allied American Corporation obtained the Ford dealership for the Soviet Union. The personal friendship between Charles Sorensen, Ford's foreign sales manager, and Armand and Julius Hammer did much to foster Ford's trust and confidence in this trade. Indeed, much of Ford's early optimism over this market was the result of Hammer's enthusiastic reports.[56] Although sales through Allied American were undoubtedly hampered by Ford's refusal to extend any credit to the Soviet government, the firm nonetheless reported a "considerable turnover . . . in Ford cars and tractors."[57]

Even before the conclusion of the trade concession, Allied American had dispatched a representative to southeastern Russia to investigate the sale of Fordsons, as well as the possibility of "covering [that] section of Russia with service stations."[58] By the beginning of June 1923, Allied American had handled the sale and shipment of between 300 and 400 Fordson tractors to Novorossisk alone.[59] By the end of 1925 over 11,000 Fordson tractors had been delivered to the Soviet Union, over two-thirds of them having arrived in 1924 and 1925. Although the Allied American Corporation had handled a considerable percentage of these sales, by 1925 Armand Hammer admitted that he could no longer compete with the official Soviet purchasing organization, Amtorg.[60] In mid-1924, as private purchasing organizations such as Hammer's were being phased out and state purchasing organs took over, Ford's sales of tractors to Soviet Russia increased substantially. A manifestation of the overall drive to modernize Soviet agriculture, the growing number of tractors purchased was also due to Amtorg's ability to obtain credit from several of the New York banking houses. Amtorg was granted its first substantial bank credit of $2.5 million in mid-1924. The Equitable Trust Company provided $2 million of this with the stipulation that it had to be put toward the purchase of tractors from Ford. The effect that the availability

Table 8.1   Ford's Exports to Soviet Russia

	Automobiles	Trucks	Tractors	Total
1922	261	56	268	585
1923	30*	192	404	624
1924	61	154	3,108	3,323
1925	162	463	10,515	11,140

Source: Wilkins and Hill, *American Business Abroad: Ford on Six Continents*, p. 212.

*The abrupt decline in the sale of Ford automobiles in 1923 was the result of a vigorous campaign to reduce Soviet purchases abroad and, specifically, an embargo on the importation of foreign automobiles. Julius Hammer to Henry Ford, 1 June 1923, FMCA, Acc. 38, box 47.

of credit had on Soviet purchases is striking, and in the case of Ford's Russian business is amply illustrated by tractor sales figures in Table 8.1.

The Allied American Corporation played a crucial role in the development of Ford's business with Soviet Russia. In addition to handling the first large consignments of Ford cars and tractors, Hammer's firm acted as an important intermediary in Ford's early discussions with the Soviets on the subject of constructing a plant in the USSR. Even before the revolution, Henry Ford had entertained the idea of manufacturing in Russia.[61] In the spring of 1923 Ford again expressed his interest in building a factory there. Julius Hammer was dispatched to Russia shortly thereafter to investigate conditions, to find a suitable site for a plant, and to bring the subject to the attention of the Soviet government. Reporting on his progress, Hammer wrote that the Soviets were convinced of the superiority of the Ford automobile and tractor for Russian conditions and needs, but economic considerations made large purchases abroad difficult. As a result, a policy had been adopted to diminish imports of machinery and to cultivate their construction in Russia. The production of Ford automobiles and tractors on Soviet territory employing Russian materials and labor would, therefore, "be a great boon to the nation and every assistance and opportunity would be granted . . . to facilitate [its] profitable operation."[62]

By 1925 Soviet Russia had become one of Ford's largest foreign purchasers of tractors, and was reportedly using Fords "almost exclusively." Of the approximately 24,500 tractors in the USSR in mid-1926, 20,148— some 82 percent—were Fordsons.[63] Moreover, the Soviets had apparently become a reliable credit risk. Early that year, Ford—who was against extending credit even to his own domestic dealers—had begun to investigate some means to finance his trade with the Soviet Union. The company's rather sudden effort to secure bank export credits for Amtorg can be partially explained by the development of a serious depression in the automobile industry, which had forced a number of manufacturers to reduce their monthly output schedule in mid-1924. Ford, however, was convinced that any sharp decline in domestic sales could be offset through his overseas business. Other manufacturers shared the view that it was essential for "greater attention than ever before [to be] given to export markets"—attention that certainly included the extension of credits to the Soviets.[64]

Ford's chief rival in Russia, International Harvester, certainly did not dismiss that market, despite the substantial losses it suffered there.[65] Even after the company's decision to close its Lubertsy plant in May 1923, International Harvester continued to maintain an office in Moscow in order to "keep in close touch with the Soviet government on its plans to meet the agricultural needs of the country as well as to provide a base for servicing and instructing on its machinery."[66] Moreover, that company was also known to be offering the Soviets liberal terms as early as 1924. By August 1925 the company required only 50 percent down three months after the purchase had been made. By 1926 competition had apparently become so stiff that International Harvester was forced to revise those terms, extending two-year credit with only 20 percent down.[67]

No longer willing or able to pay cash for foreign purchases, the Soviets had made it clear that any firm wishing to do business with them would have to offer credit. Competition in the Russian market had led a number of American firms, like Ford and International Harvester, to extend or arrange credit in an attempt to secure that business. Moreover, international competition over the postwar Russian market had been instrumental in lifting the blockade in 1920 and, by the end of the year, had prompted both Britain and the United States to seek more "normal" economic relations with the Soviet Union.[68] More than anything else, however, it was the satisfactory and indeed profitable trade that kept British and American merchants coming back for more, making the Soviet Union a preferred and trusted customer by the late 1920s.

The Significance of Early Soviet Trade

Between 1921 and the 1924–25 Soviet fiscal year, the total Soviet trade turnover increased nearly five times, from 228.5 million gold roubles to 1,282.1 million gold roubles.[69] Despite the unsettled nature of Anglo-

Soviet relations and the continued American policy of nonrecognition, Britain and the United States together accounted for an average of 33 percent of the entire Soviet trade turnover between 1921 and 1924–25.[70] Although the United States purchased only 1.5 percent of the total value of goods exported from the Soviet Union during this period, it provided nearly 17 percent of all imports. Britain, on the other hand, took an average of nearly 30 percent of all Russian exports, while providing nearly 22 percent of the total value of goods imported. These numbers compare favorably with those statistics of Russia's primary prewar trading partner, Germany, which provided a market for almost 18 percent of all Russian exports and accounted for nearly a quarter of all Russian imports for those years.

Taken in terms of total American and British trade turnovers, however, Soviet Russia occupied only a minor place in the foreign commerce of those countries, accounting for an average of only 0.6 percent and 1.1 percent of their respective total turnovers between 1921 and 1924. These figures tend to illustrate the importance of Britain and the United States to Soviet trade, while implying that Russian trade was of little consequence to these countries. However, as has been shown, this early trade can hardly be described as "insignificant." Perceived as an eldorado, pursued despite the inherent risks, and valued highly enough to provoke considerable international competition, the postrevolutionary Russian market was seen by government and private traders alike as being of definite significance during the period 1918 to 1924.

Despite the deteriorating state of relations, Anglo-Soviet trade grew considerably during the 1920s, the total trade turnover increasing from just over £6 million in 1921 to nearly £31 million in 1924. However, as is evident from the returns given in Table 8.2, Anglo-Russian trade continued to fall short of the 1913 level. It is nonetheless worth noting that imports of Russian goods grew substantially faster than did British exports to that country, increasing more than sevenfold between 1921 and 1924. While this expansion is in no small part due to Soviet Russia's increasing ability to export, it also goes far to illustrate its renewed importance to Britain as a supplier.

Soviet imports into Britain accounted for 41 percent of the total turnover (by value) of Anglo-Soviet trade in 1921. By 1924 this had increased to 64 percent. The balance of trade became steadily worse for Britain after 1921, with Soviet imports being more than one and a half times greater than U.K. exports by 1924. It was remarked that, if these Russian exports represented new production, "her position must be more favourable than we are disposed to believe."[71]

Table 8.2   United Kingdom Trade with Russia (in Millions of Pounds Sterling)

	1913	1921	1922	1923	1924
Imports from Russia	40.3	2.7	8.1	9.3	19.8
As % of total U.K. imports*	7%	.4%	1%	1%	2%
Export of U.K. produce to Russia	18.1	2.2	3.6	2.5	3.9
As % of total U.K. produce exported*	5%	.5%	.8%	.5%	.8%
Reexports to Russia	9.6	1.2	1.0	2.0	7.2
As % of total U.K. reexports*	10%	1%	1%	2%	6%
Total exports to Russia	27.7	3.4	4.6	4.5	11.1
As % of total U.K. exports*	6.5%	.6%	.9%	.7%	2%
Turnover with Russia	68.0	6.1	12.7	13.8	30.9
As % of total U.K. trade turnover*	6.7%	.5%	1%	1%	2%

Source: Data from U.K. Parliamentary Papers, *Annual Statement of the Trade of the United Kingdom.*

*Percent of total consigned to or from foreign countries—that is, does not include U.K. trade with British Dominions and Possessions.

The United Kingdom purchased increasing quantities of those food-stuffs and raw materials that were imported from Russia before the war.[72] Indeed, the Soviet Union quickly resumed its importance as Britain's primary foreign source of manganese ore, with imports that were exceeded only by those from British India. As early as 1921 Russia was again providing nearly one-third of all manganese imported into the United Kingdom from foreign countries—that is, not including British possessions—and by 1922 was Britain's primary foreign supplier, providing over half of all that ore imported.[73] The Soviet timber industry had likewise made "startling progress" during the early 1920s, with the industry said to be "developing more rapidly than money can be found to finance it in Russia."[74] Russia again became an important source of timber for the United Kingdom, supplying 14 percent of all Britain's imports by 1924. It is interesting to note that, if timber imports from Finland and the Baltic states—formerly part of the Russian Empire and thus included in the prewar timber trade returns—are taken in conjunction with those from Russia, the imports of this commodity for this

Table 8.3   British Trade with Russia and Succession States (in Thousands of Pounds Sterling)

Kind of Trade	1913	1920	1921	1922	1923	1924*
Imports from Russia	40,271	33,523	2,695	8,103	9,266	13,346
Exports to Russia	27,694	16,833	3,391	4,610	4,481	7,699
Imports from Finland	—	—	7,721	10,434	13,210	9,627
Exports to Finland	—	—	2,902	3,468	4,832	4,104
Imports from Estonia	—	—	730	1,136	1,874	1,875
Exports to Estonia	—	—	4,269	1,886	1,366	724
Imports from Latvia	—	—	1,618	3,005	5,628	4,631
Exports to Latvia	—	—	946	1,400	1,874	1,677
Imports from Lithuania	—	—	344	1,116	817	583
Exports to Lithuania	—	—	54	118	220	258
Imports from Poland**	—	—	1,840	2,863	5,360	5,740
Exports to Poland**	—	—	4,869	3,072	3,694	3,525
Total Imports	40,271	33,523	14,948	26,657	36,155	35,802
Total Exports	27,694	16,833	16,431	14,055	16,467	17,927

Source: *Board of Trade Journal*, 16 October 1924, p. 447.

*Figures for 1924 are for January to September only.
**Includes Danzig.

period closely approximate the prewar levels.[75] Indeed, taking the combined returns of those areas that formerly composed the Russian Empire, Anglo-Russian trade for the period 1921–24 compares favorably against the 1913 returns. A fair proportion of goods imported by Britain prior to the war, such as flax and timber, originated from areas of the empire that subsequently became independent and were no longer included in British returns for "trade with Russia." The effect of their loss on the volume of Anglo-Soviet trade may be inferred from Table 8.3.[76]

Although Britain's exports to Soviet Russia increased by nearly three and a half times between 1921 and 1924, most of this gain was accounted for by the rapid growth in reexports to Russia. In 1921, reexported goods accounted for approximately 36 percent of all U.K. exports to the Soviet Union, a percentage that increased to 72 percent by 1925. A large proportion of these reexports were consignments of U.S. cotton, a commodity that accounted for well over half of Britain's reexports and some 37 percent of its total exports to Russia in 1924.[77] Moreover, manufactured goods produced in Britain comprised only 26 to 27 percent of the total domestic U.K. exports to Russia for this period, the majority of which was made up of goods that had "little significance to British industry" —that is to say, primarily foodstuffs and coal.[78] The low proportion of exports of U.K. manufactured goods to Russia may be attributed in part to the stagnation of Britain's trade generally.[79] Taken on the basis of 1913 prices, Britain's total annual exports to all countries of domestically man-ufactured goods remained well below the prewar value throughout the period 1921 to 1924.[80] Given this depressed state of Britain's overall global trade, combined with the British disinclination to extend long-term credit and the Soviet preference to buy American, it is not surprising that British exports to Russia likewise failed to achieve their prewar value.

Though it amounted to only 40 percent of Britain's Russian-bound prewar exports and accounted for only 2 percent of Britain's total exports in 1924, Soviet trade was nonetheless considered to be significant. In-deed, even in terms of volume and value it was openly admitted that the statistics of trade do not always mean what they seem to imply. As dis-cussed earlier, even after the conclusion of the trade agreement, British merchants continued "to a large extent" to conduct their business through non-Russian ports, and the actual volume of this trade was officially suspected of being "considerably more than the statistics seem to show." There is good evidence that transit trade accounted for almost as much again as the officially recorded trade.[81] While there is no way to deter-mine precisely how much transit trade was actually done, there is no doubt that it was substantial.

That both the government and private traders in Britain *perceived* the postwar Russian market as having tremendous potential is clear. Its antic-ipated value caused even those businessmen who had suffered expropria-tion or nationalization to reinvolve themselves in that market. Bolshevik or not, Russia as a market was "bound to be of immense value in the future."[82] Throughout the postrevolutionary period Russia did not lose its appeal as an "eldorado" for British business.[83] The predicted impact that reopening this trade was to have on relieving economic difficulties in Britain should not be underestimated. It is evident that industry and government alike ascribed considerable importance to this business as a means of alleviating unemployment. The perception of Russia as a rem-edy for Britain's economic ills continued to be of considerable importance throughout the period prior to recognition. As late as September 1923 it was maintained that, while Anglo-Soviet trade was as "yet inconsiderable as compared with the volume of prewar trade," it was, "nevertheless, a not inconsiderable asset in a period of slump like the present."[84]

The argument that more "normal" Anglo-Soviet relations would have a positive effect on domestic economic conditions ran as a common refrain during the first half of the decade. Advocates of a trade agreement repeatedly pointed out the effect that the resultant huge Russian orders would have on unemployment in Britain. Even within the government, there were many who believed that once an agreement was concluded —one that included provisions for the import and disposition of Soviet gold—it was "probable that orders would be placed which would considerably effect unemployment." On the other hand, "it may be taken as certain that the extent of unemployment at the present moment would intensify the disappointment if the negotiations break down." Nor was this disappointment to be limited to labor only; there were "a good many indicators" that there had been a distinct "change of mind" in commercial, industrial, and financial circles. Even the *Financial Times* had felt it necessary to run a leader "urging the necessity of resumption of trade relations." In light of the "very serious commercial and financial position" it was "not surprising . . . that opinions should have changed."[85]

Many in the government likewise hoped to capture some of the Soviet orders that were going to other countries. In fact, Britain's representative in Moscow thought this business so important that he gave a diplomatic visa to Professor Lomonossoff, a Soviet emissary who came to England in late 1920 to conduct business. Though he later admitted that this was a mistake, Hodgson explained that he did so "because Lomonossoff had placed some £40 million worth of orders in Germany" and his visit to Britain was in connection with "several important contracts."[86] Hodgson did attempt to vindicate himself, however, pointing out that this expedient was not without its payoff; while in Britain, Lomonossoff concluded agreements with Armstrong-Whitworth and Leeds Forge Company worth over £1 million. In the case of Armstrong-Whitworth, it was understood that this contract would make a "considerable difference" to the financial position of that company.[87]

Despite the failure of the trade agreement to bring about any dramatic increase in Soviet orders placed in Britain, unemployment continued to be an argument used in favor of closer relations between the two countries. It was one of Lloyd George's primary concern's at the economic conferences at Genoa and The Hague.[88] Further, the issues of unemployment and general economic stagnation in Britain went on to form the basis of the case for de jure recognition. It was argued that there were a number of factors arising from the "absence of normal diplomatic relations with Russia" that prevented "a re-opening of the Russian markets of which our industry stands in urgent need." Despite the difficulties inherent in this absence, the fact that a "fairly considerable volume of business" had been conducted was cited as an indication of what could be done once normal relations were resumed.[89]

Russia was more than just a chimerical market, however. Soviet business was of considerable tangible importance to a variety of industrial sectors in Britain. Indeed, in a number of cases, contracts concluded with the Soviets had a definite impact on the immediate economic health of the company involved.

As mentioned previously, British textile manufacturers had found a lucrative market in Russia during the civil war, with the value of textiles exported to Russia during 1920 accounting for 1 percent of the total value of U.K. exports to all countries that year. More significantly, Russia accounted for nearly 3.5 percent of the total value of woolen and worsted goods exported. The cancellation of existing orders for the counterrevolutionary armies and the loss of this market after the civil war hit the textile manufacturers hard, worsening their already depressed state by the end of 1920. Willing to pay cash on substantial orders, the Bolsheviks provided a ready and welcome market for this industry. Despite the "risky nature" of the transactions, the state of unemployment compelled many textile manufacturers to take these risks.[90] The effect that Soviet orders had on this business is without question; it was estimated that Britain had sold—directly and indirectly—£2.3 million worth of textiles and clothing to Russia in 1921, or some 1.6 percent of all U.K. exports of cotton, woolen, and worsted manufactures. In comparison, the 1913 value of these exports to Russia was £1.9 million—some 1.1 percent of textile exports to all countries.[91]

Although textile manufacturers probably benefited most from this early trade, it was the heavy industries that pushed the hardest for the normalization of relations with Soviet Russia. There is evidence that companies like Higgs, Whisha & Company, Cammell Laird, Armstrongs, and Vickers were involved in considerable contracts—directly or indirectly—for Soviet Russia.[92] Here again, this early business was of considerable immediate importance not only to the individual manufacturers but to whole industries as well.[93] Exports of U.K. machinery, for example, had fallen steadily between 1920 and 1924—from £37.6 million to £22.6 million. The impact of Soviet purchases of such machinery is shown by the fact that Soviet Russia claimed an increasing proportion of these exports after

1922: accounting for less than 1 percent of the total value in 1920, Russia received 3.4 percent of U.K. machinery exported in 1924. Although the value of U.K. machinery exported to Russia in 1913 was some ten times greater than in 1924, early transactions with the Soviets were still highly significant for some U.K. machine makers. Soviet Russia was, for example, the leading foreign market for British spinning and weaving machinery between 1923 and 1925.

The wire rope industry was also "badly in want of work" as export orders had "fallen off considerably" by the autumn of 1920. Informing the Foreign Office that the Soviet Trade Delegation was interested in purchasing "a very large quantity of steel wire rope, amounting to over £200,000," one manufacturer indicated that "this important contract would be very welcome to the trade, and would avoid the closing down of wire rope works, which has already commenced."[94] Industrial belting manufacturers were in similar straits. One concern, which had been "very large exporters" to Russia and Siberia before the revolution, claimed that this business had "very often . . . kept one of our departments entirely occupied for months at a time." Now forced to lay off employees and cut back production, the firm ventured to suggest that if it were receiving orders from Russia "as in the old days," it would be working full-time; "until trade is opened with Russia . . . we can see no prospect of very much improvement."[95]

Even those firms that did not have any previous dealings with Russia were anxious to gain unrestricted access to this market. For example, Birmingham Small Arms was eager to become involved in whatever way possible for the purpose of "securing the goodwill of the Soviet Government in view of considerable prospective business in motor cars, cycles, steel, tools and other of our products, which we hope to secure at least a share of."[96]

Whether these attempts were by companies intent on recouping some of their earlier losses in Russia or on gaining an initial foothold in that market is irrelevant. What all these efforts do indicate is an increased confidence in commercial and trade relations with the Bolsheviks.

At first glance, Russian-American trade appears to have always been of more importance to Russia than to the United States. Imports from Russia never exceeded 1.2 percent of the total American imports, and exports to Russia—though much greater in value—were also of relatively little importance as compared with the total exports of the United States. In addition, the United States consistently exported more than it imported from Russia, a condition that became more pronounced after the

Table 8.4   U.S.-Russian Trade, 1910–1924 (in Thousands of Dollars)

	Exports to Russia	% of Total U.S. Exports	Imports from Russia	% of Total U.S. Imports
1910–14*	$24,604	1%	$20,865	1%
1919	82,463	1%	9,663	.2%
1920	28,278	.4%	12,481	.2%
1921	15,584	.4%	1,312	.05%
1922	29,896	.8%	964	.03%
1923	7,618	.2%	1,619	.04%
1924	42,104	.9%	8,169	.2%

Source: Worked from returns in U.S. Department of Commerce, *Foreign Commerce and Navigation of the United States*, 1925.

*Five-year average, 1910–14.

revolution.[97] Indeed, U.S. exports to Russia accounted for 92 percent of the total U.S.-Soviet trade turnover by value in 1921. While this proportion fell to 84 percent in 1924, the balance of Soviet-American trade was increasingly disproportionate, with U.S. exports being more than five times that of its imports from the Soviet Union.

Despite the fact that "chaotic conditions" prevailed throughout Russia and trade was possible with only a certain small portion of the country, the United States still managed to export over $82 million worth of goods to Russia in 1919.[98] While the Bolshevik victories and the growing disenchantment with the counterrevolutionary movements resulted in a decline in U.S. trade with Russia in 1920, the value of exports to that country nevertheless exceeded that for the prewar period. As can be seen from Table 8.4, it was not until 1921 that American exports again fell below prewar levels. U.S.-Soviet trade hit its lowest point of the 1920s in 1923, when the entire trade turnover amounted to only a little more than $9 million. This decline was a direct result of the Soviet government's decision to reduce foreign expenditure and to hold out on purchases until credit was offered, a policy reflected in the overall drop in Soviet purchases abroad.

Although Soviet-American trade was somewhat irregular during the period 1921–24, the turnover for 1924 was nearly three times that for 1921—a difference largely accounted for by a sudden, dramatic increase in U.S. exports to Russia. Indeed, U.S. exports in 1924 were some 70 percent larger than the prewar average; moreover, it should also be remembered that after 1920, these returns do not include trade with Finland, the Baltic states, or Poland. They reflect only direct trade with the Soviet Union, and make no allowance for the substantial transit trade that was known to exist between American merchants and businessmen and the Soviet buying organizations in Northern Europe and England. These European intermediaries remained important in the conduct of Soviet-American commerce, even after the restrictions on this trade were removed in 1921. Germany and Britain especially continued to handle vast amounts of American goods bound for Soviet Russia. Indeed, as late as 1924, transactions valued at $20 million were known to have been concluded with American firms through Soviet trade missions in Britain and other countries.[99] The continued use of Britain and Germany especially was in no small part due to the greater leniency of banks in those countries in extending credit to the Soviets. It was because of this availability of credit that a considerable amount of the business handled by the Allied American Corporation was conducted in the British markets.[100]

The extension of credit by American banks and manufacturers in 1924 had an immediate and visible impact on the volume and value of Soviet-American trade. Soviet purchases in the United States increased by five and a half times between 1923 and 1924; and during the 1924–25 Soviet fiscal year, the United States provided nearly 28 percent of all Soviet imports by value—nearly twice as much as any other country, and four times that of the preceding year.[101] The effect of this credit on boosting direct U.S. sales to the USSR is particularly dramatic in the case of cotton. With the extension of a substantial line of credit to the All-Russian Textile Syndicate in early 1924, cotton exports to the Soviet Union jumped from just over $1 million in 1923 to $36.7 million in 1924. The secretary of the syndicate, Victor Nogin, observed that the Americans had established credit relations that they evidently found to be "highly satisfactory" as they were not even demanding the endorsement by the Soviet State Bank of the syndicate's bills.[102]

By 1924 cotton had recaptured its prewar position as the principle American export to Russia, accounting for $38 million of the $41 million worth of U.S. goods imported by the Soviet Union between January and October 1924.[103] While direct sales to Soviet Russia represented only 4 percent of the total value of cotton exported by the United States in 1924, the value of this market was fully recognized; the depressed state of the American cotton industry had made the Soviets welcome buyers. Indeed, American cotton growers had found "a sorely needed outlet in Russia," one that was later attributed with having "materially served to sustain the cotton market."[104] Nor was the importance of Soviet custom lost on the government. The Department of Agriculture had gone so far as to assure the Soviets that a representative would be "invited to all conferences on the cotton question."[105]

While the value and volume of Soviet-American trade remained only a small proportion of total U.S. trade, Soviet Russia as a market was none-theless seen by many as having considerable bearing on American trade and industry. As in Britain, the postwar economic slump and resultant unemployment exaggerated this importance and helped to promote the image of Russia as a virtually bottomless market with little regard to economic reality. Even so, Soviet purchases did have a definite positive impact on a number of individual firms and, indeed, entire industries.

Soviet Russia was an early valued market for certain light consumer articles. American leather goods found a ready market in that country, accounting for $8.4 million of the $15.6 million worth of U.S. exports to Russia in 1921. More significantly, Soviet Russia absorbed over one-third of the $29.5 million worth of leather goods exported by the United States that year. The American shoe industry particularly benefited from this business, with footwear alone accounting for $7.8 million of the total U.S. exports to Russia.[106] The new importance of this market was further illustrated by the fact that the average monthly value of shoe exports from the United States in 1921 was over seven times greater than that for 1913.[107] Indeed, one major Boston manufacturer, Endicott Johnson, had secured at least two Soviet orders for a total of approximately 3 million pairs of shoes at an average price of $3 per pair on terms of cash against documents in New York. Placed over the course of six months, these two orders constituted a sizable business for the company.[108] Moreover, the total value of American footwear sold to Soviet Russia was undoubtedly greater than official returns indicate: there is evidence that large consign-ments of shoes were shipped through Reval. In one instance alone, 250,000 pairs and another "large consignment" were transferred to a vessel in Stockholm for delivery to the Soviet agent in Reval.[109] A further 5 million pairs of shoes and 1,000 tons of leather, all part of a single order from the United States, were reported to have passed through Reval in the spring of 1921.[110]

Although the value of leather goods sold to Russia declined subsequent to 1921, Americans continued to sell impressive quantities of shoes and leather to the Soviet government. As late as 1924, what was re-ported as "perhaps the largest order for any commodity received by Americans was that for 17 million pairs of footwear purchased with gold by the Soviets. These shoes are in process of delivery, and each American ship arriving carries from 200,000 to 500,000 pairs of shoes. They are of excellent quality, of standard makes, Endicott Johnson shoes predominating."[111]

While cotton was to remain by far the largest U.S. export to Russia throughout the 1920s, sales of American heavy industrial goods continued to increase, with iron and steel manufactures and machinery accounting for the second largest class of exports to the Soviet Union. The machine tool industry was characteristic of those manufacturers of highly specialized goods who frequently competed for Russian business. One machine tool manufacturer informed the Department of Commerce that he did not care if the total amount of trade with Russia *was* insignificant. The Soviets he declared, were "in the market for $350,000 worth of machine tools. If we land this order it will keep several of our shops busy for four months. . . . From the standpoint of international trade statistics, it may be very little business for a country like Russia, and your economic data are all very well in their place, but from the standpoint of individual manufacturing concerns, this is a whale of an order and we are going after it."[112]

Agricultural machinery manufacturers were another of these highly specialized industries interested in establishing themselves in the Soviet market. Totaling nearly $1.6 million in 1924, agricultural machinery and implements were second only to cotton as the single largest *specific* commodity exported to the USSR. The United States had traditionally been a major supplier of these goods and, along with Canada, had provided over 80 percent of Russia's prewar requirements of all manner of harvesting machines.[113] One firm eager to regain its foothold in this market was International Harvester.

Although the International Harvester plant at Lubertsy near Moscow continued to operate, albeit unprofitably, the company's American exports to Russia did not cease. Indeed, over the course of 1921, International Harvester shipped $1.5 million worth of agricultural machinery to Russia and was paid in dollars.[114] This market was particularly important to International Harvester as the depressed state of American agriculture in 1921 had caused the firm's domestic sales to dry up; in fact foreign sales represented the company's only profit that year. A more important motivation for the company's early return to the Russian market can no doubt be found in the desire to avoid losing the favor it had built up with Russian farmers over a long period of years. As early as 1919 International Harvester officials were already planning for a reentry in the market as soon as conditions would permit: "Whenever the doors for commercial intercourse are re-opened the Harvester distributing organizations, already extending lines toward the border of Russia, will be prepared to aid in supplying the needs of agriculture in that great potential market."[115]

Though a relative newcomer to the market, Ford quickly came to value Soviet Russia as a major customer for its tractors, the sales of which in the United States and Europe had declined seriously in the early 1920s. Indeed, it was the sale of increasing numbers of Fordsons that saved the company from the recession that hit the automotive industry in the spring of 1924; while a number of his competitors were left bankrupt, Ford's Russian sales had increased more than five times that year. The significance of this market to Ford is clearly apparent from the fact the USSR bought up no less than 4 percent of the Ford Motor Company's total 1924 tractor production, a proportion that increased to a staggering 10 percent in 1925.[116] From the company's perspective, there was considerable truth in the assertion that Soviet orders were "helping to keep the wheels turning in America."[117]

Moreover, future Soviet business was seen as valuable enough for Ford to reconsider his stand against extending credit. By mid-1925, the Soviets were clearly dissatisfied with Ford's cash-only terms. Indicating that they would pay cash if they had to on an order for 3,800 Fordson tractors, they pointed out that such a move would "cripple" them for future purchases. At a time when credit from other American tractor manufacturers was readily available, Ford was easily persuaded to extend credit rather than to risk losing one of his most valuable foreign tractor markets — a market that accounted for 38 percent of his foreign sales in 1925. As Ford's New York manager pointed out, "They are going to have a lot of business for us, as there is plenty of it to be had over there, and I don't think we are taking very many chances."[118] In light of the growing volume of these sales — a single contract for $6 million worth of tractors, plows, and spare parts having been concluded in December 1925 — it is not surprising that Soviet Russia was seen as having the potential to develop into a "market for Ford products which . . . may someday surpass in volume all the rest of Europe and Asia combined."[119]

This early Soviet trade was certainly not insignificant. To be sure, the volume and value of Anglo-Soviet trade remained well below prewar levels throughout the 1920s, and American exports to Russia — which accounted for the majority of this turnover — did not attain the prewar percentage of total U.S. exports until the middle of the decade. Even so, that the market was *perceived* as significant is indisputable. The importance that both government and traders attached to the normalization of economic relations was great. Moreover, sales to Russia had a definite impact on the economic health of a number of individual companies and even whole industrial sectors. Indeed, in some cases—like that of Ford —trade with the young Soviet regime *exceeded* the company's prewar Russian business.

Prelude
to Trade

Although the recorded trade with Soviet Russia accounted for only a very small proportion of the overall volume and value of British and American foreign trade between 1918 and 1924, it was certainly not "insignificant." The competition between Britain and the United States over the postrevolutionary Russian market reveals its economic importance to foreign governments and traders. Even before the war, merchants in both countries were keenly aware of the business opportunities in Russia that were controlled by the Germans. American interest was further heightened by the massive volume of Russian wartime purchases. The fact that U.S. exports to Russia had increased ten times between 1914 and 1916 was certainly not lost on American businessmen or their government.

Britain and the United States moved quickly after the war to secure an economic foothold in Russia, taking advantage of the absence of Germany to establish themselves there. The Bolshevik revolution mattered little and was seen as no more than a passing phase that posed no real threat to the Allies' long-term economic aspirations. Russia's postwar economic potential was still regarded as being tremendous, and a sharp rivalry over this market soon developed not only between British and American merchants, but also between the two governments.

With the possible initial exception of the Russian North, the Allied intervention was to a large extent a manifestation of these economic aspirations. The control of those areas of Russia in which Britain or the United States had particular interest and the immediate initiation of economic and commercial undertakings either with the support or at the behest of the respective government indicate the extent to which economic motives played a role in the intervention. Despite the division of the intervention into virtual "spheres of influence," competition in Russia remained fierce. Indeed, competing British and American interest over the oilfields of South Russia provoked a particularly heated rivalry, which continued well into the 1920s, causing much friction and discord between the two allies.

British and American interest in postwar Russia was not limited to the support of counterrevolutionary factions. The wisdom of continuing to back a failing cause was increasingly questioned by both governments. Moreover, frequently disastrous business encounters with the Whites had elicited numerous complaints from merchants. Goods purchased or delivered by Western businessmen were held up and even requisitioned in non-Bolshevik Russia, and normal trade was rendered impossible by widespread corruption among the local counterrevolutionary government officials. Evidence that the neutrals were confidently conducting profitable business with the Soviet regime, coupled with British and American merchants' own growing experience of satisfactory dealings with the Bolsheviks, resulted in increased pressure being brought to bear on the governments to reopen unrestricted trade with all of Russia. By the end of 1919 the choice was clear: either remove the blockade of Soviet Russia or lose this budding trade to the neutral states.

Although Russia was initially seen to be more important to Britain as a supplier, the worsening economic conditions of 1920 shifted the focus of attention to its potential as a market for British goods. Pressure from business circles increased as the economic conditions worsened in 1920; the lure of cash sales was a strong one, and business with the Bolsheviks was certainly no more risky than trading with the Whites. Indeed, the Soviets proved ultimately more dependable, and their business more profitable than recent dealings with such corrupt counterrevolutionary governments as that of Denikin's Volunteer Army.

Concurrent with the worsening economic conditions in 1920 was the British government's decision to seek more normal economic relations with the Soviet government. Largely seen as an attempt to gain an initial commercial advantage in Soviet Russia, this move was met with considerable American suspicion. British overtures toward the Soviets provoked the U.S. government to modify accordingly its own restrictions on this trade in an effort to prevent Britain from stealing a march. The continuing postwar recession and the evaporation of European markets only sharpened this rivalry.

Characteristic of much of the British and American approach to the "Russian question," this competition was the cause of considerable friction and suspicion between the allies, each suspecting the other of scheming to gain an unfair advantage in Russia. That conflicting commercial interests rather than any political disagreements were the source of most difficulties between the United States and Britain goes far to show their commitment to furthering their own economic interests in Russia.

The interaction between politics and economics during this period has been described in the examination of the policy toward the Russian question as it developed in the United States and Britain. Although political and economic relations were closely linked, they were not dependent upon one another. The openly anti-Bolshevik policy of the Allies from 1918 to 1920 was pursued despite a growing interest in trade with Russia and, indeed, in the face of developing indirect commercial activities with Soviet Russia. Although the trade agreement was to have "paved the way for the resumption of direct business," the British attempt to place Anglo-Soviet trade in the context of a formalized agreement resulted in no real benefit to Great Britain.[1] The parallel development of American trade with the Soviet Union, the problems that arose over the Bolsheviks' revolutionary activities abroad, and the failure to reach any satisfactory agreement concerning the settlement of Russian debts and obligations all support the assertion that the agreement was more a Soviet diplomatic victory over the British government than anything else. Indeed, the failure of the U.S. government to respond to the numerous Soviet overtures to negotiate some sort of agreement had little effect on the development of trade. In 1924—trade agreement and de jure recognition notwithstanding—the volume and value of American exports to the Soviet Union exceeded those of Great Britain by a substantial margin.

Trade with geographical Russia from 1918 to 1924 was perceived to be of considerable consequence. Commercial activity in Russia generally did not cease with the revolution or at any time thereafter. Further, taking into consideration the possible volume and value of British and American trade with Soviet Russia as indicated by the amount of transit trade and Soviet gold movements, this market was of greater commercial importance than the official returns would indicate. Although Soviet trade generally was still only a fraction of the Russian prewar level, it nonetheless had a significant impact on certain industries in Britain and the

United States, and was essential in establishing Soviet Russia as a trust-worthy trading partner.

The explosion of trade that took place between the West and Soviet Russia during the second half of the 1920s was the result of a carefully laid foundation of experience and trust. More than anything else it was the successful conduct of a considerable volume of indirect commerce that prompted the West to accept Soviet Russia as a responsible trading partner, opening the way for the rapid expansion of Soviet purchasing abroad. While the postwar depression had much to do with generating the exaggerated impression of Russia as a bottomless market, the contin-ued punctilious observation by the Soviet government of its financial responsibilities, even during the period of the famine, did much to elevate it into a position of respectability and earned it a reputation as a trusted business partner with an enviable credit rating. This confidence is reflected in the growing number of British and American businessmen who chose not only to deal directly with Soviet purchasing organs but also to extend to them limited credit facilities that had previously been denied. With the end of the relief shipments in 1923, transit trade was never again to occupy such an important position in Soviet foreign trade.[2]

The Soviet trade boom that took off in the middle of the 1920s is apparent in the U.S. returns. Soviet-American trade rose steadily after 1923, increasing nearly threefold between 1924 and 1930. Continuing to account for the overwhelming proportion of the Soviet-American trade turnover, U.S. exports to the USSR had reached $114.4 million in 1930—some 82 percent of the $138.8 million turnover. Moreover, the huge expansion in Soviet foreign purchasing had a definite impact on the United States: while total American exports declined 27 percent between 1929 and 1930, exports to the USSR gained 35 percent. Accounting for 3 percent of the total value of U.S. exports, Soviet Russia was America's eighth best overall customer.[3]

The Soviet market had become even more valuable to certain American industries.[4] By 1925 the USSR already ranked as the fourteenth largest consumer of U.S. industrial equipment; by 1929 it counted as the third largest foreign market for this equipment, surpassed only by Canada and the United Kingdom. The USSR was also the largest market for American agricultural machinery and supplies in 1930. Business with the Soviets was apparently considered by some firms to be so valuable that they agreed to "desist from all claims whatsoever" in regard to nationalization or confiscation. In the case of International General Electric, the com-pany agreed to waive its claims as part of its contract with the Soviet government for the sale of at least $25 million in goods over seven years.[5]

The overall effect of the boom on Britain was somewhat less dramatic. While Anglo-Soviet trade had increased from some £29.9 million in 1924 to just over £43.5 million in 1930, the overwhelming majority of this trade was accounted for by imports from Russia. Indeed, the proportion of this trade accounted for by Soviet imports had increased—from 65 percent in 1924 to 79 percent in 1930.[6] Even so, the USSR continued to be of considerable significance to British industry as an important market for a variety of manufactured goods. By 1924–25, the USSR had become a primary market for U.K. steel manufactures generally. The Soviet Union was the second largest purchaser of steel wire by 1925; and the renovation and modernization of the Soviet oil industry had made that country second only to Japan in the value of steel tubes, pipes, and fittings it purchased that year. A major market for a variety of industrial equipment, such as British textile spinning and weaving machinery, the Soviet Union had also come to represent the single largest foreign purchaser of goods from a number of British companies—such as oil-drilling and petroleum-refining equipment from Vickers, and electrical generating equipment from its subsidiary company Metropolitan-Vickers.[7]

While this early trade may have represented an effort by British and American business to recoup losses suffered as a result of the revolution in Russia, it nonetheless demonstrates that there was enough confidence in the Soviet regime to have extensive dealings with it, with an increasing number of these transactions being conducted on credit. The extension of such credit was the most significant aspect in the development of these early economic relations. Businessmen and banks alike were impressed and encouraged by the Soviet government's scrupulous observation of its commercial obligations. Though at first gradually and cautiously offered by British and American producers, credit was increasingly made available to the Soviets. The willingness to offer better terms—requiring smaller advances on larger sums over longer periods—directly reflects the confidence that the West increasingly put in its dealings with Soviet Russia, and signaled the acceptance of the Soviet Union as a responsible business partner.

The Soviet government's policy of scrupulously meeting all of its incurred obligations had begun to pay off in America by late 1921, when the Equitable Trust Company extended limited credit to a Soviet purchasing agency.[8] By 1924, short-term credits up to about eighteen months were generally available to the Soviet trade agencies. Indeed, Soviet trade operations were "readily financed by the American banks, which grant both merchandise credit and credit against bills of exchange," the latter exceeding $10 million in 1924.[9] By mid-1925 it was estimated that approximately 70 percent of American transactions with Soviet Russia were conducted on credit.[10]

While it was officially reckoned that British sales to Arcos up to 1924 had been done "almost entirely on a basis of cash against documents," it was noted that the "practice of granting credits" was becoming more widespread, and that "British firms [had] no serious ground for complaint."[11] British banks had indeed been extending limited credit to the Soviets for some time. Arcos had reportedly done a "fair amount of business" on short-term credit under conditions that generally stipulated 25 percent with the order and the rest in six-month bills.[12] Even though the Export Credit Scheme was not applied to Soviet Russia, even after formal British recognition of that government, it was nonetheless the case that "export trade from Great Britain to Russia has been proceeding during the last three years without any guarantee of payment by Russia from H.M. Government, and that a very considerable turnover has been done. No case of failure on the part of the importing Russian concerns . . . to discharge all due obligations, has been reported to the Department of Overseas Trade, whether terms have been cash or, as is frequently known to have been the case during the past twelve months, partly cash combined with trade credit against acceptances."[13]

By the middle of the decade, competition for Soviet business had become so intense that any attempt to limit credit would have only meant the loss of a potentially lucrative contract. Indeed, the increasing number—if not the sheer size—of Soviet orders demanded that normal credit facilities be extended, and by 1926 firms were regularly offering long-term credit arrangements. The effect that the extension of normal —and, indeed, preferred—lines of credit to Soviet Russia had on British and American industries is apparent from the business that resulted. Without the accompanying long-term credit, both Vickers and International General Electric would have certainly lost the huge Soviet orders for electrical generating equipment and plant. In the case of International General Electric, the 1928 contract alone was worth at least $25 million over seven years.[14] At the same time, the Soviets would have been in a dire position by 1924 without this credit.[15] The amount of gold being "processed" through Sweden had dropped sharply in 1923, indicating that reserves of that metal were beginning to run out. Thus it was the increasing availability of long-term credit that enabled the Soviet government to realize the full potential of its program of rapid industrialization in the late 1920s.

The increasing interest in concessions and technical aid contracts underscored the growing American and British trust in Soviet Russia. Within four years of the Bolshevik nationalization and expropriation of foreign property in Russia and its repudiation of all debts and obligations, Western businessmen were already making moves to acquire concessions in Soviet Russia. A number of British and American agricultural machinery manufacturers, for example, had expressed an interest in restarting their Russian operations on a concession basis as early as 1921.[16] Even the oil companies, which had ostensibly formed a united front against the Soviets, were competing for concessions in the Soviet oilfields by 1922. Far from advising British businessmen against such arrangements, the Department of Overseas Trade had encouraged companies with industrial concerns in Russia to enter into negotiations with the object of operating their businesses on a concession basis.[17] Between 1922 and 1926 some 330 concessions were granted, and in all these cases the foreign operator was again required to invest money in capital and plant in Russia. Given the earlier losses suffered by Western businessmen at the hands of the Bolsheviks, the conclusion of these contracts represent a remarkable achievement for the Soviets.

Even so, the attempt to attract substantial foreign investments through concessions was not very successful.[18] Much more was gained through the increasing number of technical aid contracts that were concluded during the late 1920s. These agreements not only supplied the Soviets with the advanced products and methods of the West, but also provided the foreign technical advisors to set up and make operational the factories, plants, and power generating stations, as well as to train the Soviets. Such major multinationals as Ford, Vickers, International General Electric, and the Radio Corporation of America were among the many that had found the prospects of this business too tempting to resist.

The success and results of this early trade had a considerable impact on the development of future economic relations between the West and Soviet Russia. The Soviet government's prompt execution of its obligations made a strong impression on Western businessmen, and did much to counter memories of expropriation and repudiation. Without the trust nurtured during these early dealings with the Soviet regime, the trade boom of the latter part of the decade could scarcely have occurred. Nor would it have been possible for the Soviets to have secured the goods and technology that were especially vital to the rapid development of Soviet industry during the late 1920s and early 1930s.

NOTES

Abbreviations

DBFP   *Documents on British Foreign Policy*, 1st series, ed. E. L.
          Woodward and R. Butler (London, 1947–).

Cab.   Cabinet records, Public Record Office, London.

FMCA   Ford Motor Company Archives, Archives Record Center, Henry
          Ford Museum, Dearborn, Michigan.

FO   Foreign Office papers, Public Record Office, London.

FRUS   *Papers Relating to the Foreign Relations of the United States*
          (Washington, D.C., 1936–).

NARG   National Archives Record Group, National Archives, Washington,
          D.C.

Introduction

1. There are a number of outstanding works that deal with early Soviet relations with the West, but they generally dismiss the early attempts at trade and
economic relations as being of little or no consequence. See, for example, Carr,
The Bolshevik Revolution; Ullman, *Anglo-Soviet Relations*, vol. 3; and Kennan,
Soviet-American Relations, vol. 2.

Chapter 1

1. See, for example, Girault, *Emprunts russes et investissements français*; McKay,
Pioneers for Profit; Crisp, *Studies in the Russian Economy*; Ol', *Inostrannye
kapitaly v Rossii*; Eventov, *Inostrannye kapitaly v rosskoy promyshlennosti*. Paul
Gregory's study, *Russian National Income*, takes issue with, among other things,
the commonly held notion that Russian industrial and economic development

was largely dependent on foreign investments and provides an interesting contrast to the previously mentioned works.

2. Danishevskii, *Lesnoy eksport SSSR*, pp. 8–10.

3. Pasvolsky and Moulton, *Russian Debts and Russian Reconstruction*, p. 99.

4. Ibid., p. 98.

5. Ibid., p. 100.

6. Kennard, *The Russian Yearbook*, 1911, p. 166.

7. Margaret Miller, *The Economic Development of Russia*, p. 61.

8. Pasvolsky and Moulton, *Russian Debts and Russian Reconstruction*, p. 83.

9. Kennard, *The Russian Yearbook*, 1913, p. 301.

10. Despite the fact that Germany had gained an advantage over the United Kingdom in this regard, Britain still occupied a major position in Russia's foreign trade. Together, Germany and the United Kingdom accounted for a significant proportion of all Russia's trade, absorbing up to 60 percent of all the empire's exports and providing up to 70 percent of all its imports.

11. Pasvolsky and Moulton, *Russian Debts and Russian Reconstruction*, p. 76.

12. Ibid., pp. 77–78; and Soboleff, "The Foreign Trade of Russia," p. 311. Soboleff's article appears as part of a volume of reports on key Russian industries, such as agriculture, flax, timber, and mining and metallurgy; each essay was written by a Russian specialist in the particular field. Raffalovich himself was a Russian privy councillor and the president of the Russian Chamber of Commerce of Paris.

13. Davis, *Open Gates to Russia*, pp. 123–24.

14. Worked from returns given in the *Annual Statement of the Trade of the United Kingdom*, 1913.

15. Soboleff, "The Foreign Trade of Russia," p. 318; and Kryukov', *Russko-angliiskaya torgovaya palata*, pp. 17–21. The United States, Canada, Russia, and Argentina were the four most important suppliers of grain to the U.K. market.

16. Soboleff, "The Foreign Trade of Russia," pp. 120, 318; Kryukov', *Russko-angliiskaya torgovaya palata*, pp. 40–41; and Fride, *Inostrannye kuryatnye i yaichnye rynki*.

17. Pelferoff, "Agriculture," p. 42.

18. Soboleff, "The Foreign Trade of Russia," p. 320.

19. See especially Jones, *The State and the Emergence of the British Oil Industry*; and Jones and Trebilcock, "Russian Industry and British Business."

20. Soboleff, "The Foreign Trade of Russia," p. 322.

21. Worked from returns given in the *Annual Statement of the Trade of the United Kingdom*, 1914.

22. Soboleff, "The Foreign Trade of Russia," p. 323.

23. Kennard, *The Russian Yearbook*, 1913, p. 303.

24. Ibid., p. 305.

25. Soboleff, "The Foreign Trade of Russia," p. 323.

26. Worked from returns given in the *Annual Statement of the Trade of the United Kingdom*, 1914.

27. Kennard, *The Russian Yearbook*, 1913, p. 301.

28. Ibid., p. 782; and Soboleff, "The Foreign Trade of Russia," p. 323.

29. Munting, "Ransomes in Russia," pp. 257–58.

30. For a case study of these two firms' involvement in Russia, see Carstensen, *American Enterprise in Foreign Markets*.

31. *Times Book of Russia*, p. 24.

32. Ibid., p. 25.

33. Kennard, *The Russian Yearbook*, 1912, p. 324.

34. Soboleff, "The Foreign Trade of Russia," p. 303. The expansion of the Russian Volunteer Fleet during the last decade before the war, combined with the growing number of Danish and Dutch lines serving the Russian ports, accounted for an increasing volume of Russian shipping at the expense of the British share.

Chapter 2

1. Just how much of a gap in Russo-German trade was created by the war is open to debate. There exists substantial evidence of continued German economic and commercial presence in Russia, despite the official severing of relations and the freezing of German assets by the Russian government. German firms, however, continued to do a considerable business there, albeit indirectly, through neutral affiliates and branches that conducted their transactions under Scandinavian names. According to the *Torgovo Promyshlennaya Gazetta* of 17 February 1916, the Swedish electrical industry provided one outlet through which the Germans had successfully maintained their interests in the Russian market. Having established a large plant in Sweden, this particular German electrical manufacturer was able to continue to sell its own products in Russia merely by marketing them under the Swedish name. There were also instances reported where items of German origin were sold in Russia using brand names that alluded to English or Russian manufacture, and sometimes even carried patriotic inscriptions. See Sack, *America's Possible Share in the Economic Future of Russia*, p. 24; and Davis, *Open Gates to Russia*, pp. 78, 124. Sack was director of the Russian Information Bureau in the United States.

2. See Carstensen, *American Enterprise in Foreign Markets*.

3. See especially Wilkins, *The Emergence of Multinational Enterprise*.

4. U.S. Department of Commerce, *Foreign Commerce and Navigation of the United States*, 1900 and 1910. The returns for January–September 1910 show that manufactured goods for the first time made up over 50 percent of all U.S. exports.

Unless otherwise specified, all U.S. statistics given are derived from U.S. returns as reported in the U.S. Department of Commerce, *Foreign Commerce and Navigation of the United States*.

5. Lebedev, *Russko-amerikanskiy ekonomicheskiy otnosheniya*, p. 43; and Sack, *America's Possible Share in the Economic Future of Russia*, pp. 18–19. The rouble value was converted at a rate of fifty-one cents to the rouble.

6. The United States was the single largest purchaser of Russian licorice root, absorbing 27.73 million pounds of the 29.24 million pounds total weight exported in 1910.

7. Lebedev, *Russko-amerikanskiy ekonomicheskiy otnosheniya*, p. 43. A similar case can be made with regard to Russian exports of hides and skins. After Germany and the United Kingdom, Russia was the third largest supplier of hides and skins to the American market. Here again, Germany reexported a considerable percentage of the Russian hides it imported, which in turn undoubtedly made up a substantial proportion of that country's exports of hides to the United States.

8. According to Department of Commerce statistics, Russia was second only to the United Kingdom as a supplier of scrap and refuse rubber to the United States.

9. *Foreign Commerce and Navigation of the United States*; Sack, *America's Possible Share in the Economic Future of Russia*, p. 19; and Lebedev, *Russko-amerikanskiy ekonomicheskiy otnosheniya*, pp. 43–44.

10. A more striking example of the end result of this practice can be found in the case of Russian fur imports. Official Russian returns offer no data on American-bound fur exports, the overwhelming majority of Russian pelts being exported via Germany to all other European—and American—destinations. The Department of Commerce, on the other hand, gives considerable information relating to the import of Russian furs to the United States. See Sack, *America's Possible Share in the Economic Future of Russia*, p. 16.

11. Official Report of the Ministry of Finance on Russian Trade with the United States, as quoted in ibid., pp. 16, 18. For the value of Russian exports according to U.S. consulates in Russia, see Snodgrass, *Russia*, p. 18.

12. Davis, *Open Gates to Russia*, pp. 133–34.

13. U.S. Department of Commerce, *Diplomatic and Consular Report for the Moscow District*, 1913, pp. 18–19; Kennard, *The Russian Year Book*, 1916, p. 737; and U.S. Department of Commerce returns in *Foreign Commerce and Navigation of the United States*. Bremen in particular was a major transit port for Russian-bound American cotton, handling on average one-fifth of the total Russian imports of cotton over European frontiers between 1895 and 1905, and growing in importance to handle nearly one-half of this trade between 1910 and 1912.

14. U.S. Department of Commerce and Bureau of Statistics, *Statistical Abstracts of Foreign Countries*, 1909; and Snodgrass, *Russia*, p. 18.

15. European middlemen again account for this difference: "Part of the American machinery, after being reloaded in Germany, England or Denmark, is registered in our statistics as coming from those countries and not from the United States." "Report of the Russian Ministry of Finance on Trade with the United States," as quoted in Sack, *America's Possible Share in the Economic Future of Russia*, pp. 20–21.

16. Snodgrass, *Russia*, p. 18. The United States had competed successfully with Germany and the United Kingdom for this market, capturing the bulk of Russia's

purchases of complex agricultural machinery—particularly harvesters, reapers, and binders—by the end of the nineteenth century. By 1910–11, the United States had begun to undermine seriously the overall position of both the United Kingdom and Germany in the Russian agricultural machinery market: though Russian imports of these goods reflected considerable growth, both Britain and Germany exported less to Russia in 1911 than in 1910, the difference being made up by increased American exports to that country.

17. Such discrepancies caused by the use of European agents are evident in the returns of nearly all the articles imported from the United States. Although Russia was not normally noted as being an importer of foodstuffs (especially grain), a remarkable case can be found in Russian imports of American wheat flour. While Russian statistics put the yearly average of all flours (except potato flour) imported from the United States during the five years 1906–10 at 15.7 million pounds, the Department of Commerce gives that of wheat flour *alone* as 75.81 million pounds for the same period. The flour was exported predominantly to Finland and, because of the lack of direct trade with the United States, these imports were registered in Finland as having come from Germany. This is supported by official German trade reports. See U.S. Department of Commerce, *Foreign Commerce and Navigation of the United States*; and Sack, *America's Possible Share in the Economic Future of Russia*, pp. 21, 22.

18. Snodgrass, *Russia*, p. 18.

19. The 1832 trade agreement was terminated by the United States because of the Russian government's systematic persecution of Jews.

20. NARG 59 [State Department], file 611.6131, contains letters from industrialists and traders protesting the termination of the 1832 trade agreement.

21. U.S. Chamber of Commerce to the Secretary of State, 31 December, 1912, NARG 59, file 611.6131/40. The American Chamber of Commerce gives an extremely conservative 20 percent as the portion of these exports bound for Russia.

22. Russian Foreign Minister S. D. Sazonov, as reported by U.S. Ambassador Curtis Guild. *FRUS, 1911*, p. 695, as cited in Tuve, "Changing Directions in Russian-American Economic Relations," p. 56.

23. *New York Times*, 13 July 1913.

24. Narkomfin, *Narodnokhozyaystvo v 1916g.*, pp. 218–39.

25. Charles Wilson, St. Petersburg, to Secretary of State, 24 August 1914, NARG 59, file 611.613/75.

26. The United States, which had been without an ambassador in the Russian capital since the abrogation of the trade agreement in January 1913, had dispatched George Marye to take up the post soon after the war had broken out. He had been specifically entrusted with negotiating a new treaty. See Tuve, "Changing Directions in Russian-American Economic Relations," pp. 59–60.

27. Ibid., p. 60.

28. Nolde, *Russia in the Economic War*, p. 147.

29. For a rather more critical assessment of the British conditions, see Stone, *The Eastern Front*, pp. 153–54.

30. Lebedev, *Russko-amerikanskiy ekonomicheskiy otnosheniya*, p. 160. Aschberg, a Swedish banker and financier, had close ties with the Russo-Asiatic Bank as well.

31. Ibid., p. 163.

32. Tuve, "Changing Directions in Russian-American Economic Relations," p. 61; and Ganelin, *Rossiya i SShA*, p. 22.

33. See, for example, Kalamantiano, *Possibilities of Success of Import and Export Trade between Russia and the USA*. Kalamantiano was associated with the Russian Association of Commerce and Industry.

34. The Russian-American Chamber of Commerce was reportedly recognized as an organ of the Russian government, which it used to promote direct Russian-American trade. Tuve, "Changing Directions in Russian-American Economic Relations," p. 61.

35. A number of other institutions followed suit, extending credit to the Russian government on terms similar to those reached with National City Bank. Lebedev, *Russko-amerikanskiy ekonomicheskiy otnosheniya*, pp. 251–52; Nolde, *Russia in the Economic War*, p. 145; and Tuve, "Changing Directions in Russian-American Economic Relations," p. 65.

36. Seleznev, *Ten' dollara nad rossiey*, p. 24.

37. Long-standing publications such as the *New York Commercial* and *Moody's Magazine* devoted ample space to this theme, often supplying no more than the most basic information about Russia. Such journals aimed to create a familiarity; one article in *Moody's* went so far as to compare Petrograd with Chicago. *Moody's Magazine*, August 1916, p. 473, as cited in Tuve, "Changing Directions in Russian-American Economic Relations," p. 62.

38. *Russia*, May 1916, p. 17, and *Russian Review*, July 1917, p. 17, as cited in Tuve, "Changing Directions in Russian-American Economic Relations," pp. 61–63. It is interesting to note that a number of such publications came into existence shortly after the war started.

39. *Russia*, May 1916, as cited in Tuve, "Changing Directions in Russian-American Economic Relations," p. 61. Tuve goes on to reason that such optimism was at least partially justified because of the "growing efficiency" of peasant labor and the increase in savings bank deposits, which was brought about by the prohibition of vodka.

40. Seleznev, *Ten' dollara nad rossiey*, pp. 10–11.

41. Gaston Plantiff to Liebold. Stockholm, 26 July 1916, FMCA, Acc. 572, box 16. Similar sentiments were echoed by the Cadillac Motor Car Company in a letter to the State Department in which it urged the speedy conclusion of a trade agreement: "Our Company expects Russia to be one of her greatest foreign markets subsequent to the War." Cadillac Motor Car Co., Detroit, to Secretary of State, 29 May 1917, NARG 59, file 611.6131/138.

42. One of these schemes, undertaken by the American International Corpora-

tion was promoted by Frances Vanderlip, whose bank—National City Bank —had contributed half of the $50 million capitalization of the company. Lebedev, *Russko-amerikanskiy ekonomicheskiy otnosheniya* p. 220; and Tuve, "Changing Directions in Russian-American Economic Relations," p. 63.

43. *Times Book of Russia*, p. 19; and Beable, *Commercial Russia*, p. 6. Beable organized the Anglo-Russian Trade Commission.

44. Beable, *Commercial Russia*, p. 1.

45. Rozhansky, *British Opportunities in Russia*, p. 5.

46. Ibid., p. 5. While the British consular reports coming from Russia were also optimistic about the commercial future in the country, they were frequently tempered with advice to British merchants to reassess their old business methods. Pointing out that the Americans had met with success by adjusting their commercial practices to suit Russian needs and customs, the consular reports went on to warn that the market would indeed be lost to Britain if similar changes were not made. See U.K. Parliamentary Papers, Diplomatic and Consular Reports, Russia: *Report on the Trade of the Consular District of Batoum*, 1914; *Report on the Trade of the Consular District of Novorossisk*, 1914; and *Report on the Trade of the Consular District of Odessa*, 1914.

47. With the U.S. entry into the war, all legal and diplomatic obstacles in the way of granting direct government aid to Russia were removed, and $325 million worth of credit was quickly extended to the Russians for the financing of their war purchases in the United States. It is worthwhile noting that the new provisional government that was established after the March Revolution had a moral credibility for Wilson, enabling him to give his wholehearted support to the regime. For a discussion of Wilsonian policy, see Link, *Wilson the Diplomatist*; and Levin, *Woodrow Wilson and World Politics*.

48. See especially *Russko-amerikanskaya torgovlaya palata v Moskva*; *Otchet o deyatel'nosti russko-amerikanskoy torgovoy palat'i za 1916g.*; *Commercial Russia*, the official organ of the American-Russian Chamber of Commerce of New York; and *Vestnik Russko-Amerikanskoe Torgovoy Palat'i*.

49. This is not to say that these relations were totally without discord. There was a good deal of Russian suspicion of American motives as well; resentment rapidly developed over the domineering approach of the Stevens Commission, which was sent to aid the Russians in operating the trans-Siberian railway. The growing presence of ostensibly philanthropic organizations such as the Red Cross and the YMCA also drew fire from the Russians. Rumors concerning the true nature and objectives of these groups spread quickly, and the American charitable presence was soon attributed with a wide range of ulterior commercial motives. *FRUS*, 1918, Russia, 1:111; and Lebedev, *Russko-amerikanskiy ekonomicheskiy otnosheniya*, pp. 348–49. The British, it must be pointed out, not only agreed with these views but positively encouraged them.

50. Beable, *Commercial Russia*, p. 8; Kennard, *Russian Year Book*, 1916, p. 741; and Davis, *Open Gates to Russia*, pp. 77–78.

51. Plantiff, Stockholm, to Liebold, 26 July 1916, FMCA, Acc. 572, box 16.

52. Francis, *Russia from the American Embassy*, p. 25. The American ambassador to France echoed these sentiments after he learned that British companies were "teaching their employees Russian in expectation of future commercial opportunities there." Accordingly, he advised his government that "a large group of Americans [should be] stationed in Russia specifically to counter British economic efforts." See Sharp to Wilson, 8 August 1918, Wilson Papers, Library of Congress.

53. Moulton and Pasvolsky, *Russian Debts and Russian Reconstruction*, p. 102. At the same time the postwar potential of Russia was being exhorted as being the new eldorado, the wartime realities for some were anything but profitable. The war seriously disrupted a number of businesses, causing considerable losses and indeed not a few failures. A notable example of where the war created less than favorable conditions for profitable business can be found in the case of the Singer Sewing Machine Company in Russia. Although business in the country had been a great success up to 1914, the war years witnessed a dramatic decline in sales and profits. In addition to being unable to import finished machines or to manufacture profitably in Russia, the company was also faced with increasing difficulties in collecting the installment payments due on the machines sold on credit. By the summer of 1917 things were so bad that the company began to reconsider doing business in that country. According to a memorandum entitled "The Reasons Compelling the Singer Co. to Discontinue Its Business in Russia," the company lost over 17 million roubles during the three years of the war—an amount that exceeded the profits of the company during its entire presence in Russia. See Fithian, "Soviet Economic Relations," p. 18.

54. Baker, *Woodrow Wilson*, 7:349. In a letter to Representative Frank Clark, Wilson wrote, "I have not lost faith in the Russian outcome by any means. Russia, like France in a past century, will no doubt have to go through some deep water but she will come out upon firm land on the other side." Ibid., p. 355.

55. Wardrop, Moscow, to the Foreign Office, 24 January 1918, FO 368/1970.

56. As late as mid-1919 there was evidence of considerable transactions in these scrips: Russian government, railway, and municipal bonds such as the 5 percent loan of 1906 were still traded, as well as 4 percent Russian government loan bonds, 6 percent Russian city bonds, and 8 percent railway and 2 percent "rentes" bonds. The mines included the Kyshtim, the Irtysh, the Russo-Asiatic, the Spassky, the Caucasus Copper, and the Lena Gold companies; and among the oil companies still active on the London Exchange were the Baku-Russian, the Russian Petroleum, the North Caucasian, the Ural Caspian, Spies, New Schibaieff, Black Sea Amals, Anglo-Maikop, and the Maikop Pipeline Company. See *Russian Outlook*, 19 July 1919, p. 261.

57. Richard Crawford, British Embassy, Washington, to Lord Euston Percy, Foreign Office, 30 July 1918, FO 371/4367.

58. Richard Crawford, British Embassy, Washington, to Lord Euston Percy, Foreign Office, 23 August 1918, FO 371/4367. It is interesting to note that along with the expansion of British export trade, Crawford advocated "confining our

imports exclusively to real essentials. . . . It is the only sound way in which we shall be able to meet our liabilities incurred in this war."

59. The British and United States governments kept their channels of communications with the Bolsheviks open through their unofficial agents, R. Bruce Lockhart and Raymond Robins. Through these representatives, both countries continued to sound the Soviet government throughout the spring—and, indeed, even after the signing of the Brest-Litovsk Treaty. While undoubtedly concerned with attempting to bring Russia back into the war, these agents were also entrusted with the protection and promotion of their country's economic interests in Russia. Robins in particular was credited with attempts to foster economic cooperation between the United States and Soviet Russia, and his representations along these lines are believed to have forestalled the nationalization of several American concerns in Russia, including International Harvester, Singer, and Westinghouse Brake Company. See William A. Williams, *American-Russian Relations*; Meiburger, *Efforts of Raymond Robins toward the Recognition of Soviet Russia*; Hard, *Raymond Robins Own Story*; Furaev, *Sovetsko-amerikanskie otnoshenniya*. For details concerning the unofficial British agent Lockhart, see Ullman, *Anglo-Soviet Relations*, vol. 1; and Lockhart, *Memoirs of a British Agent*.

Chapter 3

1. See Sir Auckland Geddes, Evidence Presented to a War Cabinet Meeting, May 1919; and Victor Wellesley to Sir Eyre Crowe, 14 June 1919; FO 368/2253.

2. Hoff-Wilson, *Ideology and Economics*, and Sutton, *Wall Street and the Bolshevik Revolution*, come the closest to being exceptions to this. Hoff-Wilson's work, however, dismisses the early American pro-Soviet trade lobby, and argues that the American business community failed to have any appreciable influence on the development of U.S.-Soviet relations. Sutton, on the other hand, is primarily concerned with the clandestine efforts by major banking and industrial circles to support and promote the Bolshevik movement as a means of extending monopoly control. According to Sutton, this group believed that the Bolsheviks would effectively reduce Russia to a "captive technical market."

3. The Allied intervention in Russia has spawned a number of varying interpretations. By no means an exhaustive listing, the following works can be taken as a representative selection of studies on the early phase of Allied-Soviet relations, and should be referred to for a more detailed analysis of the events and governmental decision making that lead up to the intervention: Coates and Coates, *Armed Intervention in Russia*; Kennan, *Soviet-American Relations*; Mints, *Angliiskaya interventsiya i severnaya kontr-revolyutsiya*; Strakhovsky, *Intervention in Archangel*, and *The Origins of American Intervention in North Russia*; Ullman, *Anglo-Soviet Relations*; Unterberger, *America's Siberian Expedition*; and John Albert White, *The Siberian Intervention*.

4. The increasing paralysis of the Russian transportation network in 1916–17

had prevented these supplies from being shipped to the front. The congestion at these ports was so bad that the limited warehouse space had long ago been filled, and goods were often piled directly on the docks. Needless to say, the condition of these goods suffered greatly from months of exposure to the elements and pillage, and a large percentage of the supplies was found to be worthless by the Allies when they occupied the port. See Kennan, *Soviet-American Relations*, 2:17, 20.

Trotsky, in one of his many sessions with Lockhart, had agreed to provide timber and other raw materials in exchange for the Allied stores in Russia. See Lockhart to Undersecretary of State, Moscow, 4 April 1918, FO 371/3285.

5. Even in the case of Lenin's assertion that a state of war existed between Britain and Soviet Russia, the British government nonetheless instructed its agent, R. H. Bruce Lockhart, to maintain as far as possible his "existing relations with the Bolshevik Government. Rupture or declaration of war should come, if it must, from Bolsheviks not from Allies." Undersecretary of State to Lockhart, 8 August 1918, FO 371/3278. See also, Lockhart, *Memoirs of a British Agent*.

Although Lockhart was repeatedly referred to as an "unofficial representative" so that the Bolsheviks would not misconstrue his appointment as an act of recognition, it is interesting to note that he was initially appointed as "the representative of His Majesty's Government in Petrograd in maintaining informal relations with the de facto government." See Parliamentary Question by Mr. Joseph King, 11 March 1918, FO 371/10470.

6. *Board of Trade Journal*, 17 November 1917.

7. Ullman, *Anglo-Soviet Relations*, 1:232.

8. Francis, Vologda, to Secretary of State, no. 1118, 11 July 1918, NARG 59, file 861.00/2575; and Balfour to Reading, Washington, telegram no. 4316, 11 July 1918, in Wiseman papers, as cited in Ullman, *Anglo-Soviet Relations*, 1:233.

9. Licenses for the export of Russian goods, especially seeds, were still being regularly granted for transit through Sweden and Finland. E. Howard, Stockholm, to Foreign Office, no. 12, 3 January 1918, FO 368/1967.

10. See Chapter 2 above for particular reference to the development of these routes prior to the war. For a description of the postrevolutionary use of these routes, see Commercial Report 62, Copenhagen, 12 January 1918, FO 368/1969; and my Chapter 6.

11. Vauxhall Motor Co., Ltd., to Secretary of the Treasury, 13 May 1918, FO 371/3294; Vauxhall Motor Co., Ltd., to Foreign Office, 23 July 1918, and same to same, [August 1918], FO 368/1969; and Picton Bagge, Odessa, to Undersecretary of State, no. 5, 4 January 1918, FO 371/3283; Kodak Company to Foreign Office, 16 July 1918, FO 368/1974; and B. Hayton Fleet, Special Department of Overseas Trade Consul, Siberia, to Foreign Office, [received 27 February 1920], FO 371/4049.

12. Robins was specifically mentioned as the intervening force who prevented the nationalization of these properties. Fischer, *The Soviets in World Affairs*, 1:300.

Anglo-Russian Cotton Factories Ltd., Petrograd, to Foreign Office, 28 January

1918, FO 368/1968. For an insight into the International Harvester Company's operations in Soviet Russia, see Pickering, "The International Harvester Company in Russia."

13. Wardrop, Petrograd, to Foreign Office, 20 December 1917, FO 368/1969.

Obviously counting on some future Russian government to honor its predecessors' obligations, this same institution had been paying the semiannual interest on $25 million of Imperial Russian Five Year, 5.5 Percent Bonds held in the United States. In contrast, the British government froze the assets of the previous Russian government and associated institutions in early January 1918—well before the decree of 10 February annulling all state debts. The British government also assumed liability for 82 percent of the face value of the £17.5 million in privately subscribed Treasury Bills that were issued on behalf of the Russian government. See I. V. Bubnoff, Manager, London Branch, Moscow Narodny Bank to U.S. Embassy, London, no. 9690, 13 August 1918, NARG 59, file 661.4115/1; and Ullman, *Anglo-Soviet Relations*, 1:56, 69–70.

14. Minutes on Report Forwarded from H.M. Consul General, Moscow, no. 299, 29 December 1917, FO 368/1969. Similar plans to gain control of key industries by purchasing Russian banks had been considered by the British as early as November 1917. With the blessings of the Foreign Office, the British Embassy in Petrograd had been actively involved with Karol Yaroshinsky and H. A. F. Leech, financiers of shady reputations, in their scheme to purchase five banks that had branches in "friendly territory." It was argued that this would enable the government to extend its financial support to the local non-Bolshevik forces as well as "obtain control of important industrial resources in South Russia." See Kettle, *The Allies and the Russian Collapse*, pp. 139–42.

15. "Memorandum on the Tzaritzin Works," [circa February 1924]. Vickers Archives, Envelope b-40, "War Work. Vickers Ltd. and the Imperial Russian Government."

16. M. Romanoff, Kyshtim, to Russo-Asiatic Consolidated Ltd., London, via Lindley, Petrograd, no. 131 Russtrade, 15 January 1918, FO 368/1965.

17. Lindley, Petrograd, to Foreign Office, no. 131(R), 15 January 1918, FO 371/3294; and Lindley to Department of Overseas Trade, no. 130(R), 15 January 1918, FO 368/1965.

18. Clark to Wellesley, 23 April 1918; Comptroller General, Department of Overseas Trade Memorandum to Foreign Office, 26 April 1918; and Department of Overseas Trade to Foreign Office, 2 May 1918; FO 368/1972; and Foreign Office Memorandum, January 1918, FO 368/1969.

19. See Minute by W.H.S., 21 January 1918, FO 368/1969; and Minute by E. H. Carr, 6 May 1918, FO 371/3477.

The impression of a commercial presence was apparently considered to be as important as its actual maintenance. When a Dutch newspaper interpreted the departure of sixty English factory managers from Russia as a sign that the British intended to cut back on their industrial activity in that country, the News Department of the Foreign Office thought enough of the report to issue a prompt denial through Reuters. Commercial Report no. 62, Copenhagen, "Summary of a Series of Articles Appearing in *Berlingske Tidende*," 12 January 1918, FO 368/1969.

20. Minutes, War Cabinet Meeting, no. 294, 7 December 1917, Cab. 23/27.

21. *FRUS*, 1918, Russia, 1:397; and Memorandum by Lansing, 7 December 1917, in Lansing Papers, Library of Congress.

22. Newton D. Baker to Peyton C. March, 7 September 1917; and Baker, "Personal Observations about the North Russian and Siberian Expeditions," 11 November 1924, enclosed in Baker to Mrs. John Casserly, 15 November 1924; Newton D. Baker Papers, Library of Congress, as cited in Trani, "Woodrow Wilson and the Decision to Intervene in Russia," p. 443.

The administration was by no means alone. Similar doubts concerning the efficacy of the intervention were expressed by notable members of the American business community. According to M. A. Oudin, International General Electric Company along with twenty other firms—all with interests in Russia—favored economic assistance rather than military intervention. Among the companies named by Oudin were New York Life Insurance, Chase National Bank, Vacuum Oil, Baldwin Locomotives, International Harvester, and Singer. M. A. Oudin, Vice-President, International General Electric, to Secretary of Commerce Redfield, 3 June 1918, NARG 40, file 77295; and Lord Reading, Washington, to Foreign Office, no. 2585, 8 June 1918, FO 371/3286.

23. Commander U.S. Naval Forces in North Russia to Force Commander, 28 November 1918, NARG 45, WA-6, file 75-56; same to same, "General Intelligence Report," 20 December 1918, NARG 45, WA-6, box 605, file 136-56; Intelligence Report no. 338, Vladivostok, 4 June 1919, NARG 45, WA-6, folder 20978/305; American Consul, London, to Secretary of State, 3 May 1918, NARG 59, file 661.119/415a; and same to same, 23 July 1919, NARG 59, file 661.4115/4a.

24. General Poole, Archangel, to Secretary of State. no. 572, 13 November 1918. *FRUS*, 1918, Russia, 2:567.

25. Lockhart, "Memorandum on the Internal Situation in Russia," 1 November 1918, Milner Papers, box C-2.

26. "Report by Acting Naval Attaché for Imports and Exports from Archangel during the Navigation Season, 1918," no. 1303, Archangel, 10 February 1919, NARG 59, file 661.00/10.

27. Board of Customs and Excise to Foreign Office, "Trade with Areas under Hostile Occupation," 23 May 1918; and Minutes; FO 368/1971.

28. Wishaw, Archangel, to Foreign Office (via Wardrop, Moscow), 24 June 1918, FO 368/1967.

29. E. Schluter & Co., London to Foreign Office, 9 January 1918; and Minutes; FO 368/1968.

In other cases in which a company may have expressed an interest in cutting its losses and selling, the Foreign Office response was much the same: although the government was unable to advise in the matter, it would "naturally view with regret the disappearance of British interests in Russia." See the Anglo-Russian

Cotton Factories Ltd. to Foreign Office, 11 March 1918; and Balfour to the Anglo-Russian Cotton Factories Ltd., 20 March 1918; FO 368/1966.

30. The British practiced a "robber policy" in more than one way: in addition to exporting valuable goods that the Bolsheviks could have sold for much needed foreign currency or could have themselves bartered, during the spring of 1918 the British also stripped Petrograd clean of almost all metals, metal goods, rubber, machinery, industrial plant—in short, anything that could be shipped. The British officer in charge of this systematic plundering stated that less than 40 percent of the war stores and valuable goods in Petrograd remained by mid-1918. For the three months April to June 1918, he claimed to have shipped away to the North between 4 and 4.5 million poods of such goods. DeFalber (Restriction of Enemy Supplies Department) to Carr, no. 9197, 6 September 1918; and Enclosure, "Report by Captain Schwabe"; FO 371/3313; John Field, War Office Memorandum, 0149/430, "Evacuation From Petrograd of Metals and other Military Stores in 1918," 8 February 1924, FO 371/10488; and Lt. P. I. Bukowski, Petrograd, to Lt. Col. James A. Ruggles, Chief of American Military Mission, Vologda, 1 June 1918, NARG 84, American Consulate, Petrograd, box 4.

31. F. N. Best & Co, London, to Foreign Office, June 1918, FO 368/1973; and Board of Trade, Timber Supply Department, to Foreign Office, "Notes on the Russian Timber Position," 29 November 1918, FO 368/1974.

32. Mints, *Angliiskaya interventsiya i severnaya kontr-revolyutsiya*, p. 140.

33. "Minutes of a Meeting Held at the Ministry of Shipping to Discuss the Question of Free Trading in the White Sea," 15 July 1919, FO 371/4022.

34. Ullman, *Anglo-Soviet Relations*, 2:24.

35. Ibid., 2:26; and Francis to Secretary of State, 27 October 1918, NARG 59, file 861.51/436.

36. Commander, U.S. Naval Forces in North Russia to Force Commander, 28 November 1918, NARG 45, WA-6, box 605, file 74-56; and same to same, "General Intelligence Report," 20 December 1918, NARG 45, WA-6, box 605, file 136-56.

37. Cecil's Minutes on Résumé from Vice-Consul Nash, Ekaterinburg, [?May or June 1918], FO 371/3292.

38. The Russia Committee, "Notes on Allied Policy in Siberia," 23 April 1918, FO 371/3292.

39. Vice-Consul Nash, Irkutsk, to Foreign Office, 28 January 1918, FO 371/3291.

40. Sir C. Greene, Tokyo to Foreign Office, no. 435, 27 April 1918, FO 371/3292; and Sir J. Jordan, Peking, to Foreign Office, no. 50, 13 June 1918, FO 371/3292. It was noted by Jordan that such an arrangement would avoid any question of recognition as well. This proposal bears a striking resemblance to the Supreme Economic Council's decision in January 1920 to allow trade through the Russian cooperative societies.

41. Because of "geographical considerations" and "economy of tonnage," it was understood that "the main burden must fall on the United States and

Japan." J. D. Gregory, Foreign Office Memorandum, December 1919, *DBFP*, 3:723–25.

As early as September 1918, George Clerk of the Russian Department at the Foreign Office noted that, because of the existing "tonnage difficulties" and the "infinite stocks of material" the United States had available for export to Siberia, "we can gain only by joining up our organisation with the Americans or rather . . . letting the Americans into our organisation." Balfour agreed with Clerk's estimation. See G. R. Clerk to Lord Robert Cecil, Russian Department, no. 78, 24 September 1918, FO 371/3367.

42. Sir Rupert Llewelyn Smith to Lord Robert Cecil, 27 July 1918; and Minute by H.A.B., 20 August 1918; FO 368/1974.

43. *DBFP*, 3:724.

44. Foreign Office to Elliot, Vladivostok, no. 210, 12 December 1918, FO 371/3367.

45. American Consulate, London, to Secretary of State, 28 July 1919, NARG 59, file 661.411/5.

46. American Consulate, Harbin, to Secretary of State, 12 November 1921, NARG 151, box 2734, file 611; see also the relevant correspondence in FO 371/3977; FO 371/3987; and WO 0149/7335. A similar bank scheme, though on considerably greater scale, was seriously considered by the British government in 1919. See Chapter 4.

47. Further aid in financing Siberian trade was expected from the Hong Kong and Shanghai Banking Corporation, which had applied for permission to open a branch in Vladivostok in September 1918. The government was more than willing to give assurances that it would "do its best to protect this bank from penalty in the event of any Russian government which may be formed taking legal or other steps against them." C. S. Addis, Hong Kong and Shanghai Banking Corporation, to Foreign Office, 2 October 1918, FO 371/3366.

48. See File 91, Russia, Political, 1919, FO 371/3956.

49. Originally detained in Russia as prisoners of war, those Czechoslovakian nationalists who were willing to take up arms against Germany were in Siberia awaiting transportation to the western front. After the revolution, however, Bolshevik neutrality and the Brest-Litovsk Treaty with Germany dictated that these troops be "repatriated" through Vladivostok. It was en route to Vladivostok on the Trans-Siberian railway that the Czechoslovak troops became embroiled in the civil war. See Kennan, *Soviet-American Relations*, vol. 2.

50. John F. Stevens [chairman of the U.S. Advisory Committee of Railway Experts to Russia], "Russia during the World War," John F. Stevens Papers, Hoover Institution Archives.

Wilson's moral stand on Russia was outlined in his Fourteen Points Address to the United States Congress, 8 January 1918; the "Aide Memoire" to Allied ambassadors cites the Czechoslovaks as the administration's reason for suddenly reversing its earlier position on intervention in Siberia. Secretary of State to Allied

Ambassadors, "Aide Memoire," 17 July 1918, *FRUS*, 1918, Russia, 2:287–90; and Morely, *The Japanese Thrust into Siberia*.

51. Department of Commerce, Bureau of Foreign and Domestic Commerce, General Press Release, 30 November 1918, NARG 151, file 882. The U.S. government was early on quite clearly concerned over the possibility of Britain gaining a commercial edge in Russia. A fair number of requests were fired off to the Consulate in London for information on "measures taken by Great Britain to promote the resumption of its trade with non-Bolshevik Russia" as well as for details concerning the Siberian Supply Company. See State Department to U.S. Consulate, London, 31 May 1918, NARG 59, file 661.119/415a; State Department to U.S. Consulate, London, 23 July 1919; and U.S. Consulate, London, to State Department, 24 July 1919, NARG 59, file 661.4115/4a.

52. Secretary of State to Allied Ambassadors, "Aide Memoire" concerning the Russian Bureau, 10 October 1918, NARG 182, box 1550. While the Russian Bureau was initially set up to handle American trade in North Russia as well as Siberia, British economic domination of the Murmansk province effectively prevented the bureau from having any extensive dealings there. For details of the organization and operations of the bureau, see Killen, *The Russian Bureau*.

53. Acting Secretary of State Polk to American Consul, Omsk, 3 February 1919, NARG 59, file 611.61171/11.

54. B. F. Johnson, Vladivostok, to L. V. Lang, New York, 16 August 1918, intercepted letter, NARG 165, box 48, file 20978/305, "Confidential Files. Financial and Economic Conditions in Siberia."

55. Killen, *The Russian Bureau*, pp. 70–72. Representatives of the National City Bank did indeed go to Vladivostok in mid-November 1918 to open a branch there.

56. USS *Brooklyn* to Secretary of the Navy, for State and Ordnance Departments from Preston, I.N. 2067, 2 August 1918, NARG 45, WA-6, box 607; and same to same, I.N. 2438, 13 August 1918, NARG 45, WA-6, box 614(b).

57. USS *Brooklyn* to Secretary of the Navy, for State and Ordnance Departments from Preston, I.N. 2438, 13 August 1918, NARG 45, WA-6, box 614(b). It is also apparent that the government was not averse to dealing with the Bolsheviks in order to acquire platinum. According to an intelligence report filed from Stockholm, the Soviet Minister of Finance had arrived in that city with "18 trunks said to contain . . . a certain amount of platinum. . . . Advise Department of Commerce and U.S. War Trade Board that Dr. Huntington will remain [in] Stockholm another week. He has been for platinum in Russia and understands the situation." Naval Attaché, Christiania, to Naval Intelligence, no. 5672, 27 September 1918, NARG 45, WA-6, box 602. Huntington was concerned with Russian affairs at the Bureau of Foreign and Domestic Commerce.

58. My italics. War Department to Chief Military Intelligence Branch, Executive Division. "Platinum," 27 August 1918, NARG 165, MID, box 168, file 184-20.

59. Bureau of Foreign and Domestic Commerce to Foreign Trade Advisor, Department of State, 12 June 1918, NARG 151, file 882; and Fithian, "Soviet Economic Relations," pp. 41–46.

60. See, for example, correspondence from the Lied Corporation, the Russian-Siberian Merchants Association, and the American-Siberian Export and Import Company, Inc., in NARG 59, file 611.61171/20 and NARG 59, file 611.1124/4. All these firms were chartered specifically to take advantage of commercial opportunities in Siberia. See also the intercept from B. F. Johnson, Vladivostok, to L. V. Levy, New York, 16 August 1918, "Confidential Files and Economic Conditions in Siberia," in NARG 45, WA-6, box 48, file 20978/305.

61. Ansel R. Clark to Bureau of Foreign and Domestic Commerce, no. 102, 28 July 1919, NARG 151, box 2558, file 511.

62. Memorandum by Major General P. de Radcliffe, Director of Military Operations, 13 November 1918, Cabinet Paper GT 6274, Cab. 24/69.

63. From remarks made by Lord Curzon, at the 40th Meeting of the Eastern Committee, 2 December 1919, Cab. 27/24.

64. Remark concerning Baku made by Lord Robert Cecil, at the 40th Meeting of the Eastern Committee, 2 December 1919, Cab. 27/24.

65. Jones, *The State and the Emergence of the British Oil Industry*, pp. 50, 61–62. Jones draws his statistics from Ol', *Inostrannye kapitaly v Rossii*, pp. 44–54.

66. George Tweedy, Managing Director, Anglo-Maikop Corporation, to the Assistant Secretary, Commercial Relations and Trade Department, 14 December 1918, FO 368/1974.

Tweedy also informed the government about the properties and interests of the corporation that were to be involved in the transaction—some 2,376 acres of oil-bearing lands and leaseholds in the Maikop region, some 999 acres in the Kuban, as well as a pipeline and transport company, various refineries in the region, and distribution and storage facilities in Moscow and Petrograd.

67. H. Fountain, Board of Trade, to George Tweedy, Commercial Relations and Treaties Series (CRT 7657), 20 November 1918, FO 368/1974.

68. J. Cadman for W. Long, Petroleum Executive to the Comptroller, Foreign Trade Department of the Foreign Office, 10 December 1918, FO 368/1974.

69. Balfour to the Petroleum Executive, 13 December 1918, FO 368/1974.

Originally not included in the nationalization decree of 20 December 1917, the Narodny Bank and other specialized banking and credit institutions were free to conduct business much as before the revolution. The Bolsheviks feared that any threat to these institutions would turn the peasantry against them. Even after they were officially nationalized in December 1918, the cooperative societies and their financial organs were allowed to continue operations relatively unscathed. The Moscow Narodny Bank was one of the only remaining financial links with the West and was essential in the conduct of trade with the Russian cooperative societies when it was permitted in January 1920. As it became clear that the British would receive a Russian trade delegation representing Centrosoyus—but not one representing the Soviet government—it was imperative that the illusion of distinction between these two bodies be maintained. See Epstein, *Les banques de commerce russes*, pp. 74–108; and Carr, *The Bolshevik Revolution*, 2:138, 239–40.

70. Department of Commerce, Bureau of Foreign and Domestic Commerce, no. 81, "British Trade with Russia," London, 25 June 1919, NARG 151, box 2239, file 448, "United Kingdom, 1919–1929."

71. Preston, Ekaterinburg, to Foreign Office, 11 July 1918, FO 368/1971.

72. U.S. Embassy, Constantinople, to Secretary of State, no. 5402, 24 November 1919, NARG 59, file 661.4115/15.

73. Board of Trade, "War Risk Insurance Scheme," 21 June 1919, FO 371/4022; and "British Trade with Russia," London, no. 81, 25 June 1919, NARG 151, box 2239, file 448.

74. Consul General Skinner, London, to State Department, 25 June 1919, NARG 59, file 661.4115/12.

75. U.S. Bureau of Foreign and Domestic Commerce to Department of Shipping Trades, 23 June 1919; and reply, 30 June 1919; NARG 151, box 2558, file 511.

Even in the case of exporting Russian goods already loaded onto ships or dockside in some Black Sea ports—goods that were to be used as credit against supplies and materials received from the United States—there was no organization, save the feeble Russian Bureau, to facilitate any exchange. Complaints about the lack of any official attempts to redress these conditions came not only from the merchants pursuing such trade but from the Russian Embassy as well. Chargé, Russian Embassy, New York, to Acting Secretary of State, 6 March 1919, NARG 59, file 661.119 Vessels/178.

76. Memorandum by Trade Commissioner Gary, London, to Commerce Department, Bureau of Foreign and Domestic Commerce, 27 May 1919; and "Memorandum" by Trade Commissioner Gary, London, 29 May 1919, NARG 151, box 2025, "Business Conditions."

77. Department of Commerce, Bureau of Foreign and Domestic Commerce, no. 81, "British Trade with Russia," London, 25 June 1919, NARG 151, box 2239, file 448, "United Kingdom, 1919–1929."

Chapter 4

1. Field Marshal Lord Ironside, Diary Entry for 7 November 1918, as cited in Ullman, *Anglo-Soviet Relations*, 2:5–6. Ironside was given the temporary rank of brigadier general in North Russia.

2. Imperial War Cabinet, 45th Meeting, 23 December 1918, 3 P.M., Cab. 23/42. By the end of 1918 Britain had an estimated 14,000 troops in North Russia; 4,000, including Canadians, in Siberia; and at least 20,000 troops in the Caucasus.

3. The Supreme Economic Council's Report, 7 June 1919, *FRUS*, 1919, Russia, pp. 149–51; and Ullman, *Anglo-Soviet Relations*, 2:288.

4. War Cabinet Minutes, WC 489, 18 October 1918, noon, Cab. 23/8.

5. Lord Robert Cecil, Parliamentary Undersecretary of State at the Foreign Office, in "Memorandum on Russian Policy," 20 October 1918, Cabinet Paper GT 6050, Cab. 24/67; and Sir Henry Wilson, "Memorandum on Our Present and Future Military Policy in Russia," Cabinet Paper, 13 November 1918, GT 6311, Cab. 24/70.

6. Balfour Memorandum, 1 November 1918, as recorded in War Cabinet Minutes, WC 511, 10 December 1918, noon, Cab. 23/8.

7. Lord Milner, Minutes of the Meeting at the Foreign Office, 13 November 1918, 3:30 P.M., in WC 502, 14 November 1918, Cab. 23/8. More detailed accounts of the military operations can be found in the following works: Bennett, *Cowan's War*; Denikin, *Ocherki russkoi smuty*; Graves, *America's Siberian Adventure*; Ironside, *Archangel, 1918–1919*; Maynard, *The Murmansk Venture*; Melchin, *Amerikanskaya interventsiya v 1918–1920gg.*; and Parfenov, *Grazhdanskaya voina v Sibiri*.

8. Secretary of State to the American Delegation, Paris, for the Allied Powers, no. 2714, 2 August 1919, *FRUS*, 1919, Russia, pp. 155–57. It is interesting to note that, while the Americans were no longer willing to participate in the blockade, the U.S. government repeatedly asserted that the Allies were free to enforce it themselves.

9. Sir Arthur Steel-Maitland to Sir Auckland Geddes, 1 May 1918, FO 371/3477; Director, Military Intelligence (MI5), War Office, to Undersecretary of State for Foreign Affairs, 0149/5739, 13 November 1918, FO 371/3365; and "Report on Raw Materials and Their Sources," 1918, FO 368/2038.

10. Steel-Maitland to Sir Auckland Geddes, 1 May 1918, FO 371/3477.

11. Board of Trade, Department of Overseas Trade, Memorandum, 20 May 1919, FO 371/4022.

12. The development of an especially sharp rivalry between the Board of Trade, the Foreign Office, and the Department of Overseas Trade was the cause of considerable governmental concern in the spring of 1919. See Chapter 3.

13. Villiers's Minutes of an interview with the Representatives of the All-Russian Central Union of Consumers Societies at the Foreign Office, 3 February 1919, FO 371/3994.

14. It is worth noting, however, that there were reports of an active American interest in securing timber concessions in the White Sea region. The British government clearly took this information to heart: when the American Ambassador in London requested a copy of a report on the timber industry and exploitable forest regions of northern Russia, the Foreign Office was loath to part with the report. "I don't see why we should, but it is rather difficult to invent a good excuse for refusing." Ultimately, the request was refused on the grounds that the report was "confidential" and "unofficial." See Professor Stebbing, "Memorandum on

White Sea Timber Trade," 11 January 1919; American Embassy, London, to Foreign Office, 30 July 1919; and Minutes; FO 371/2171.

15. Reilly, New York, to Bagge, no. CKC 416, 10 May 1919, FO 371/3987.

16. Parliamentary Question put to Cecil Harmsworth by Lt. Cmdr. Kenworthy, 5 August 1919, FO 371/3961. Assistant Secretary of State Phillips made a similar statement, declaring that "so far as the United States is concerned, no blockade exists." Reply by Phillips to Senator Wandsworth, 4 November 1919, State Department Russian Series, no. 2, as in Cumming and Pettit, *Russian-American Relations*, p. 351.

17. *Daily Herald*, 9 July 1919, and Minute by W. H. Selby, 15 July 1919, FO 371/4002. See also Minutes of the Council of Four, 17 June 1919, 4 P.M., in *FRUS, Paris Peace Conference*, 6:530–32.

18. Edsel Ford to R. S. Neely [manager of Ford's Foreign Department in New York], 31 March 1919, FMCA, Acc. 49, box 1. Ford went on to instruct Neely "to keep in as close touch with Russia through various channels in New York as possible," and to "keep this agreement confidential for the present."

19. See Ivan Stacheef and Co. Agreement, 14 March 1919, FMCA, Acc. 49, box 1. Even without the instability in Russia, the financial terms of the agreement were extremely liberal for Ford at the time—25 percent against ocean bills of lading, 25 percent upon arrival at ocean destination, and 50 percent ninety days after arrival at ocean destination. Henry Ford, it should be noted, was loath to extend credit to even his own dealers! For an examination of Ford's business in Russia, see Christine White, "Ford in Russia."

20. "Russian Trade and Industrial Opportunities," *Dearborn Independent*, 26 April 1919.

21. Simultaneous with the company's various dealing with non-Bolshevik organizations, Ford's personal secretary was also negotiating with the Soviet trade representative along similar lines. See Chapter 5.

22. Baker to Bliss, 3 March 1919, 861.-602/1, Bliss Papers, Russia, box 248, Library of Congress, as cited in Killen, *The Russian Bureau*, pp. 138–39. See also "British Trade with Russia," Report no. 81, London, 25 June 1919, Department of Commerce, Bureau of Foreign and Domestic Commerce, NARG 151, box 2239, file 448 (United Kingdom), 1919–29.

23. For British suspicions concerning the Red Cross and the YMCA especially, see British Embassy, Washington, to Secretary of State for Foreign Affairs, 23 August 1918, FO 371/4367; Pinder, Rostov, to Foreign Office, 22 October 1919, and others in FO 368/2173; and FO 371/3367. The British were not especially pure on this score either. In May Lindley complained that some of the YMCA personnel sent out to Archangel had been "far from satisfactory," and had "amassed very large sums of roubles in circumstances . . . which appear to me most suspicious." Lindley to Foreign Office, no. 310(R), 13 May 1919, FO 371/4015.

24. Joint Secretary of the Russo-British Co-operative Information Bureau, to Sir Arthur Steel-Maitland, 10 April 1919, FO 368/2176.

25. London Chamber of Commerce to Undersecretary of State for Foreign Affairs, 12 April 1919, FO 368/2171.

26. Bagge, Odessa, to Steel-Maitland, "Anglo-Russian Economic Relations," 14 May 1919, FO 371/4022.

27. Ibid. As mentioned in Chapter 3, things were apparently set afoot in early 1918 when the British Embassy in Petrograd authorized Colonel Keyes to participate in a scheme for the purchase of shares in the Siberian Bank. Yaroshinsky was instrumental in this project as well, though his credibility appears to have survived intact despite the subsequent scandal surrounding this earlier undertaking. See Kettle, *The Allies and the Russian Collapse*, pp. 139–44.

28. Arthur Steel-Maitland, Memorandum to Foreign Office. It was also believed that the success of the scheme would "depend on the establishment of a strong central government in Russia." It is interesting to note that some in the Foreign Office shared Bagge's conviction that the restoration of the monarchy in Russia was "inevitable." See Minute by Leeper, 4 June 1919, FO 371/4022.

29. Minute by J.A.S., 5 July 1919, FO 371/4022. All the minutes on Bagge's memorandum indicate that the scheme was considered "worth supporting." Although the British industrialist Dudley Docker was named as the "competent financial authority" consulted on this matter, no record of his evaluation was found among these papers.

30. Ibid.

31. Ibid.; and Minute by Tilley, 6 June 1919, FO 371/4022.

32. Selby of the Foreign Office even declared that he could "see no political objection whatsoever to giving such approval" and thought that that office could "certainly go as far as saying that if both the Treasury and financial interests here are satisfied we will give M. Yaroshinski our fullest support." Minute, 4 July 1919, FO 371/4022. The British were undoubtedly counting on the possibility of reaching some sort of agreement with the French that would provide for the repayment of the huge Russian debt to France.

33. Reilly, New York, for Bagge, no. CKC 416, 10 May 1919, FO 371/3987; and Bagge, Odessa, to Steel-Maitland, no. 2, Supplementary to "Anglo-Russian Economic Relations," 15 May 1919, FO 371/4022. It is also apparent that the Americans suspected that something was up when official inquiries were made concerning a spate of British purchasing of Russian industrial securities. See Sir C. Marling, Copenhagen, to Foreign Office, no. 904, 10 April 1919, FO 371/4008.

34. Gunther, The Hague, to Secretary of State, no. 6527, 3 July 1919, NARG 59, file 661.419/orig.

35. Minutes of a Meeting at the Ministry of Shipping, 31 May 1919, FO 371/4022.

36. Mints, *Angliiskaya interventsiya i severnaya kontr-revolyutsiya*, p. 133.

37. Commander Naval Forces in North Russia, to Force Commander, "General Intelligence Report," 20 December 1918, NARG 45, WA-6, box 605, file 136-56.

38. Foreign Office to Lindley, Archangel, no. 18, 9 January 1919, FO 371/3952. Export licenses would be granted subject to the condition that, first, the sellers

were paid in sterling in Britain (a written undertaking to this effect "being insisted upon in all cases") and, second, it was understood that the grant of licenses implied no guarantee that tonnage would be available.

39. Restriction of Enemy Supplies Department to Foreign Office, no. 401, 23 April 1919, FO 371/4008.

40. Mints, *Angliiskaya interventsiya i severnaya kontr-revolyutsiya*, p. 134; Cole to War Trade Board, 11 December 1918, NARG 182, box 1590; and Memorandum, "Economic Rehabilitation," 19 November 1918, box 1551. While agreeing to a British request that the United States supply 3,000 tons of food to Murmansk, the War Trade Board stipulated that unless the British altered their politics on the Supply Committee, the food would be distributed by an American representative. See Killen, *The Russian Bureau*, p. 58, n. 22.

41. It is interesting to note that Canada was next, accounting for 28,750 tons of commercial cargo received at that port, whereas Britain shipped only 15,074 tons. U.S. Embassy, Archangel, to Secretary of State, "Report by Acting Naval Attaché for Imports into and Exports from Archangel during the Navigation Season of 1918," no. 1301, 10 February 1919, NARG 59, file 661.00/10.

42. Edward J. Lusby to Sir Victor Wellesley, 9 January 1919, FO 368/2238.

43. H.M. Chargé d'Affaires Kennard, Helsingfors, to Curzon, no. 4 Commercial, 4 September 1919, FO 368/2177; and Department of Overseas Trade, Development and Intelligence, to Acting Consul Bell, 20 May 1919, FO 368/2176.

44. Report from Commercial Attaché Birse, 2 April 1919, in Lindley, Archangel, to Balfour, no. 44, 3 April 1919, FO 371/3995. Included in this report was a list of goods worth over $1.5 million which the North Russian Provisional Government was planning to purchase in the United States.

45. Underscored in original. Sir S. D. Waley, Treasury, to Selby, 6 February 1919, FO 371/3952.

46. Mints, *Angliiskaya interventsiya i severnaya kontr-revolyutsiya*, p. 133. Other examples of British interference with U.S. shipping to North Russian ports can be found in NARG 59, file 661.119/Vessels/118.

47. Hoare, Acting Commercial Attaché, Archangel, to Undersecretary of State for Foreign Affairs, no. 101, 7 July 1919, FO 371/3953.

48. Board of Trade to Lindley, Archangel, no. 111, 18 February 1919; and Lindley to Board of Trade, no. 120, 21 February 1919; FO 371/2171.

49. Lindley, Archangel, to Foreign Office, no. 105(R), 11 February 1919; and Ministry of Shipping to Lindley, 20 February 1919; FO 371/3997.

50. Lindley to Foreign Office, no. 145, 6 March 1919, FO 371/3997.

51. Foreign Office to Hoare, no. 382(R), 26 June 1919; and Hoare to Foreign Office, no. 432, 26 June 1919; FO 371/4011.

52. Minutes of a Meeting at the Ministry of Shipping, 15 July 1919, FO 371/4022.

53. Lindley to Foreign Office, no. 363, 14 June 1919, FO 371/4022.

54. American Consulate, Vladivostok, "Report on Trading Conditions in Siberia," [circa January 1919], NARG 165, MID, box 1440, file "Russia. Siberia."

55. Gabriel A. Bashkiroff, Co., in *Russian Economic Bulletin*, March 1920, Russia, Posol'stvo (U.S.), box 9, file 3, Hoover Institution Archives.

56. Hinton, Vladivostok, to Foreign Office, no. 706(R), Overseas 104, 7 August 1919, FO 371/4115.

57. American-Siberian Export and Import Co., Inc., New York, to State Department, 26 July 1919, NARG 59, file 661.1124/4; and Lied, Inc., New York, to State Department, 11 November 1918, NARG 59, file 611.61171/20. On the notification of the company's incorporation received at the State Department, Bullitt noted that he "assumed we are keeping an eye on Lied."

58. Snow to Judd, Guarantee Trust Company, 16 November 1918, NARG 151, file 611.

59. District Office Manager, Port of New York, to Bureau of Foreign and Domestic Commerce, Department of Commerce, 28 July 1919, NARG 151, box 2558, file 511, "Russia."
A comparison of cargoes is also most revealing. Whereas the ships bound for North Russian ports were listed as carrying cargoes classified primarily as relief supplies, cargoes for Vladivostok contained a wide variety of consumer goods and other manufactures. The manifests included such things as Ford automobiles and trucks, tires, tools and hardware, agricultural equipment, haberdashery and cheap jewelry, clocks, photographic materials, and office goods and equipment. Another indication that Siberia was perceived to be a paying consumer market is evident from the fact that the United States exported over $40,000 worth of confectionery alone to Asiatic Russia in 1919. See *Russian Economic Bulletin*, March 1920, Russia, Posol'stvo (U.S.), box 9, file 3, Hoover Institution Archives.

60. Confidential Intelligence Report, Vladivostok, "Financial and Economic Conditions in Siberia," 4 June 1919, NARG 45, WA-6, box 48, file 20978/305. Several large syndicates had also expressed their willingness to organize credit for Siberia. One such syndicate—an Anglo-American combine of banks representing Baring Brothers, National City Bank, and the Equitable Trust—was understood to have offered a $10 million loan to the Omsk government in July 1919. A more spectacular offer was also made by the American Mercantile Corporation, which reportedly declared itself willing to organize a loan of up to $500 million to the Russian government at Omsk. These offers go far to indicate that even professional financial circles held Siberia to be a viable market, capable of handling such obligations. Perhaps even more significant, however, was the certainty that the counterrevolutionary forces would undoubtedly win—a conviction held even in the face of the advancing Red Army, the increased discord among the White factions, and the ultimate withdrawal of Allied interventionist forces from Russia. See O'Reilly, Vladivostok, to Foreign Office, no. 676, 29 July 1919, FO 371/4113; and Hoare, Archangel, no. 451, Intercept of telegram from Russian Minister at Stockholm to Minister of Finance at Omsk, 23 August 1919, FO 371/4115.

61. According to one source, the credit was to cover the purchase "of quantities of clothing, manufactured goods, etc., representing surplus of war supplies no

longer needed by U.S. government." See Hinton, Vladivostok, to Foreign Office, no. 706(R), Overseas 104, 7 August 1919, FO 371/4115.

62. Barou, *Russian Co-operation Abroad*, p. 62. Barou was the director of the Moscow Narodny Bank in London.

63. Lindsay, Washington, to Foreign Office, no. 1369(R), 20 September 1919, FO 371/4115.

64. Barou, *Russian Co-operation Abroad*, p. 62.

65. "American Assistance to Russia," *Russian Outlook*, 19 July 1919, p. 260.

66. Sir Beilby Alston, Commercial Commissioner, Vladivostok, to Department of Overseas Trade, Military, no. 53, 15 September 1918, FO 371/3367.

67. Director of Military Intelligence, War Office, to the Undersecretary of State for Foreign Affairs, 13 November 1918, FO 371/3365.

68. Alston, Vladivostok, to Foreign Office, no. 135, 8 October 1918, and Minute by J. D. Gregory, 11 October 1918, FO 371/3367.

Upon the Bolshevik evacuation from the region, it was discovered that the Ural mining industries had been left relatively intact, with "mining machinery and plant surprisingly little damaged as nationalisation saved works from pillage." Consul at Ekaterinburg, no. 1, enclosed in Alston, Vladivostok, no. 702, Overseas, [circa January 1919], FO 368/2171.

69. Irtysh Corporation, Ltd., to Secretary of the Treasury, 19 November 1918; and Foreign Office and Department of Overseas Trade Minutes; FO 368/1974.

70. Hinton, Vladivostok, no. 417, 4 May 1919, FO 368/2175; and "Mining in Siberia," *Russian Outlook*, 19 July 1919, p. 260.

71. Board of Trade to Derby, Paris, no. 69, "Trade with Siberia," 26 January 1919, FO 371/4110.

72. Clerk to Cecil, Russia Department, no. 78, 24 September 1918, FO 371/3367.

73. Foreign Office Memorandum, "Policy of His Majesty's Government on Exports for Allied Siberian Economic Relief Operations," January 1919, FO 371/2171.

74. Barou, *Russian Co-operation Abroad*, p. 22; Merchant Trading Corporation to Foreign Office, 2 July 1919, and Minutes, FO 371/3987; and Foreign Office to British High Commissioner, Vladivostok, no. 37(R), 17 June 1919, FO 371/4112.

75. Foreign Office to High Commissioner, Vladivostok, no. 37(R), 17 June 1919, FO 371/4112.

76. Hinton, Commercial Commissioner, Vladivostok, to Department of Overseas Trade, 8 August 1919, FO 368/2175.

77. G. R. Clerk to Cecil, Russia Department, no. 78, 24 September 1918, FO 371/3367.

78. See File 11, *Siberia*, 1919, FO 371/4096. It seems that these accusations were not entirely groundless: within the organizations themselves there were a number of persons who were suspected of pursuing their own economic interests. See the collections pertaining to the activities of the American Red Cross and

YMCA in Siberia, as contained in the "Archival Collections Relating to Siberia" in the Hoover Institution Archives.

79. Knox, Omsk, to War Office, no. 9005, 1 August 1919; and War Office to British Mission, Vladivostok, for Knox, no. 80251, 5 August 1919, WO 33/967.

80. Ullman, *Anglo-Soviet Relations*, 2:50–51.

81. Brinkley, *The Volunteer Army and Allied Intervention in South Russia*, p. 94.

82. Minutes by Balfour, 7 February 1919, on a recommendation put forward by Colonel Blackwood, British Mission to General Denikin, 20 January 1919, FO 371/3977.

83. Commercial Attaché, Constantinople, to State Department, no. 5402, 24 November 1919, NARG 59, file 661.4115/15. In addition to commandeering rolling stock and securing permits from the local Russian authorities, the British military authorities in South Russia were ready to use their influence in other ways as well. According to the testimony of returning American and British business-men, "British influence with Denikin, through British officers, [was] not only derogatory to American trade, but created a false impression about American sympathy with the Bolsheviks." See American Embassy, Constantinople, to Secretary of State, no. 5402, 24 November 1919, NARG 59, file 4115/15.

84. Department of Overseas Trade to Foreign Office, Russian and Scandinavian Section, 10 January 1919, Memorandum concerning the Meeting of the Inter-Departmental Conference on Russian Affairs, 23 December 1918; and Minutes; FO 371/3989.

85. Steel-Maitland to Curzon, "First Memorandum," 31 January 1919, FO 371/3994. While the decision to lift the embargo on exports from Britain to South Russia had not yet been announced, General Poole in Constantinople reported that Allied merchant vessels had commenced private trade in the Black Sea as early as January. See Poole, Constantinople, to Foreign Office, [January 1919], FO 371/3977.

86. Steel-Maitland to Curzon, "Second Memorandum," 31 January 1919, FO 371/3994.

87. Steel-Maitland to Curzon, "First Memorandum," 31 January 1919, FO 371/3994.

88. Clive, Stockholm, to Foreign Office, no. 24(R), 4 January 1919, and Min-utes; and Admiralty to Foreign Office, no. 14117, 24 January 1919, and Minutes; FO 371/3667.

89. Bagge, Odessa, to Foreign Office, February 1919; and Cooke, Odessa, to Foreign Office, no. 155, 5 March 1919; FO 368/2171.

90. R. Tweed, "Report to H.M. Petroleum Executive on the Petroleum Mining Industry of South Russia," 30 July 1919, FO 368/2175. This passage was scored by the Foreign Office.

91. Foreign Office Minutes on Bagge, Odessa, no. 1A, 9 January 1919, FO 371/3994; and *Board of Trade Journal*, 20 February 1919, p. 235.

92. Villiers, Foreign Office, to Lord Granville, Athens, no. 166, 4 March 1919,

FO 368/2173; and Interdepartmental Conference on Russian Affairs, 27th Meeting, 3 April 1919, Minutes, FO 371/3978.

93. Villiers to High Commissioner, Constantinople, no. 385(R), 4 March 1919, FO 368/2173. There were reportedly "frequent opportunities" for commercial passengers to proceed from Constantinople to Batum and other South Russian Black Sea ports on British and French government transports. See Admiral Webb, Constantinople, to Foreign Office, no. 480(R), 6 March 1919, FO 368/2173.

94. *Board of Trade Journal*, 20 February 1919, p. 235.

95. Admiral Webb, to Foreign Office, no. 537, 12 March 1919; Lord Granville, Athens, to Foreign Office, 15 March 1919, and Minutes, FO 368/2173.

96. 62nd Report of the Directors, 31 December 1919, delivered at the Annual Meeting of Shareholders, 23 January 1920, Lloyds Bank Archives, File "USSR." It was noted that, at the time of its inauguration, the South Russian Banking Agency "appeared to have prospects of establishing a good business . . . and considerable transactions chiefly of a barter character took place, but recent disturbances have checked this."

97. Board of Trade Circular, "Announcement of War Risks Insurance Scheme," 21 June 1919, FO 371/4022; Department of Commerce, Bureau of Foreign and Domestic Commerce, Report no. 81, "British Trade with Russia," London, 21 June 1919, NARG 151, box 2239, file 448, "United Kingdom, 1919–1929"; and H. S. Brock, American Embassy, London, to B. S. Cutler, Bureau of Foreign and Domestic Commerce, "South Russian Trade Conditions," 13 June 1919, NARG 151, box 2025.

There was also a considerable British interest in developing trade between the various Black Sea ports. Between April and June 1919, there was "a noticeable increase in trade at Novorossisk," and in October, the demand for shipping was so great that the Lloyd Triestino Line had extended its existing freight service between Taranto and Batum to include a fortnightly service from Batum to Poti, Novorossisk and Northern Black Sea ports. See Rear Admiral, Commanding, Black Sea, to Admiralty, no. 413/120, "Trade Conditions at Novorossisk, 8–14 July 1919," 18 July 1919; and P. Stevens, Batum, to Foreign Office, no. 65, 11 October 1919, FO 368/2173.

98. Russian Trade (Insurance) Committee, 1st Meeting, 14 August 1919, Minutes, FO 371/4002. It is not surprising that private insurers were so accommodating: with the government compelled to insure cargoes at the standard rate, irrespective of the risk, private underwriters were free "to cream off the best risk cargoes." See Supple, *The Royal Exchange Assurance*, pp. 419–21.

99. For examples of profitable British commercial expeditions, see Department of Commerce, Report no. 81, "British Trade with Russia," 21 June 1919, NARG 151, box 2239, file 448; Trade Commissioner Gary to Brock, memorandum concerning an interview with M. Barsh, London Manager of the Russian Transport Company Ltd., 29 May 1919, in which it was reported that one British firm had recently dispatched £500,000 worth of merchandise to South Russia. NARG 151, U.S. Department of Commerce, "Business Condi-

tions," box 2025; and Martin, London, to Foreign Office, November 1919, FO 368/3173.

100. Department of Overseas Trade, "Memorandum on the Resumption of Trade with Russia," R.4, Appendix 1, [circa 17 January 1920], FO 371/4033.

101. Vice-Consul, Novorossisk, to Foreign Office, 15 March 1919, FO 368/2171.

102. It was noted that commerce with the region was effectively controlled by the Government of the Volunteer Army and its officials, "most of whom are connected with trading concerns themselves or trade on their own account." Pinder to Foreign Office, 7 September 1919, FO 368/2173. Some British merchants were likewise guilty of corruption: in an attempt to "monopolise" the trade available, they had themselves "doled out goodly bribes in Novorossisk and elsewhere, instead of relying on the strong official support offered." See Pinder to Newton, 22 August 1919, FO 368/2173.

103. Major Pinder, British Military Mission to South Russia, Economic Section, Rostov-on-Don, to B. C. Newton, Comptroller-General, Department of Overseas Trade, 22 August 1919, FO 368/2173.

104. Pinder to Undersecretary of State for Foreign Affairs, 7 September 1919, FO 368/2173.

105. Pinder to Newton, no. R/101/156, "End of Year Situation," 30 December 1919, FO 371/4038. The plight of the Anglo-Continental Produce Company provides a classic example of the difficulty that a number of British firms had found themselves in by the end of the year. Having dispatched three shiploads of goods to the Black Sea and disposed of them on what it thought to be favorable terms, the company was left holding 50 to 55 million roubles in Russia, which were effectively worthless as the company was unable either to obtain goods to an equivalent value for export or even to export the roubles.

106. British Consul, Rostov-on-Don, to Foreign Office, Overseas Trade no. 13, 8 September 1919, FO 368/2173. The shipments were made on the understanding that the buyers would provide the equivalent value in Russian produce. In light of the existing restrictions on exports, as well as the recent government prohibition on the export of grain from the region, the consul remarked that it was doubtful whether the Russians would be able to meet these obligations. The Foreign Office was more blunt, declaring that there could be no business on any large scale until they had something to export. See William S. Walton, Vice-Consul, Rostov-on-Don, to Newton, Overseas Trade no. 17, 15 September 1919, FO 368/2173.

107. From returns in FO 368/2173; and Department of Overseas Trade, "Memorandum on the Resumption of Trade with Russia," R.4, Appendix 1, [circa 17 January 1920], FO 371/4033.

108. The Allied nature of this intervention was stressed by the British government, despite its protective jealousy over these operations. The hasty addition of French and American advisors to the British staff ensured that the force could be landed in the name of the Allies. The American chosen to represent the United States was Wilber E. Post, a physician formerly attached to the American Relief

Commission in Persia. For an account of the experiences of these advisors, see Post et al., "A Resumé of Events in the Caucasus since the Russian Revolution," manuscript in the Hoover Library.

109. Sinderskii to Shcherbachev, 9 September 1919, Wrangel Military Archives, file 71, Hoover Institution Archives.

110. The Office of the Financial Agent was founded in January 1917. In November 1920 it took over the functions of the Division of Supplies, and after June 1922, when the Russian Embassy was closed, it remained the only Russian representative in the United States that was officially recognized by the U.S. government. See the papers of the Russian Financial Agent, in Russia, Posol'stvo (U.S.), boxes 129–31, Hoover Institution Archives.

111. See "Otchet' o deyatel'nosti otdel po snabzheniyu pri rossiiskom posol'stvo v Vashington," vol. 3 (1 May 1918 to 1 July 1919) and vol. 4 (1 July 1919 to 1 November 1920) in the file on the Financial Agent, Russia, Posol'stvo (U.S.); and Wrangel Military Archives, files 121 and 122, both in the Hoover Institution Archives. For details of the credit arranged, see State Department, Foreign Affairs Section, NARG 59, file 861.24/121.

112. See Killen, *The Russian Bureau,* pp. 107–8; Memorandum no. 18, NARG 182, box 1551; Huntington to Kennedy, 3 February 1919, NARG 151, Bureau of Foreign and Domestic Commerce; and "Reconstruction—Russia," NARG 151, file 882.

113. L. B. Gary, London, to Brock, Department of Commerce, 27 May 1919, NARG 151, box 2025, "Business Conditions"; and Department of Commerce, Bureau of Foreign and Domestic Commerce, Report no. 81, "British Trade with Russia," 25 June 1919, NARG 151, box 2239, file 448.

114. The new U.S. Consul to Odessa, for example, arrived in that city with no less than six vice-consuls. See Bagge, Odessa, no. 121 Russtrade, 30 March 1919, FO 371/3989.

115. Chargé d'Affaires, Russian Embassy, New York, to Acting Secretary of State Polk, 6 March 1919, NARG 59, file 661.119, Vessels/178.

116. R. I. Roberge, *Reminiscences,* Ford Archives Oral History, 1919 Series, FMCA; and Christine White, "Ford in Russia," pp. 81–82.

117. Pinder, British Military Mission, Economic Section, Rostov, to Foreign Office, "Foreign Competition," 22 October 1919, FO 368/2173.

118. Ibid.

119. Pinder to Department of Overseas Trade, R/101/102, 8 November 1919, FO 368/2173.

120. Pinder to Foreign Office, "Foreign Competition," 22 October 1919; Pinder to Department of Overseas Trade, R/101/102, 8 November 1919; and Pinder to Department of Overseas Trade, R/101/119, 18 November 1919; FO 368/2173. It was also pointed out that the scale of these undertakings and the risks that the Americans were taking to secure this control "were of good augury for the success of their enterprise."

121. Villiers's Minutes of an interview with the Representatives of the All-

Russian Central Union of Consumers Societies at the Foreign Office, 3 February 1919, FO 371/3994.

122. C. B. Jarram, Acting British Consul, Novorossisk, to Foreign Office, no. 62 Russtrade, 2 November 1919, FO 368/2173.

123. Stevens, Batum, to Foreign Office, no. 8, 10 March 1919; and Minutes; FO 368/2174.

124. Hoover, *An American Epic*, 3:404. This method of providing relief was arguably more economical; the transaction yielded the Americans more than 8,000 tons of foodstuffs, which, if shipped from the United States, would have cost the relief organization approximately $1 million.

125. Minute by P. V. Emerys-Evans, on Glyn, Mills, and Currie to the Foreign Office, 4 November 1919, FO 368/2173. Although British traders doing business with Russia were warned that they "must not look for fresh credits or guarantees," no restrictions were placed on British commercial or financial circles to devise means for financing and organizing further trade. In essence, Russia was being left to "merchant adventurers" who had in the past opened up trade with undeveloped regions of the world. See MacKinder, British High Commissioner to South Russia, Constantinople, to Foreign Office, 29 December 1919, Memorandum on an Interview with A. G. H. Dickson of the British Trade Corporation, FO 371/3980.

126. In February 1918 it was reported that, due to the inability of the Russian Empire to effect any exports during the war, there was enough manganese above ground to cover normal, prewar exports of the ore for three years. See Department of Overseas Trade, Memorandum, 4 February 1918, FO 368/2754.

127. State Department to Office of the Foreign Trade Advisor, 5 May 1919; and reply; NARG 59, file 661.001/14.

128. See protests made by the British firm of Forwood and Sellar in August and September 1919, in FO 368/2174.

129. Wardrop, Tiflis, to Foreign Office, no. 7, 10 September 1919; and Wardrop to Foreign Office, no. 65(R), 7 October 1919; FO 368/2174.

130. British Trade Corporation to Foreign Office, Ref. no. 139654/C/138, 24 October 1919; and the Georgian government's announcement of the manganese export monopoly awarded to the British Trade Corporation, 12 November 1919; FO 368/2174.

131. Foreign Office to Wardrop, no. 98(R) Urgent, 22 November 1919; Forward and Sellar to Foreign Office, [October 1919]; and Foreign Office Minutes; FO 368/2174.

132. See, for example, Commercial Attaché, Constantinople, "Commerce Report," 30 November 1921, Regional Economics Division, Eastern Europe, NARG 151, box 219, file 21.000, Russia, Caucasus, 8300, Manganese.

133. Pearsons was apparently also convinced of the temporary nature of the unrest; in January 1920 the company had begun to consider the possibility of resuming petroleum prospecting on the island of Sakhalin. H. Colyn to J. Evelyne

Coates, 10 October 1919, Shell Papers; and Lord Murray to Sir Trevor Dawson, 16 January 1920, Pearson Papers, C15, both as cited in Jones and Trebilcock, "Russian Industry and British Business," p. 88.

134. Ural Caspian Oil Corporation to Secretary of the Treasury, 21 January 1919, FO 368/2173; H. G. Trew, Spies Petroleum Co., to Secretary of Capital Issues Committee at the Treasury, 4 March 1919; North Caucasian Oilfields Ltd., to Capital Issues Department, the Treasury, 10 April 1919; and Foreign Office Minutes; FO 368/2174.

135. J. Cadman, Petroleum Executive to Undersecretary of State for Foreign Affairs, 16 January 1919, FO 371/3995.

136. "Co-operation of British Firms in South Russia," Notes of a Meeting at the Offices of the Petroleum Executive; and Minutes by E. Weakley, Villiers, and Curzon, 11 April 1919; FO 371/3670.

137. Mitchell-Innes to Maitland-Edwards, 13 March 1919, FO 368/3670. Mitchell-Innes was the representative of a Baku Petroleum Producers' Association.

138. The Petroleum Executive to The Anglo-Persian Oil Company, 24 July 1919, FO 371/4025.

139. Minutes by E. Weakley, 18 March 1919, on Mitchell-Innes to Lt. Col. Maitland-Edwards, 13 March 1919, FO 371/3670.

140. Including the Anglo-Persian Oil Company's foreign holdings, Britain controlled only about 4 percent of the total world production of petroleum. See Minutes by Weakley, 24 March 1919, on Weakley to Clark, Memorandum, 24 March 1919, FO 371/3670.

The government apparently agreed with the sentiment that Britain should "conserve as much as possible British oil bearing lands and profit as much as possible by oilfields outside British territory which we may be able to control through financial or political interests." Mitchell-Innes to Maitland-Edwards, 13 March 1919; and Enclosure; FO 371/3670.

141. Weakley to Clark, Memorandum, 21 March 1919; and Minute by Weakley, 24 March 1919; FO 371/3670. See also Foreign Office Minutes on Interview with Maitland-Edwards concerning Nobel Properties, "British Participation in Baku Oilfields," 21 March 1919, FO 371/3670.

The fact that the firm L. Hirsch & Company was willing to finance the combine's purchase of the Russian properties goes far to show that the scheme was considered not only possible but economically sound as well. Even while the business was being discussed in the earlier stages, the company had undertaken "to find several millions of money." T. H. Lowinsky, L. Hirsch & Co., to Maitland-Edwards, 25 March 1919, FO 371/3670.

142. Minute by Weakley, 24 March 1919 on Weakley to Clark, Memorandum, 21 March 1919, FO 371/3670.

143. Mitchell-Innes to Foreign Office, [March 1919], FO 371/3670.

144. Mitchell-Innes to Maitland-Edwards, 13 March 1919, FO 371/3670. It was also remarked that the Standard Oil Company would "soon have the most

modern methods [of refining] installed. It is hardly necessary to point out that the better the refining methods employed the cheaper the consequent products." See Mitchell-Innes to Foreign Office, [March 1919], FO 371/3670.

145. Mitchell-Innes to Foreign Office, [March 1919], FO 371/3670.

146. Anglo-Maikop Oil Corporation to Foreign Office, 7 March 1919, FO 371/4015.

147. R. Tweed, "Report to H.M. Petroleum Executive on the Petroleum Mining Industry of South Russia," Anglo-Persian Oil Company, 10 July 1919, Enclosure in Petroleum Executive to the Undersecretary of State for Foreign Affairs, 15 July 1919, FO 368/2175. It appears that these charges were well founded. During the autumn of 1919 the British Military Authorities had been negotiating with the Azerbaijan government for supplies of oil, presumably for local use. When the British failed to obtain the terms that they required, they stopped the pipeline for fifteen days, throwing the entire industry into confusion and rendering impossible the arrangements for exporting considerable supplies, "the shipment of which has been decided to be of urgent importance." Further, the French had complained that a British officer described as the "Oil Controller" had placed "all possible obstacles in the way of French shipments of oil" from Batum. It is interesting to note that the Petroleum Executive had no information about this officer or the functions that he had been appointed to perform. See Sir John Cadman, Petroleum Executive, to Undersecretary of State for Foreign Affairs, no. S 332, 20 December 1919, FO 371/3666.

148. War Office to Department of Overseas Trade, Ref. 14773/3564/RSS, 30 September 1919, in Department of Overseas Trade to Foreign Office, "Note in Regard to the Importance and Possibility of Immediate Export of Petroleum from South Russia," 15 October 1919, FO 368/2175.

149. Unsigned, undated Foreign Office Minute [circa 6 October 1919] on War Office, "Note in Regard to the Importance and Possibility of Immediate Export of Petroleum from South Russia," 30 September 1919, FO 371/3667. The same author also noted that he could not "make out what is at the back of this, but it looks like an attempt to combine the interests of Marcus Samuel and the Shell group with the anti-Caucasian Republic policy of the War Office." Curzon left no doubt about his perception of the scheme, calling it an "immoral proposal." It appears that there was a particularly strong pro-Shell lobby in the War Office, which those in the Foreign Office "were anxious to check." See Foreign Office Minutes on Stevens, Batum, to Foreign Office, 1 December 1919, FO 371/3666.

150. Petroleum Executive to Foreign Office, 3 December 1919; and Foreign Office to Petroleum Executive, 11 December 1919; FO 371/3666.

151. Brinkley, *The Volunteer Army and Allied Intervention in South Russia*, p. 378, n. 72.

152. Gillett, "The Political Origins of American-Soviet Trade," p. 86. Standard agreed to pay $320,000, half of which was to be paid upon conclusion of the agreement.

153. The Foreign Office remarked that "perhaps British Companies might not

be disinclined to do the same." Minutes on Interview with Maitland-Edwards concerning Nobel Properties, "British Participation in Baku Oilfields," 21 March 1919, FO 371/3670.

154. Petroleum Executive to Foreign Office, Ref. S 434, 15 July 1919, FO 368/2175; Petroleum Executive to War Office, 8 April 1919; and Petroleum Executive to War Office, no. S 374, 16 April 1919; FO 371/3670.

155. War Office to Petroleum Executive, MI6a/TRADE/2660, 23 April 1919; and War Office to Petroleum Executive, 2 May 1919; FO 371/3670. The Foreign Office likewise stated that it had no objections to the Standard Oil's purchase, though it warned that the company was no doubt "anxious to secure supplies for their trade in the Levant which was a very extensive one before the war."

156. Remarking upon the ultimately counterproductive British action, R. Tweed of the Anglo-Persian Oil Company noted that as a result of the refusal of the Military Authorities (who controlled all petroleum transport in the region) to assist with this transaction, the British were increasingly being blamed for the unsatisfactory state of the oil industry. This belief is not without foundation: despite the fact that the pipeline had been used to shift fuel oil since the spring, and that the transport of kerosene to Batum had been severely restricted since that time, the consul at Batum was nonetheless able to report as late as December that "the quantity of illuminating oil at this port which is available for shipment is great," and that the "supply of kerosene at Batum at present is in excess of the demand." See R. Tweed, "Report to H.M. Petroleum Executive on the Petroleum Mining Industry of South Russia," Anglo-Persian Oil Company, 10 July 1919, Enclosure in Petroleum Executive to the Under-Secretary of State for Foreign Affairs, 15 July 1919, FO 368/2175; and P. Stevens, Batum, to Secretary of State for Foreign Affairs, 1 December 1919, FO 368/3666.

157. U.S. Commercial Attaché, London, to Bureau of Foreign and Domestic Commerce, 18 September 1919, NARG 151, box 1548, file 276.

158. Data worked from statistics given in *Annual Statement of the Navigation and Shipping of the United Kingdom*, 1919, table 6.

159. Department of Overseas Trade, Development and Intelligence to Foreign Office, Ref. 7341/5639, 19 May 1919, FO 368/2175.

160. Pinder to Foreign Office, "Foreign Competition," 22 October 1919, FO 368/2173.

161. Exports to Asiatic Russia had accounted for $52.2 million of the $82.4 million total U.S. exports to Russia in 1919, whereas European Russia—exclusive of the Baltic states and the Ukraine—received goods to the value of $30.3 million from the United States. In either instance, U.S. exports to these regions alone represented a greater value than the prewar five-year average (1910–14) of $25 million for all of Russia. See U.S. Department of Commerce, *Foreign Commerce and Navigation of the United States*, 1910–14, 1919.

162. *House of Commons, Debates*, 5 November 1919.

163. All of the major counterrevolutionary armies operated from non-Russian ethnic areas. Expecting to recruit a proportion of their forces from the local

population, the White commanders had failed to consider the possibility of nationalist or separatist movements. The political leaders of the counterrevolutionary groups envisaged a "united" Russia that would reincorporate all of the outlying, non-Russian ethnic areas. In a number of cases, it was the prospect of this future that determined the eventual support for the Bolsheviks among those populations, as the Soviet government repeatedly declared themselves to be in favor of establishing independent republics. This, along with the heavy-handed nature of the British occupation, undoubtedly hastened the fall of Transcaucasia. According to one British oilman, "the bulk of our people are bolshies at heart and in any case, we dare not put a rifle into their hands for defence against the natives for fear it should be used against us." Spies Petroleum Company's Representative in Grozny, letter to his wife forwarded via the Foreign Office, circa July–August 1919, FO 371/3671.

164. Minutes by Hoare, 22 January 1920, on Pinder to Department of Overseas Trade, Ref. R/101/146, 14 December 1919, FO 368/2173.

165. Brinkley, *The Volunteer Army and Allied Intervention in South Russia*, p. 221; and *FRUS*, 1919, Russia, pp. 775–76.

166. Minutes of Consular Corps Meeting, Vladivostok, 18 November 1919, FO 368/2177.

167. Indeed, British and American merchants had built up a considerable transit trade with Soviet Russia during the course of 1919. This important element of early Soviet trade will be discussed fully in Chapter 7.

Chapter 5

1. The prime minister's annual speech at the Lord Mayor's Banquet at the Guildhall, 8 November 1919, as printed in the *Times*, 10 November 1919.

2. *House of Commons, Debates*, 13 November 1919.

3. *Times*, 17 January 1920.

4. The moral mechanics of this decision were not lost on the United States. The State Department was quick to note that trade through the cooperative organizations served as an effective way of restating moral principle while at the same time exploiting business opportunities. "Export Restrictions. U.S. Trade with Russia. Decision of the Supreme Council," 29 January 1920, NARG 151, file 861.

5. Epstein, *Les banques de commerce russes*, pp. 74–108. The Bolsheviks were apparently loath to nationalize these organizations because of the possible repercussions of this action on peasant support.

6. The percentage of the Russian population that was served by the cooperative societies rarely fell below 50 percent; and in the prime agricultural areas of Central Russia, some 72 percent of the population was served by these organizations. "A General History of the Russian Co-operatives," [n.d.], FO 371/4009.

7. Barou, *Russian Co-operation Abroad*, p. 21. The Zakupsbyt, along with the

Centrosoyus, had also taken part with British commercial interests in the so-called Kara Sea Expedition in 1919. See Chapter 4.

8. *Manchester Guardian*, 18 June 1919; and American Legation, Copenhagen, no. 43, 3 July 1919, NARG 165, box 168, file 184-20(MID).

9. Enclosure in Sir M. Findlay, Christiania, to Foreign Office, no. 73, 18 February 1920, "Resumés of Two Articles from *Morganbladet* of 11 and 12 February 1920," FO 368/2175.

It is interesting to note that news of the recent establishment of a branch of Centrosoyus in Norway gave rise to the speculation that it was "prompted by the desire to transfer considerable sums of money lying at their disposal in belligerent countries (England, the United States) to a neutral country where their financial transactions would be less handicapped." Memorandum by Evelyn Reynolds, Enclosure in Findlay, Christiania to Foreign Office, no. 40, Overseas Trade "A," 5 May 1920, FO 371/4035.

10. London City and Midland Bank to Moscow Narodny Bank, Ltd., 24 May 1918; Moscow Narodny Bank to London City and Midland Bank, Ltd., 17 July 1918; and reply. Midland Bank Archives, London, File 181(10), "Moscow Narodny Bank." According to Midland Bank's archivist, Mr. Edwin Green, the Moscow Narodny Bank accounted for approximately 1 percent of the £349 to £350 million held on deposit by the bank at the time.

11. Barou, *Russian Co-operation Abroad*, pp. 21–22, 70.

12. Moscow Narodny Bank to London Joint City and Midland Bank, 18 November 1919; Moscow Narodny Bank to London Joint City and Midland Bank, 5 March 1920; and Midland Bank to Moscow Narodny Bank, Ltd., 18 May 1920; Midland Bank Archives, File 181(10), "Moscow Narodny Bank."

13. Barou, *Russian Co-operation Abroad*, p. 79.

14. *Manchester Guardian*, 17 January 1920.

15. The Foreign Office had in fact received confirmation from the representatives of Centrosoyus in London that the cooperative had "received permission from the Soviet government to enter into direct commercial relations with Co-operative Societies as well as with private firms of Western Europe, America and other countries; they also received all guarantees concerning the protection of all goods exported and imported by the Central Union of Co-operative Societies." Centrosoyus to Birkenheim, London, 23 January 1920, FO 371/5434.

16. Lord Hardinge, Undersecretary of State for Foreign Affairs, to Derby, Paris, for Curzon, no. 177, 20 January 1920, FO 371/4032.

17. According to Wise, the possibility of famine in Central Europe especially was *not* due to any world shortage of grain but rather due to a lack of foreign exchange necessary to purchase it from the United States and Canada. See Ullman, *Anglo-Soviet Relations*, 3:17; and "Memorandum on Economic Aspects of British Policy concerning Russia," E. F. Wise, Ministry of Food, 6 January 1920, FO 418/54, part II.

18. Indeed, Wise was not the only one to express such fears. A memorandum circulated a few days after the Supreme Council's decision pointed out that there

were numerous drawbacks: "A monopoly is created by the Centrosoyus in both buying and selling and it is by no means certain that goods will be exchanged primarily with Great Britain, France and Italy. When supplying goods to North Russia last year the Centrosoyus showed a marked tendency to deal with the United States and Scandinavia in preference to the Allies and we had suspicions of their obtaining goods indirectly from Germany." Memorandum by Birse, 20 January 1920, FO 371/4032. See also Chapter 3.

19. "Memorandum on Economic Aspects of British Policy concerning Russia." E. F. Wise, Ministry of Food, 6 January 1920, FO 418/54, part II.

20. Lloyd George at the Council of Premiers, 16 January 1920, Inter-Allied Conference Documents, DBFP, 2:912.

21. The Foreign Office blamed the French for the delay in informing the neutral states of the Allied decision to allow trade with Russia. The French had refused to issue a joint communiqué—a move that put Britain in an "invidious position." Britain "did not wish to take the whole onus of making initial advances to [the] Bolsheviks. It is, however, notorious that His Majesty's Government took the lead and are still taking the lead in arrangements for the resumption of trade, and there is no doubt that the strongest suspicion is felt abroad that we are trying to get our trade with Russia started in advance of, and to the disadvantage of, foreign trade." Minutes by Owen O'Malley, 26 March 1920, on Barclay, Stockholm, no. 85, March 1920, FO 371/4033.

22. It was not until late April that the Admiralty sent orders to the Senior Naval Officer in the Baltic, instructing him "that in view of altered condition, H.M. Ships are not to interfere with trade in the Baltic with the exception that any vessel suspected of carrying guns or munitions consigned to the Soviet Government or its agents is to be searched and if necessary sent to Danzig for further orders." Admiralty to First Light Cruiser Squadron, 23 April 1920, FO 371/3618.

Despite its attempts to continue the "bluff blockade," however, a number of neutral states had already refused to take part in any reestablishment of the blockade. Some, like Sweden, had actively expressed disapproval of the Allied cause as early as mid-1919 by refusing to load any further war matériel for the White Armies of Siberia. See Report no. 93, "Wireless News," MI1A (DMI), Agent CW 195, 18 June 1919, FO 371/4095; and August 1919, file 117180, FO 371/4115.

23. Interdepartmental Russia Committee, Draft Resolutions for Inclusion in the Minutes of the 1st Meeting, 24 January 1920, FO 371/4032. This resolution was curiously overridden, however, when the committee stated that the government had no objection to British merchants trading "direct from the Baltic States with Co-operatives in Russia"; and that the Foreign Office would grant passports to the Baltic states for this purpose. As will be discussed later, the government was fully aware that a considerable trade was being conducted with the Bolsheviks through the medium of the newly independent Baltic states. See Chapter 6.

24. See H. Fountain, Department of Overseas Trade, to Foreign Office, CRT 4091, 11 September 1920, Commercial Relations and Treaties; Joseph Gregory

[head of the Foreign Office Russia Department], to Fountain, 21 October 1920; Lonergan, Reval, to Foreign Office, no. 271, 25 October 1920; and Fountain, Memorandum to the Foreign Office, CRT 4091, 1 November 1920; all in FO 371/5435.

25. See file 142549 in FO 371/4032.

26. "Memorandum on Russian Policy," O. O'Malley, 20 May 1920, FO 371/3961.

27. Minute by Joseph Gregory, on Supreme Council's announcement, 19 January 1920, FO 371/4032. The Minutes of the Supreme Allied Council's discussions of the matter were not forwarded to the Foreign Office until 16 February 1920. See FO 371/4032, file 172293/162549/38.

28. Hardinge to Lord Derby, Paris, for Curzon, no. 177, 20 January 1920, FO 371/4032.

29. Derby, Paris, (from Curzon) to Hardinge, 22 January 1920, FO 371/4032.

30. Department of Overseas Trade, "Memorandum on the Resumption of Trade Relations with Russia," [circa 17 January 1920], FO 371/4033.

31. Minute by Gregory, 19 January 1920, FO 371/4032.

32. Lindsay, Washington, to Foreign Office, no. 48, 21 January 1920, FO 371/4032.

33. General Keyes, Novorossisk, to Foreign Office, no. 7, 19 January 1920; and Foreign Office Minute; FO 371/4032.

34. *Agreement between His Britannic Majesty's Government and the Soviet Government of Russia for the Exchange of Prisoners*, 1920, U.K. Parliamentary Papers, Cmd. 587, 12 February 1920.

35. Statement by the Supreme Council, 24 February 1920, *New York Times*, 25 February 1920, in Cumming and Pettit, *Russian-American Relations*, p. 361.

Lloyd George was unmistakably the author of this resolution. As Ullman points out, the original draft suffered few alterations before being accepted by the Supreme Council. See Ullman, *Anglo-Soviet Relations*, 3:31, n. 42.

36. Memorandum by E. F. Wise, R.112, Confidential, 21 April 1920, Confidential Print, FO 418/54.

The majority of the cooperative officials abroad were anticommunist, and a number of them had also actively supported the counterrevolution. The papers of Joseph Okulich and Ivan Emil'ianov, both who were intimately involved in the affairs of the Russian cooperative societies, provide an interesting insight into this. These archives are under the trust of the Museum of Russian Culture in San Francisco.

37. When asked in the House of Commons what provisions had been made for the initiation of trade negotiations between the Soviet and British government, Lloyd George replied that the Soviet government had made no such request, but that the "Central Board" of Russian cooperative organizations had asked permission to send its delegation to Britain. Privately, however, the prime minister made no distinction, and in an unguarded moment Lloyd George admitted that the Russian trade delegation represented not the cooperatives but the "Soviet, un-

doubtedly." *House of Commons, Debates,* 15 March 1920, as cited in Ullman, *Anglo-Soviet Relations,* 3:41, n. 68; and entry of 6 March in Riddell, *Lord Riddell's Intimate Diary,* p. 175.

38. No effort will be made to discuss the general political questions or negotiations. A detailed account of the events and the negotiations between the two governments can be found in Ullman, *Anglo-Soviet Relations,* vol. 3.

39. The Allies agreed to authorize the arrival of representatives of the Russian trade delegation with the aim of opening trade relations "between Russia and other countries through the Co-operative Societies and otherwise." "Decision of the Supreme Council at San Remo, on 26 April 1920," no. 20, 194884/N38, FO 371/5434.

40. O'Malley to Gregory, "Memorandum Submitted to San Remo Conference, Drawing Attention to Salient Points in the Question of the Resumption of Russian Trade," 21 April 1920, FO 371/4034.

41. O'Malley to Gregory, Foreign Office Memorandum, "Trade with Russia," 27 April 1920, FO 371/4034.

42. Prime Minister's Statement in the House of Commons, as cited in the *Times,* 30 April 1920.

43. The government's main objective was to prevent Europe from starving; and starvation could "only be prevented by the opening up of Russia. Therefore we ought to direct the whole of our diplomacy to this end." Indeed, as late as April a number of government officials were still referring to this policy as an almost quid pro quo arrangement: "Stated it its simplest terms the present position now seems to be as follows. We want Russian grain; Russians want British locomotives." Memorandum by Gregory, 19 February 1920, FO 371/3961; and O'Malley to Gregory, "Memorandum Submitted to San Remo Conference," 21 April 1920, FO 371/4034. See also L. A. Davis, Export Credits Department, to E. F. Wise, 23 March 1920, FO 371/4633.

44. Question for Law Officers from the Inter-Departmental Russian Trade Committee, 31 May 1920; and Opinion of the Law Officers of the Crown, Gordon Hewart and Ernest M. Pollock, Law Officers' Department, to E. F. Wise, for the Prime Minister, 4 June 1920; FO 371/5434.

45. Treasury to Foreign Office, Confidential, 8 June 1920, FO 371/4035.

46. Treasury to Foreign Office Northern Department, no. 1227, 5 November 1920, FO 371/5420.

47. "No gold could obtain world market price unless it was given an export license." "A Summary of Relations between His Majesty's Government and the Soviet Government, from September 12, 1920 to December 22, 1920." H. F. B. Maxse, no. 82, 30 December 1920, FO 418/54.

48. See, for example, the British Baltic Commercial Corp., Ltd., to O'Malley, 19 April 1920; and Minutes by Maxse, 5 May 1920; FO 371/4034.

49. Sir Robert Horne, Board of Trade, to Curzon, 20 May 1920, FO 371/4035.

50. Minutes by Gregory, 21 May 1920, on Horne to Curzon, 20 May 1920, FO 371/4035.

51. Gregory to Kershaw, Stockholm, 2 November 1920; and Minutes by Sir Eyre Crowe, 5 November 1920; FO 371/5433.

52. Neither side was averse to using the threat of breaking off negotiations as a political weapon during the Russo-Polish conflict. See Ullman, *Anglo-Soviet Relations*, vol. 3, "Poland and Trade."

53. That the government was loath to jeopardize the progress it had made in these negotiations is clear from its decision to allow Kamenev to return to Britain —despite his unsavory political activities. Refusal to do so would have certainly led to the termination of the negotiations, "which at present hold out some prospects for useful results." "Notes of a Conference with the Russian Trade Delegation," 10 Downing Street, 10 September 1920, *DBFP*, 8:783–91, as cited in Stephen White, *Britain and the Bolshevik Revolution*, pp. 10–11.

54. See the *Sunday Times*, "Trade with Russia. Why There is a Delay," 12 December 1920; "Why We Must Trade with Russia"; and "The Negotiations. Obstacles to an Agreement," 19 December 1920.

55. It is interesting to note that there was a number of instances in which the Foreign Office complained that British traders, in circumventing the government's restrictions on trade with Russia, were using neutrals as agents. While this itself was accepted, their annoyance lay in the subsequent loss of potential profits to foreign intermediaries. See the case of Birnbaum and Co., December 1920, [no. N4992/207/38], FO 371/5435. The same holds true with regards to the willingness of those countries to accept Soviet gold. See the Minutes by Crowe and O'Malley, 30 December 1920, on no. N4645/207/38, FO 371/5435.

56. In addition to a number of Liverpool leather companies, firms such as Cammell-Laird, William Allen and Co., and "many others of equal importance" had business with the Soviets arranged in such a fashion. See John Cull and Co., to Board of Trade, 19 June 1920; and Cyril Davies and Co., to Sir William Clark, Comptroller General of the Department of Overseas Trade, 18 March 1920; FO 371/4036.

57. Kershaw, Stockholm, to Foreign Office, Overseas Trade "A," no. F.R. 2234, 1 December 1920, FO 371/5421. See Chapter 6.

58. Secretary of the India Tea Association, to Clark, 6 December 1920, FO 371/5434. The association urged that "every effort should be made to bring about closer trading relations with Russia." It was further pointed out that the consequences of this lapse in business would be far reaching, not only resulting in a depression in the tea industry, but causing a decline in British sales to India as well. Secretary of the India Tea Association to Foreign Office, no. 4637, 6 December 1920, FO 371/5434.

59. *Special Weekly Report on Unemployment*, no. 9, Week ended 10 December 1920, Cabinet Paper C.P./2297, Cab. 24/116, as cited in Ullman, *Anglo-Russian Relations*, 2:433–44.

60. Krasin pointed out that a contract had been concluded in September with five Yorkshire firms for the supply of broadcloth. The contract was reportedly worth "nearly a million sterling" and was payable in cash. Krasin, *Voprosy*

vneshney torgovli, pp. 251–52; Shishkin, *Sovetskoe gosudarstvo i strany zapada v 1917–1923gg.*, pp. 186–87; and *Times*, 29 September 1920.

61. Sir William Clark to Foreign Office, 21 December 1920; and Minute by O'Malley; FO 371/5434. The unemployment in the Midlands and the North was cited by a number of concerns as the reason why—despite the risks involved —firms there entered into contracts with the Soviets. See M. Oldroyd and Sons to Foreign Office, 25 February 1921, FO 371/6901.

62. *House of Commons, Debates*, 18 November 1920, and 29 November 1920.

63. Restriction of Enemy Supplies Department to Foreign Office, "Flax through Esthonia to Reval," 4 July 1919, FO 368/2172; Board of Trade to Flax Control Board, 25 September 1920, FO 368/2173; and the complaint from the U.S. Linen and Thread Producers Association to the Secretaries of State and Commerce, May 1920, NARG 151, box 1469/1626-3, Flax.

64. "Memorandum on Economic Aspects of British Policy concerning Russia," E. F. Wise, Ministry of Food, 6 January 1920, Confidential Print, FO 418/54, part II. While the United States, Canada, and Argentina also grew flax, their crops were primarily for seed and, in the case of the United States, failed to meet even domestic requirements for that fiber. The U.S. linen and thread industries likewise suffered from the shortage of Russian flax. See Linen and Thread Producers Association to Secretaries of State and Commerce, May 1920, NARG 151, box 1469/1626-3, Flax; and Taylor, "The Commercial Importance of Russia," p. 453.

65. Heavy industry suffered the worst in Britain during the economic slump of the early 1920s. Shipbuilding and the iron and steel manufacturers were by far the hardest hit, with nearly 37 percent unemployment in both industries by the end of 1920. Engineering works followed with 27 percent unemployment. Not surprisingly, the geographical areas of Britain that experienced the highest rate of unemployment—Scotland, with 21 percent, and the Midlands and Northeast with 18 percent each—reflected the predominance of those industries on the local economy. *Third Winter of Unemployment*, pp. 16–17, as cited in Mowat, *Britain between the Wars*, p. 126. The orders placed in Sweden in the spring of 1920 were primarily for heavy industrial and engineering goods.

66. Despite the fact that a large proportion of the footwear and fabric ordered was undoubtedly meant to outfit the Red Army—a point bitterly made by the War Office—the government appears to have supported these transactions, the Polish crisis notwithstanding. "Contracts for the Supply of Goods to Soviet Russia," Board of Trade, 27 September 1920, C.P. 1890, as cited in Ullman, *Anglo-Soviet Relations*, 2:435.

67. See Krasin, *Voprosy vneshney torgovli*, pp. 248–49; and Sir C. Ottley of Armstrong-Whitworth to Gregory, 31 December 1920, FO 371/6885. The Foreign Office and Board of Trade both received numerous complaints from British manufacturers concerning the "loss" of Soviet orders to other countries. It was argued that a large proportion of the orders that the Russian Trade Delegation had placed elsewhere could have been placed with British firms had the agreement

been in existence or, indeed, had British policy been less ambiguous. See Lord D'Albernon, Berlin, no. 1141, 6 November 1920, on growing German competition for the Armstrong-Whitworth contract; and the British Baltic Corporation Ltd. to O'Malley, 19 April 1920, concerning British agricultural machinery; FO 371/4034. That such a situation existed was admitted by the Foreign Office: "The reason Krasin will not place orders in this country to the full limit of Russia purchasing capacity in present circumstances is that the Soviet government expect —quite rightly—to be able to place orders on more favourable terms after the signing of the agreement." Minutes by O'Malley on N4645/207/38, 30 December 1920, FO 371/5434.

68. The decline in foreign trade was closely linked to the growing unemployment in Britain. It was believed that the root of the problem was "not overproduction, but under-consumption"; therefore, it seemed quite logical to seek relief by increasing exports. The *Observer* pointed out that the development of trade with Soviet Russia would help alleviate this crisis, predicting that orders "up to one hundred million pounds" would be obtained in the first year after trade had been renewed. Indeed, British manufacturers and merchants who were suffering from the depressed economy had "turned their attention seriously to Russia as being practically the only market at present available for the absorption of their wares. . . . The seriousness of the industrial situation in England . . . is the driving force impelling . . . firms to trade with Russia." Cabinet Minutes, 24 December 1920, Cab. 77(29) 2 & 3, Cab. 23/23, "Business and Trade Conditions in 1920." Statement at the Annual Meeting of Shareholders, Birmingham, 2 February 1921; Lloyds Bank Archives, London; *Observer*, 5 November 1920; Enclosure in Barclay, Stockholm, to Foreign Office, no. 933, 29 December 1920; FO 371/6878.

69. See especially the *Times* editorials of 19 December 1920 and 2 January 1921, where the opinion is expressed that "if a long period of trade depression" was to be avoided, "it was imperative that trade with Russia should be resumed forthwith." It went on to describe the issue as primarily "one between a group of financiers and the trading interests of the country. The urgency of the question is made clear by the fact that if we will not trade other countries will capture the market." On 2 January, contrary to its normally restrained and pro-City disposition, the *Times* published yet another editorial along similar lines, only this time going so far as to support the extension of credit to Russia. It declared that it was "false economics to take everything from a country which has gone through such terrible upheavals as Russia and give nothing in return. With obligations recognised on both sides so definitely, as the new settlement promises, there is created an atmosphere in which trust and confidence can be born again—without which there can be no trade."

70. *House of Commons, Debates*, 22 December 1920. It appears that even Horne was moved by the argument at one point, when he defended the trade agreement as enabling Britain to sell "all the manufactures which our people work into fabrics by their hands that we should especially at present time be able to give increased employment to our people."

71. One cannot overlook the effect that Curzon's overwhelming hatred for the Bolsheviks had in the department—but in the department it largely remained. Throughout 1920–21, Britain's Russia policy was firmly in the hands of Lloyd George, who pointedly ignored the recommendations of the Foreign Office, and Curzon in particular.

72. Ullman, *Anglo-Soviet Relations*, 3:432. It was noted by the *Times* that "for every Member of Parliament who rises to demand the Soviet Government acknowledge all Russian debts, there are a half a dozen others who will speak out to insist that the economic health of their constituencies depend on the early revival of Anglo-Russian trade." *Times*, 22 December 1920.

73. H. F. B. Maxse, Foreign Office Memorandum, "The Political Aspects of Trading with Russia," 22 November 1920; and Minutes by O'Malley, 22 November 1920; FO 371/5434.

74. Cabinet Minutes, 17 November 1920, Cab. 61(20), Cab. 23/23. Bonar Law, himself a businessman, declared that trade with Russia was "still more desirable now, when there is a state of unemployment. . . . This country must do its best to get its share of the trade." *House of Commons, Debates*, 15 November 1920.

75. *House of Commons, Debates*, 28 March 1921. Remarking on the "great impression" that the New Economic Policy had produced in Europe, Krasin observed that in Britain it was thought that "the Bolsheviks have at last come to their senses and that it is now possible to have dealings with them." Report on Krasin's speech in Moscow, in *Izvestiya*, no. 97, 7 May 1920.

76. While the Kronstadt rebellion earlier that month was seen by some as the beginning of the end for the Soviet regime, Churchill's suggestion that the government "should not hasten the conclusion of the agreement" elicited a sharp response from the Cabinet: the government had "already suffered delay in this matter," and the issue should "now be forced to a conclusion." Cabinet Minutes, 14 March 1921, Cab. 13(21) 1, Cab. 23/24, as cited in Stephen White, *Britain and the Bolshevik Revolution*, p. 22.

77. Even so, the Soviet government did declare that it recognized "in principle" that it was "liable to pay compensation to private persons who have supplied goods and services to Russia for which they have not been paid." See "Declaration of Recognition of Claims," amended to the Trade Agreement between His Britannic Majesty's Government and the Government of the Russian Socialist Federal Soviet Republic, 16 March 1921, FO 418/55.

78. Ullman, *Anglo-Soviet Relations*, 3:456.

79. It appears that the British and American governments were not alone in suffering interdepartmental differences of opinion. There was considerable disparity between the Commissariat for Foreign Affairs and the head of the Russian trade delegation. "The Commissariat of Foreign Affairs—especially Litvinov—were inclined to view the delegation as a Trojan horse, inside which a political embassy of the Soviet Government was to be smuggled into England. The commercial side . . . was just clever bait." Krasin, however, "regarded the whole mat-

ter quite differently, and set as his goal the conclusion of tangible commercial deals with the British." By Krasin's own account, "all of the efforts of the Soviet foreign delegation were concentrated upon the achievement of an agreement with England." Liberman, *Building Lenin's Russia*, p. 119; and Krasin, *Voprosy vneshney torgovli*, pp. 249–50.

80. Aspects of this debate can be followed in periodic exchanges published in *Izvestiya* between November 1920 and February 1921, and in the proceedings of the eighth–twelfth party congresses. See also Karpova, *L. B. Krasin—Sovetskii diplomat*.

81. Central Soviet Committee Meeting, 28 December 1920, as reported in no. CX/233/V, SIS Report D/178 (Copenhagen), 28 December 1920, FO 371/6877.

82. Lenin's speech at the Eighth Congress of Soviets of the RSFSR, December 1920, as cited in Ullman, *Anglo-Soviet Relations*, 3:397.

83. Gorodetsky, *The Precarious Truce: Anglo-Soviet Relations, 1924–1927*, p. 14.

84. Lenin, *Polnoe sobranie sochineniyi*, 39:209; and 40:152, as cited in Furaev, *Sovetsko-amerikanskie otnosheniya, 1917–1939*, p. 54. Such sentiment may have been due to the awareness of a possible problem of supply in Britain. Commenting on the goods readily available for export to Soviet Russia, the Department of Trade noted that "machinery products of all kinds are difficult to obtain. Comparatively small quantities may be available of machine tools, saws, axes, locomotives (standard type) and possibly cranes. Very little agricultural machinery can be supplied at once compared with what must be the Russian demand, and it is unlikely that electrical plant, mining plant or locomotives of Russian type can be available within less than 12 months." See Department of Trade to Foreign Office, "Note on the List of Goods Required for Import into Russia, Handed in by Krasin. Supplies Available from U.K.," 9 June 1920, FO 371/4035.

85. It was further noted with some alacrity that "relations with the Americans seems to be good . . . 200 locomotives recently arrived at Reval, intended for Soviet Russia." Enclosure no. 3 in Admiralty to Undersecretary of State for Foreign Affairs, 30 September 1920, Mediterranean Letter, no. 6250/11, 15 August 1920, "Report From Naval Intelligence Group, Crimea," Sevestopol; FO 371/3984.

86. Lindsay, Washington, to Foreign Office, no. 48, 21 January 1920, FO 371/4032.

87. Funsten Bros., International Fur Exchange, Chicago, to E. F. Sweet, Assistant Secretary of Commerce, 14 February 1920, NARG 151, file 861. One of the largest fur auction houses in the world, this company had a considerable interest in Russian trade. There is no question that the International Fur Exchange was "directly and seriously" affected by the Allied governments' decision. The rivalry that developed between the Hudson's Bay Company and the International Fur Exchange over Siberian furs became so bitter that in 1923 the British were accused of foul play.

88. Lindsay, Washington, to Foreign Office, no. 327, 1 March 1920, FO 371/4049.

89. Acting Secretary of State to U.S. Embassy, London, for transmission to the Foreign Office, 10 March 1920, FO 371/4033.

90. Wilson to Polk, 4 March, 18 March, and 19 March 1920, Wilson Papers; and Polk Diary, 8 April 1920, as cited in Killen, *The Russian Bureau*, p. 141.

91. Secretary of Commerce Alexander to Secretary of State Polk, 24 April 1920, NARG 59, file 861.61323/28.

92. Foreign Office Memorandum to Curzon regarding the Visit of Mr. Williams [American Embassy], 7 April 1920, FO 371/4033.

93. William Phillips, Assistant Secretary of State, to Wadsworth, 4 November 1919, NARG 59, file 861.48/977. American policy was described as one of "non-intercourse" with territory under Bolshevik control. The effective embargo on trade as a result of the government's refusal to issue export licenses or clearance papers to cargoes or vessels bound for Soviet ports amounted to much the same thing.

94. Redfield was appointed chairman of the American-Russian Chamber of Commerce soon after his resignation.

95. Confidential Memorandum for Dr. MacElwee, from the Trade Commissioner, Bureau of Foreign and Domestic Commerce, 4 June 1920, NARG 151, file 861, box 3219.

96. "We hear much of what the British are doing in planning for the trade invasion of Russia." H. W. Adams, Acting Commercial Attaché, Paris, 29 March 1920, NARG 151, box 3219, file 861.

97. Both the State Department and Commerce Department had received numerous demands for the removal of all restrictions on trade with Soviet Russia. See, for example, W. E. Aughinbaugh [foreign editor of the *New York Commercial*] and the Philadelphia Chamber of Commerce to J. W. Alexander, 25 March 1920; Portland Oregon Chamber of Commerce to Department of Commerce, 31 March 1920; and Alexander to Chamber of Commerce, New York, 5 June 1920; NARG 40, file 77295.

98. *New York Times*, 3 January 1920. There were, however, a number of powerful organizations that remained opposed to trade with the Bolsheviks, including the American-Russian Chamber of Commerce, the American Manufacturers Export Association, and the American Federation of Labor.

99. Harold Kellock to Senator Borah, 20 May 1920, as cited in Fithian, "Soviet Economic Relations," pp. 52–53.

100. Department of State Press Release, 7 July 1920, as printed in the *New York Times*, 8 July 1920. This announcement left no doubt as to the American attitude toward the British negotiations with the Bolsheviks: the State Department's action "in no way constitutes recognition of the validity of industrial or commercial concessions granted by any existing Russian authority." In other words, the government refused to recognize the legal sanctity of whatever concession British businessmen were able to secure in Russia, leaving them open to liability for compensation or damages. Further, the United States chose to distance itself as much as possible from its ally's negotiations with Krasin: the State

Department refused to allow any American representation at the meetings between the British and the Soviet Trade Delegation in London. Even a specific request from the Bureau of Foreign and Domestic Commerce to allow the commercial attaché in London to attend was denied. See Lincoln Hutchinson, Office of the Commercial Attaché, London, to O. P. Hopkins, Assistant Director, Bureau of Foreign and Domestic Commerce, 16 July 1920, NARG 151, file 861.

101. The British ambassador in Washington was quick to note these continued restrictions, and remarked that the American decision "must be regarded as a political move rather than as a measure directed to bring about an immediate exchange of commodities to any serious degree." Rather, its importance lay "in the attention it directs to Russia as a market for American goods in the future and it may be confidently expected that U.S. exporters will at once begin to make preparations against the time when regular trade with Russia becomes possible." See Sir A. Geddes, Washington, to Comptroller General, Department of Overseas Trade, no. 481, Overseas Trade "B," 16 July 1920, FO 371/4037.

102. Secretary of State Colby to Italian Ambassador Avezzana, 10 August 1920, *FRUS, 1920*, 3:463–68.

103. Boris Baievsky, Russian Division, Bureau of Foreign and Domestic Commerce to U.S. Commercial Attaché, London, 7 January 1921, NARG 151, box 2237, file 6012.

104. State Department to S. P. Gilbert, Treasury Department, 16 December 1920. Cited in Gilbert to Assistant Secretary of State Dearling, 25 March 1921, *FRUS, 1921*, 2:764–68. The decision to accept such gold only made legal the process that the government had been looking at through its fingers since the beginning of 1920.

105. Secretary of State Hughes to U.S. Consulate, Reval, for Litvinov, 25 March 1921, *FRUS, 1921*, 3:768.

106. See Fithian, "Soviet Economic Relations," pp. 65–66.

107. To be sure, American business circles generally found the Bolshevik philosophy loathsome. Unlike the British, however, a considerable number of these businessmen were early on able to overlook the moral repugnance of the regime in favor of trade, an ability that may have been due to the fact that American losses as a result of the revolution were substantially less than those suffered by the British.

108. Martens was appointed as the Soviet government's official representative in the United States on 2 January 1919. "Translation of Credentials sent by L. C. A. K. Martens to the State Department," 19 March 1919; and "Memorandum Sent to the State Department by L. C. A. K. Martens, 19 March 1919," both in Cumming and Pettit, *Russian-American Relations*, pp. 320–29.

109. Item no. 1291 in NARG 165, box 305, file 10110-137/137.

110. *New York Times*, 3 February 1920; *Standard Daily Trade Service*, 5 February 1920, FO 371/4050; and Jennings, Lehigh Machine Co., to State Department, 15 January 1920, NARG 165, box 1793, file 2515-u-10. Martens filed his list with the Subcommittee of the Senate Foreign Relations Committee in early February 1920 as evidence supporting the renewal of trade relations.

111. *New York Times*, 16 November 1919.

112. War Department, Office of the Chief of Staff, MI2, to Department of Commerce, "On the Resumption of Trade with Soviet Russia by the Allied Nations," 10 May 1920, NARG 151, file 861.

113. Capt. John B. Trevor, MID, New York, to the Director of Military Intelligence, 14 May 1919, NARG 165, box 3051, file 10110-1194/81, 1919.

114. *New York Herald*, 27 June 1919, and *New York Times*, 27 June 1919, as cited in Wilkins and Hill, *American Business Abroad*, p. 209.

115. Like other manufacturers, Ford suffered a sharp decline in sales at the end of the year. Initially closed for inventory on 24 December, it was announced in early January that the Ford Company would remain closed indefinitely due to the "lack of orders" and the "general financial and business conditions." Nevins and Hill, *Ford: Expansion and Challenge, 1915–1933*, pp. 154, 157.

116. The People's Industrial Trading Corporation, which was contacted in connection with this deal, was expected "to waive any claim for commission or discount" on the sale. Further, the acceptance of this order by the People's Industrial Trading Corporation did not "invalidate the Memorandum of Agreement between the Ford Motor Company and Ivan Stacheef and Co., dated March 14 1919." Ford Motor Company, New York, to People's Industrial Trading Corporation, 9 November 1920, FMCA, Acc. 49, box 1.

117. The Products Exchange Corporation and the People's Industrial Trading Corporation were incorporated in New York in 1919; Centrosoyus America, originally the New York branch office of the cooperative society, was incorporated as a joint-stock company in New York at the beginning of 1920, as a result of the extension of its trade activities to cover "the whole of Russia." Centrosoyus America had an authorized capital of $500,000, of which $300,000 was paid up. Barou, *Russian Co-operation Abroad*, pp. 62–63; and Ropes, "American-Soviet Trade Relations," pp. 89–94.

118. Colby to Bruno Schill, Russia and Baltic Corporation, New York, 22 April 1920. See also Guaranty Trust Co., New York, to Department of State, 12 May 1920; and reply; International Harvester Co., Chicago, to Secretary of State, 26 April 1920; and Amdur, Tachna, and Ellis to State Department, 7 July 1920; NARG 59, file 660.i-119/.

119. Traders were informed that the "old Baltic provinces . . . are not included in the present division 'European Russia,' and commodities may be exported to those provinces without individual export licenses." See Glushanok and Hill, Importers and Exporters, New York, to Department of State, 17 February 1920; and reply from the Bureau of Exporters, 21 February 1920; NARG 59, file 660.i-119/1. As there was no way of controlling the reexport of these goods once they were in the Baltic, merchants and government alike chose to ignore the fact that the majority of these goods were indeed being contracted for by the Soviet government—a fact that was ruefully noted by the British. "It appears that Esthonia has lodged a large order in the United States for locomotives and agricultural implements, and there is reason to believe that as she has no need of these herself

she will probably sell them to the Soviet Government at a large profit." "War Office Summary of Brig. Gen. A. Turner's Report on Present Conditions in Soviet Russia," 27 March 1920, FO 371/4004.

Chapter 6

1. In the case of the official returns listed in the United Kingdom Trade with Foreign Countries, the prewar geographical classification of "Russia" was adhered to until 1 January 1921, and incorporated trade with those territories formerly included in the prewar Russian Empire but which had subsequently become independent. It was admitted that a "certain amount of transit trade [with Soviet Russia], principally via the Baltic States, may be wrongly but unavoidably credited to the latter states." See Reyntiens, Department of Overseas Trade, to O'Malley, 14 November 1924, Enclosure, "Statistics of Trade with Russia," FO 371/10470.

2. Transit trade had accounted for a considerable proportion of American imports into that country prior to the war. See Chapter 2; and Commercial Report, no. 62, Copenhagen, 12 January 1918, FO 368/1968.

3. "You *Must* Help Russia: A Plea for Russia, the Land of Golden Opportunity," *Kelly's Monthly Trade Review*, 27 July 1918 (published by Kelly Trading Company, Ltd.).

4. The Swedish government regarded this trade as valuable enough to conclude a comprehensive trade agreement with the Soviet government in October. In addition to anticipating 15 million kroner (nearly £826,000) worth of trade, the agreement set important precedents: concluded by both governments as equal partners, with the same rights of access to harbors provided to both parties, the agreement also recognized the Soviet government's monopoly of foreign trade. According to the trade office attached to the Soviet Mission in Stockholm, forty-two transactions were concluded before the Soviet Mission was closed in January 1919. See Fischer, *The Soviets in World Affairs*, 1:248; Shishkin, *Sovetskoe gosudarstvo i strany zapada v* 1917–1923gg., pp. 82–84, 110, 117–18; Schuman, *American Policy towards Russia since* 1917, p. 148; Navy Department, Office of Naval Intelligence to Secretary of State, no. 1127, 1 February 1919, NARG 45, WA-6, box 607; *Izvestiya*, 15 July 1918; *Dokumenty vneshnei politiki*, vol. 1, 1917–1918, pp. 446, 448.

5. William Hurley, Copenhagen, to War Trade Board, no. 2672, 24 August 1918, NARG 59, file 661.59171/orig.-; "Report on Danish Commercial News," no. 1774, 22 August 1918, War Department, General Staff, Military Intelligence Division, 1917–41, NARG 165, box 79, file 2057-36; American Legation, Christiania, to Office of Naval Intelligence, no. 114, 28 August 1918, NARG 45, file 2066-38, box 846; and Office of Naval Intelligence to State Department, no. 1098, 11 January 1919, NARG 45, file WA-6, box 607.

6. Article translated from *Ekonomicheskaya Zhizn'*, 29 July 1919, in Patrick

Ramsay, Stockholm, to Foreign Office, no. 283 Commercial, 30 July 1919, FO 368/2176; Sir Coldridge Kennard, Stockholm, to Foreign Office, no. 260 Commercial, 5 July 1919, FO 368/2194.

7. Ford also had plans for trade with South Russia; proposed regional headquarters in Odessa were to serve the territory of the Ukraine, the Caucasus, and Central Russia. R. I. Roberge, *Reminiscences*, p. 31. Ford Archives Oral History, 1919 Series, FMCA; and "Report on Foreign Sales," Ford Motor Company, Great Britain, 17 June 1919, FMCA, Acc. 572, box 18, file 11.15; and Knudson [Ford's foreign manager], to Edsel Ford and Frank L. Klingensmith, "Report on Foreign Operations," 18 October 1919, Office of the President, FMCA, Acc. 6, box 260.

8. N. L. Anderson, *Baltic Trade after the War*; and "American-Baltic Trade after the War," *Board of Trade Journal*, 2 January 1919, p. 7. For reports of shipments from New York to Copenhagen, and the U.S. assessment of the significance of that port in American transit trade, see War Department, General Staff, Military Intelligence Division, Item no. 2057-455, "Commercial," 13 March 1919, NARG 45, box 791.

9. See *Official Gazette* (Copenhagen), 24 June 1919, in R. H. Hoare, Archangel, to Balfour, no. 115, 23 July 1919, FO 368/2175.

10. J. N. F. Larsen, Managing Director of International Clearing House, Ltd., Copenhagen, to Secretary of State, 15 November 1919, NARG 59, box 6159, file 661.4116/115. A number of similar companies had branches in major commercial cities, including New York, Stockholm, and Petrograd, to facilitate the handling of orders for Soviet Russia.

Krasin likewise supported the formation of a "clearinghouse" for Soviet trade at Copenhagen. Suggesting that this should take the form of a limited company, Krasin proposed that Russian gold should be held on deposit as a guarantee for the shareholders. It was pointed out that this would ensure that the Allies "would have a firm control over the whole affair." *Washington Post*, 18 June 1920.

11. War Trade Intelligence Department to Foreign Office, Ref. AT/12291/DL, 26 July 1919, Enclosure, "Russian Business through Swedish Firms," Stockholm, 25 July 1919, FO 368/2176.

12. Montgomery Grove, Gothenburg, to Patrick Ramsay, no. 18, 20 August 1919, translation of an article in the *Morgonpost* of 16 August 1919, FO 368/2194; and "Russian Business through Swedish Firms," Stockholm, 25 July 1919. Enclosure in War Trade Intelligence Department to Foreign Office, 26 July 1919, Ref. AT/12291/DL. The *Morgonpost* thought it "suggestive that the harbor of Gothenburg has been visited this year [1919] by a number of American vessels which had discharged here, while the British flag has been comparatively little seen."

13. The Finns were ambivalent in their pursuit of war against the Red Army, and the small skirmishes that did occur on the border had "little importance" and attracted "no attention." It was widely believed that unless the Bolsheviks were provoked, they would not embark on any aggression toward Finland. See Sir Coldridge Kennard, Chargé d'Affaires, Helsingfors, to Foreign Office, no. 100, 4 September 1919, FO 371/3731.

14. G. F. Greaves, British Consulate, Helsingfors, to Foreign Office, no. 68, 28 August 1919, FO 368/2176.

15. When asked to what Russian port the American goods were destined, Kennard replied: "Goods are destined for Petrograd." Sir Coldridge Kennard, Helsingfors, to Curzon, no. 4 Commercial, 4 September 1919; Foreign Office to Kennard, no. 644(R), 24 September 1919; and Kennard to Foreign Office, no. 527(R), 8 October 1919; FO 368/2177.

There was considerable American commercial representation in Petrograd and Moscow as well—despite the U.S. government's prohibitions on travel in Soviet Russia. As early as October 1918, "over 600 new American commercial men" were reported to be in Petrograd; and in August 1919, an American "commission" was reputed to be in Moscow, keeping an eye on the prospects for American exports to Russia. The Americans were believed to have "prepared the ground well" and to have already hired depots and warehouses at Petrograd in anticipation of future trade. See report filed by E. P. Stebbing, 24 October 1918, FO 368/2171; and *Stockholm Dagblad*, 13 August 1919, in Ramsay, Stockholm, to Foreign Office, no. 325, 15 August 1919, FO 371/4029. Ramsay noted that this tallied with information received earlier.

16. Other early transit routes favored by the United States were through Norway and Holland. See, for example, Consul General George E. Andersen, Rotterdam, 16 November 1922, NARG 59, file 661.5616/2; and Kilmarnock, Berlin, to Foreign Office, no. 2583 FR, 2 February 1921, FO 371/6876. In this connection, it is interesting to note that, because of the uncertainty of the blockade and transportation through Russia in 1919, goods that were bought and paid for by the Soviets were frequently stored in warehouses in the neutral states to await future shipment. See "Notes of a Meeting between Allied Representatives and Delegates of the Russian Co-operative Organisations," 2nd Session, (R.104), 8 April 1920, FO 371/4034.

17. The railway lines serving parts of the Baltic region were of the same gauge as that used in greater Russia, eliminating the costly need of transferring goods to carriages of the Russian gauge at the frontier.

18. *Dokumenty vneshnei politiki*, vol. 2, 1918–1920, p. 225.

19. Correspondence between Chicherin, Trotsky, and Lenin, in Meijer, *Trotsky Papers*, 1: nos. 397, 399, 403, and 409–12, as cited in Ullman, *Anglo-Soviet Relations*, 2:284.

20. Carr, *The Bolshevik Revolution*, 3:153.

21. See Intelligence Reports for December 1919, in file 67181, FO 371/3619; and Commander Smythies, Reval, no. 15/30, 2 March 1920, FO 371/3620.

22. It was made clear that the Soviets did not consider the gold as an indemnity or reparations payment. In his discussions with the Estonians, Joffe reportedly declared: "If we meet you on the question of the gold fund it is not because we feel that you really have a claim but on account of *other considerations*. . . . Firstly, you must state what sum you want and then we must say whether we can give you as much. . . . We agree to pay you *but our reasons for doing so are our business*"

[my italics]. Their reasons were certainly tied up with the reopening trade, and the decision to handle it this way was undoubtedly to avoid setting a precedent for reparations.

23. Bruno Schill, "Esthonia and Her National Aspiration." Schill was the president of the Russian-Baltic Company.

24. Inter-Allied Committee Meeting, 12 December 1919, *DBFP*, 2:748; and Russian Department to Foreign Office, July 1919, FO 368/2172. It is also interesting to note that when asked whether British merchants were permitted to ship goods to Estonian ports for eventual sale to Soviet Russia, Lloyd George sidestepped the real issue by reiterating that "goods may be exported to Esthonia without licenses." Parliamentary Question put to the Prime Minister by Commander Kenworthy, 20 January 1920; and statement prepared by the Foreign Office as a reply; FO 371/4032.

25. F. Thelwall, British Military Mission, Berlin, to Comptroller General, Department of Overseas Trade, O.T. no. 42, 29 October 1919, FO 368/2177. American commercial interest in the Baltic had been apparent since April 1919, when an American "commission" arrived in Libau. They were reportedly interested in establishing a free port at Reval. See Bosanquet, Reval, to Foreign Office, no. 6, 17 April 1919, FO 371/3967.

26. Tallents, Riga, to Foreign Office, no. 243, 24 November 1919; and Minute by C. A. Harvey, 25 November 1919, FO 371/3626.

27. Ward, Kovno, to Foreign Office, no. 29(R), 29 December 1919, FO 371/3630.

28. Estonian businessmen were likewise keen to restart this commerce and had "declared themselves willing to do all in their power to facilitate transit traffic." Patrick Ramsay, Stockholm, to Foreign Office, no. 296 Commercial, 5 August 1919, FO 368/1276. See also *The Importance of Reval from the Point of View of the World's Transit Trade with Russia* (Reval, 1921), in NARG 59, file 660i.0025 1/39.

29. See Ronimois, *Russia's Foreign Trade and the Baltic Sea*, and "The Baltic Trade of the Soviet Union: Expectations and Probabilities"; Anderson, "The USSR Trade with Latvia: The Treaty of 1927"; and Hinkkanen-Lievonen, *British Trade and Enterprise in the Baltic States, 1919–1925*.

30. John Thors, American Relief Administration Representative, Reval, to Bureau of Foreign and Domestic Commerce, 24 June 1924, NARG 151, file 448x.

31. Narodnogo Komissariata Vneshney Torgovli, *Vestnik*, no. 1, January 1921, p. 51; and "Revel'skaya gavan' bolsheviki. Estonskaya tranzitnaya torgovlya." Maklakov Manuscripts, box MS, folder HE 558/T28 R45, Hoover Institution Archives. There is considerable discrepancy even among Soviet sources as to this early trade. Contemporary sources put Soviet imports for 1920 as high as 5,923,000 poods—some 97,000 metric tons. A more recent official statistical report, however, puts Soviet imports for that year at 85,549.14 tons. The discrepancy may be accounted for insofar as the later statistics include trade that took place only from the ratification of the peace, that is, from the spring of 1920. See Kaufman, *Vneshnyaya torgovlya Rossii*, pp. 15, 19–20; and Vneshtorg,

Vneshnyaya torgovlya za 1918–1940gg., p. 21. Contemporary reports of the volume and value of transit trade also vary considerably from figures found in later Soviet statistical publications. In the case of Estonia in 1920, the older data show more than double the volume of goods as having passed through that country to Soviet Russia. One can only assume that this difference is due to the Soviets' later ascribing those imports to the countries from which they originated as opposed to the contemporary practice of crediting them to the country from which they were last shipped. See Kutuzov, *Vneshnyaya torgovlya soyuza SSR za X let*, pp. 101, 302–6; *Vestnik*, no. 1, January 1921; and Kaufman, *Vneshnyaya torgovlya Rossii*, pp. 15–22.

32. *Vneshnyaya torgovlya soyuza SSR za X let*, p. 302; and Fischer, *The Soviets in World Affairs*, 2:501. By volume, Sweden accounted for more than 17 percent of all Russian imports for that year. See *Vestnik*, no. 1, January 1921, p. 51.

33. Thomas Sammons, American Consul General, Melbourne, to Secretary of State, no. 479, "Shipment of American and British goods to Russia via Sweden," 2 February 1921, NARG 59, file 661.4117/2.

34. Charles Albrecht, American Consul, Reval, to State Department, no. 234, "Goods in Transit to Russia through Reval," 19 August 1921, NARG 59, file 660i.00251/33.

35. H. Kershaw, Commercial Secretary, Stockholm, to Barclay, "British Trading with the Baltic Provinces via Sweden," 1 December 1920, FO 371/5421. Kershaw also remarked that "a great many details regarding these transactions will never come to light owing to the devious channels through which they are, in the present abnormal conditions, compelled to be carried on."

36. "Baltic Trade—First Step in Re-Opening Trade with Russia," *Journal of Commerce*, 4 June 1919; and Board of Trade, Report no. 9, week ending 28 January 1920.

37. Minute by E. W. Birse, 25 February 1920, FO 371/4032. By using the border states as a kind of "clearinghouse" for trade, the British government hoped to avoid the question of consular representation in Soviet Russia. See unsigned Minute no. 191081, 13 April 1920, FO 371/4033. Further, as Joseph Gregory pointed out this would also enable Britain to continue to use trade as a political lever against Soviet Russia, manipulating it "as circumstances demanded." Minute by Gregory, [?27 April 1920], FO 371/4034.

38. Foreign Office to Stephen Tallents, Riga, no. 59, 26 February 1920, as cited in Tallents to Foreign Office, no. 60, 15 March 1920, FO 371/6318.

39. E. F. Wise, Memorandum, [?20 January 1920], FO 371/4032.

40. Resolution by the Estonian Government, 21 January 1920, FO 371/3631. While the Foreign Office had received a copy of the resolution on 23 January, the Board of Trade did not learn of this development until 16 February—and then only through the press!

41. Chamberlain to Meierovics, as cited in Sampts, "The Achievement of Meierovics' Last European Trip," p. 250, as quoted in Hinkkanen-Lievonen, *British Trade and Enterprise in the Baltic States, 1919–1925*, p. 112.

42. See, for example, "City Notes" in *Times*, 5 January 1920; "Trade with Finland," *Manchester Guardian Commercial*, 17 June 1920; "Sad Plight of Esthonia: Hopes Founded on Trade with Russia," *Manchester Guardian Commercial*, 29 July 1920; "New Baltic States & Russian Trade," *Times Trade Supplement*, 19 February 1921; and "Russian Trade—A Possible Start," *Manchester Guardian Commercial*, 3 February 1921. Britain considered commercial relations with Estonia important enough to warrant an exchange of notes concerning reciprocal "most favored nation" treatment of citizens and commerce as early as July 1920. This is hardly surprising considering that the Baltic handled 75 percent of all Britain's trade with Russia prior to the war. See American Consul, Riga, to State Department, no. 144, 9 September 1920, NARG 59, 641160i31/-; and the Memorandum by General Wrangel, December 1918, FO 371/3954.

Similarly, much the same can be said of Estonia's value to the Bolsheviks. An editorial in *Izvestiya* remarked that "though Esthonia herself could supply little more than paper and leather—and then only to a rather limited extent," the peace treaty made it possible to increase the amount of foreign purchases. *Izvestiya*, no. 21, February 1921.

43. Gukovsky to Piip, [circa 9 January 1920], as reported in Smythies, Reval, to Foreign Office, no. 15/30, 2 March 1920, FO 371/3620.

44. Reyntiens, Department of Overseas Trade, to O'Malley, Enclosure, "Statistics of Trade with Russia," 14 November 1924, FO 371/10470.

45. Minutes by O'Malley, 1 November 1920, on Lucien Woolf to Foreign Office, 20 October 1920, FO 371/5443.

46. Minutes by Gregory, 1 January 1920, on Tallents's Memorandum on his discussion with Tilden Smith, National Metal and Chemical Bank, FO 371/3630.

Declaring this to be "all for the good," Gregory went on to note that Britain had "no engagements of any kind towards our Allies to conflict with this." See Chapter 4 for an earlier case—the Yaroshinsky scheme—where the Foreign Office demonstrated a similar blindness toward the friction that would have inevitably arisen over such a move.

47. Fortington, National Metal and Chemical Bank, to Foreign Office, "Memorandum on the Baltic Scheme of the National Metal and Chemical Bank," 1 January 1920, FO 371/3630.

48. Minute by Evans, 1 January 1920, on Fortington, Memorandum on the Baltic Scheme of the National Metal and Chemical Bank, FO 371/3630. Further, it was noted that the "effect of a commercial penetration of the Baltic Provinces by British trading on the scale contemplated . . . would give to Great Britain an effective if not a decisive voice in the tariff policy of the states which lie between Russia and Germany."

49. My italics. Minutes by Gregory, 1 January 1920 on Tallents, Riga, Memorandum on a discussion with Tilden Smith, National Metal and Chemical Bank, FO 371/3630. For a detailed discussion scheme, see Hinkkanen-Lievonen, *British Trade and Enterprise in the Baltic States, 1919–1925*, pp. 148–70.

50. Sir Robert Horne, Board of Trade, to Lord Curzon, 25 November 1920, FO 371/5378.

51. Kaufman, *Vneshnyaya torgovlya Rossii*, p. 15.

52. Admiralty to Senior Naval Officer in the Baltic, 23 April 1920, FO 371/3618.

53. "Russian Trade through Reval," *Evening Sun* (New York), 19 April 1920. An example of this can be found in the *Journal of Commerce*, 25 June 1921, which reported that contracts for 50,000 tons of coal for Russia had been placed with American exporters through British concerns.

54. A "large trade" in khaki cloth was also being conducted through the Netherlands. See George E. Andersen, American Consul General, Rotterdam, to State Department, 15 January 1920, NARG 59, file 661.5616/-.

55. H. Fountain, Board of Trade, to Foreign Office, CRT 4091, 11 September 1920; Minute by O'Malley, 13 October 1920; Minute by Gregory, [n.d.]; and Gregory to Board of Trade, 21 October 1920; FO 371/5435.

56. Board of Trade to Foreign Office, 1 November 1920, FO 371/5435.

57. Lonergan, Reval, to Foreign Office, no. 271, 25 October 1920; and Foreign Office to Lonergan, no. 294, 29 October 1920; FO 371/5435.

58. Director of Military Intelligence, "Summary of Information Regarding Soviet Russia," [circa May 1920], FO 371/4004; and Political Report CX 711/V, Secret, 15 December 1920, FO 371/6846.

59. A. B. Cox, Acting Director, Military Intelligence, to War Department, Office of the Chief of Staff, M.I.2., 10 May 1920, NARG 151, box 86. Cox reported on a statement made by the Soviet representative in Berlin, Victor Kopp. For details of the activities of the Soviet Bureau in the United States, see Chapter 5.

60. Apparently, this was not much of a hardship initially: according to official U.S. returns, American transactions direct with Russia through Siberia, the Caucasus, and the Baltic provinces for the eleven months July 1919 to May 1920 amounted to some $80 million. See Boris Baievsky, Russian Division, Bureau of Foreign and Domestic Commerce, Memorandum for Dr. MacElwain, Director, no. 21, 17 July 1920, NARG 151, box 1880, file 400, Russia, Trade Promotion.

61. As early as 1919 International Harvester had already concluded a contract with Glavmetal for the sale of the entire production of its Lubertsy plant for the 1920 planting season. Some 5,000 mowers and 7,000 reapers were delivered to the Soviet organization between October 1919 and October 1920 under this agreement. See Pickering, "The International Harvester Company in Russia," pp. 269, 297.

62. See Morris and Co., New York, to American Consulate, Reval, 25 December 1920; and Albrecht, Reval, to Morris and Co., 6 January 1921, NARG 59, box 6142, file 660i.00251/ia. A number of other Northern European governments allowed this courtesy as well. See Findlay, Christiania, to Foreign Office, no. 413, 13 October 1920, FO 371/5420.

63. International Harvester, Chicago, to State Department, 26 April 1920; and reply, 13 May 1920; NARG 59, file 660i.119/6. Certain American firms like the

Russian and Baltic Company of New York were quite frank in indicating their desire to do business with "Esthonian firms in Esthonia who are exporting to Russia." See Bruno Schill, Russia and Baltic Company, New York, to State Department, 21 April 1920; and reply; NARG 59, file 660i.119/4.

64. *Evening Sun*, 19 April 1920. Prominent among these negotiations were those with representatives of Morgans (United States) for the sale of locomotives —a deal which was "variously stated as [involving] a total of 5,000 or . . . 300 to 400 a month for an unspecified number of months." The Soviets clearly anticipated no difficulty in taking delivery of this purchase: as early as January 1920 the Soviet representative in Reval, Gukovsky, pointed out that Russia was able to receive rolling stock through Estonia. See Director of Intelligence, "Summary of Information regarding Soviet Russia," [circa April–May 1920], FO 371/4004.

65. People's Industrial Trading Corporation, New York, to R. I. Roberge, 6 December 1920, FMCA, Acc. 49, box 1. As pointed out earlier, the People's Industrial Trading Corporation acted as a purchasing agent in the United States for the Soviets. See Chapter 5.

66. American Consulate, Reval, to Secretary of State, no. 42, "Shipments of Medical Supplies to Russia," 9 November 1920, NARG 165, box 137, file 164.386/1. This was preceded by the arrival at Reval of a shipment of drugs and medical supplies worth over $51,700 which was dispatched directly from New York by the Allied Drug Company. The consignment was "held up for some time" in Reval before the license was issued for shipment to Soviet Russia.

67. As mentioned, British firms acted as intermediaries for this American trade. A small percentage of U.S. goods—agricultural machinery, in particular—was also shipped through Canadian import-export houses. Further, International Harvester was known to ship agricultural machinery to Stockholm, where it was then transported to Reval for ultimate delivery to Soviet Russia. See Philadelphia Chamber of Commerce to H. Brock (assistant director of Department of Commerce), 27 March 1920, NARG 151, box 861; Commissioner Young, Riga, to Secretary of State, 15 June 1920, NARG 59, file 661.00/13; Vice-Consul Nielson, Stockholm, to Secretary of State, Report no. 30142, 19 May 1921, NARG 151, box 2240, file 448; and Consul Murphy to Secretary of State, 29 July 1921, NARG 59, file 661.5816/6.

68. See Wilton to Foreign Office, 24 March 1921, Enclosure, "Goods Available for Export from Russia and Goods Ordered by Russian Representatives Abroad. Purchase and Sales Commission, Foreign Countries, Moscow"; "Translation of a Confidential Report Compiled by Soviet Authorities for Their Own Use"; FO 371/6877.

69. Although the returns for 1920 do not include trade conducted with the former Russian duchies of Poland and Finland, they do incorporate U.S. trade with the Baltic states. It is also interesting to note that of the nearly $23 million worth of goods exported from the United States to Russia in 1920, more than $13 million was bound for Asiatic Russia. Data as compiled from U.S. Department of Commerce, *Foreign Commerce and Navigation of the United States*,

1921; and Albrecht, U.S. Consulate, Reval, 11 January 1922, NARG 59, file 660.0251/35.

70. A. W. Kliefoth, Riga, to State Department, "Russian Trade," 1 March 1921, NARG 59, file 661.00/22.

71. More than anything, this decision was made as a response to the earlier British move to initiate negotiations for a trade agreement with the Bolsheviks. See Chapter 5.

72. By the end of the year American businessmen were apparently not content to risk the whole of their Russian business through intermediaries and were negotiating directly with the Soviets in Moscow as well as with the Soviet Mission in Reval. Albrecht, U.S. Consulate, Reval, to Secretary of State, "Trade with Soviet Russia," no. 101, 28 December 1920, NARG 59, box 6143, file 660i61/-.

73. *Russian Information and Review*, October 1920. The Board of Trade frequently pointed out that not all cases of successful business transacted with the Soviets were likely to have been reported.

74. Restriction of Enemy Supplies Department to Secretary of the Treasury, no. 9099/2, 13 August 1918, FO 368/1970.

75. This is in addition to the heavy demands for platinum from the medical and dental professions. See U.K. Ministry of Munitions, *History of the Ministry of Munitions*, vol. 7, part III, "Non-Ferrous Metals" (HMSO, 1922).

76. Admiralty to the Secretary of the Restriction of Enemy Supplies Department, no. L.32721, 23 July 1918; Treasury to Undersecretary of State, 24 June 1918; BRITSUP, Petrograd, to RUSPLYCOM, London, no. P.67, 10 June 1918; Enclosure from McAlpine; and Minutes by Lord Reading, 16 August 1918, on RESD Memorandum, no. 9099, 3 July 1918; FO 368/1970.

77. In connection with this, Lockhart's earlier attempts at negotiations with Trotsky in March 1918 also included the topic of platinum. When discussing the possibility of establishing British aid for the Red Army against Germany, Lockhart wrote that "in particular, I asked him [Trotsky] about the platinum at Ekaterinburg, and he promised that this would be arranged at once." Lockhart, Moscow to Secretary of State, no. 23, 8 March 1918, FO 371/3285.

78. Despite this warning, the Ministry of Munitions nonetheless authorized the purchase of 12.5 poods of platinum from the Bolsheviks at £30 an ounce. Clive, Stockholm, to Undersecretary of State, no. 2839, 26 September 1918; and Ministry of Munitions to Foreign Office, 3 October 1918; FO 368/1970. Lord Reading concurred, pointing out that the platinum should be purchased "while there is still time." Sir William Mitchell-Thomson of the RESD also held this view. See Lord Reading's Minute on the Ministry of Munitions to Foreign Office, 3 October 1918, FO 368/1970; and RESD to Foreign Office, 7 October 1918, FO 368/1970.

79. By April 1922 the sale of church relics and art had realized some 20 million gold roubles for the Bolsheviks. See *Russian Information and Review*, 15 May 1922, pp. 364–65; and *Pravda*, 17 May 1922. For a fascinating account of the sale of Russian art in the U.S., see Robert Williams, *Russian Art and American*

Money, 1900–1940. Other goods that found a ready market in the West included vintage French champagnes and caviar. See Charles Albrecht, Reval, no. 203, 18 June 1921, NARG 59, 660i.0025 1/18; and Hammer, *Romanov Treasure,* and *Witness to History.*

80. Ramsay, Stockholm to Foreign Office, no. 258(R), 17 September 1920, FO 371/4037. See also J. Edgar Hoover, Department of Justice, to Colonel Hicks, Director of Military Intelligence, 23 September 1920, NARG 165, box 2616, file 10058-717/2.

81. Negotiations between the Bolshevik Mission in Reval and the DeBeers representative reportedly involved some 40,000 to 50,000 carats worth of diamonds. See Peter Leslie, Reval, to Foreign Office, no. 1994 F.R., 30 October 1920, Enclosure, Vice-Consul Dilley, Reval, 25 October 1920, FO 371/5433; and U.S. Consulate, Reval, to Secretary of State, no. 91, 18 December 1920, NARG 59, file 661.621/-.

82. "Report on Bolshevik Diamond Smuggling," no. 1586, 7 November 1920, NARG 59, file 861.51/850.

83. War Trade Intelligence Department to Secretary of State, 30 September 1919, Enclosure, Report from Viborg, 8 September 1919, FO 368/2177. The War Trade Intelligence Department also remarked that valuta speculations were "managed by Bolshevists. . . . English valuta has been wanted from time to time in amounts approximately from 10,000 to 20,000 pounds at Stockholm." See War Trade Intelligence Department to Secretary State, 27 January 1919, FO 371/3950.

84. Moscow Narodny Bank to Undersecretary of State, 9 October; and extracts from the *Morning Post,* 22 October 1920; FO 371/5433. The *Morning Post* reported that the "authority for the sale of the bonds had been given in January 1920." A Foreign Office Minute declared this to be "a correct account." See Minute by Maxse, 25 October 1920, FO 371/5433.

85. *Federal Reserve Bulletin,* June 1922, p. 659.

86. "Circular Instruction," Serial no. 9, 28 January 1921, NARG 59, file 861.51. Replies to this circular are largely found in NARG 165, box 2616.

87. It was further noted that, although the greater part of this gold was in the form of currency of Allied nations, it was "perfectly possible—and in fact the obvious thing to do—for the Bolsheviks to obtain gold of other than Russian nationality in return for Russian roubles or bullion deposited here. A small commission paid would certainly enable them to effect such a transaction." See William Phillips, The Hague, to Secretary of State, "29-Gold," "Shipment of Bolshevik Gold to the United States," 8 February 1921, NARG 165, box 2616, file 10058-710/22.

88. U.S. Consul General, Paris, to Secretary of State, 1 August 1921, NARG 165, box 2616, file 10058-710/116. For its part, the Foreign Office gave credence to reports that "practically the entire quantity of gold which the Soviet government has succeeded in disposing has passed through the hands of the French Bank Lyons Allemand." See Hodgson, Moscow, to Foreign Office, Memorandum on his Conversation with Mr. Bloomfield, 22 July 1921; and Minute by Maxse; FO

371/6879. Bloomfield visited Soviet Russia twice, reportedly at the request of President Harding, to report on conditions there. He was known to be "on friendly terms" with Armand Hammer and had undertaken "several interviews with both Mr. Chicherin and Mr. Litvinov." Not surprisingly, he was in "favour of a resumption of commercial relations between the U.S. and Russia." William Peters, Moscow, to Foreign Office, no. 868, 6 November 1922, FO 371/8214.

89. Charles D. Westcott, Economic Consul, Paris to Secretary of State, "Decrease in Russian Gold Invoiced to America through Paris Consulate General," 16 February 1922, NARG 165, box 2616, file 10058-710/124.

90. Office of Naval Intelligence, Report no. 1099, 11 January 1919, NARG 45, WA-6, box 607.

91. "Gold Movements in 1920–22 According to Customs Statistics of Sweden, Switzerland, France and the United States," in Amtorg Trading Corporation, *Russian Gold*, pp. 57–60.

92. C. Barclay, Stockholm, to Undersecretary of State, no. 904, 6 December 1920, Enclosure, H. Kershaw, "British Trading with the Baltic Provinces via Sweden," 1 December 1920, FO 371/5421. Kershaw based his information on "particulars officially supplied by the Swedish Commercial Department."

93. Consul Walter H. Sholes, Göteborg, to Secretary of State, no. 301, 21 April 1921, NARG 165, box 2616, file 10058-710/40.

94. C. Barclay, Stockholm, to Undersecretary of State, no. 242, 27 April 1921, Enclosure, H. Kershaw, Stockholm, no. 228, 27 April 1921, FO 371/6879; Consul General Murphy, Stockholm, to Secretary of State, "Trade with Soviet Russia," 11 April 1921, NARG 59, file 661.5816/5; and NARG 165, box 2616, file 10058-710/34.

Considerably disturbed by this outpouring of Soviet gold, Maxse noted that "there will not be much left with which to finance Anglo-Russian trade if this goes on." Reginald Leeper, however, took a more philosophical view, observing that "gold is exported from Russia for political or trading purposes, and it gravitates naturally to America for economic reasons, as part of the tribute of a debtor old world to the creditor new world." Minutes by Maxse, 7 May 1921, and R. C. Leeper, 9 May 1921, on Kershaw, FO 371/6879.

95. Sweden apparently enjoyed a special arrangement: while the Assay Office remained under instruction to refuse gold it suspected of being of Russian origin—an option it regularly exercised against gold from Germany—both the Treasury and the Mint "ruled that the Assay Office may not refuse to purchase [Swedish] gold." *New York Times*, 2 April 1921.

96. Boris Baievsky, Russian Division, Bureau of Foreign and Domestic Commerce, to U.S. Commercial Attaché, London, 7 January 1921, NARG 151, box 2837, file 601.2.

97. See, for example, the report concerning National City Bank's successful test shipment of gold reminted in Copenhagen given in Grew, Copenhagen, to Secretary of State, 27 June 1921, NARG 165, box 2616, file 10058-710/93.

98. *New York Tribune*, 2 April 1921; and *New York Times*, 2 April 1921.

99. Reported in *Dagens Nyheter*, 1 December 1920, as conveyed in Barclay, Stockholm, to Foreign Office, no. 904, 6 December 1920, FO 371/5421.

100. Department of State to Brigadier General Nolan, Military Intelligence, 15 July 1921, NARG 165, box 2616, file 10058-710/92.

101. See *Our Vanishing Gold Reserves*, pamphlet issued by the American Mining Congress, 1920.

102. Commercial Attaché, Paris, to Secretary of Commerce, 17 December 1920, NARG 151, box 2837, file 601.2.

103. Albrecht, Reval, to Secretary of State, "Trade with Soviet Russia," no. 101, 28 December 1920, NARG 59, file 660i.61/-.

104. Russian Division, Department of State, "Memorandum of Information," 30 April 1921, p. 11, NARG 165, box 2616, file 10058-710/39.

105. Ibid.; and Charles D. Westcott, Paris, to Secretary of State, 28 June 1921, NARG 165, box 2616, file 10058-710/110.

106. This figure represents the compilation of the volume and value of gold shipped to the Equitable Trust Company's account, as reported by U.S. consular officials. Although care has been taken to weed out any duplicate reports as well as any less reliable sources, this is in no way represents a definitive figure. Rather, lacking access to the bank's own records, it stands as a "best guess" estimate of the approximate volume of Russian gold that the Equitable received, as derived from other reliable sources. The consular reports concerning the movement of Russian gold that were used in deriving this estimate may be found in NARG 165, box 2616.

107. Market price for gold was $665 per kilogram in Washington and 104 shillings per ounce in London. C. Barclay, Stockholm, to Undersecretary of State, no. 242, 27 April 1921, Enclosure, H. Kershaw, Stockholm, no. 228, 27 April 1921, FO 371/6879; and Ullman, *Anglo-Soviet Relations*, 3:431, n. 78.

108. Moscow Narodny Bank to Secretary of State, 4 May 1920; and reply, 8 May 1920; FO 371/4034; and Minutes from the Meeting with the Russian Trade Delegation, 3rd Meeting, 3 December 1920, FO 371/5434.

109. Treasury to Foreign Office, Confidential, 8 June 1920, FO 371/4035; William F. Malcolm and Co. to Foreign Office, 22 July 1920; and Minutes by Maxse, 23 July 1920; FO 371/3635.

110. Treasury to Foreign Office, no. F.1311, 22 January 1921, FO 371/6878.

111. Foreign Office Memorandum on Russian Gold, June 1920, FO 371/4035.

112. Minute by Maxse, 21 July 1920, on Findlay, Christiania, Overseas Trade "A," no. 66, 13 July 1920, FO 371/4036.

An indication of how out of touch the Treasury was on this issue is evident from the fact that, as late as November, it continued to believe that "the difficulties in the way of giving title to the gold have effectively prevented the Soviet government from disposing of any but insignificant amounts in any direction." Treasury to Northern Department, Foreign Office, no. 1227, 5 November 1920, FO 371/5420.

113. Treasury to Foreign Office, no. F.1311, 22 January 1921, FO 371/6878; Barclay to Secretary of State, 2 February 1921, FO 371/6879; and Leslie, Reval,

to Foreign Office, no. (R), 17 June 1920, FO 371/4035. The government's official explanation for this distinction was that it chose to regard the Estonian government as a "mine." See Memorandum by Mr. B. P. Blackett, Treasury, 2 June 1920, Cabinet Paper 1394; and Clark to O'Malley, [circa July 1920]; and Blackett to Chapman, 12 August 1920; FO 371/3633.

114. The Treasury apparently thought better of informing the United States about such official differentiation. See U.S. Ambassador Rodgers, London, to O'Malley, 13 March 1921; and Waley, Treasury, to O'Malley, 7 April 1921; FO 371/6869.

115. Moscow Narodny Bank, Ltd., London, to Litvinov, Copenhagen, no. 3, 29 March 1920, FO 371/4051.

116. U.S. Consul General, London, to Secretary of State, "Financial Sources of the Russian Government," no. 12127, 22 November 1921, NARG 59, box 6159, file 661.4116/150.

117. Minutes from the Meeting with the Russian Trade Delegation, 5th Meeting, 10 December 1920, FO 371/5435; and Maxse, "Memorandum on Policy to be Adopted towards Gold Originating in Russia," 14 July 1920, FO 371/4036.

118. Minute by O'Malley on Sir Eyre Crowe, 30 December 1920, FO 371/5434.

119. Minute by Maxse, 1 November 1920, on Paper N 1877/1164/38, FO 371/5444.

120. Minutes from the Meeting with the Russian Delegation, 3rd Meeting, 3 December 1920, FO 371/5434.

121. It was also reported that they had "cargoes of flax, bristles, copper, etc., waiting now in Petrograd . . . and also 100,000 cubic meters of timber." Report from Wise in Grant-Watson, Copenhagen, no. 15, 17 April 1920, FO 418/54. In addition to these goods, oil was also mentioned as a possible cash-raising export. Barclay, Stockholm, to Foreign Office, no. 871, 23 November 1920, FO 371/5436.

122. Russian Corporation, Ltd., London, to Hoare, 27 May 1920; and Enclosure; FO 371/4035; and U.S. Consul, Copenhagen, 25 May 1920, NARG 59, file 661.5916/19.

123. Sir A. Geddes, Washington, to Foreign Office, no. 1228, 8 October 1920, Enclosure, Memorandum, 6 October 1920, FO 371/5420.

124. O'Malley, "Resumption of Trade with Soviet Russia," Foreign Office Memorandum, 21 December 1921; and Minutes; FO 371/5434.

125. See, for example, Industrial and Commercial Bank of Esthonia, Ltd., Reval, to E. H. Archer, 9 June 1920, FO 371/3635; and Russian Corporation, Ltd., London, to Foreign Office, 27 May 1920, FO 371/4035.

126. Minute by Maxse, Minute no. 214307, 13 September 1920, FO 371/4048. See also Hugessen, The Hague, no. 160, 14 September 1920, FO 371/4037.

127. Minute by Maxse, 6 September, on Findlay, Christiania, no. 181, 2 September 1920, FO 371/4037.

128. C. Barclay, Stockholm, to Undersecretary of State, no. 242, 27 April 1921, Enclosure, H. Kershaw, Stockholm, no. 228, 27 April 1921, FO 371/6879. It was realized in official circles that the amount of Bolshevik literature that was re-

ported by certain "reliable sources" to have been exported and the amount that had actually been seized differed considerably. Commenting on the purported seizure of some 300,000 kilograms of Bolshevik propaganda bound for New York, one U.S. intelligence official observed that, "often, the amount of gold that is reported to be shipped into the Western countries is said to be for propaganda purposes . . . [but] no quantity of 300 kilograms or even less has been seized for many months past." Military Intelligence, April 1921, NARG 165, box 2622, file 10058-999/4.

129. Fischer, *The Soviets in World Affairs*, 2:560.

130. U.S. Commercial Attaché, Paris, to Russian Division, Bureau of Foreign and Domestic Commerce, 17 December 1920, NARG 151, box 2837, file 601.2.

131. Amtorg Trading Corporation, *Russian Gold*, pp. 57–60. In Sweden alone the Soviets were reported to have over $100 million to their account, with a further $7 million said to be on deposit with a New York banking concern. *New York Times*, 7 June 1921.

132. The total quantity of Russian gold delivered to the Osaka Mint for recoinage during 1920 was equivalent to $24,660,000. See U.S. Ambassador, Tokyo, 10 June 1921, NARG 165, box 2616, file 10058-710/95.

133. *Report of the United States Senate Commission on Gold and Silver Inquiry*, p. 206.

134. Estimates worked from U.S. consular and intelligence reports in NARG 165, box 2616. See n. 106.

135. Minute by Maxse, 6 September 1920, on Findlay, Christiania, no. 181, 2 September 1920, FO 371/4037.

136. H. Kershaw, Stockholm, no. 86, Overseas Trade "A," 1 December 1920, in Department of Overseas Trade no. F.R. 2234, 10 December 1920, FO 371/5421.

Chapter 7

1. *Times*, 20 December 1923.

2. In fact, these relations were officially maintained up to 1933. The records of the Russian Financial Agent, Sergie Ughet, provide a detailed account of these relations. These records can be found in the papers of Russia, Posol'stvo (U.S.) at the Hoover Institution Archives.

3. J. D. Gregory to the Law Officers of the Crown, no. 66, 13 April 1921; and "Report of the Law Officers," 18 April 1921; FO 418/55. This report went on to state that the Law Officers thought that "it necessarily follows that direct diplomatic relations can be established between representatives of the Soviet Government and the Secretary of State for Foreign Affairs."

4. Court of Appeals, Aksionairnoyo Obschestvo A. M. Luther v. James Sagor and Co., Judgment of Lord Justice Bankes, 12 May 1921, Law Report, *Times*, 13 May 1921. Lord Justice Scrutton concurred with this judgment, declaring that "at a time when the British Government took so much in taxes and death duties

the morality of Soviet confiscations could hardly be questioned!" Ullman, *Anglo-Soviet Relations*, 3:453, n. 120.

It is worth noting that this ruling on Soviet title had the effect of boosting British imports of raw materials from Russia. Imports of timber, grain, and petroleum, for example, amounted to only £882,863 in 1921, but had increased to £2,765,061 in 1922. See *House of Commons, Debates*, 17 July 1923, as in FO 371/9352.

5. "Report from the Proceedings of the Tenth Meeting between the British and Russian Representatives Held at the Board of Trade," 5 January 1921; and the Report of the Eleventh Meeting, 10 January 1921; FO 371/68677; and Sir Robert Horne, "Gold Letter to Krasin," Confidential, 11 January 1921, FO 371/6868.

6. High Court of Justice, Chancery Division, *A. G. Marshall v. Mary Grinbaum and Others*, Judgment by Mr. Justice Peterson, 13 July 1921, Law Report, *Times*, 14 July 1921.

7. "Gold Letter." Horne stressed this point again on the eve of the signing of the trade agreement, stating that he hoped Krasin "thoroughly understood that gold brought to England was not to be used to finance purchases from other countries, but it was for the purpose of buying British goods." Although Krasin was "perfectly willing" to accept this clause of the "Gold Letter" in its present general form, he pointed out that "if it was interpreted strictly great practical difficulties might arise." See the "Report from the Proceedings of the Fourteenth Meeting between the British and Russian Representatives Held at the Board of Trade," 15 March 1921, FO 371/6878.

8. Krasin's assessment of the situation was upheld by the Legal Advisor to the Foreign Office. See Home Office to Gregory, 8 June 1921, Intercept, Krasin to Union of Siberian Creamery, London, 4 April 1921; Minutes by Maxse, 11 June 1921; and H. Sherman, Legal Advisor, 15 June 1921; FO 371/6941.

9. "The Position and Work of Our Trade Delegation in Great Britain," interview with Krasin in Moscow, *Izvestiya*, no. 97, 7 May 1921. A similar report was carried in *Ekonomicheskaya Zhizn'* on the same day.

10. "The Position and Work of Our Trade Delegation in Great Britain," *Izvestiya*, no. 97, 7 May 1921.

11. The Prime Minister's Statement to the House of Commons, 19 October 1921, FO 371/6856.

12. Parliamentary Question and the Prime Minister's Reply, 20 October 1921, FO 371/6855; and Parliamentary Question and Prime Minister's Reply, 24 October 1921, FO 371/6856. The House was informed that "considerable purchases [had] been made in this country since the conclusion of the Trade Agreement with the Soviet government." See Lloyd-Greame's reply to L. Lyle, House of Commons, 6 June 1921, FO 371/6878.

13. According to the Soviets, a steady "stream of offers and inquiries" had developed after the conclusion of the trade agreement, and Arcos was "in touch with many thousands of firms, including practically every important British concern in the industries connected with engineering, textiles, leather, chemicals,

scientific instruments and agricultural supplies." "Work of Arcos," in *Russian Information and Review*, 1 October 1921, p. 19. Published by the Information Department of the Russian Trade Delegation.

14. Department of Overseas Trade, Memorandum, no. 7344 F.R., 24 April 1923, FO 371/9351; and Reyntiens, Department of Overseas Trade, to Foreign Office, 22 November 1923, FO 371/9353.

15. The classifications were prewar Russia, including Finland; prewar Russia, except Finland; postwar Russia, including the Ukraine and the Far Eastern Republic; and territories of the RSFSR. This last group was subjected to further division: trade across European frontiers, trade with Russia in Europe, and trade with Russia in Asia are the more common. In short, there were about as many different geographical classifications describing where this trade took place in Russia as there were sets of data.

16. See, for example, the *Official Report* as cited by Lt. Buckley in the House of Commons, 7 May 1923, FO 371/9352.

17. "The Position and Work of Our Trade Delegation in Great Britain," in Moscow, *Izvestiya*, 7 May 1921. Indeed, there was a noticeable absence of Soviet orders for such heavy goods as locomotives and rails. Even the contract with Armstrong-Whitworth for the repair of Soviet locomotives had "very little probability" of being executed. See Hodgson, Moscow, no. 34(R), 22 August 1921, FO 371/6929.

18. *Izvestiya*, 7 May 1921. It had also been made clear to the British that if credit facilities were available the Soviets would not hesitate to place considerable orders regardless of the higher prices. See Hodgson, Moscow, no. 221, "Economic and Commercial Situation in Russia during 1922," 26 March 1923, FO 371/9364; and Hugh Ledward, Foreign Office Memorandum, "The Monopoly of Foreign Trade," December 1923, FO 371/10469.

Reporting the government's position, *Ekonomicheskaya Zhizn'* noted that "in order to develop our trade relations abroad, the question of credit has to be raised. We have taken steps to obtain credit and take the line that we cannot work without it. Insofar as Great Britain is interested in trade with Russia, its traders must give us credit." *Ekonomicheskaya Zhizn'*, 7 May 1921.

19. *Russian Information and Review*, 1 October 1921; and Department of Overseas Trade, "Statistical Notes on the Extent and Importance of the Foreign Trade of Russia," Russian Purchases in the United Kingdom according to Figures Published by the Russian Trade Delegation, March 1922, FO 371/8175.

20. Résumé of speeches by Kamenev and Trotsky at the Special Meeting of the Moscow Soviet, 30 August 1921, in Hodgson, Moscow, to Curzon, no. 84, 3 September 1921, Enclosure, William Peters, Commercial Secretary, Moscow, "Memorandum Respecting the Economic Situation of Soviet Russia," FO 418/56.

21. This had a curiously legitimizing effect on Russian gold: Krasin observed that "if America accepts our gold coin at its face value, we may be sure that other powers, and consequently European banks, will do the same." Krasin, *Vneshtorg i vneshnyaya ekonomicheskaya politika sovetskogo pravitel'stva*, pp. 11–16.

22. A further $4 million had been allotted by Congress, raising the U.S. governmental contribution to $24 million; $12 million in gold was provided by the Soviets; and nearly $17 million collected in charitable contributions. See Hoover to President Harding, 10 February 1922, NARG 151, box 200, "Regional Economics," file 0400-A, "American Relief, Special Administration, 1918–1923."

23. Secretary of State Hughes, 2 September 1921, NARG 59, file 841.48/1601.

24. Résumé of speeches by Kamenev and Trotsky at the Special Meeting of the Moscow Soviet, 30 August 1921, in Hodgson, Moscow, to Curzon, no. 84, 3 September 1921, Enclosure, Commercial Secretary Peters, "Memorandum Respecting the Economic Situation of Soviet Russia," FO 418/56.

25. Hodgson, Moscow, to Curzon, no. 14, 10 August 1921, FO 371/6920.

26. Ibid.

27. Karl Radek lambasted the Allies' proposed commission as a "fool's comedy" —appointed "to study the question of how long a starving people can wait for the Christian and civilized peoples of the West." *Na Pomosch*, a special government publication devoted to the famine, gave prominence to a telegram from H. G. Wells that rendered "the vacillating and inhumane policy of [the] Entente" responsible for the Soviet government's inability "to deal effectively with this sudden catastrophe." See Karl Radek, "The Supreme Council and the Famine in Russia," in *Pravda*, 17 August 1921; *Na Pomosch*, 29 August 1921, as reported in Hodgson to Curzon, no. 44(R), 30 August 1921, FO 418/56; and the résumé of speeches by Kamenev and Trotsky at the Special Meeting of the Moscow Soviet, 30 August 1921, in Hodgson, Moscow, to Curzon, no. 84, 3 September 1921, Enclosure, Commercial Secretary Peters, "Memorandum Respecting the Economic Situation of Soviet Russia," FO 418/56. Both Kamenev and Radek were quick to point out the immediate offers of aid from the United States.

28. "Report on the Meeting of the International Commission for Russian Relief at Brussels," Appendix B, 14 October 1921, FO 418/56. Significantly, there were no Russians on the Commission, nor on the Commission of Enquiry that was eventually appointed to investigate the extent of the famine.

29. Prime Minister's Speech to the House of Commons, *House of Commons, Debates*, 16 August 1921.

30. Minute by Gregory, 12 September 1921, on R. A. Leeper, Memorandum, "Political Aspects of the Russian Famine Question," 12 September 1921, FO 371/6851.

31. R. A. Leeper, Memorandum, "Political Aspects of the Russian Famine Question," 12 September 1921, FO 371/6851.

32. Minutes by Leeper, 24 September 1921, on Mr. London to Foreign Office, no. 37, 23 September 1921, FO 371/6924. When faced with the possibility of the Soviets agreeing to honor the prewar debts conditional upon de jure recognition and the extension of credit, the Foreign Office was thrown into a panic. Remarking that if the Soviets did undertake such an action, the British government would be exposed "to very serious charges if we do not immediately take cognizance of this step and adopt some measures to respond to the *beau geste* made by the

Soviet government." But as the conditions for credit included that the Soviets agree to the admission of a commission of inquiry and the provision of adequate security, as well as the recognition of all debts and obligations, the Foreign Office reasoned that there was "no commitment to the recommending of credits" if only two of the conditions were fulfilled. See Foreign Office minute by R. Leeper, concerning intercepted Soviet telegrams, 27 October 1921; and telegram from Soviet Representative, "Recognition of Debts by Soviet Government," 28 October 1921; FO 371/6933.

33. Report of the International Red Cross and Red Cross Society of Great Britain, September 1922, FO 371/8150. The original value of the supplies donated by the British government was put at £100,000, but due to inflation, the par value at prevailing prices had risen to £194,431.11.6. This figure represents the total value of the aid contributed by the government for famine relief in Russia.

34. E. C. Wilton, Riga, to Gregory, 30 November 1921, FO 371/6926. While the government's contribution to famine relief was somewhat less than impressive, private contributions of £12,000 to £15,000 a month were collected. These charitable contributions did little to assuage Soviet bitterness over the official British policy, but rather were seen as confirming the Soviet's conviction that the *people* of England were friendly to Russia, while the government alone was antagonistic. Hodgson warned of this possibility as early as August. See Lord Emmott, Chairman, Russian Famine Relief Fund, to Lloyd George, 14 December 1921, FO 371/6928; and Hodgson to Curzon, no. 14, 10 August 1921, FO 371/6920.

35. See Gregory to the British Red Cross Society, 3 November 1921, FO 371/6925; File 12 (1922) on the Russian Famine, in FO 371/8150; E. C. Wilton, Riga, to Gregory, 30 November 1921, FO 371/6926; and Lord Emmott to Lloyd George, 14 December 1921, FO 371/6928.

36. *Resolution Adopted by the Supreme Council at Cannes*, U.K. Parliamentary Papers, British White Paper, Cmd. 1621.

37. "Declaration of Recognition of Claims," Trade Agreement between His Britannic Majesty's Government and the Government of the Russian Socialist Federated Soviet Republic, 17 March 1921. The trade agreement also provided the Soviet government with the reciprocal right to press the claims "of its nationals against the other party in respect of property or rights in respect of obligations incurred by the existing or former governments of either country." FO 418/55.

38. Lenin, on Genoa, Moscow, 6 March 1922, in Lenin, *Sochineniya*, 27:173; and Narodnyi Komissariat po Inostrannym Delam, *Materialy Genueskoi Konferntsii*, p. 19.

39. Lenin's Speech at the Opening of the Eleventh Congress of Soviets, *Pravda*, 28 March 1922. See also *Ekonomicheskaya Zhizn'*, "Russia's Foreign Trade Prospects and the Genoa Conference," 7 March 1922.

40. Lord Robert Cecil, *House of Commons, Debates*, 13 June 1922, as cited in Stephen White, *Britain and the Bolshevik Revolution*, p. 142.

Indeed, there is much to be said for the assessment of the Genoa Conference as a "businessmen's convention to explore possible terms under which oil companies, foreign industrialists and miners might resume operations in Russia." Like a number of other British businessmen who had joined the British delegation as "special advisors" to Lloyd George, Urquhart was personally interested in the outcome of the conference: he had been engaged in negotiations with the Soviets since mid-1921 for the return of his properties in one form or another. See K. H. Kennedy, *Mining Tsar*, esp. pp. 164–66.

41. "International Economic Conference at Genoa," File 646 (1922), FO 371/8186-8193. Concerning the Rapallo Accord, the Deputy Commissar for Foreign Trade declared that the Allies had finally been forced to realize that the establishment of formal economic relations between Russia and Germany, "especially under existing circumstances," was "far more important to both these countries than the problematic results of the Conference." The Entente was obliged to deal with Russia as a "great country" without whose participation the Western European countries would be unable to restore their own prosperity. The British translator observed that there seemed "to be little that can be disputed in this article. . . . Rapallo is really only the beginning of the realisation of the inevitable *status quo ante bellum*." Translation of an Interview with Froomkin, Deputy Commissar for Foreign Trade, Forwarded by Department of Overseas Trade to Foreign Office, no. FR/5248, 25 April 1922; and Translator's Note; FO 371/8190.

42. Gregory, Genoa, to Foreign Office, no. 63(R), 21 April 1922, FO 371/8188. The Soviet government further refused to admit any liability for the debts of its predecessors until de jure recognition had been accorded to it by the "powers concerned."

43. Gregory, Genoa, to Curzon, no. 37(R), 15 April 1922, FO 371/8187. The presentation of Soviet counterclaims was not totally unexpected by the British. As early as 6 March the Foreign Office "had under consideration the possible claims which the Russian Government might not inconceivably put forward at the Genoa Conference against H.M. Government in connection with the various warlike operations which were undertaken on Russian territory since the establishment of the Bolshevik regime." Foreign Office Memorandum, "Claims Which the Russian Government May Put Forward at Genoa Conference," Transmitted to the War Office, 6 March 1922, FO 371/8186.

44. Gregory, Genoa, to Curzon, no. 63(R), 21 April 1922, FO 371/8188.

45. Minute by O'Malley, *DBFP*, 19:702–3.

46. War debts were not considered by the Russians primarily because of the failure of the Allies to recognize any liability for the losses caused by the intervention and blockade. Gregory, Genoa, to Curzon, no. 179, Transmitting Russian Reply to British Memorandum, 11 May 1922, FO 371/8190.

47. Minute by Maxse, 2 July 1920, on Commander Luke, Tiflis, to Foreign Office, 29–30 June 1920, FO 371/4036.

48. Boyle to Curzon, 6 September 1921; Geoffrey Haly, Petroleum Department, to Boyle, S 583 (Secret), 26 August 1921; and Boyle to Haly, 28 August 1921; FO 371/6930. The Foreign Office apparently shared Boyle's conviction that "the interests of the Royal Dutch Shell and H.M. Government [were] identical." For-

eign Office memorandum by Maxse, "Russian Oil Interests of the Shell Group," 10 September 1921; and Minute by Maxse, 13 September 1921; FO 371/6930.

49. Gregory to Sir H. Rumbold, Constantinople, 7 November 1921, FO 371/6930; and Esmond Ovey to Krasin, 19 October 1921, as cited in Fischer, *Oil Imperialism*, p. 41.

50. Gregory to Sir H. Rumbold, Constantinople, 7 November 1921, FO 371/6930.

51. Marcosson, *The Black Golconda*, p. 119. Senator Borah remarked that the "real, moving, driving power in Genoa was oil, not political recognition, not restoration of Russia, but the question which concerned them was what amount of natural resources and raw material of Russia each one of the Allied powers could get hold of." See Borah's defense of his motion to recognize Russia, 15 May 1922, Russia, Posol'stvo (U.S.), box 9, file 5, Hoover Institution Archives.

52. See, for example, *Times*, 2 May 1922.

53. The British Memorandum of 2 May defined a "previous owner" as a company controlled by foreign nationals "at the date of nationalisation"—that is, before 1918. See British Memorandum, 2 May 1922, Clause VII, *Papers Relating to International Economic Conference, Genoa, April–May* 1922, U.K. Parliamentary Papers, Cmd. 1667, pp. 314–22; and Fischer, *The Soviets in World Affairs*, 1:437. In response to the British Memorandum, Standard hastened to remind the oil community that it had purchased Nobel properties in Russia in 1920 and that "there had been no change in the situation since that time." See *New York Herald*, 13 May 1922; for details of Standard Oil's purchase of the Nobel properties, see Chapter 4.

In the face of the demands put by the British in their memorandum, it is interesting to note that the Foreign Office admitted that it was unrealistic to expect that the Soviets would agree to return the oil lands to the original private owners. "Apart from the political suicide they would commit is the very real and indisputable argument that any such action is detrimental to the industry." See Foreign Office Memorandum by R. McDonell, 19 May 1922, FO 371/8162.

54. Memorandum prepared by Walter Teagle for presentation to the State Department, in Gibb and Knowlton, *History of the Standard Oil Company*, 2:338; and *FRUS*, 1922, 2:786–88, as cited in Carr, *The Bolshevik Revolution*, 3:379, n. 4.

55. Statement issued at Genoa by the U.S. Ambassador to Rome, as cited in Carr, *The Bolshevik Revolution*, 3:379. French and Belgian support for the American stand has generally been attributed to pressure from Washington; in the case of France, however, this was more likely due to their dependence upon Standard—through its French subsidiary—for their supply of oil. See Carr, 3:379; and Fischer, *Oil Imperialism*, p. 44.

56. Gregory, Genoa, to Foreign Office, no. 147, 4 May 1922, FO 371/8161; and Minute by O'Malley, 9 May 1922, on Sir A. Geddes, Washington, no. 214(R), 4 May 1922, FO 371/8161. Commenting on Shell's denial of its reported deal

with Russia, Curzon observed that "there can be no smoke without fire." Minute by Curzon on E. Weakley, 8 May 1922, FO 371/8161.

57. Minute by O'Malley, 9 May 1922, on Geddes, Washington, no. 215(R), 4 May 1922, FO 371/8161. The Petroleum Department agreed with this position.

58. O'Malley, 10 May 1922, on Foreign Office Minute for Reply to a Parliamentary Question by Commander Kenworthy, FO 371/8161.

59. Minute by R. A. Leeper for Sir William Tyrell's information, 4 May 1922; J. C. Clarke, Petroleum Department, to O'Malley, 15 May 1922; and Minute by R. Sperling, 18 May, on P. Lloyd-Greame to H. G. Trew, Managing Director of Spies Petroleum Co., 7 May 1922; FO 371/8161; and R. McDonell, Foreign Office Memorandum, "Petroleum," 19 May 1922, FO 371/8162.

60. Despite the general agreement reached by the delegations while still at Genoa that any country wishing to be represented "could not be excluded from the non-Russian Commission," the Soviets were pointedly excluded from the preconference discussions. Gregory, the Hague, to Foreign Office, no. 1, 15 June 1922, FO 371/8191; and file on the Hague Conference, FO 371/8194.

61. Gregory, the Hague, to Foreign Office, no. 1, 15 June 1922, FO 371/8191.

62. Stephen White, *Britain and the Bolshevik Revolution*, pp. 74–75. White describes the delegation to the Hague as a commission of "experts" rather than plenipotentiaries, with no power to take decisions.

63. Report from H.M. Mission, Moscow, 13 June 1922, in Gregory, The Hague, to Foreign Office, no. 24, 26 June 1922, FO 371/8194.

64. Editorial by Radek in *Pravda*, 18 July 1922; article by Sokolnikov in *Izvestiya*, 25 July 1922; and Report from H.M. Mission, Moscow, 13 June 1922, in Gregory, The Hague, to Foreign Office, no. 24, 26 June 1922; FO 371/8194.

65. Statement by Litvinov, *Daily Telegraph*, 27 June 1922.

66. Even this demand had been moderated somewhat, from demands for loans or credits from the Allied governments to credits from Western businessmen with governmental guarantees. *The Hague Conference, June–July* 1922, Complete Stenographic Report, VSNKh (Moscow, 1922), p. 165, as cited in Fischer, *The Soviets in World Affairs*, 1:355–56.

67. Maxse, The Hague, to O'Malley, 10 July 1922, FO 371/8195; and Sir Philip Lloyd-Greame, The Hague, Memorandum, 1 July 1922, FO 371/8194. Maxse was of the opinion that the united Allied front had finally "driven the Russians into a corner from which there is no escape." Maxse, The Hague, to Ovey, 6 July 1922, FO 371/8195.

68. The French in particular were keen on extracting an agreement that would bind the British to prevent their nationals from "taking over anybody elses' property." Such an undertaking would "be useless unless the United States were included, and on this ground alone, such an agreement can not be entertained at the moment." Maxse, The Hague, to O'Malley, 10 July 1922, FO 371/8195.

69. Maxse, The Hague, to O'Malley, 10 July 1922, FO 371/8195. The British government had clearly recognized the Soviet government's legitimate right to nationalize property when the British Court ruled in its favor in the battle over

title to Russian goods exported to Britain. See Precis Verbal of Fourth Meeting of the Non-Russian Property Commission, Sub Committee with Russians, British Delegation, The Hague, no. 50, 12 July 1922, FO 371/8195; and my n. 4.

70. Maxse, The Hague, to O'Malley, 10 July 1922; and Minute by Gregory on the effects of a separate agreement; FO 371/8195.

71. Fischer, *The Soviets in World Affairs*, 1:362. For Litvinov's Plenary Session proposal and subsequent events, see file 646 (1922) on The Hague Conference, FO 371/8195-8196; *The Hague Conference, June–July* 1922, Complete Stenographic Report, VSNKh (Moscow, 1922); and *Dokumenty vneshnei politiki*, 5, no. 216, pp. 511–12, 514.

72. Fischer attributed these remarks to Sir Sidney Chapman and Leslie Urquhart, to whom Litvinov first privately suggested this plan. See Fischer, *The Soviets in World Affairs*, 1:362.

73. By 1922 the Soviets were again able to export grain as well as other commodities. Soviet currency had also been stabilized through the issue of the chervonetz—a gold-backed rouble note. See Foreign Office Memorandum, 26 October 1922, FO 371/8199; and Hodgson, Moscow, to Curzon, no. 822, 19 October 1923, Enclosure, Peters's Memorandum on Chervonetz, FO 371/9345.

74. Memorandum from Sir Philip Lloyd-Greame, The Hague, on a conversation with Litvinov, 1 July 1922, FO 371/8194.

75. *Financial Times*, 11 September 1922; and *Morning Post*, 11 September 1922, both as cited in K. H. Kennedy, *Mining Tsar*, p. 179.

76. The Soviets were angered at not having been included in negotiations on the Eastern Crises—an issue in which they felt they had a justifiable interest. See Enclosure 1, in William Peters, Moscow, to Curzon, 10 October 1922, FO 371/8162. For a description of how it this particularly effected the ratification of the Urquhart contract, see K. H. Kennedy, *Mining Tsar*, pp. 179–92.

77. Krasin alone voted in favor of ratification. Krasin saw the rejection of the contract as a personal failure, and with his reputation coming under increasing attack as a result of his primary role in the negotiations, Krasin unsuccessfully offered Lenin his resignation. See Intelligence Report, Northern Summary no. 93, D/57 Germany, A.2, "Russia. The Krasin-Urquhart Agreement," 1 November 1922, FO 371/8163; and Carr, *The Bolshevik Revolution*, 3:432.

78. William Peters, Moscow, to Curzon, 10 October 1922; and Enclosure 1; and Lord D'Abernon, Berlin, to Curzon, no. 187(R), 11 October 1922; FO 371/8162. There is also considerable evidence that the contract was rejected on the grounds that it failed to offer more favorable terms to the Soviets. Having previously stipulated that "Urquhart should be given a concession only if we get a big loan," Lenin was certainly displeased with the terms of the contract, which offered Urquhart not only 20 million gold roubles worth of governmental assistance but also an immediate cash payment of £150,000. Indeed, Lenin subsequently informed Stalin that the contract was no more than "bondage and plunder." Lenin to Stalin, 4 September 1922; and Lenin to Stalin, 12 September 1922; in Lenin, *Sochineniya*, 45:562, 565–66, as cited in K. H. Kennedy, *Mining Tsar*, pp. 191–92.

79. See, for example, "Sheffield Refuses Russian Orders: Insistence on Cash Basis," in *Manchester Guardian*, 21 August 1923. Sheffield complained that although "several large contracts" had been carried out previously on a cash basis, the Soviet government "now declines to comply with this condition." Soviet selectivity in concessions is apparent from the fact that less than 60 (some 7 percent) of the 800 proposals for concessions received between July 1922 and January 1924 had been accepted by the Soviet government. See the interview with Krasin in the *Manchester Guardian*, 4 January 1924.

80. *House of Commons, Debates*, 24 April 1923. Comment by Mr. Riley to Lloyd-Greame, as reproduced in FO 371/9355.

81. Attributed to Lloyd George, in Coates and Coates, *A History of Anglo-Soviet Relations*, p. 103.

82. Krasin to Moscow, 23 January 1923, R. F. Karpova, *L. B. Krasin—Sovetskii diplomat*, p. 148, as in Stephen White, *Britain and the Bolshevik Revolution*, p. 148. Acutely aware of the official British antipathy, Krasin admitted that "the only reason why he had not been more openly hostile in attitude towards British at Lausanne was anxiety lest H.M.G. should do anything premature to terminate Anglo-Russian Trade Agreement." W. Strang of the Foreign Office noted with satisfaction this indication of the importance that the Soviets attached to the agreement, "particularly at a moment when we are considering whether a rupture would do enough harm to them to be effective as a counter-blast to the anti-British campaign." Military Intelligence, SIS, SW1/1 Switzerland, 16 January 1923, in no. 1057, 30 January 1923; and Minute by W. Strang, 1 February 1923; FO 371/9359.

83. *House of Commons, Debates*, 29 March 1923, as cited in Stephen White, *Britain and the Bolshevik Revolution*, pp. 150–51.

84. Hodgson to Chicherin, 30 March 1923; Weinstein to Hodgson, 31 March 1923; and Hodgson to Weinstein, 4 April 1923; FO 371/9365. See also Eudin and Fisher, *Soviet Russia and the West*, pp. 184–88; and Coates and Coates, *A History of Anglo-Soviet Relations*, pp. 102–29.

85. Minute by Gregory, "Case for a Rupture with the Soviet Government," 5 April 1923, Foreign Office Minute, FO 371/9365. Gregory had pointed out on previous occasions that the annulment of the Trade Agreement was "a weapon that could be used only once," and thus should be used only when there was a "reasonable chance of upsetting the Soviet government, or at least of dealing an effective blow to its stability." Gregory, Memorandum, 31 March 1923, FO 371/9341.

86. Curzon to Hodgson, "Very Secret," 2 May 1923, FO 371/9365. Curzon demanded the cessation of anti-British Soviet propaganda and other hostile activities; compensation for British subjects and for damage done to British fishing vessels in a recent dispute over Russian territorial waters; and the withdrawal of the recent offensive communications to Hodgson in response to his protest over the execution of clergy in Russia.

87. Hodgson, Moscow, no. 103, 13 May 1923, FO 371/9367.

88. Stating that it had no connection whatsoever to the Third International, the Soviet government denied the charges of spreading propaganda hostile to Britain in the Near East and ultimately countered with claims of anti-Soviet activities in the Caucasus and Near East. Whereas demands for compensation of British nationals were likewise met with claims against Britain for Soviet losses, the Soviets were completely supplicant on the issue of compensation for the British trawlers, and apologized for the tone of their previous correspondence with Hodgson. Two days after the receipt of the "Curzon Ultimatum" Moscow was further shaken by the assassination of its representative at Lausanne. The Soviet government was also faced with what appeared to be a British effort to provoke an incident. The House of Commons was informed that a British warship had been dispatched to the Archangel district with instructions "to prevent interference with British vessels outside the three mile limit using force if necessary." Admitting that the diplomatic standoff was certainly no more acute than in previous years, the undersecretary for Foreign Affairs could offer no explanation as to why the vessel had been dispatched with such dangerous instructions at this particularly tense moment in the relations between the two countries. Litvinov to Hodgson, 11 May 1923, FO 371/9369; and Statement by Undersecretary of State McNeill, *House of Commons, Debates*, 10 May 1923.

89. The choice of Baldwin to succeed Bonar Law undoubtedly had an effect on governmental policy—the other choice could have been Curzon. Stephen White, *Britain and the Bolshevik Revolution*, pp. 165–66.

90. *Manchester Guardian Commercial*, 24 May 1923.

91. File 3198, in FO 371/9369.

92. Urquhart to Lloyd-Greame, "Paris Resolution," 13 February 1922, FO 371/8161; the Resolution of the Association of British Chambers of Commerce, *Times Trade Supplement*, 3 November 1923; and Minute by Maxse, 8 March 1922, on the memorandum submitted by the Imperial Commercial Association, 6 March 1922, FO 371/8168.

93. Resolution of the Russo-British Chamber of Commerce, 3 January 1924, FO 371/10468. Along with this, the chamber wanted the government to make "simultaneously adequate provision for the recognition of Russia's pre-war indebtedness."

94. See *Evening Standard*, 20 December 1923; and *Westminster Gazette*, 20 December 1923.

95. Although recognition was indeed unconditional, it is clear the British government still had a number of reservations. The question of debts was again left for future negotiations, though the Soviets were warned that the maintenance of friendly relations depended upon the resolution of these issues. Representation was to be limited to chargé d'affaires only, with no ambassadors being appointed. Foreign Office to Hodgson, 1 February 1924, FO 371/10465.

Moreover, the Foreign Office maintained that to extend the government's credit scheme to Russia before a settlement had been reached would "deprive us of a very useful bargaining weapon in the forthcoming conference." See Minute by Maxse, 19 March 1924, on N.2753/39/38, FO 371/10469.

96. See Reyntiens to Gregory, "Trade with Russia," 18 January 1924, FO 371/10469; and Hodgson, Moscow, to Foreign Office, no. 507, "Zinoviev's Speech at Party Conference," 30 May 1924, FO 371/10464; and file 250 in FO 371/1083. Curzon's antipathy toward the Soviet regime was allowed to surface once more before MacDonald's government took power: when news of Lenin's death had reached London, Curzon decided to "leave it up to Mr. Hodgson to take or join in any action at Moscow that might be officially appropriate to the occasion." But, as O'Malley noted, "surely we may take it that Mr. Hodgson would not convey such a message without instructions." Because the British government had, at the moment of Lenin's death, not yet recognized the Soviet government, it was reasoned that "an official pronouncement was not appropriate." Foreign Office Minutes, W. Strang, 13 February 1924; O. O'Malley, [n.d.]; and Sir E. Crowe, [n.d.]; FO 371/10485.

97. Hodgson to Rakovsky, 21 November 1924, FO 371/10501; Hodgson, Moscow, no. 507, Zinoviev's Speech at Party Conference, 30 May 1924; and Peters, Moscow, to MacDonald, no. 1018, 30 October 1924, Enclosure, "Resumé of Speech Delivered by Sokolnikov (People's Commissary for Finance) at the Meeting of the Central Executive Committee of the Union, 20th October 1924"; FO 371/10464.

98. Eudin and Fisher, *Soviet Russia and the West*, p. 194.

99. Ibid.

100. Hardy and Ruperti, Inc., to Durand, Near East Division of the Bureau of Foreign and Domestic Commerce, "Re: Discussions with Mr. Hoover about Trade with Russia," 20 April 1922, NARG 151, box 1519; and Christian Herter to Leonard Gary, Director of Bureau, Boston, 20 July 1921, NARG 151, box 2240, file 448.

101. Address of President Coolidge to Congress, 6 December 1923, in *Congressional Record*, 65, part 1, [20 December 1923], p. 451.

102. Hoover was especially worried that American merchants would be placed at a disadvantage because of the Anglo-Soviet Trade Agreement. Hoover to Hughes, 16 March 1921, *FRUS*, 1921, 2:762.

For examples of the Department's efforts to help businessmen, see Martin, "Sale of Agricultural Implements in Foreign Countries"; and the Bureau of Foreign and Domestic Commerce, Circular, "Opportunities for American Branch Banks in the Baltic Provinces," Julius Klein, August 1921, NARG 151, box 2837, file 601.2. Estimating the foreign trade of the Baltic states to be about $10 million per month, the bureau considered that the existence of American branch banks in the Baltic would "overcome much of the difficulty in capital transfer." Indeed, one company informed the Commerce Department that it had been "refusing orders almost every day for large amounts of American products" on account of the difficulty of transferring money. See The American Baltic and Russian Import Co., Inc., New York, to Hoover, 6 June 1921; and "Opportunities for American Branch Banks in the Baltic Provinces," 1921, NARG 151, box 2837, file 601.2.

103. Hoover to Hughes, 6 December 1921, *FRUS, 1921*, 2:785–88, as cited in Hoff-Wilson, *Ideology and Economics*, p. 43.

104. Hoover to Hughes, 6 December 1921, NARG 59, file 661.6215/1.

105. *Izvestiya*, "Krasin's Report at the Congress of the Plenipotentiaries of the Central Unions," 22 July 1921; and American Consul, Viborg, to Secretary of State, no. 183, 15 August 1921, NARG 59, file 600.6115/2.

106. Minute by E. W. Birse, 25 February 1920, FO 371/4032. See also Tallents, Riga, no. 2, 13 August 1920, FO 371/3629; and Foreign Office minute on Birnbaum and Co., to Foreign Office, 30 December 1920, FO 371/5435.

107. Borah's replies to attacks on his motion "that the Senate of the U.S. favors the recognition of the present Soviet government of Russia," 15 May 1922, Russia, Posol'stvo (U.S.), box 9, file 5, Hoover Institution Archives. Even Hammer had gone this route: because of the more liberal attitude of the British banks in extending credit to the Russians, "a considerable amount" of the business handled by his corporation had originated in the British markets. As an example, Hammer cited the purchase of $1 million worth of cotton which had been purchased in England by the corporation and shipped to Russia. *New York Times*, 28 February 1924.

108. State Department to Commerce, 2 August 1923, NARG 151, box 2734, file 611. The Products Exchange Corporation (Prodexco) and the Import and Export Company of America were later combined to form Amtorg.

109. State Department to Commerce, 2 August 1923, NARG 151, box 2734, file 611; and Peters, Moscow, to Foreign Office, no. 654, 27 August 1923, Enclosure, "The Russian State Bank's Fortnightly Official Statement," FO 371/9345.

110. See Table 7.5. While this increase was largely the result of purchases made by the Soviet government and American relief organizations for the aid of the famine victims in Russia, it must be kept in mind that these exports were nonetheless *bought* from American producers. Further, American efforts in famine relief had put them at a distinct advantage over Britain, whose merchants would suffer the loss of future trade because of Russian familiarity with and preference for American manufactures.

111. Davis, "Soviet Recognition and Trade," pp. 657, 659.

112. Hugh Ledward, "The Monopoly of Foreign Trade," [December 1923], FO 371/10469.

113. My italics. Kliefoth, Riga, to Secretary of State, 3 May 1929, NARG 59, file 661.621/1. Kliefoth noted another advantage as well: the Soviets "would not dare to arrest a prominent American businessman but do not hesitate to arrest Germans."

114. Hoover to Hughes, 6 December 1921, NARG 59, file 661.6215/1.

115. *New York Times*, 16 April 1926.

116. Sol Bron, at a luncheon of the American-Russian Chamber of Commerce, Bankers' Club, New York, 17 February 1928, Gumberg Manuscripts, box 21, folder 1. See also Sutton, *Western Technology and Soviet Economic Development*, 1:140; and Carr, *The Bolshevik Revolution*, 3:280–81, 356, n.4.

117. See Walker, *Ford ili Marks*, p. 3; Maurice Hindus, "Henry Ford Conquers Russia," *Outlook*, 25 June 1925, pp. 280–83, as cited in Wilkins and Hill, *American Business Abroad*, p. 216; and Berghoff, *Reminiscences*, p. 81, Ford Archives Oral History, FMCA.

118. September 1922, file 646, The Hague Conference, FO 371/8197. Krasin opposed this decision, arguing that "without a preliminary and even prolonged acquaintance with the general Soviet landscape American capital will not come to work in Russia." Krasin to Central Committee, August 1922, as cited in Gillett, "The Political Origins of Soviet-American Trade," pp. 15–16.

119. The strengthening of the state monopoly of foreign trade can be seen as an expression of increased control over Soviet domestic policy. Even before the Hague Conference was concluded, the Soviets had undertaken to prevent any further shipments of speculative cargoes to Russian ports. Apparently, Western merchants had dispatched goods independently, negotiating with the local Vneshtorg offices for permits to import only after the goods had arrived. See Hodgson, Moscow, to Foreign Office, no. 141(R), 1 July 1922, FO 371/8217.

120. *New York Times*, 28 February 1924.

121. U.S. Department of Commerce Statement, transmitted by Sir A. Geddes, Washington, to Foreign Office, no. 643, 2 June 1922, FO 371/8175.

122. Hoover to Hughes, 6 December 1921, NARG 59, file 661.6215/1. Hoover saw the promotion of expansion of American capital overseas as a means of maintaining domestic prosperity. Russia, an underdeveloped country with vast natural wealth, offered endless opportunities for the application of the Open Door policy. See William Williams, *Tragedy of American Diplomacy*, pp. 85–86.

Chapter 8

1. See Reyntiens, Department of Overseas Trade, to Gregory, "Trade with Russia," 18 January 1924, FO 371/10469. One report that related a highly successful deal in which the British merchant was "well treated from the outset" was minuted as "not very interesting." A further minute agrees, but points out that it was "not exaggerated." See G. Knox, 9 December 1921, in Sir H. Rumbold, Constantinople, no. 1126, 11 December 1921, FO 371/6852.

2. In addition to those interests that sought representation through their local Chamber of Commerce, a number of firms were represented by organizations specifically created to "promote and protect" commercial relations between Britain and Soviet Russia. See R. Kelly, British Association of Ukraine Trade Ltd., to Foreign Office, 11 January 1923, FO 371/9353. Members of this organization included Debenhams Ltd., Ransomes, Sims & Jefferies Ltd., and the Export Corporation of British Manufacturers, Gwynnes Engineering Company, Ltd., Etringhams Ltd., Ridgways, James Spicers Ltd., United Alkali Company, William Walker & Sons; Ship Canal Portland Cement Manufacturers Ltd., London Assurance; and the Agricultural & General Engineers.

3. Joseph Gregory, Foreign Office Minute, "Case for a Rupture with the Soviet Government," 5 April 1923, FO 371/9365.

4. See Sir Philip Lloyd-Greame to Curzon, Secret, 1 May 1923, FO 371/9365; and Minute by O'Malley, 18 April 1923, on M. W. Donald, Department of Overseas Trade, Memorandum, Urgent, 17 April 1923, FO 371/9365.

5. Examples of Hudsons Bay Company and De Jersey & Company were cited. M. W. Donald, Department of Overseas Trade, Memorandum, Urgent, 17 April 1923, FO 371/9365. In addition to these arguments, it was also noted that, once relations and the trade agreement were broken off, "creditors in Britain would lose their last chance of regaining their properties"; indeed, the best chance of "getting better terms is by improving relations." "Trade or Tomfoolery," *New Statesman*, vol. 21, no. 529, 2 June 1923, pp. 224–26.

6. Further, in response to McNeill's assertion that the British representative in Moscow had little—if any—influence on trade, one member of Parliament responded that this "only proves your representative is useless." *House of Commons, Debates*, 15 May 1923.

7. *British-Russian Gazette and Trade Outlook*, December 1923, as cited in Stephen White, *Britain and the Bolshevik Revolution*, pp. 196–97.

8. Minute by O'Malley for P. Lloyd-Greame, 9 May 1923, FO 371/9366.

9. Minute by W. Strang, 28 May 1923, FO 371/9368. Accusing Curzon of having flung stones at the Bolsheviks with "his rhetorical catapult," no doubt hoping "to scare them away altogether," Lloyd George pointed out that "had it not been for the sharp intervention of traders, who were beginning to do business with Russia, and of others who were looking forward to business relations with Russia, his [Curzon's] designs would have succeeded." *Daily Chronicle*, 16 February 1924.

10. See Association of British Chambers of Commerce to Foreign Office, 12 June 1923, in which the chamber related the protests of Ruston and Hornsby, among others, FO 371/9368; and Merryfield and Ziegler and Co. (cotton brokers), Manchester, via Sir L. Scott, M.P., 11 May 1923, FO 371/9367. The firm of Ruston and Hornby was described as "representing a combine of factories in Lincoln, Grantham, Stockport, Newark and Ipswich, manufacturers of agricultural machinery and oil and gas engines." See *House of Commons, Debates*, 15 May 1923.

11. *House of Commons, Debates*, 17 May 1923; and Sir Allen Smith to Bonar Law, 18 April 1923, Baldwin Papers, as cited in Stephen White, *Britain and the Bolshevik Revolution*, pp. 165, 176.

12. *Economist*, 27 January 1923, as cited in Stephen White, *Britain and the Bolshevik Revolution*, p. 177.

13. Mr. E. D. Morel, M.P., to Mr. McNeill, 8 January 1923, FO 371/9347.

14. *Daily Telegraph*, 14 August 1923, reporting an exchange of letters between Stanley Baldwin and Sir Allen Smith, FO 371/9352.

15. *Daily News*, 5 September 1923, FO 371/9352.

16. *Financial News*, "Trade with Russia: Is It Time for a Change of Policy?," 7 November 1923.

17. Peters, Moscow, to MacDonald, no. 1018, 30 October 1923, Enclosure, Text of Sokolnikov's speech, FO 371/10487.

18. *Financial News*, 7 November 1923.

19. The engineering industries suffered some 27 percent unemployment in 1921–22. See Mowat, *Britain between the Wars*, p. 126.

20. Newman, *100 Years of Good Company*, pp. 115–16, as cited in Stephen White, *Britain and the Bolshevik Revolution*, p. 188.

21. P. M. Roberts, "Commercial Notes on the Ukraine and Caucasus," 20 August 1923; and Minutes; FO 371/9343.

22. Ibid.; see also Consul General, Warsaw, to State Department, "Warsaw as a Base for British Firms' Operations in Russia," 21 November 1922, NARG 59, file 661.4116/153; Reyntiens to Gregory, "Trade with Russia," 18 January 1924, FO 371/10469; and file 380 (1922), FO 371/8181.

23. Becos Traders was formerly the British Engineering Company of Russia and Siberia. *Railway Gazette*, 17 August 1923, FO 371/9352.

24. *Evening Standard*, 3 September 1923; and *Daily Herald*, 23 August 1923. By the spring of 1924 over 120 firms and 200 factories and works in Britain were associated with Becos.

25. *Russian Information and Review*, 27 October 1923.

26. Reyntiens to Gregory, "Trade with Russia," 18 January 1924, FO 371/10469.

27. *Evening Standard*, 31 May 1923.

28. *Ekonomicheskaya Zhizn'*, 4 September 1923; *Daily Telegraph*, 15 November 1923; *Times*, 13 November 1923; and Minutes by Gregory and O'Malley on press extracts, 21 November 1923, FO 371/9349; and Reyntiens to Gregory, Memorandum, "Trade with Russia," 18 January 1924, FO 371/10469.

29. Indeed, O'Malley could "hardly believe it." Minutes by Gregory and O'Malley, 21 November 1923, on extracts from the press, Paper N 9116/136/38, FO 371/9349. Although it was speculated that this contract represented "a foretaste of what may happen following an agreement," the Department of Overseas Trade had little doubt that "the effect of *de jure* recognition on trade will be small unless such recognition is accompanied by some system of credit." See *Westminster Gazette*, 20 December 1923; and Reyntiens to Gregory, Memorandum, "Trade with Russia," 18 January 1924, FO 371/10469.

30. Schenectady Historical Society, New York, as cited in Sutton, *Western Technology and Soviet Economic Development*, 1:204.

31. Scott, *Vickers*, pp. 144–45.

32. Under the 1921 Arms Export Prohibitions Order, the "export of certain specified articles coming under the heading of 'Arms' is prohibited . . . except by permission by license from the Board of Trade." Even so, the War Office and Admiralty supported Vickers's application—arguing that by supplying arms to Russia, Britain could exercise a degree of control over its armament. The Foreign Office, however, had made it clear that it opposed "on political grounds" the export to Russia of "any arms or ammunition of a purely military character." See Fountain, Board of Trade, to Foreign Office, 1 December 1923;

and Minutes; and Foreign Office reply to Board of Trade, 8 December 1923; FO 371/9355.

33. Vickers, Ltd., to Admiralty, 21 March 1923, FO 371/9370. The export license for these mines was granted on the grounds that they were considered "defensive weapons"! See Fountain to Foreign Office, 1 December 1923; and Minutes; FO 371/9355.

34. Fountain to Foreign Office, 1 December 1923; and Minutes; FO 371/9355. Vickers was not alone in this belief. Inquiries as to the government's attitude toward their undertaking to reequip the Russian Fleet, Barr and Stroud also pointed out that this contract "would be of great benefit to British firms and if permission is not given the Soviet government will have little trouble obtaining what they require from other countries." Admiralty to Foreign Office, 21 February 1922; and Enclosure; and Foreign Office Minutes; FO 371/8205.

35. Vickers's Russian Correspondent, 14 January 1924, Vickers Archives, Microfilm R. 215, "Russia," 1924–27.

36. Sir Vincent Caillard to Sir Eyre Crowe, Confidential, 18 January 1924; and Enclosure, Alexander Bourdt, Berlin, to Vickers, Ltd., 16 January 1924; FO 371/10473; and Lord D'Abernon, Berlin, to Foreign Office, no. 66, 25 January 1924, FO 371/10473.

37. Goodwill for future business was valued so highly that Vickers had even become involved in shady negotiations with Soviet representatives. In one instance, the Foreign Office was moved to complain that the company had been "lacking in frankness in their replies to enquiries by the Home Office . . . and have only been brought under pressure to admit that they are engaged in negotiations for the sale of machine guns to the Soviet government." Minute by Strang, 29 November 1923, FO 371/9355.

38. Vickers, Ltd., to MacDonald, 25 February 1924, FO 371/10473.

39. Sir Vincent Caillard, to MacDonald, 16 April 1924, FO 371/10473.

40. Foreign Office Memorandum, "Export of War Material to the Soviet Union," 6 October 1924; and Minutes by O'Malley, 27 October 1924; and Cabinet Minutes, 12 November 1924; FO 371/10473.

41. Sir Vincent Caillard to Sir William Tyrell, 20 November 1924; Minute by Maxse, 21 November 1924; FO 371/10473. Both the Board of Trade and the Foreign Office felt that in cases where firms had incurred expenses in preparing to carry out a definite contract for the export of war matériel—and authority to export had already been obtained from the late government—export under existing license should be allowed, and renewals of existing license be granted where necessary. William Brown, Board of Trade, to the Prime Minister's Private Secretary, 19 December 1924; and Minute by Charles Peale, 20 December 1924; FO 371/10473.

42. British businessmen also encountered considerable competition from the Germans, whose products were generally cheaper and frequently preferred in Russia. It was also suggested that British manufacturers should combine with the Germans where possible. It was "obviously better that [a British firm] should secure the order in this way than that none of it should come to the U.K. at all."

Further, it was hoped that such cooperation, if successful, would "pave the way for similar transactions in other branches of industry and might enable British manufacturers to overcome at least a portion of the German competition which they will have to meet . . . in Russia." See the Report by Commercial Secretary Thelwall, 14 June 1921, in Kilmarnock, Berlin, to Foreign Office, no. 868, 21 June 1921, FO 371/6886.

43. As from Soviet statistics, worked from data given in Kutuzov, *Vneshnyaya torgovlya soyuza SSR za X let*.

44. As from data in U.S. Department of Commerce, *Foreign Commerce and Navigation of the United States*.

45. Gordon Lee to Thomas Taylor (assistant director of the Bureau of Foreign and Domestic Commerce), 1 May 1922, as cited in Hoff-Wilson, *Ideology and Economics*, p. 46.

46. Christian Herter, Department of Commerce, to Julius Klein, 20 July 1921, NARG 151, box 2240, file 448. This attitude did much to confirm British suspicions that U.S. interests in Russia were "solely economic and commercial." See Intercept, Foreign Office to Harvey, no. 44, 4 February 1922, NARG 59, file 661.1115/369.

47. See Chapter 5; and for a discussion of Hoover's view on the matter, see Chapter 7.

48. Statement by Harry Hunt, chairman of the Committee on Russian Trade, *New York Times*, 7 October 1923.

49. As mentioned earlier, a number of U.S. firms had managed to escape nationalization and continued to operate—some quite profitably—well into the 1920s. Along with the examples of Kodak and International Harvester discussed earlier, the Westinghouse Brake Company had remained open throughout the revolution, and it was only in 1922 that the firm had "begun suffering difficulties because of their inability to recover payments from government departments owing them." See Hodgson, Moscow, to Foreign Office, no. 558, 1 August 1922, FO 371/8182.

50. Hoff-Wilson, *Ideology and Economics*, p. 98.

51. The Dollar Trading Corporation was apparently on good terms with the Soviet government, with which it admitted having "extensive dealings"—including undertaking the disposal of "large amounts" of gold. By the spring of 1922 the company had already reported the opening of an office in Moscow. Alexander Dye, Commercial Attaché, London, to Bureau of Foreign and Domestic Commerce, 4 May 1922, NARG 151, box 2240, file 448.

52. Ibid. Dye was curious to know "how many firms in America are dealing through the Dollar Trading and Finance Corporation."

53. Other concessions taken up by Hammer included an asbestos mine and a pencil manufacturing concern in Moscow. See *Russian Information and Review*, 25 August 1923; Hammer, *Romanov Treasure*, and *Witness to History*; and Harry C. Armstrong, H.M. Consul General, New York, to Foreign Office, Enclosure, [?October 1924], FO 371/10464.

54. *New York Times*, "Americans Pushing Trade with Russia," 28 February 1924. Among these early sales through the Allied American Corporation was an "initial order" for the supply of electric equipment placed with Westinghouse. These orders were "expected to aggregate upwards of $1 million." It should be noted that the concession also stipulated that imports into Russia were not to exceed exports. Apparently, this requirement was also satisfied.

55. *New York Times*, 28 February 1924. Nor was Allied American interested solely in American trade. Since the concession was obtained, the corporation had opened branches in London, Paris, and Riga. It had even requested the Department of Overseas Trade "to pass [their] name on to manufacturers etc. who may be interested in developing an export trade with Russia." See Allied American Corporation to Department of Overseas Trade, 2 October 1924, in Department of Overseas Trade to H.M. Consul General, New York, no. O.T. 96, 29 October 1924, FO 371/10464.

56. See, for example, the letter from Julius Hammer to Charles Sorensen, 3 June 1923, FMCA, Acc. 38, box 47, in which Hammer reports that he found Russia "to exceed [his] expectations." It is interesting to note that Sorensen was described within the company as being "pretty much sold on this particular Russian government." Gaston Plaintiff to E. C. Kanzler, New York, 26 February 1925, FMCA, Acc. 38, box 51.

57. Peters, Moscow, no. 632, 14 August 1923, FO 371/9349. Not merely sales agents, Allied American's Moscow office also performed the invaluable task of translating Ford manuals into Russian. Indeed, Ford's "deep interest in promoting the sale of [their] products in foreign countries" was reflected in the Allied American Corporation's efforts "to preach the Ford gospel in Russia." S. D. Winderman, Allied American Corporation, New York, to Charles Sorensen, 13 March 1923, FMCA, Acc. 38, box 47.

58. S. D. Winderman, Allied American Corporation, New York, to Charles Sorensen, 13 March 1923; and Sorensen to Winderman, 28 April 1923; FMCA, Acc. 38, box 47.

59. Julius Hammer to Manager of Foreign Department, 3 June 1923, FMCA, Acc. 38, box 47.

60. "Report of the Ford Delegation to Russia," April–August 1926, p. 223, FMCA, Acc. 49, box 1-A.

61. Ford's primary long-range interest in Russia throughout the 1920s concerned the manufacture of his products on Russia soil. See Christine White, "Ford in Russia," pp. 81–82, 86, 88–90.

62. Julius Hammer, Moscow, to Henry Ford, 1 June 1923, FMCA, Acc. 38, box 47. It should be noted that American machinery makers were quick to get into the business of supplying Soviet industry with the machinery they needed to construct these plants. By the middle of 1926, the Ford delegation that was dispatched to Russia had noted that the tool rooms at both the Red Putilov tractor plant and the Rostov agricultural implement factory were "well equipped with American machines," and that American time clocks and cards were in use in most of the plants

visited by the delegation. See "Report of the Ford Delegation to Russia," April–August 1926, pp. 51, 55, FMCA, Acc. 49, box 1-A.

63. With such a large number of tractors already on Soviet soil and the prospects of further large sales, the question of servicing quickly became a major issue. See "Report of the Ford Delegation to Russia," April–August 1926, pp. 123, 153, FMCA, Acc. 49, box 1-A; and *Ford News*, 15 August 1924, FMCA.

64. J. Dalton, "Strongly Fortified Industry Set for Any Emergency," *Automotive Industries*, 10 April 1924, pp. 804–5. For an account of Ford's efforts to obtain bank credits for Amtorg's purchases of tractors, see Christine White, "Ford In Russia," pp. 86–89.

65. The closing of International Harvester's Lubertsy plant in May 1923 and its eventual nationalization by the Soviet government in July 1924 in no way represented a hardship for the company. The cost of production at Lubertsy was far greater than that in Chicago, a situation similar to that of prerevolutionary times. Before the war, International Harvester could import American made machinery into Russia at 20–25 percent cheaper than it could be produced in Russia. In the years immediately prior to the war, the plant continued to operate only by virtue of the protection and subsidies provided by the tsarist government. Rather, the company suffered its greatest losses as a result of the sequestration of its deposits in the State Bank and other private financial institutions in Russia. See Foreign Claims Settlement Commission Claim, no. SOV-41,072, documents in support of claims as cited in Fithian, "Soviet Economic Relations," p. 25; and Foreign Office notes concerning International Harvester, FO 371/6851.

66. "Report of the Ford Delegation," p. 224.

67. Sutton, *Western Technology and Soviet Economic Development*, 1:143–44; "Report of the Ford Delegation," p. 224; and a separate report submitted by the delegation, entitled "Credits Granted to the Soviet Government to Date," p. 4, FMCA, Acc. 49, box 1-A.

68. Carr, *The Bolshevik Revolution*, 3:356.

69. These figures, cited in 1913 prices, represent a *real* increase in the value of trade. Worked from Kutuzov, *Vneshnyaya torgovlya soyuza SSR za X let*, tables I–IV.

70. Britain, the United States, *and* Germany together accounted for over 56 percent of the total trade turnover of Soviet Russia between 1921–24/25.

71. Foreign Office to Board of Trade, Enclosure, 6 March 1923; and Minute by P. M. Roberts; FO 371/9351.

72. A number of British contracts to *purchase* goods were cited as being examples of those deals that would suffer should Anglo-Soviet relations be severed in 1923: among those at stake were a £40,000 contract for the supply of eggs; negotiations concerning the import of butter; considerable advances that had been made on timber stocks; and negotiations concerning a platinum concession. See M. W. Donald, Department of Overseas Trade, to Foreign Office, Trade Memorandum GS/Urgent, 17 April 1923, FO 371/9365.

73. Worked from returns given in U.K. Parliamentary Papers, *Annual Statement of the Trade of the United Kingdom*, 1929.

74. J. C. Nellis, Acting Chief, Lumber Division, Commerce Department. Special Circular no. 180, Confidential, 16 January 1924, NARG 151, file 411.

75. The dissolution of the Russian Empire resulted in the loss of "a number of the better large tracts of forest" to Poland, Lithuania, and Latvia. Danishevskii, *Lesnoy eksport SSSR: Ego polozhenie i perspektivy*, p. 10.

76. In a report concerning the importance of Russian trade, the Department of Overseas Trade warned that, because of the loss of "certain important areas," pre- and postwar statistics of Russia's foreign trade were "not strictly comparable." Department of Overseas Trade, "Statistical Notes on the Extent and Importance of the Foreign Trade of Russia," March 1922, FO 371/8175. It has been assumed by many Soviet economists that those areas that became independent from Russia after the revolution accounted for approximately 20 percent of Russian foreign trade. While this assumption may be "substantially correct as far as the entire export is concerned," the proportion of 20 percent "cannot be assumed to be correct with regard to individual classes of goods." Birmingham Bureau of Research on Russian Economic Conditions, *The Foreign Trade of the USSR*, Memorandum no. 2, p. 10.

77. For a report concerning the volume of consignments of U.S. cotton to Britain for reexport to Soviet Russia, see Board of Trade to Foreign Office, 9 May 1924, FO 371/10469.

78. Service Report, Germany, Economic, no. 3148, 8 April 1922, NARG 151, box 1785, file 1515.

79. Britain's export trade in 1921 had declined by nearly 48 percent, and imports by nearly 44 percent as compared with trade in the previous year. See Mowat, *Britain between the Wars*, p. 125; Lloyds Bank, "Business and Trade Conditions in 1920," Annual Meeting of Shareholders for year ending 31 December 1920; and for year ending 31 December 1921, Lloyds Bank Archives. The Soviets certainly held this to be one of the reasons that their foreign trade remained so far below prewar levels. See Krasin, *Voprosy vneshney torgovli*, pp. 155–59.

80. On the basis of 1913 prices, the value of exports of U.K. manufactured goods in 1921 amounted to only 51 percent of the 1913 value, and by 1924 had increased to only 79 percent. "Fluctuations in the Trade of the United Kingdom," U.K. Parliamentary Papers, *Annual Statement of the Trade of the United Kingdom*, 1925, part I, p. vii.

81. Foreign Office Memorandum by O'Malley on possible effect of a breach of Anglo-Soviet relations, 24 April 1923, FO 371/9365. See also Minutes by P. M. Roberts, 5 March 1923, on Anglo-Russian trade statistics supplied to A. T. Davies, M.P.; Foreign Office to Secretary to the Board of Trade, 6 March 1923, Enclosure, FO 371/9351; Owen O'Malley, "Memorandum on Soviet Policy," Foreign Trade, 17 March 1923, p. 22, FO 371/9363; J. D. Gregory, "Confidential Memorandum on Russian Trade," N 751/G, 29 January 1924, FO 371/10464; Reyntiens to Gregory, "Trade with Russia," 18 January 1924, FO 371/10469; and section on transit trade in Chapter 6.

82. Maxse, "Memorandum on Policy to be Adopted towards Gold Originating in Russia," 14 July 1920, FO 371/4036.

83. Indeed, this is still largely the case today: the *Times* referred to Siberia as "the Russian El Dorado" as recently as 1978. The possibilities for British trade and technological participation there were described as great; it was only for British business to capture it from those Japanese and American interests that had long been active in the region. See *Times*, Special Report, "Siberia," 20 September 1978; 26 September 1978; and Christine White, "British Business in Russian Asia."

84. Foreign Office Memorandum, 20 September 1923, Paper no. N 7913/7913/38, FO 371/9373.

85. William H. Clark, 21 December 1920, on O'Malley, Foreign Office Memorandum, 18 December 1920, FO 371/5434.

86. Hodgson, Moscow, to Foreign Office, no. 132, 3 November 1921, FO 371/6886.

87. Hodgson, Moscow, to Foreign Office, no. 34(R), 22 August 1921; and Minute by Maxse; FO 371/6929. Although the government was certainly against according any further such privileges, it was certainly not indisposed to giving the Bolshevik trade representatives more of a free hand than Scotland Yard would have liked. The loss of trade was apparently seen as posing more of a threat than the presence of Bolsheviks in those areas hardest hit by unemployment! In response to Special Branch complaints concerning the presence of "numerous representatives of the Russian Trade Delegation in certain industrial areas," the Department of Overseas Trade pointed out that this was necessary for the "satisfactory execution by British firms of the contracts placed with them." Further, any attempt to obstruct such arrangements would "seriously prejudice the placing of subsequent orders in this country and have a detrimental effect on British trade." The Foreign Office agreed with this view. See Department of Overseas Trade to Foreign Office, Memorandum, no. 4667FR, 15 December 1921; and Minute by Maxse, 17 December 1921; FO 371/6887.

88. See Chapter 7. The Cannes Resolution declared that the "resumption of international trade" was essential in order "to increase the volume of productive trade." *Resolution Adopted by the Supreme Council at Cannes*, U.K. Parliamentary Papers, British White Paper, Cmd. 1621.

89. E. D. Morel, to McNeill, 6 December 1922, no. 8, Archives, Russia, FO 371/8147.

90. William H. Clark, 21 December 1920, on O'Malley, Foreign Office Memorandum, 18 December 1921, FO 371/5434; *Board of Trade Journal*, 11 January 1923, p. 32; and M. Oldroyd & Sons to Foreign Office, 25 February 1921, FO 371/6901; see also O'Malley, Foreign Office Memorandum, 18 December 1921, FO 371/5434; and Chapter 5.

91. Service Report, Germany, Economic, no. 3148, 8 April 1922, NARG 156, box 1785, file 1515; Department of Overseas, "Statistical Notes on the Extent and Importance of the Foreign Trade of Russia," March 1922, FO 371/8175; and

data worked from U.K. Parliamentary Papers, *Annual Statement of the Trade of the United Kingdom*.

92. See Higgs, Whisha & Co. to Sir William Clark, (R.70), 17 March 1920; and Cyril Davies to Clark, 18 March 1920; FO 371/4033; Major Farina (War Office, M.I.5) to Gregory, no. SF 400/2/UK, 11 October 1920, FO 371/5437; Sir Basil Thomson to Gregory, 18 October 1921, FO 371/5433; and William Stern, Machinery Exporters, Manchester, to Foreign Office, 16 August 1920, FO 371/4037. Cyril Davies claimed to represent "many important British manufacturers" in the Russian market.

93. Perhaps a more dramatic example can be found in the case of Lincoln, where it was claimed an estimated 90 percent of the *city's* prewar trade was done with Russia. The loss of this trade would have had an immediate devastating effect on the economic health of that city. Mr. A. T. Davies, M.P., to Gregory, 13 February 1924, FO 371/10469.

94. John and Edwin Wright, Ltd., Universal Wire Rope Works, Birmingham, to Foreign Office, 29 July 1920, FO 371/4036; and Thos. & Wm. Smith, Ltd., to Foreign Office, 29 September 1920, FO 371/4037.

95. Gandy Belt Manufacturing Co. to Foreign Office, 1 February 1921, FO 371/6877.

96. Birmingham Small Arms to Foreign Office, 22 February 1924, FO 371/10473. A number of firms also sought to promote their trade by advertising in Soviet trade journals and publications directed at the Russian market. See, for example, *Mechanical Transport*, which was touted in Britain as "a medium of trade and business propaganda." Vincent Mander to Foreign Office, 23 November 1922, FO 371/8176.

97. Condoide, *Russian-American Trade*, p. 109.

98. Boris Baievsky, Bureau of Foreign and Domestic Commerce, to Dr. MacElwee, "Russian Trade Promotion," no. 21, 17 July 1920, NARG 151, box 1880, file 400; and U.S. Department of Commerce, *Foreign Commerce and Navigation of the United States*, 1925.

99. *Ekonomicheskaya Zhizn'*, 12 November 1924. See also Consul General George E. Andersen, "Dutch Trade with Russia," 16 November 1922, NARG 59, file 661.5616/2.

100. *New York Times*, 28 February 1924, especially concerning the Allied American Corporation's sale of $1 million worth of U.S. cotton to Soviet Russia through London.

101. Kutuzov, *Vneshnyaya torgovlya soyuza SSR za X let*, table IV, p. 305.

102. Indeed, it was remarked that this credit arrangement would allow cotton to be purchased for the USSR "under normal conditions." Previous to Nogin's visit, the Soviet textile industry had been buying most of its cotton through the Bremen agency of a large American brokerage house whose terms were 25 percent cash with the balance due in sixty to ninety days. Hodgson, Moscow, to Foreign Office, no. 830, 23 October 1923, FO 371/9353; and *Daily News Record*, 10 January 1924, as reported in Eric C. Buxton, Commercial Secretary, British Em-

bassy, Washington, to Foreign Office, no. 64, Overseas Trade B, 18 January 1924, FO 371/10470.

103. *Ekonomicheskaya Zhizn'*, 12 November 1924. In fact, cotton comprised a major portion of all Russian imports from the United States until 1929, when this was surpassed for the first time by the purchase of agricultural machines.

104. William L. Clayton, Clayton-Anderson Co., to Morris Sheppard, Democratic Senator from Texas, 2 July 1924, in the Gumberg Manuscripts, box 4, folder 2. Clayton-Anderson was one of the largest cotton brokerage firms in the United States.

105. Hodgson, Moscow, to MacDonald, no. 127, 15 February 1924, FO 371/10469.

106. Worked from returns given in U.S. Department of Commerce, *Foreign Commerce and Navigation of the United States*, 1921. See also Bureau of Foreign and Domestic Commerce, District Office, New York, to Klein, 9 February 1922, NARG 151, box 2240, file 448.

107. Department of Commerce, *Trade Information Bulletin*, no. 21, 24 April 1922.

108. Leonard B. Gary, Regional Office, Boston, to Bureau of Foreign and Domestic Commerce, Washington, 20 July 1921, NARG 151, box 2240, file 448. While Klein (director of the bureau) initiated a "secret and confidential investigation," Hoover reminded the bureau that "we have not the slightest objection to shoes being shipped to Russia," and that the Department had "no desire to pry into the private affairs of the shoe concerns." See Klein to District Office, Boston, 19 July 1921; and Christian Herter to Klein, 20 July 1921, NARG 151, box 2240, file 448.

109. These transshipments also included "a cargo that must have been sorely needed in Soviet Russia, i.e., 10,000 cases of American soap." Consul General Murphy, Stockholm, no. 29408, 30 March 1921, NARG 151, box 2240, file 448.

110. This order was handled by "a certain Mr. Edward Gibson," who had recently established a branch in Moscow to facilitate this business. The Bolsheviks had paid in gold for these orders. *Posledniya Novosti*, 5 April 1921, NARG 151, box 2240, file 448.

111. John Thors, American Relief Administration Representative in Reval, 24 June 1924, NARG 151, file 448X, "Russian Trade with US, 1919–1922."

112. L. J. Lewery to Hoover, 22 September 1924, Russian File, Herbert Hoover Commerce Department Papers, Herbert Hoover Presidential Library, as cited in Hoff-Wilson, *Ideology and Economics*, p. 68.

113. Hodgson, Moscow, to Foreign Office, no. 524, "Memorandum on Russian Agricultural Machinery Business," 5 June 1924, FO 371/10470.

114. See Vice-Consul Nielsen, Stockholm, no. 30142, 19 May 1921, NARG 151, box 2240, file 448; Consul General D. I. Murphy, Stockholm, 29 July 1921, NARG 59, file 661.5816/6; and Fithian, "Soviet Economic Relations," p. 28.

115. Fithian, "Soviet Economic Relations," p. 28; International Harvester, *Annual Report*, 1919, p. 19, as cited in ibid., p. 27.

116. "Sales Statistics," FMCA, Acc. 572, box 24. It is interesting to note that by 1927 over 85 percent of the trucks and tractors in the USSR were U.S.-manufactured Fords. See Sutton, *Western Technology and Soviet Economic Development*, 1:140.

117. Sorensen to "Dear Eynon," 16 June 1925, FMCA, Acc. 38, box 51.

118. Gaston Plantiff to Edsel Ford, 22 July 1925, FMCA, Acc. 38, box 51.

119. "Report of the Ford Delegation," 1926, FMCA, Acc. 49, box 1A. The Department of Commerce agreed with the delegation's assessment of the Soviet Union as representing "perhaps the greatest possibility for the sale of tractors of any foreign country." See Charles D. Martin, "Foreign Markets for Tractors," U.S. Department of Commerce, *Trade Information Bulletin*, no. 502, p.3.

Chapter 9

1. Minute by O'Malley on Department of Overseas Trade, no. 7344 F.R., 24 April 1923, FO 371/9351.

2. American Consul Reval, "Decrease in Esthonian Transit Trade with Soviet Russia," 25 June 1923, NARG 59, file 660i.0025 1/46; Edward Hunt, "The Volume and Value of Russian Transit Trade through Esthonia," 14 November 1928, NARG 59, file 660p.6125 1/1; and Hinkkanen-Lievonen, *British Trade and Enterprise in the Baltic States*, p. 138.

3. American-Russian Chamber of Commerce, *Economic Handbook of the Soviet Union*, p. 124.

4. With the onset of the Great Depression in 1929, interest in the Russian market again grew considerably. Initially little effected by the depression, the Soviet demand for goods remained high, and the industrial economies of Britain and the U.S. had a real need to dispose of their goods. Resonant of the depression in 1921, the Soviet market was once more hailed as the solution for the depressed economies. See Lovenstein, *American Opinion of Soviet Russia*, especially the chapter on "The Depression in the U.S. and the First Five Year Plan."

5. From photostat of original agreement, 9 October 1928, in Gumberg Manuscripts, box 6A, folder 2.

6. Anglo-Russian trade had in fact reached its highest point for that decade in 1925, when the turnover amounted to nearly £44.6 million, 57 percent of which was accounted for by imports.

7. Jones and Trebilcock, "Russian Industry and British Business," pp. 87, 90.

8. Eastern District Manager to Edsel Ford, 22 July 1925, FMCA, Acc. 66, box 1.

9. American Legation, Riga, "Soviet Trade with America," 19 November 1924, NARG 59, file 611.61/2. American banks had reportedly "expressed their readiness to open credit to the newly established Arcos America to promote the development of trade between America and the USSR." Wireless News, New York, 17 January 1924, FO 371/10489.

10. *Commercial and Financial Chronicle*, 8 August 1925, p. 600.

11. Minute by P. M. Roberts, 5 January 1924, FO 371/10468.

12. See Reyntiens to Foreign Office, 22 November 1923, FO 371/9353; and J. G. Buchanan Diaries, entries for 15 and 28 December 1922, Midland Bank Archives, 30/377.

13. Department of Overseas Trade to Foreign Office, no. 9560/F.R., 3 July 1924, FO 371/10470.

14. From photostat of original agreement, Gumberg Manuscripts, box 6A, folder 2. Small businesses were at a disadvantage in terms of commercial credit throughout the decade. Huge American companies such as General Electric, Ford, and International Harvester could finance their trade independent of American banks or were able to arrange long-term credit through the larger American banks. See Hoff-Wilson, *Ideology and Economics*, p. 55. This may be exactly why the larger American firms remained fairly indifferent to the question of recognition throughout the decade; they needed no government guarantees or assurances, and they all had the international trade connections necessary to conduct this trade irrespective of the government's official position. Moreover, by *opposing* recognition, the larger firms were able to eliminate possible competition by keeping out those companies less able to finance or arrange credit.

15. There remained considerable disagreement among the "Old Guard" as to just how far the Soviet government should be prepared go in order to get foreign credit. Krasin believed that they should be prepared "to go so far as to satisfy the claims of former owners of nationalized enterprises." Indeed, he claimed that the "main objective of [Soviet] foreign policy is to obtain credits, which we need for restoration of agriculture, for transport, for industry and for stabilization of our rouble." Trotsky, however, remained firmly opposed to inviting foreign capital or capitalist back into the country: Russians could rebuild Russia themselves. Karpova, *L. B. Krasin—Sovetskii diplomat*, p. 125; and Krasin at the twelfth Party Congress, April 1922, as cited in Gillette, "The Political Origins of American Soviet Trade," p. 9.

16. See *Ekonomicheskaya Zhizn'*, 11 November 1921; Hodgson, Moscow, to Foreign Office, no. 19, 13 August 1921, FO 371/6928; Grove, Moscow, to Foreign Office, no. 36, "Concession to Manufacture Agricultural Machinery," 14 January 1922; R. T. Elsworthy, 24 February 1922; FO 371/8161; E. F. Wise to O'Malley, Memorandum concerning an Interview with Jonas Lied, 24 March 1921, FO 371/6848; and Political Report no. 21, "Trade Policy of the Soviet Government," 12 February 1921, FO 371/6846.

17. See R. T. Elsworthy to Department of Overseas Trade, 8 November 1921; and Foreign Office Minutes; FO 371/6928.

18. For an account of the various types of concessions that were offered and taken up, as well as their varying success and ultimate fate, see Sutton, *Western Technology and Soviet Economic Development*, vol. 1.

BIBLIOGRAPHY

Unpublished Sources

Private Papers

American Engineers in the Soviet Union, Hoover Institution Archives, Stanford, California.
Balfour Papers, British Library, London, and Public Record Office, London.
Bank of England Archives, London.
BECOS Traders Archives, Gane, Jackson & Scott, London.
M. V. Bernatskii Papers, Columbia University Library, New York; and Hoover Library, Stanford, California.
Lord Robert Cecil Papers, Public Record Office, London.
Ivan Emil'ianov Papers, Museum of Russian Culture, Inc., San Francisco.
Ford Motor Company Archives, Henry Ford Museum, Dearborn, Michigan.
Gumberg Manuscripts, Wisconsin Historical Society, Madison, Wisconsin.
Khorvat Papers, Museum of Russian Culture, Inc., San Francisco.
Kodak Archives, Harrow, Middlesex; and Rochester, New York.
Krasin Archive, Internationaal Instituut voor Sociale Geschiedenis, Amsterdam.
Lansing Papers, Library of Congress, Washington, D.C.
Lloyds Bank Archives, London.
MacDonald Papers, Public Record Office, London.
Maklakov Manuscripts, Hoover Institution Archives, Stanford, California.
Midland Bank Archives, London.
Milner Papers, New College, Oxford.
National Metal and Chemical Bank Papers, Montague Investment Management, London.
Okulich Papers, Museum of Russian Culture, Inc., San Francisco.
Pearson Papers, The Science Museum, London.
Russia. Posol'stvo (U.S.), Hoover Institution Archives, Stanford, California.
John F. Stevens Papers, Hoover Institution Archives, Stanford, California.
Trotsky Archives, Harvard University, Cambridge, Massachusetts.
Vickers Archives, Cambridge University Library, Cambridge, England.

Woodrow Wilson Papers, Library of Congress, Washington, D.C.
Wrangel Military Archives, Hoover Institution Archives, Stanford, California.

Government Records

United Kingdom: Public Record Office, London.
  Board of Trade: Department of Overseas Trade (BT 60).
  Cabinet Office: Cabinet Papers (Cab. 24); War Cabinet (Cab. 23).
  Committees: General Series (Cab. 27).
  Confidential Print (FO 418).
  Foreign Office: General Political Correspondence (FO 371).
  Trade and Commercial Correspondence (FO 368).
United States: National Archives, Washington, D.C.
  Department of Commerce, Record Group 40.
  Department of Commerce, Bureau of Foreign and Domestic Commerce,
    Record Group 151.
  Department of the Navy, Naval Collection of the Office of Naval Records and
    Library, Record Group WA-45.
  Department of State, Consular Post Files, Record Group 84.
  Department of State, U.S. Department of State Decimal File, and Record
    Group 59.
  War Department, Records of the General Staff and Military Intelligence Divi-
    sion, Record Group 65.
  War Trade Board, Russian Bureau, Inc., Record Group 182, Suitland Annex.

Published Sources

American Mining Congress. *Our Vanishing Gold Reserves*. Washington, D.C.,
  1920.
American-Russian Chamber of Commerce. *Economic Handbook of the Soviet
  Union*. New York, 1931.
Amtorg Trading Corporation. *Economic Review of the Soviet Union*. Published
  twice monthly. New York, 1926–34.
———. *Economic Statistics of the Soviet Union*. 2nd ed. New York, 1928.
———. Information Department. *Russian Gold: A Collection of Articles, News-
  paper Editorials and Reports, and Statistical Data Regarding the Russian
  Gold Reserve and Shipments of Soviet Gold*. New York, 1928.
Anderson, N. L. [American Trade Commissioner, Stockholm]. *Baltic Trade after
  the War*. U.S. Department of Commerce Report, no. 280. Washington, D.C.,
  29 November 1918.
Browder, Robert Paul, and Alexander F. Kerensky, eds. *The Russian Provisional
  Government, 1917*. Documents. 3 vols. Stanford, California, 1961.

Committee on Russian-American Relations. *The United States and the Soviet Union: A Report on the Controlling Factors in the Relations between the United States and the Soviet Union.* New York, 1933.

Cumming, C. K., and Walter W. Pettit, eds. *Russian-American Relations, March 1917–March 1920. Documents and Papers.* New York, 1920.

Danishevskii, K. Kh. *Lesnoy eksport SSSR: Ego polozhenie i perspektivy.* 2nd ed. Moscow, 1926.

Davies, Roland R. *American Agricultural Implements in Europe, Asia and Africa.* U.S. Department of Commerce and Labor, Bureau of Manufactures. Special Agent Series, XXII. Washington, D.C., 1909.

Degras, Jane, ed. *Soviet Documents of Foreign Policy.* 2 vols. London, 1951–52.

Dokumenty vneshnei politiki SSSR. Vols. 1–6. Moscow, 1957–63.

Eudin, X. Y., and H. H. Fisher, eds. *Soviet Russia and the West, 1920–1927.* Stanford, California, 1957.

Istoriya sotsialisticheskoy ekonomiki SSSR: Sovetskaya ekonomika v 1917–1920gg. Vol. 1. Moscow, 1976.

Istoriya sotsialisticheskoy ekonomiki SSSR: Vosstanovlenie narodnogo khozyaystva SSSR, 1921–1925gg. Vol. 2. Moscow, 1976.

Kennard, Howard P., ed. *The Russian Year Book.* London, 1911–16.

Lenin, V. I. *Polnoe sobranie sochineniyi.* 5th ed. 55 vols. Moscow, 1958–65.

———. *Sochineniya.* 2nd ed. 35 vols. Moscow, 1930–35.

Lewery, L. J. "Foreign Capital Investment in Russian Industries and Commerce." U.S. Department of Commerce Miscellaneous Series, no. 124. Washington, D.C., 1923.

Materialy po vneshney torgovle: Sobrannye zagranichnymi kontorami CCKS "Zakupsbyt." Sibdel'gostorga. Moscow, 1923.

Ministry of Trade and Industry [Imperial Russian Government]. *Bulletin de l'office d'information pour le commerce extérieur. 1912, 1913.*

Narkomfin, Institute ekonomicheskikh isledovanii. *Narodnokhozyaystvo v 1916g.* Vypusk VII. Petrograd, 1922.

Narodnyi Komissariat po Inostrannym Delam. *Genuezskaya Konferentsiya: Materialy i dokumenty.* Moscow, 1922.

———. *Materialy Genueskoi Konferntsii.* Moscow, 1922.

National City Bank of New York. *Russia and the Imperial Russian Government: Economic and Financial.* New York, 1916.

Obzor vneshney torgovli Rossii po evropeiskoy i aziatskoy granitsam. Published annually. St. Petersburg and Moscow, 1906–10.

Otchet o deyatel'nosti russko-amerikanskoy torgovoy palat'i za 1916g. Moscow, 1917.

Russko-amerikanskaya torgovlaya palata v Moskva. Spravka o deyatel'nosti. Moscow, 1918.

Snodgrass, John H. [American Consul General, Moscow]. *Russia. A Handbook on Commercial and Industrial Conditions.* U.S. Department of Commerce Special Consular Report, no. 61. Washington, D.C., 1913.

The Soviet Union Information Bureau. *The Soviet Union: Facts, Descriptions and Statistics*. Washington, D.C., 1929.

United Kingdom. Cabinet Papers. *Special Weekly on Unemployment*. No. 9 Week Ended 10 December 1920. C.P./2297.

United Kingdom. Ministry of Munitions. *History of the Ministry of Munitions*. Vol. 7, *The Control of Materials*, part 3, *Non-Ferrous Metals*. London, 1922.

United Kingdom. *Annual Statement of the Navigation and Shipping of the United Kingdom*.

————.Parliamentary Papers. *Annual Statement of the Trade of the United Kingdom*. Accounts and Papers.

————. Cmd. 587. *Agreement between His Britannic Majesty's Government and the Soviet Government of Russia for the Exchange of Prisoners*. 1920.

————. Cmd. 1621. *Resolution Adopted by the Supreme Council at Cannes, 6 January 1922, as the Basis of the Genoa Conference*. 1922.

————. Cmd. 1667. *Papers Relating to International Economic Conference, Genoa, April–May 1922*. 1922.

————. Diplomatic and Consular Reports, Russia: *Report on the Trade and Commerce of the Consular District of Moscow, 1913*.

————. Diplomatic and Consular Reports, Russia: *Report on the Trade of the Consular District of Batoum, 1914*.

————. Diplomatic and Consular Reports, Russia: *Report on the Trade of the Consular District of Novorossisk, 1914*.

————. Diplomatic and Consular Reports, Russia: *Report on the Trade of the Consular District of Odessa, 1914*.

————. *House of Commons, Debates*. Hansards. London, 1918–25.

United States. Congress. *Congressional Record*.

United States. Department of Commerce. *Diplomatic and Consular Report for the Moscow District, 1913*. Washington, D.C., 1914.

————. *Foreign Commerce and Navigation of the United States*. Washington, D.C., 1900–1930.

————. *Statistical Abstracts of the United States*. Washington, D.C, 1921.

————. *Trade Information Bulletin*. Washington, D.C., 1922–30.

————. Bureau of Foreign and Domestic Commerce. *Foreign Commerce Yearbook*. Washington, D.C., 1926.

United States. Department of Commerce and Bureau of Statistics. *Statistical Abstracts of Foreign Countries*. Washington, D.C., 1909.

United States. Department of State. *Papers Relating to the Foreign Relations of the United States*. 1918–32. Washington, D.C., 1931–52.

————. *Papers Relating to the Foreign Relations of the United States. The Lansing Papers*. 1914–20. Washington, D.C., 1939.

United States. Federal Trade Commission. *Report on Foreign Ownership in the Petroleum Industry*. Washington, D.C., 1923.

United States. Senate. *Report of the United States Senate Commission on Gold and Silver Inquiry*. Serial 9, vol. 2. Washington, D.C., 1924.

Vneshtorg. *Vneshnyaya torgovlya SSSR za 1918–1940gg.* Moscow, 1960.
Woodward E. L., and R. Butler, eds. *Documents on British Foreign Policy: 1919–1939.* 1st series, vols. 1–11. London, 1947–61.

Newspapers and Journals

Board of Trade Journal.
The Bulletin of the Russian Information Bureau.
The Coast Banker.
Commercial and Financial Chronicle.
Commercial Russia.
Dagens Nyheter.
Daily Herald.
Daily Telegraph.
Dearborn Independent.
The Economist.
Ekonomicheskaya Zhizn'.
Engineers and Engineering.
Evening Standard.
Evening Sun.
Federal Reserve Bulletin.
Financial News.
Izvestiya.
Journal of Commerce.
Kelly's Monthly Trade Review.
Manchester Guardian.
Manchester Guardian Commercial.
Messenger of Finance.
Moody's Magazine.
The Morning Post.

Nautical Gazette.
New Statesman.
New York Commercial.
New York Herald.
New York Times.
New York Tribune.
The Observer.
Pravda.
Russia.
The Russian Economist.
Russian Information and Review.
Russian Outlook.
The Russian Review.
The Times.
The Times Trade Supplement.
Torgovo Promyshlennaya Gazeta.
Vestnik, Narodnogo Komissariata Vneshney Torgovli.
Vestnik Finansov, Promyshlenosti i Torgovli.
Vestnik Russko-Amerikanskoe Torgovoy Palat'i.
Washington Post.
Westminster Gazette.

Secondary Sources

Books and Pamphlets

Apostol, P., and A. Michelson. *La lutte pour le pétrole et la Russie.* Paris, 1922.
Baker, Ray Stannard, ed. *Woodrow Wilson, Life and Letters.* 8 vols. New York, 1927–39.
Barou, N. *Russian Co-operation Abroad: Foreign Trade, 1912–1928.* London, 1930.

Bauer, Robert A., ed. *Interaction of Economic and Foreign Policy*. Charlottesville, Va., 1975.

Baykov, Alexander. *The Development of the Soviet Economic System: An Essay on the Experience of Planning in the USSR*. Cambridge, 1946.

——. *Soviet Foreign Trade*. Princeton, N.J., 1946.

Beable, William Henry. *Commercial Russia*. New York, 1919.

Bennett, Geoffrey. *Cowan's War: The Story of British Naval Operations in the Baltic, 1918–1920*. London, 1964.

Bernstein, S. A. *The Financial and Economic Results of the Working of the Lena Goldfields Company, Limited*. London, 1931.

Birmingham Bureau of Research on Russian Economic Conditions. *The Foreign Trade of the USSR*. Memorandum no. 2. Birmingham, 1931.

——. *The Foreign Trade of the USSR*. Memorandum no. 9. Birmingham, 1934.

Brinkley, George A. *The Volunteer Army and Allied Intervention in South Russia, 1917–1921: A Study in the Politics and Diplomacy of the Russian Civil War*. Notre Dame, Ind., 1966.

Bron, Sol G. *Soviet Economic Development and American Business: Results of the First Five Years under the Five Year Plan and Further Perspectives*. New York, 1930.

Budish, J. M., and Samuel Shipman. *Soviet Foreign Trade, Menace or Promise?* New York, 1931.

Carr, E. H. *The Bolshevik Revolution: 1917–1923*. 3 vols. London, 1950–53.

——. *The Interregnum. 1923–1924*. London, 1954.

——. *Socialism in One Country: 1924–1926*. 3 vols. London, 1958–64.

Carrol, E. Malcolm. *Soviet Communism and Western Opinion: 1919–1921*. Edited by F. B. M. Hollyday. Chapel Hill, N.C., 1965.

Carstensen, Fred V. *American Enterprise in Foreign Markets: Studies of Singer and International Harvester in Imperial Russia*. Chapel Hill, N.C., 1984.

Coates, W. P., and Zelda Coates. *Armed Intervention in Russia, 1918–1922*. London, 1935.

——. *A History of Anglo-Soviet Relations*. London, 1943.

Cockfield, Jamie H., ed. *Dollars and Diplomacy: Ambassador David Rowland Francis and the Fall of Tsarism, 1916–1917*. Durham, N.C., 1981.

Committee on Russian-American Relations. *The United States and the Soviet Union: A Report on the Controlling Factors in the Relations between the United States and the Soviet Union*. New York, 1933.

Condoide, Mikhail V. *Russian-American Trade: A Study of the Soviet Foreign Trade Monopoly*. Columbus, Ohio, 1946.

Crisp, Olga. *Studies in the Russian Economy before 1914*. London, 1976.

Davis, Malcolm W. *Open Gates to Russia*. New York, 1920.

Day, R. B. *Leon Trotsky and the Politics of Economic Isolation*. Cambridge, 1973.

Denikin, A. D. *Ocherki russkoi smuty*. 5 vols. Berlin, 1921–26.

Diesen, Emil. *Exchange Rates of the World.* Christiania, Norway, 1922.

Dockrill, Michael L., and J. Douglas Goold. *Peace without Promise: Britain and the Peace Conferences, 1919–1923.* London, 1981.

Epstein, E. *Les banques de commerce russes.* Paris, 1925.

Eventov, L. Ya. *Inostrannye kapitaly v russkoy promyshlennosti.* Moscow, 1931.

Faas, V. V. *Russian Export Trade in Timber.* New York, 1919.

Falkus, M. E. *The Industrialisation of Russia, 1700–1914.* London, 1972.

Feis, Herbert. *Europe, the World's Banker, 1870–1914: An Account of European Foreign Investment and the Connection of World Finance with Diplomacy before the War.* New Haven, Conn., 1930.

———. *Petroleum and American Foreign Policy.* Commodity Study no. 3. Stanford, Calif., 1944.

Filene, Peter G. *Americans and the Soviet Experiment, 1917–1933.* Cambridge, Mass., 1967.

Fischer, Louis. *Oil Imperialism: The International Struggle for Petroleum.* New York, 1926.

———. *The Soviets in World Affairs: A History of the Relations between the Soviet Union and the Rest of the World.* 2 vols. London, 1930.

Francis, David R. *Russia from the American Embassy.* New York, 1921.

Fride, M. A. *Inostrannye kuryatnye i yaichnye rynki: Materialy i izsledovaniya vipusky. Angliya i Londonskiy rinok'.* St. Petersburg, 1912.

Friedman, Elisha M. *Russia in Transition: A Businessman's Appraisal.* London, 1933.

Furaev, V. K. *Sovetsko-amerikanskie otnosheniya, 1917–1939gg.* Moscow, 1964.

Ganelin, R. Sh. *Rossiya i SShA, 1914–1917gg.: Ocherki istorii russko-amerikanskikh otnosheniy.* Moscow, 1969.

Gerretson, C. *Geschiedenis der "Koninklijke."* Baarn, 1973.

Gerschenkron, A. *Economic Backwardness in Historical Perspective.* Cambridge, Mass., 1966.

———. *Europe in the Russian Mirror.* Cambridge, 1970.

Gibb, George Sweet, and Evelyn H. Knowlton. *History of the Standard Oil Company (New Jersey).* 2 vols. New York, 1956.

Gindin, I. F. *Russkie kommercheskie bank, iz istorii finansogo kapitala v Rossii.* Moscow, 1948.

Girault, René. *Emprunts russes et investissements français en Russie, 1887–1914.* Paris, 1973.

Goldstein, Joseph M. *America's Opportunities for Trade and Investment in Russia.* New York, 1919.

Gorodetsky, Gabriel. *The Precarious Truce: Anglo-Soviet Relations, 1924–1927.* Cambridge, 1977.

Graves, William S. *America's Siberian Adventure, 1918–1920.* New York, 1931.

Gregory, John D. *On the Edge of Diplomacy: Rambles and Reflections, 1902–1928.* London, 1929.

Gregory, Paul R. *Russian National Income, 1885–1913.* Cambridge, 1982.

Hammer, Armand. *The Quest of the Romanoff Treasure.* New York, 1932.

Hammer, Armand, with Neil Lyndon. *Hammer, Witness to History.* New York, 1987.

Hard, William. *Raymond Robins Own Story.* New York, 1920.

Heller, A. A. *The Industrial Revival in Soviet Russia.* New York, 1922.

Hinkkanen-Lievonen, Merja-Liisa. *British Trade and Enterprise in the Baltic States, 1919–1925.* Helsinki, 1984.

Hoff-Wilson, Joan. *Ideology and Economics: U.S. Relations with the Soviet Union, 1918–1933.* Columbia, Mo., 1974.

Hoover, Herbert. *An American Epic.* Vol. 3, *Famine in 45 Nations: The Battle on the Front Line, 1914–1923.* Chicago, 1961.

Hovi, Olavi. *The Baltic Area in British Policy, 1918–1921.* 2 vols. Helsinki, 1980.

Huntington, W. Chapin. *The Prospects of British and American Trade with the Soviet Union.* School of Slavonic and Eastern European Studies, Monograph no. 7/8. London, 1935.

Hwang Jen, M. *Le regime des concessions en Russie Sovietique.* Paris, 1929.

Ironsides, Field Marshal Lord. *Archangel, 1918–1919.* London, 1953.

Izvestiya obshchestva sblizheniya mezhdu Rossey i Amerikoy. Petrograd, 1915.

Jones, Geoffrey. *The State and the Emergence of the British Oil Industry.* London, 1981.

Kalamantiano, S. K. *Possibilities of Success of Import and Export Trade between Russia and the U.S.A. after Present Events.* Odessa, 1914.

Karpova, R. F. *L. B. Krasin—Sovetskii diplomat.* Moscow, 1926.

Kaufman, M. Ya. *Vneshnyaya torgovlya Rossii, 1918–1921gg.* Petrograd, 1922.

Kennan, George F. *Soviet-American Relations, 1917–1920.* 2 vols. Princeton, N.J., 1956–58.

Kennedy, K. H. *Mining Tsar: The Life and Times of Leslie Urquhart.* Sydney, 1986.

Kennedy, Paul. *The Realities behind Diplomacy: Background Influences on British External Policy, 1865–1980.* London, 1981.

Kettle, Michael. *The Allies and the Russian Collapse, March 1917–March 1918.* London, 1981.

Keynes, John Maynard. *The Economic Consequences of the Peace.* London, 1924.

Killen, Linda. *The Russian Bureau: A Case Study in Wilsonian Diplomacy.* Lexington, Ky., 1983.

Krasin, Leonid B. *Blizhayshie perspektivy russkogo eksporta.* Moscow, 1923.

———. *Osnovnye tsifry vneshney torgovli.* Moscow, 1925.

———. *Vneshnyaya torgovlya SSSR.* Moscow, 1924.

———. *Vneshtorg i vneshnyaya ekonomicheskaya politika sovetskogo pravitel'stva.* Petrograd, 1921.

———. *Voprosy vneshney torgovli.* Moscow, 1928.

Kryukov', N. A. *Russko-angliiskaya torgovaya palata: Angliya. Kak' rynok' sel'skokhozyaystvennikh' produktov'.* St Petersburg, 1910.

Kutuzov, A. I. *Vneshnyaya torgovlya soyuza SSR za X let. Sbornik materialov.* Moscow, 1928.

Langer, William L. *The Diplomacy of Imperialism.* 2 vols. New York, 1935.

Lebedev, V. V. *Russko-amerikanskiy ekonomicheskiy otnosheniya, 1900–1917gg.* Moscow, 1964.

Leites, K. *Recent Economic Developments in Russia.* Oxford, 1922.

Levin, Gordon N. *Woodrow Wilson and World Politics: America's Response to War and Revolution.* New York, 1968.

Libbey, James K. *Alexander Gumberg and Soviet-American Relations, 1917–1933.* Lexington, Ky., 1977.

Liberman, Simon. *Building Lenin's Russia.* Chicago, 1945.

Lied, Jonas. *Siberian Arctic: The Story of the Siberian Company.* London, 1960.

Link, Arthur. *Wilson the Diplomatist.* Baltimore, 1957.

Lockhart, R. H. Bruce. *Memoirs of a British Agent.* London, 1932.

Lovenstein, Meno. *American Opinion of Soviet Russia.* American Council on Public Affairs. Washington, D.C., 1941.

Lyashchenko, P. I. *A History of the National Economy of Russia to the 1917 Revolution.* New York, 1949.

McKay, John P. *Pioneers for Profit: Foreign Entrepreneurship and Russian Industrialization, 1885–1913.* Chicago, 1970.

Maddox, Robert J. *William E. Borah and American Foreign Policy.* Baton Rouge, 1969.

Malle, Silvana. *The Economic Organization of War Communism, 1918–1921.* Cambridge, 1985.

Marcosson, I. *The Black Golconda.* New York, 1923.

Margold, Stella K. *Let's Do Business with Russia: Why We Should and How We Can.* New York, 1948.

Mayer, Arno J. *Politics and Diplomacy of Peacemaking: Containment and Counter-revolution at Versailles, 1918–1919.* London, 1967.

Maynard, Sir C. *The Murmansk Venture.* London, 1928.

Mayzel', B. *Mirovaya torgovlya i nashe uchastie v ney.* Leningrad, 1928.

Meiburger, A. V. *Efforts of Raymond Robins toward the Recognition of Soviet Russia and the Outlawry of War, 1917–1933.* Washington, D.C., 1958.

A. I. Melchin. *Amerikanskaya interventtsiya v 1918–1920 gg.* Moscow, 1951.

Michelson, Alexander M., V. N. Kokovzov, Paul N. Apostol, and Michael W. Bernatsky. *Russian Public Finance during the War.* New Haven, Conn., 1928.

Miller, Margaret. *The Economic Development of Russia, 1905–1914.* London, 1926.

Mints, Isaak. *Angliiskaya interventsiya i severnaya kontr-revolyutsiya.* Moscow, 1931.

Mishustin, A., ed. *Torgovye Otnosheniya SSSR s kapitalisticheskimi stranami.* Moscow, 1938.

Morely, James William. *The Japanese Thrust into Siberia, 1918.* New York, 1957.

Mowat, Charles Loch. *Britain between the Wars, 1918–1940*. Chicago, 1955.

Neilson, Keith. *Strategy and Supply: The Anglo-Russian Alliance, 1914–1917*. London, 1984.

Nevins, Allan, and Frank Ernest Hill. *Ford: Expansion and Challenge, 1915–1933*. New York, 1957.

Newman, Edward Polson. *Britain and the Baltic*. London, 1930.

Nolde, Boris. *Russia in the Economic War*. New Haven, Conn., 1928.

Ol', P. V. *Inostrannye kapitaly v narodnom khozyastvo govoennoi Rossii*. Leningrad, 1925.

———. *Inostrannye kapitaly v Rossii*. Petrograd, 1922.

O'Malley, Sir Owen. *The Phantom Caravan*. London, 1954.

P. S. Parfenov. *Uroki proshlogo: Grazhdanskaya voina v Sibiri, 1918, 1919, 1920 gg*. Harbin, China, n.d.

Poletaev, M. I. *Tsentrosoyus v Amerike*. Amerikanskaya torgovlaya promishlennost', no. 1. June 1926.

Parrott, Bruce. *Politics and Technology in the Soviet Union*. Cambridge, Mass., 1983.

Pasvolsky, Leo, and Harold G. Moulton. *Russian Debts and Russian Reconstruction: A Study of the Relation of Russia's Foreign Debts to Her Economic Recovery*. New York, 1924.

Phillips, D. C., and D. Grace. *Ransomes of Ipswich*. Reading, 1975.

Pigou, A. C. *Aspects of British Economic History, 1918–1925*. London, 1974.

Ransome, Arthur. *Six Weeks in Russia*. London, 1919.

Riddell, Lord. *Lord Riddell's Intimate Diary of the Peace Conference and After, 1918–1923*. London, 1933.

Rodgers, Hugh I. *Search for Security: A Study in Baltic Diplomacy, 1920–1934*. New Haven, Conn., 1975.

Ronimois, H. E. *Russia's Foreign Trade and the Baltic Sea*. London, 1946.

Rozhansky, Louis A. *British Opportunities in Russia*. London, 1916.

Sack, Alexander J. *America's Possible Share in the Economic Future of Russia*. New York, 1919.

Sayers, Richard S. *The Bank of England, 1891–1944*. Vol. 1. Cambridge, 1976.

Schuman, Frederick L. *American Policy towards Russia since 1917: A Study of Diplomatic History, International Law and Public Opinion*. London, 1928.

Scott, J. D. *Vickers, A History*. London, 1962.

Seleznev, G. K. *Ten' dollara nad rossiey: Iz istorii amerikano-russikh otnosheniy*. Moscow, 1957.

Shishkin, B. A. *Sovetskoe gosudarstvo i strany zapada v 1917–1923gg*. Leningrad, 1969.

———. *B bor''be s blokadoy o stanovlenii sovetskoy vneshney torgovli*. Moscow, 1979.

———. *V. I. Lenin i vneshne-ekonomicheskaya politika sovetskogo gosudarstva, 1917–1923gg*. Leningrad, 1977.

Shtein, B. E. *Russkiy vopros v 1920–1921*. Moscow, 1958.

———. *Torgovaya politika i torgovye dogovory sovetskoy rossii, 1917–1922.* Moscow, 1923.

Soedinennye Shtaty Ameriki i SSSR: Ikh politicheskie i ekonomicheskie vzaimootnosheniya. Moscow, 1934.

Sokolnikov, Gregory, ed. *Soviet Policy in Public Finance, 1917–1928.* Stanford, Calif., 1931.

Sorensen, Charles E. *Forty Years with Ford.* London, 1957.

Stone, Norman. *The Eastern Front, 1914–1917.* London, 1975.

Strakovsky, Leonid I. *Intervention in Archangel: The Story of Allied Intervention and Russian Counter-Revolution in North Russia 1918–1920.* Princeton, N.J., 1944.

———. *The Origins of American Intervention in North Russia.* Princeton, N.J., 1937.

Sumner, B. H. *Russia and Europe.* Oxford Slavonic Papers, no. 1. Oxford, 1948.

Supple, Barry E. *The Royal Exchange Assurance: A History of British Insurance, 1720–1970.* Cambridge, 1970.

Sutton, Anthony C. *Wall Street and the Bolshevik Revolution.* New Rochelle, N.Y., 1974.

———. *Western Technology and Soviet Economic Development.* Vol. 1, 1918–1930. Stanford, Calif., 1968.

Tallents, Stephen. *Man and Boy.* London, 1943.

Third Winter of Unemployment. Report of an Enquiry Undertaken in the Autumn of 1922 by a Group of Economists and Industrialists. London, 1922.

Thompson, A. Beeby. *The Oilfields of Russia and the Russian Petroleum Industry.* London, 1908.

Thompson, John M. *Russia, Bolshevism, and the Versailles Peace.* Princeton, N.J., 1966.

The Times Book of Russia: Finance, Commerce, Industries. London, 1916.

Tolf, Robert W. *The Russian Rockefellers: The Saga of the Nobel Family and the Russian Oil Industry.* Stanford, Calif., 1976.

Ullman, Richard H. *Anglo-Soviet Relations, 1917–1921.* 3 vols. Princeton, N.J., 1961–72.

Unterberger, Betty Miller. *America's Siberian Expedition.* Durham, N.C., 1956.

Walker, Jacob. *Ford ili Marks.* Moscow, 1925.

White, John Albert. *The Siberian Intervention.* Princeton, N.J., 1950.

White, Stephen. *Britain and the Bolshevik Revolution: A Study in the Politics of Diplomacy, 1920–1924.* London, 1979.

Wilkins, Mira. *The Emergence of Multinational Enterprise: American Business Abroad from the Colonial Era to 1914.* Cambridge, Mass., 1970.

———. *The Maturing of Multinational Enterprise: American Business Abroad from 1914–1970.* Cambridge, Mass., 1974.

Wilkins, Mira, and Frank Ernest Hill. *American Business Abroad: Ford on Six Continents.* Detroit, 1964.

Williams, Robert C. *Russian Art and American Money, 1900–1940.* Cambridge, Mass., 1980.

Williams, William Appleman. *American-Russian Relations, 1781–1947.* New York, 1952.

———. *The Tragedy of American Diplomacy.* New York, 1959.

Yanson, J. D. *Foreign Trade in the USSR.* London, 1934.

Zarnitskii, S. V., and L. I. Trofimova. *Sovetskoy strany diplomat.* Moscow, 1968.

Zemskaya torgovlya zhelezem i sel'skokhozyaystvennymi mashinami i oridiyami v 1901–1911gg. Kharkov, 1912.

Ziv, V. S. *Inostrannye kapitaly v gornopromishlennaya rossii.* Petrograd, 1918.

———. *Inostrannye kapitaly v rosskoy gornozavodskoy promyshlennosti.* Petrograd, 1917.

Articles

Anderson, Edgar. "The British Policy toward the Baltic States, 1918–1920." *Journal of Central European Affairs* 19, no. 3 (September 1959): 276–89.

———. "The USSR Trade with Latvia: The Treaty of 1927." *Slavic Review* 21, no. 2 (June 1962): 296–321.

Barkai, H. "The Macro-Economics of Tsarist Russia in the Industrialisation Era: Monetary Developments, the Balance of Payments, and the Gold Standard." *Journal of Economic History* 33, no. 2 (June 1973): 339–72.

Cadieux, François. "Western Technology and Early Russian Pipelines, 1877–1917." *Journal of European Economic History* 15, no. 2 (Fall 1986): 335–44.

Crisp, Olga. "The Russian Liberals and 1906 Anglo-French Loan to Russia." *Slavonic Review* 39, no. 93 (June 1961): 497–511.

Dalton, J. "Strongly Fortified Industry Set for Any Emergency." *Automotive Industries.* 10 April 1924.

Davis, Donald E., and Eugene P. Trani. "The American YMCA and the Russian Revolution." *Slavic Review* 33, no. 3 (September 1974): 469–91.

Davis, Malcolm W. "Soviet Recognition and Trade." *Foreign Affairs* 5, no. 4 (July 1927): 650–62.

Debo, Richard K. "Dutch-Soviet Relations, 1917–1924: The Role of Finance and Commerce in the Foreign Policy of Soviet Russia and the Netherlands." *Canadian Slavic Studies* 4, no. 2 (Summer 1970): 199–217.

Delaisi, Francis. "Oil and the Arcos Raid." *Foreign Affairs* [London] 6, no. 1 (October 1927): 106–8; and 6, no. 2 (November 1927): 137–38.

Falkus, M. E. "Russia's National Income, 1913: A Re-evaluation." *Economica* 35, no. 137 (February 1968): 52–73.

Fisher, Richard B. "American Investments in Pre-Soviet Russia." *American Slavic and East European Review* 8, no. 2 (April 1949): 90–105. [Now published as *Slavic Review.*]

Fursenko, A. "The Beginning of International Competition in Oil." In *Proceed-*

ings of the 7th International Economic History Congress at the University of Edinburgh, 1978, edited by Michael Flinn, pp. 46–52. Edinburgh, 1978.

———. "Iz istorii russko-amerikanskikh otnosheniy na rubezhe XIX–XX vv." *Iz istorii imperializma v Rossii* (Moscow, 1965).

Garvey, George. "Banking under the Tsars and Soviets." *Journal of Economic History* 32, no. 4 (1972): 869–93.

Gay, Jules E. "Anglo-Russian Economic Relations." *Economic Journal* 27, no. 106 (June 1917): 211–37.

Gefter, M. Ya. "Iz istorii proniknovleniya amerikanskogo kapitala v tsarskey rossii do pervoy mirovoy voiny." *Istoricheskye Zapiski* 35 (Moscow, 1961): 62–86.

Gillette, Philip S. "American Capital in the Contest for Soviet Oil." *Soviet Studies* 24, no. 4 (April 1973): 477–90.

Glenny, M. V. "The Anglo-Soviet Trade Agreement, March 1921." *Journal of Contemporary History* 5, no. 2 (April 1970): 63–82.

Goldstein, Edward R. "Vickers Limited and the Tsarist Regime." *Slavonic and East European Review* 57, no. 4 (October 1980): 561–71.

Gregory, Paul. "Economic Growth and Structural Change in Tsarist Russia: A Case of Modern Economic Growth?" *Soviet Studies* 23, no. 3 (January 1972): 418–34.

Heyking, Baron A. "The Economic Resources of Russia with Special Reference to British Opportunities." *Royal Statistical Society Journal*, series A, 80 (March 1917): 187–221.

Heyman, Hans. "Oil in Soviet-Western Relations in the Interwar Years." *American Slavic and East European Review* 7, no. 4 (December 1948): 303–16.

Jones, Geoffrey, and Clive Trebilcock. "Russian Industry and British Business 1910–1930: Oil and Armaments." *Journal of European Economic History* 2, no. 1 (Spring 1982): 61–103.

Kabanov, V. V. "Oktyabr"skaya Revolyutsiya i Kooperatsiya (1917–Mart 1919gg.)." *Istoricheskye Zapiski* 82 (1968): 3–26.

Kahan, Arcadius. "Governmental Policies and the Industrialisation of Russia." *Journal of Economic History* 27, no. 4 (1967): 460–77.

Kaser, Michael. "A Volume Index of Soviet Foreign Trade." *Soviet Studies* 20, no. 4 (April 1969): 523–26.

Kelly, William J., and Tsuneo Kano. "Crude Oil Production in the Russian Empire: 1818–1919." *Journal of Economic History* 6, no. 2 (Fall 1977): 307–38.

Kirby, David. "A Great Opportunity Lost? Aspects of British Commercial Policy towards the Baltic States, 1920–1924." *Journal of Baltic Studies* 5, no. 4 (1974): 362–78.

Kochan, Lionel. "The Russian Road to Rapallo." *Soviet Studies* 2, no. 2 (October 1950): 109–22.

Kolz, Arno W. F. "British Economic Interests in Siberia during the Russian Civil War, 1918–1920." *Journal of Modern History* 48, no. 3 (September 1976): 483–91.

Landes, David S. "Some Thoughts on the Nature of Economic Imperialism." *Journal of Economic History* 21 (1961): 496–512.

Libbey, James K. "The American-Russian Chamber of Commerce." *Diplomatic History* 9, no. 3 (Summer 1985): 233–48.

Liubimov, N. "The Soviets and Foreign Concessions." *Foreign Affairs* 9, no. 1 (October 1930): 95–105.

McKay, John P. "Baku Oil and Transcaucasia Pipelines, 1883–1891: A Study in Tsarist Economic Policy." *Slavic Review* 43, no. 4 (Winter 1984): 604–23.

———. "Foreign Enterprise in Russian and Soviet Industry: A Long Term Perspective." *Business History Review* 48, no. 3 (Autumn 1974): 336–56.

Maisky, I. M. "Anglo-Sovetskoe Torgovoe Soglashenie, 1921 goda." *Voprosy Istorii* 5 (May 1957): 60–77.

Martin, Charles D. "Sale of Agricultural Implements in Foreign Countries: Future Prospects." *Trade Information Bulletin*, no. 58 (4 September 1922).

Miller, Charles. "The Foreign Trade of Soviet Russia." In *Soviet Russia: Legal and Economic Conditions of Industrial and Commercial Activity in Soviet Russia*, edited by P. Apostol, V. N. Kokovzov, Charles Miller, A. Michelson, P. Gronsky, M. Bernatsky, A. Miller, and A. Pilenko, 55–156. New York, 1928.

Munting, R. "Ransomes in Russia: An English Agricultural Engineering Company's Trade with Russia to 1917." *Economic History Review*, 2nd series, 31, no. 2 (May 1978): 257–69.

Owen, G. L. "The Metro-Vickers Crisis: Anglo-Soviet Relations between Trade Agreements, 1932–1934." *Slavonic and East European Review* 49, no. 114 (January 1971): 92–112.

Pelferoff, J. J. "Agriculture." In *Russia, Its Trade and Commerce*, edited by Arthur Raffalovich, 17–64. London, 1918.

Queen, George S. "The McCormick Harvesting Machine in Russia." *Russian Review* 23 (1964): 164–81.

Rachkov, B. "The Soviet Union—A Major Exporter of Petroleum and Petroleum Products." *Soviet and Eastern European Foreign Trade* 1, no. 1 (January–February 1965): 26–38.

Radosh, Ronald. "John Spargo and Wilson's Russian Policy, 1920." *Journal of American History* 52 (1965): 548–65.

Ronimois, H. A. "The Baltic Trade of the Soviet Union: Expectations and Probabilities." *American Slavic and East European Review* 4, nos. 10–11 (December 1945): 174–78.

Roosa, Ruth A. "Russian Industrialization and State Socialism." *Soviet Studies* 23, no. 3 (January 1972): 395–417.

Ropes, E. C. "American-Soviet Trade Relations." *Russian Review* 3, no. 1 (Autumn 1943): 89–94.

———. "The Shape of US-Soviet Trade, Past and Future." *Slavonic Review* 22, no. 59 (August 1944): 1–15.

Rubenstein, N. "Sovetskaya Rossiya na Genuzkoy Konferentsii." *Voprosy Istorii*, nos. 2–3 (1946): 3–32.

Scheffer, Paul. "American Recognition of Russia: What It Would Mean to Europe." *Foreign Affairs* 9, no. 1 (October 1930): 27–41.

Schill, Bruno. "Esthonia and Her National Aspiration." *Nautical Gazette*, 23 August 1919.

Schinnes, Roger. "The Conservative Party and Anglo-Soviet Relations, 1925–7." *European Studies Review* 7, no. 4 (October 1977): 393–407.

Scoon, Robert. "Those Communist Model A's." *The Restorer* 14, no. 6 (March–April 1970): 9–22.

———. "More about Those Communist Model A's." *The Restorer* 15, no. 6 (March–April 1970): 6–11.

Soboleff, M. "The Foreign Trade of Russia." In *Russia, Its Trade and Commerce*, edited by Arthur Raffalovich, 298–328. London, 1918.

Sontag, J. P. "Tsarist Debts and Tsarist Foreign Policy." *Slavic Review* 27, no. 4 (December 1968): 529–41.

Spurr, Josiah Edward. "Russian Manganese Concessions." *Foreign Affairs* [London] 5, no. 3 (April 1927): 506–7.

Sweet, David W. "The Baltic in British Diplomacy before the First World War." *Historical Journal* 13, no. 3 (1970): 451–90.

Taylor, Alonzo E. "The Commercial Importance of Russia." *American Economic Review* 12, no. 3 (September 1922): 447–59.

Trani, Eugene P. "Woodrow Wilson and the Decision to Intervene in Russia: A Reconsideration." *Journal of Modern History* 48, no. 3 (September 1976): 440–61.

Trebilcock, R. C. "British Armaments and European Industrialisation, 1890–1914." *Economic History Review* 26 (1973): 364–79.

Turin, S. P. "The Foreign Trade of the USSR." *Slavonic and East European Review* 10, no. 29 (December 1931): 338–43.

Tuve, Jeanette E. "Changing Directions in Russian-American Economic Relations, 1912–1917." *Slavic Review* 31, no. 1 (March 1972): 53–70.

Viner, Jacob. "International Finance and Balance of Power Diplomacy, 1890–1914." *Southwestern Political and Social Science Quarterly* 9, no. 4 (March 1929): 407–51.

Weissman, Benjamin. "Herbert Hoover's 'Treaty' with Soviet Russia: August 20, 1921." *Slavic Review* 28, no. 2 (June 1969): 276–88.

White, Christine A. "British Business in Russian Asia since the 1860s: An Opportunity Lost?" In *British Business in Asia since 1860*, edited by G. G. Jones and R. P. T. Davenport-Hines, 68–91. Cambridge, 1989.

———. "Ford in Russia: In Pursuit of the Chimeral Market." *Business History* 28, no. 4 (October 1986): 77–104.

White, William C. "American Big Business and the Soviet Market." *Asia* 30 (November 1930): 747–800.

———. "Economics vs. Politics in American-Soviet Business." *Asia* 30 (December 1930): 846–73.

Wilson, J. H. "American Business and the Recognition of the Soviet Union." *Social Science Quarterly* 52, no. 2 (September 1971): 349–68.

Zolotarev, V. I. "Main Stages of the Development of USSR Foreign Trade, 1917–1967." *Soviet and Eastern European Foreign Trade* 4, no. 2 (Summer 1968): 3–34.

Theses and Dissertations

Dohan, Michael R. "Soviet Foreign Trade in the N.E.P. Economy and Soviet Industrialisation Strategy." Ph.D. dissertation, Massachusetts Institute of Technology, 1969.

Fithian, Floyd James. "Soviet Economic Relations, 1918–1933: American Business in Russia during the Period of Non-Recognition." Ph.D. dissertation, University of Nebraska, 1964.

Gillette, Philip S. "The Political Origins of American-Soviet Trade." Ph.D. dissertation, Harvard University, 1969.

Pickering, Elizabeth Cowen. "The International Harvester Company in Russia: A Case Study of a Foreign Corporation in Russia from the 1860s to the 1930s." Ph.D. dissertation, Princeton University, 1974.

Scott, David W. "The Role of the United States in the Development of the Soviet Economy: The American-Russian Chamber of Commerce and American Russian Trade, 1916–1935." M.A. thesis, University of Wisconsin, 1959.

INDEX